Joachim Schneider

Public Private Partnerships for Urban Rail Transit

GABLER EDITION WISSENSCHAFT

Baubetriebswirtschaftslehre und Infrastrukturmanagement

Herausgegeben von Professor Dr.-Ing. Dipl.-Kfm. Dieter Jacob
Technische Universität Bergakademie Freiberg

Für internationales Zusammenwachsen und Wohlstand spielt gutes Infrastrukturmanagement eine zentrale Rolle. Erkenntnisse der baubetriebswirtschaftlichen Forschung können hierzu wichtige Beiträge leisten, die diese Schriftenreihe einem breiteren Publikum zugänglich machen will.

Joachim Schneider

Public Private Partnership for Urban Rail Transit

Forms, regulatory conditions, participants

With a Foreword by Prof. Dr.-Ing. Dipl.-Kfm. Dieter Jacob

Deutscher Universitäts-Verlag

Bibliografische Information Der Deutschen Bibliothek
Die Deutsche Bibliothek verzeichnet diese Publikation in der Deutschen Nationalbibliografie; detaillierte bibliografische Daten sind im Internet über <http://dnb.ddb.de> abrufbar.

Dissertation Techn. Universität Bergakademie Freiberg, 2003

1. Auflage April 2004

Lektorat: Brigitte Siegel / Stefanie Loyal

Der Deutsche Universitäts-Verlag ist ein Unternehmen von Springer Science+Business Media.
www.duv.de

Umschlaggestaltung: Regine Zimmer, Dipl.-Designerin, Frankfurt/Main

Gedruckt auf säurefreiem und chlorfrei gebleichtem Papier

ISBN-13:978-3-8244-8050-0 e-ISBN-13:978-3-322-81708-2
DOI: 10.1007/978-3-322-81708-2

Foreword

Suburbs and inner city redevelopment zones of cities are heavily reliant on Urban Rail Transit links, which are of decisive importance for their development and prosperity. Simultaneously, owners are dependent on such links for growth in the value of their properties. How is it possible for the public sector in times of tight budgets to achieve such infrastructure links by way of a win – win situation? This is where PPP – schemes can offer a way forward.

In his research, Joachim Schneider describes and analyses successful PPP – schemes abroad for this particular application: namely TJD (Transit Joint Development), TOD (Transit oriented Development) and DBOM – schemes (Design, Build, Operate, Maintenance or Concession type contracts). These schemes are illustrated with actual examples from the United States and the United Kingdom. The theory of New Institutional Economics is applied to elaborate on the efficiency of these schemes.

Dipl.-Ing. Joachim Schneider's many years of experience in transport ministries at state level, e.g. being accountable for the Urban Rail Transit Network of Berlin-Brandenburg and now at the European Commission, Directorate-General for Energy and Transport, in Brussels, assures that his work is not confined to the ivory tower of academics. Nevertheless, J. Schneider has had sufficient time for structured thoughts and research in the United States and Great Britain on the basis of generous support by way of a Deutsche Bank – Diebold grant for a one-year sabbatical. Next to such valuable support I have to express my gratitude at this point to my colleague Horst Brezinski, who has contributed greatly to the method of the scientific approach adopted in this work.

All of the above has brought about a piece of work, which in its sum has become a valuable and interdisciplinary contribution to the German discussion on the ideal structure, finance and operation of urban rail transit systems in the context of urban development. This book can be recommended without reservation to anyone who is interested at a professional level.

Prof. Dr. Dieter Jacob

Preface

This study would not have been feasible without the help of Deutsche Bank, in conjunction with the US-based Diebold Institute for Public Policy Studies. Both institutions wanted to promote the idea of public private partnerships through a mid-carreer fellowship for professionals working in the infrastructure field. The fellowship was set up in the late 1990s, and I had the honor to be the first German fellow in that program. I owe special thanks to Ronaldo Schmitz, at the time a member of the Deutsche Bank board, as well as Klaus Deutsch and Steffen Kern of Deutsche Bank Research.

The fellowship had a strong impact on my professional and personal life. After returning in mid 2000 from the one year study-period, I continued to follow the issue, initiated a comparative European study with the funding support of the EU-commission and started to refine the findings.

The interest in the matter encouraged me. I was invited to many presentations before national and international audiences and in this way encountered Prof. Jacob, who suggested to deepen the results scientifically and base a doctoral thesis on the topic. Prof. Brezinski has helped me to develop an appropriate theoretical basis for the transferability-analysis and the political recommendations on which they are based.

Long before applying for the fellowship, several close US colleagues and friends had stimulated the interest in the matter and the enthusiasm to study in depth US developments. Most notably, I have to mention Gina Martinez of the Massachusetts State Investment Bank, now with Beacon Residential Properties in Boston and Steve Davies, Vice President of the New York based Project for Public Spaces. Steve and I have been organising German Marshall Fund sponsored exchanges to study transit oriented urban development trends in the USA and Germany. The very tangible results of those exchanges created the basis of the study approach.

Carsten Gertz of the Technical Universities in Berlin, and later Hamburg, now with the Bremen Senate of Transport and Economic Development, has strongly supported the fellowship application, based on contacts during his

PhD at UC Berkeley. He has continuously been following my studies and was the executive partner of the subsequent EU-funding application.

At the beginning of my time in the US, I was very lucky to have been supported by the former head of New York City Transit, Alan Kiepper, who has made it possible for me to work out of the New York based US head quarter office of Parsons Brinckerhoff, the largest transportation engineering firm in the US. There I met the former Chief Executive Officer, Henry Michel, as well as Vice President, Yuval Cohen. All three of them have helped me to obtain easy access to the most relevant national and regional institutions, and to widen the horizon of my study.

During my frequent stays in Washington D.C., John Diebold, the nationally eminent policy consultant and head of the Diebold Institute, took care that I was very generously hosted by the American Academy of Educational Development, AED.

Finally, the case studies themselves would not have been possible, hadn't I found very active support in each case study city. Peter Cap and Rick Mariani of Newark/ NJ, Alvin Mc Neal, Robert Dunphy and Paul Marx of Washington/ D.C., Helen Preston Tapp and Paul Vespermann of Atlanta/GA, Bud and Annie Melton of Dallas/TX, Rajiv Batra and Marc Guichard of Portland/OR, Geoff Inskip of Manchester/UK and Scott McIntosh of London stand for a large number of very knowledgeable, supportive, enthusiastic colleagues all over the USA and in the UK.

Last but not least my family, and first and foremost, my wife, Jean, was very supportive and accepted me to complete those studies during difficult times and besides my obligations as a government employee.

I hope the study will make a contribution to the development of public transport, for which, I'm convinced, the market will grow if the private sector comes in.

Joachim Schneider

Content

Illustrations

Tables

List of Abbreviations

APTA	American Public Transit Association
ARC	Atlanta Regional Commission
BART	Bay Area Rapid Transit
BEV	Bundeseisenbahnvermögen
BFO	Build-Finance-Operate
BOT	Build-Operate-Transfer
BRT	Bus Rapid Transit
CA	State of California
CEO	Chief Executive Officer
CUTA	Canadian Urban Transit Association
D.C.	District of Columbia
DART	Dallas Area Rapid Transit
DBAG	Deutsche Bahn Aktiengesellschaft
DBOM	Design-Build-Operate-Maintain
DEIS	Draft Environmental Impact Statement
DOT	Department of Transportation (federal or state level)
EBA	Eisenbahnbundesamt
EIM	Eisenbahn Immobilien Management
EIS	Environmental Impact Study
EPA	Environmental Protection Agency
FHWA	Federal Highway Administration
FTA	Federal Transit Administration
GA	State of Georgia
GDP	Gross Domestic Product
GMPTA	Greater Manchester Public Transit Authority
GRTA	Georgia Regional Transportation Authority
HOV	High Occupancy Vehicle
ISTEA	Intermodal System Transportation Efficiency Act (1991)
LEM	Location Efficient Mortgage
LID	Local Improvement District
LIRR	Long Island Railroad

LRT	Light Rail-transit
LRV	Light Rail Vehicle
LT/TfL	London Transport/Transport for London
LUTRA	Land-use, Transportation, Air Quality Connection
MARC	Maryland Railway Company
MARTA	Metropolitan Atlanta Rapid Transit Authority
MAX	Metropolitan Area Express
MIT	Massachusetts Institute of Technology
MPO	Metropolitan Planning Organization
MTA	Metropolitan Transportation Authority
MTC	Metropolitan Transportation Commission
MTDB	Metropolitan Transit Development Board (of San Diego / CA)
MTS	Metropolitan Transit System
NEPA	National Environmental Policy Act
NJ	State of New Jersey
NY	State of New York
NYCTA	New York City Transit Authority
NYMTC	New York Metropolitan Transportation Commission
ON	State of Ontario (Canada)
OR	State of Oregon
PATH	Post-Authority TransHudson Cooperation
PDC	Portland Development Corporation
PFI	Private Finance Initiative
PID	Public Improvement District
RFP	Request for Proposals
ROW	Right-of-way
RPA	Regional Plan Association (New York City)
RTP	Regional Transportation Plan
SANDAG	San Diego Association of Governments
SEIS	Supplemental Environmental Impact Statement
SEPTA	Southern Pennsylvania Transportation Authority
SIB	State Infrastructure Bank
STA	State Transit Assistance

STPP	Surface Transportation Policy Project
TCL	Tramtrack Croydon Limited
TCRP	Transit Cooperative Research Program
TDA	Transit Development Act
TEA 21	Transportation Efficiency Act (1998)
TIF	Tax Increment Finance
TIFIA	Transportation Infrastructure Finance and Innovation Act (1998)
TJD	Transit Joint Development
TOD	Transit-oriented Development
TRB	Transportation Research Board, Subdivision of the National Academy of Sciences)
Tri-Met	Tri-County Metropolitan Transportation District
TSAP	Transit Station Area Program
TTC	Toronto Transit Commission
TX	State of Texas
UITP	Union International des Transports Publics
ULI	Urban Land Institute
UMTA	Urban Mass Transit Administration
VMT	Vehicle Miles Traveled
VRE	Virginia Railway Express
WMATA	Washington Metropolitan Area Transit Authority

1. Theoretical and methodological introduction

1.1 Private infrastructure financing and regional development – classification of the study with consideration of the current debate about public transport deregulation

In order to help the reader in properly classifying this study, a certain framework regarding the topic's scope must be constructed.

The identified aspects of cooperation with private investors in the United States can be separated into 3 categories (groups): (1) Management and financing of new railroad lines (i.e. mainly Light Rail), (2) Suitable local transit use of railway real estate property, and (3) Urban development near railway stations. Both of the latter two categories may also include financial participation on behalf of parts of the infrastructure, especially stations, through beneficiaries. In each of the three groups an overview about frequencies, diversity and regional relevance of cases as well as a more detailed prime example, will be presented.

During the course of the study's investigations it became apparent that a broader-based study would deliver more suitable results than the originally intended detailed single-case study. Various findings originated from broader compilations of the case frequencies and of comparisons of different forms of public private cooperations in the transit field.

In order to understand the partnerships that emerged in the United States, it was necessary to compare findings in the U.S. in two of the three categories mentioned above with European cases of the same type. The management and financing of new urban railroad lines (i.e. Light Rail) needed to be compared with new British Light Rail systems, which are among the most advanced examples of transit-related public partnerships in Europe. The management of transit agencies' real estate property and the possibility to base partnerships on this transit asset needed to be compared with the policy of the largest real estate owner among transit agencies in Europe, the Deutsche Bahn AG.

As a general observation one might say that for transit infrastructure investments it is extremely difficult to obtain private participation on a large scale due to various political influences on the transit sector, but also due to the low market position of public transit. While this especially applies in the United States, there is also a similar tendency in Germany as well as in other European countries.

Direct co-financing or purely private financing of rail transit projects has only recently been promoted; the interest to earn money with the respective infrastructure and its operation has increased as a result. Very little is known about initial experiences or actual concepts of successful projects.

The goal of this study therefore is not only to examine which conditions could maximize the private capital use for transit infrastructure. The goal is also, and perhaps more importantly, to investigate how private capital can be attracted to urban rail systems in order to contribute to its financing and utilization.

As a result of this overview-type study, a very complex picture emerges of the interaction among factors influencing private participation. Furthermore, even if the evidence does not exist in all the examined projects, one sees, nevertheless, a basic thesis uniting a multitude of conceptual initial attempts through the examined projects: the task of involving private capital to develop urban rail systems cannot simply be based on the goal of maximizing ridership revenues.

The task must be based on additional goals, the most important one being the possibility to increase real estate property values in proximity of proficient urban rail systems. This transit-related real estate value is not mutually exclusive from the issues of housing density, the function of the inner cities, and the position of important traffic origin and destination points.

The potential ridership numbers and the resulting revenues in urban transit are on the one hand a result of these complex geographic-functional development conditions. On the other hand, the construction or extension of transit systems is capable, more than any other capital investment, of influencing the geographical patterns of cities and regions and the distribution of the use and the purpose of land in that space (area). Therefore, the rail-transit investments have a self-reinforcing effect.

As Denver Mayor Wellington E. Webb stated at the New Traditions Biennial Conference in Berlin on March 19, 2000: “In Denver, our focus is on development of a transit system not only to enhance the mobility of our residents, but also to shape land use and support economic development. To that end, we have initiated a station development program which has brought together city agencies, the Regional Transportation District, the Colorado Department of Transportation, and the private sector. The goals are to revitalize those areas of the central city served by rail and to enhance ridership of the system. In this way, we can address transportation, housing, jobs, and containment of urban sprawl".

These remarks from the Mayor of a city that until recently was one of the showcases for car-oriented urban development, underline the highly political nature and meaning of transit decisions and transit partnerships. They illustrate how complex transit developments are and, therefore, how complex the research configuration of these developments indeed is.

This complexity makes it necessary to rely on an adequate theoretical framework to systemize questions and findings and to create a basis of comparison and conclusion from findings in the U.S. and the UK. As will be explained more in detail in the following subchapters, the Neo-Institutional Economics (NIE) provides a theoretical framework that allows focus on institutional conditions of these developments and thus to specify classical economic analysis.

On this basis it is possible to answer some of the questions about the current German debate on the introduction of market conditions in the transportation sector. However, due to the absolute lack of respective U.S. experience, it is not possible to derive any knowledge in two of the most important fields of the current national German debate: the separation of infrastructure and operation, seen by some as the prerequisites for competition and private business management and operation, and the introduction of competition for transit service as such.

In addition, many other aspects will be explored that play an important role in the German debate, including tax financing versus user financing, private risk and public risk reduction, voluntary versus involuntary mobility, freedom or limitation in the choice of the needed transportation mode, transit infrastructure and location choice, stirring instruments versus market development, and private or public management.

This study attempts to uphold objectivity and a suitable emotional distance from the subject matter. The author's basic assumption is that public transport can be a vital element of urban and regional transportation modes. It increases the choice of transportation modes and can contribute to the improvement of the quality of life. As mentioned before, rail transit can also contribute to the shape and function of urban areas and may, more than bus transport, encourage car drivers to switch to public transit. Public transport in general and rail transit in particular may also contribute to the sustainability of urban areas and to the improvement of ecological standards.

Whether or not the installation of new urban rail systems will ultimately contribute to substantial changes, and if it is even possible to measure successes, cannot be judged at this point. But it can be said that at least in urban regions of the Eastern and Western Coast the desire to make a change becomes the basis for new locations of businesses and homeseekers. And it is important to notice that this is not only a result of planning and political concepts, but rather of the market itself. The investigation of how the market develops through the financing and use of transit systems directly contributes to the overriding discussion about private financing perspectives for the public infrastructure.

As will be described more in detail in this and the following chapter, the research is conducted on the basis of literature reviews, internet resources, site visits, and, most of all, interviews with private and public project participants. Case Studies are conducted in seven specifically relevant North American metropolitan areas (New York, Washington, D.C., Atlanta, GA, Dallas, TX, San Diego, CA, Portland, OR, and Toronto, CA). In order to add relevant examples and create a basis for comparison, additional case studies were undertaken in two British and two German metropolitan areas (Greater Manchester, London, Berlin/Brandenburg and the Ruhr area).

1.2 Reorganizing public tasks through public private partnerships (PPP)- Definitions

Expectations are high for privatization and regulatory reform as the solution to the problem of poor performance by public utilities, and as the means to improve service and lower prices. These expectations may not always be met because of the way political and social institutions - executive, legislative, judicial systems as well as informal norms of public behavior - interact with regulatory processes and economic conditions. They may fail because conditions for private investors are unattractive or because the public institutions may lack control over the private sector. The expectations may also focus too much on privatization of entire systems and underestimate the type of cooperation between the public and the private sector that may improve the efficiency of systems that remain public.

The origin of the idea of privatizing public facilities and services is generally ascribed to the Thatcher-Reagan era of the 1980s and early 1990s, but in 1993, HEINZ still stated that it was not possible to find a commonly accepted definition of the concept of public private partnerships. HEINZ (1993) found out that "the clear increase in partnerships in the area of municipal development and renewal projects, especially in the 1980s, was the result of a range of conditions and prerequisites, that were found in similar forms in the majority of countries surveyed. These included:

- A transformation in economic structures associated with rapid growth of the service sector;
- The resulting necessity for improvements in housing and infrastructure, accompanied by a simultaneous increase in demand for new office, business, and retail premises on the one hand, and for adequate cultural and recreational facilities on the other hand;
- A boom in the construction and real estate businesses which went hand in hand with rising property prices that promised good profits for all concerned;
- And last but not least, a shift in central government policy and ideology towards an emphasis on deregulation and on the self-regulating forces of the free market.

He distinguished the types of cooperation between the public and the private sector according to the degree of institutionalization involved:

- A comparatively informal mode of cooperation among local business and public leaders, associated with precursory forms of partnership co-operation;
- A type of cooperation based on agreements and contracts worked out in collaboration (the most common form in all countries surveyed); and finally

- A merging of public and private interests into joint corporations (HEINZ 1993, p. 23)

Even though the term *public private partnership* is nowadays used very readily, it was found in the course of this study that different individuals and organizations have different ideas of what actually constitutes such a partnership. Definitions found in the literature show a similar divergence – or simply a lack of detail, which would allow a clear distinction between what is actually considered a PPP and what is not. A sample of definitions found in the literature is provided in the following table.

Table 1.1 Possible definitions of Public Private Partnerships (PPPs)

Irish Business and Employers Confederation (1998, p.3)	*"A partnership between public sector organizations on the one hand and private sector investors and businesses on the other, for the purpose of designing, planning, financing, constructing and/or operating an infrastructure project or a service normally provided by the State."*
EU Select Committee Final Report on the Financing Options for the Trans-European Networks (1997)	*"A partnership forged between different public bodies on the one hand and legal entities from the private sector on the other for the purpose of conceiving, planning, constructing, financing and/or operating infrastructure projects".*
KYREIN (1998)	*"PPP is the organized cooperation of persons and institutions from very different areas of the private and the public sector for the common solving of complex problems in urban and regional development, which none of the actors involved could solve on their own."*

Source: GAFRON 2002

For the purpose of this study, the first definition is too narrow since rail-based urban development projects - which are incorporated into the scope of a PPP - are not necessarily limited to facilities normally provided by the public sector, such as railway stations, but can also include residential and business developments.

The second definition is wider in scope, but does not specify the actual mechanisms that make such a partnership work. These mechanisms are not addressed in the following definition either, but KYREIN stresses an important aspect of PPPs - that of generating synergies that make the entire project bigger than the sum of its components. The idea that a PPP is always the *only* solution for the development "problem" at hand is, however, not necessarily supported by the findings of the study. It might be that a PPP is seen as the *best* way to fulfill certain urban development tasks or provide certain facilities and is thus chosen over alternative solutions.

HÖRHAGER (1998) stated that PPPs could range between the provision of certain services under the continued full public ownership on a contractual basis and the design, building, operation and maintenance (DBOM) of structures or services including private investment or full private ownership and operation. In addition, it should be taken into consideration that PPPs are neither a simple dialogue between the public and the private sector nor full-scale privatization.Instead they can range from passive private investment over joint ventures to passive public investment (ibid.). In combination with the definitions already discussed, the partnerships investigated for this study can best be described in a common definition as follows:

PPPs are a partnership between public bodies and legal entities from the private sector, forged for mutual benefit and for the purpose of conceiving, planning, constructing, financing and/or operating infrastructure projects, which the public sector would not be able to provide in the same form on its own. PPPs are neither restricted to simple dialogue between the two sectors nor do they entail full-scale privatization, ranging from passive private investment to joint ventures to passive public investment.

Potential advantages of Public Private Partnerships

As the term partnership implies, the different actors in a PPP participate in the expectation that they will derive a benefit from the cooperation greater than if they acted alone. In the case of the private partners this benefit would generally include the speeding-up of the project; specific public decision making processes (such as the processing of planning applications); and a greater investment security due to increased certainty about planning decisions. The public side might also be able to contribute some capital and/or land at favorable conditions in return for some control over the development. These factors would be expected to result in earlier and/or increased financial profits.

From the public point of view, the potential advantages of PPPs over traditional procurement are generally thought to include risk transfer, innovation, and value for money. A more detailed list would include:

- mobilizing private resources (financial, managerial efficiencies) – and thus the provision of facilities and/or services the public sector would otherwise not be able to afford the potential to speed up and make more efficient the implementation of large and complex developments,
- creating greater focus and enhancing coordination of administrative processes,
- a share in profits and benefit of increased land values,
- the parallel implementation of economically viable and uneconomic elements of a project,
- the possibility to influence the implementation processes as well as the urban development and structural qualities of the project,
- the possibility to influence the management of the development after completion,
- opening up new arenas of activity, which entails a further qualification and professionalization of the public actors (knowledge transfer and project management),
- politically attractive transparency of the implementation process (see also SCHELTE, 1999; p.155)

It is the aim of this study to show whether and which of these advantages are generated through PPPs in the field of urban rail transport.

1.3 State of Research about Transit Related Partnerships in the US

Research in the US about public private partnerships for land transportation systems started in the 1980's when public funding sources for the further extension of the Federal Highway System as well as the extension or new start of urban rail systems decreased.

The most important part of this research was initiated and financed through federal transportation research programs, in particular the Transportation Cooperative Research Program (TCRP). In addition, research was organized through the Transportation Research Board, a subdivision of the National

Academy of Sciences. A very important contribution to the transport/ land use complex and its impact on investors has also been delivered through the Institute of Urban and Regional Development at Berkeley University in California and the Urban Land Institute in Washington D.C.

The topics and discussions concentrated on three fields: benefit sharing through joint development at urban railway stations, joint financing and development of transportation/transit-infrastructure and transit oriented real estate development.

Research and discussions about co-financing of the transit-infrastructure and co-operation with real estate developers at or in proximity of urban rail stations were strictly separated. This is similar in the US and Europe.

The first substantial comparison of concepts, tools and results of "the funding of urban transport through contributions from external beneficiaries" was organized by the International Metropolitan Railway Committee of the UITP and presented by the former head of London Transport, Prof. RIDLEY, at their 47th international meeting 1987 in Lausanne.

As will be explained later in detail, the majority of examples stems from the US, featuring, in particular, contributions from real estate owners and developers to the development of urban railway stations. Robert Cervero, Peter Hall and John Landis of the University of Berkeley had undertaken a very detailed study about Transit Joint Development in the United States in 1992. Both research projects and many other smaller studies in the same context show, however, that the financial impact of real estate contributions was far from becoming a substantial or at least important source of financing for urban rail infrastructure. This is the reason why since then, the possibilities and results of benefit sharing have never been deeply investigated after this IURD-study.

Instead, after 1995 the majority of partnership studies concentrated either on the impact of transit for land use development (Transit Oriented Development, TOD) or the new financing or delivery concepts for urban rail infrastructure, mentioned above.

As opposed to the studies about benefit sharing, the focus of the TOD-studies was the question of how to generate urban densities through urban rail transit systems. The focus goal was to stop urban sprawl through new incentives to settlement in inner city areas or in areas with (existing or planned) rail transit facilities. The feasibility of this policy on a large-scale basis has been and is still strongly disputed (see e.g. GRAVA 1999).

By 1977 basic and still relevant research on the context of urban densities and the transportation value and financial liability of urban rail systems had been undertaken by Pushkarev and Zupan (Public Transportation & Land Use Policy). Almost 20 years later, the "Congress of New Urbanism", inspired by the Californian Architect Peter Calthorpe, requested the construction of denser, socially and functionally mixed, transit oriented residential and activity centers as a basic principle for new suburban locations. This movement influenced federal policies on housing and urban development and in the marketing of the most desired new neighborhoods, those with transit access. But it contributed relatively few research results to the promotion of transit-oriented development.

Nevertheless – during the last few years a huge number of TOD-studies have been undertaken, most descriptive, some analyzing the real estate impact of rail transit (e.g. the IURD in Berkeley: Deakin et al. 1997), some investigating the impact of land use regulations, some renewing Pushkarev/Zupan's approach to figures and orientations and simulation models for the evaluation of the land use impact of new transit systems (e.g. Parsons/Brinkerhoff1996).

Over approximately five years many conferences, debates in the transportation and budget commissions of the US-Congress and Senate, and policy measures tried to evaluate and enhance the possibilities of public private partnerships for highway and transit infrastructure. The emphasis of politicians, administrations, engineers and construction firms was to create investment schemes, tools and pilot cases. Unlike the co-financing of highways, very few studies have been undertaken to evaluate the conditions and possible results of public private partnerships for public transit investments.

Nevertheless – Universities (e.g. Massachusetts Institute of Technology or Rutgers University) have delivered some case descriptions about the financing of Light Rail Lines and new project delivery methods in the transit field. In 1998 the Federal Transit Administration published a systematical overview on Innovative Transit Financing that helped distinguish the diverse tools and to evaluate their potential results.

Studies with clear estimations of the financial impact of certain joint development efforts or of expected and necessary profit rates of participating investors don't exist. This makes it very difficult to draw a precise picture of the impact of public efforts to attract private money, for transit or transit related investments.

This study contributes to the discussion in the US itself and in Europe through the systematic overview of the different fields of private involvement and the case-based integrated perception and evaluation of this involvement.

The study is based on two approaches: review of studies, statistics and press-articles and interviews with investors, transit experts and politicians. The goal is not to get a quantitative but a qualitative picture of the (potential) interest of private investors to contribute to transit funding and development and of the (potential) results of public policies to attract private money.

1.4 New institutional economics as a tool to analyze the topic

Despite the enormous economic importance, relatively few studies have been made to analyze the public sector and the branches of the economy that are directly steered or dominated through national, regional and local governments from a neo-institutional perspective. Such studies exist for the telecommunications sector as well as for the energy sector, which in some cases have also been subject to a comparative analysis of regulation in different countries. Both sectors were strongly publicly dominated before the deregulation and, in many cases, still remain publicly owned.

The public transport sector has not yet been the focus of neo-institutional analysis, or only in a relatively general perspective (Strobach 2001). The sector differs from telecom and energy to the extent that in countries with accessible private cars industry functioning depends heavily on public subsidies. This makes for a relatively difficult case for private participation but a fairly interesting case for neo-institutional analysis of the type of partnerships that are being realized or may be realized.

It is connected with a diverse range of topics that will be examined more closely - deregulation of public utilities (as mentioned before), infrastructure financing, and public private partnerships.

The examples in this study represent a variety of possible role sharing models to improve the efficiency of public transport systems, such as the share of investment tasks to build up and modernize urban rail transit systems. In order to analyze these properly and to draw conclusions for the applicability to other countries, namely Germany, it is necessary to look at the institutional framework in which they take place. The framework is set by the government systems, the structure and goals of public economic entities, regulatory design, and the regulatory governance. To evaluate the relevance of the institutional setting, it is also necessary to evaluate the economic context. The case studies therefore focus on the following questions:

The following results of the study are expected to be relevant for transportation policy in European countries:

1) What types of cooperation exist between the public and the private sector in order to build and use public (urban rail) infrastructure?
   This includes an overview of current fields and results of the integration of private investors and an estimation of future trends of private cooperation.

2) Which players are involved and what is the character of the relationship between these players (e.g. contracts or informal relations)?
   This includes a case-based description of typical organizations of partnerships between transportation companies, investors, local initiatives and/or communities and an evaluation of what roles the implied institutions played to accelerate or to slow down the developmental process

3) Which cooperation results have actually been achieved in the analyzed cases and which institutional framework has influenced these results positively or negatively (e.g. laws, political networks, confidence, and local economic power)?

   The following aspects are considered:

- A description of the legal framework and techniques to attract private capital and to reduce high risks that lead to the withdrawal of private investors.

- An overview and a description of legal tools in the USA to levy project-related fees, taxes and private contributions to increase the project-funding capacity of communities and an estimation of their financial role, their public acceptance, and their potential applicability in Europe.

- Examples of how real estate properties of transit agencies and/or communities can link commercial and transit usefulness, i.e. stimulate investments that attract transit passengers.

- An evaluation of the (potential) role of a closer cooperation between transit companies and the private real estate sector in the general context of private participation in the construction, renewal, and use of rail transit infrastructures.

- An evaluation of how far regulatory conditions on the local, regional, national and supranational level serve to limit or promote public private partnerships.

4) Which conclusions have to be drawn to strengthen the role of the private sector to achieve rail transport tasks in Germany?

The methodological approach of neo-institutionalism offers valuable insight in order to analyze the above mentioned research topics. Neo-institutional economics, with its emphasis on the analysis of the institutional framework of the actions and the performance of companies and individuals corresponds to the needs of systemizing the results of the case studies. The purpose of the case studies is influenced by the granted scholarship itself-- The assessment and evaluation of examples both in the U.S. and in Great Britain of privately co-financed public infrastructure. On the other hand, this purpose is also a result of the issues involved when dealing with rail transport and its "institutionalized" specific needs; the latter are dependent on the following criteria:

Dependence on public subsidies (public transport generally calls for subsidies in areas where income and supply allow for the ownership of privately owned cars),

Dependence on city's structure, density, perspectives of city's development as well as the respective underlying economic and institutional framework,

Dependence on the economic players responsible for the development of city structures,

The great political influence on the players involved in the public transport market.

The case studies shed light on this influential system and thus offer an empirical basis for a neo-institutional analysis.

1.5 Basic elements of the new institutional economics (NIE)

"While it would be incorrect to say that traditional analysis is abstracted completely from institutional structure there can be little doubt that the usual treatment of institutions is superficial. The existence of political, legal, monetary, and other systems was certainly recognized; but either these systems were regarded as neutral in their effect on economic events and ignored, or they were taken as given and then specified in so perfunctory a way as to suggest that institutional influence was not of much importance. By contrast, the new institutional economics seeks, at a minimum, to demonstrate that institutions truly matter. Each distinct organizational structure is said to affect incentives and behavior but, beyond this, institutions are themselves regarded as legitimate objects of economic analysis." (FURUBOTN/RICHTER 1991, p. 2)

As of the 1970s, "New institutional economics" (NIE) has acquired increasing importance, mainly due to the work of Oliver WILLIAMSON and Douglas NORTH. Based on the concept of transaction costs, NIE has introduced the notion of an institution in a theoretical framework compatible with standard economics (EGGERTSSON, 1991). Williamson has extended the traditional study of optimization of a production function to the comparative examination of the costs of planning, adaptation and control activities in alternative organizational forms. The term "governance structure" indicates in Williamson (1996 p.139) the explicit or implicit contractual framework in which a transaction takes places. Therefore, the analysis of transaction costs becomes an action of institutional comparison in the awareness of the existence of a variety of different transactions and of 'governance structures'. Incomplete contracting is seen as ineluctable because of bounded rationality and the impossibility to handle the complexity of all contractual aspects (WILLIAMSON, 1986 p.141).

The main premises of neo-institutionalism can be divided into two categories: those premises adhering to the neo-classical approach and those premises that oppose the neo-classical approach: Individual utility maximization, individually bounded rationality, and methodological individualism as common basis and asymmetrical information dissemination, opportunism and transaction costs as the neo-institutional differentiating contributions to the neo-classical theoretical structure/framework (182/183).This differentiation will help evaluate the "institutional aspects" of the economic development, that is the influence of different institutional stipulations/prerequisites on the successful achievement or failure of economic goals (the term "economic goal" is used in a broader sense here - in this case it is the realization of rail infrastructure and corresponding services). Based on the existing assessment and analyses, recommendations can finally be derived for the design of the institutional framework to increase private economic commitment to the development and utilization of public transport. FURUBOTN and RICHTER explain these premises more in detail:

Methodological individualism. An entirely new interpretation is given to the role of individual decision-makers within an organization. The central idea is that "society", "the state", "the people", "the firm", or "parties" are not to be understood as collective entities that behave as though they were individual actors. The organization or collectivity no longer is the main focus. Rather, the theory of such social units must start with and base its explanations on the positions and actions of the individual members involved.

Utility maximization. Individuals are assumed to seek their own interests and to maximize utility subject to the constraints established by the existing organizational structure. Contrary to conventional practice, the dichotomy between the theory of consumer choice and the theory of the firm is ended by extending the utility maximization hypothesis to all individual choices. Thus, an individual, whether he is the manager of a government bureau or a capitalist entrepreneur, is understood to make his own choices and to pursue his own goals within the limits allowed by the system in which he is operating.

Bounded rationality. To approach the conditions of the real world of institutions more closely, it is important to come to terms with the idea that individuals have only limited ability to acquire and process information". ... "A boundedly rational individual attempts to maximize but finds it costly to do so and, unable to anticipate all contingencies, and aware of this inability, provides ex ante for the (almost inevitable) time ex post when an unforeseen contingency will arise.

Opportunistic behavior. As Williamson (1975) has pointed out, while bounded rationality prevents the writing of complete contracts, there could be general reliance on incomplete contracts if economic agents were wholly trustworthy. In fact, however, some individuals (either principals or agents) are likely to be dishonest in the sense that they may disguise preferences, distort data, deliberately confuse issues, etc. There is, in Williamson's phrase, "self-seeking with guile", and since it is normally very costly to distinguish opportunistic from non-opportunistic actors ex ante, comprehensive contracting must break down".(Ibid, p.4)

"An institution is understood as a system of norms with respect to a particular set of activities. In North's definition (1989, p. 239), an institution consists, fundamentally, of informal constraints, formal rules, and the enforcement characteristics of both. Institutions are, of course, crucial to economic development because they regulate, even if imperfectly, the social behavior of individual citizens. Precisely how institutions arise represents an intriguing question, and different theories exist. On one extreme, institutions can be viewed as arising "spontaneously" on the basis of the self-interest of decision-makers — i.e., they may organize themselves. On the other extreme, the idea is that institutions may be organized in their entirety by a central authority. Proponents of the new institutional economics generally tend to accept the hypothesis of the spontaneously developing institutional structure (evolutionary rationalism). Williamson (1985) calls the other extreme "legal centralism", while Hayek (1973) refers to it as "constructivist rationalism". No matter which hypothesis is preferred, though, those interested in the economic analysis of institutions recognize that the creation of institutions is driven by the search for organizational structure that will, in some sense, optimize the social behavior of people."

Modern institutional economics focuses on the institution of property, and on the system of norms governing the acquisition or transfer of property rights. Understandably, acquisition or transfer of rights can come about in a variety of ways, such as through inheritance or gifts, by purchase agreements, by order of a central authority, through tortuous acts, etc. These distinctions have practical importance validity and indicate whether analysis is best undertaken within the theory of the firm, public choice theory, the economic analysis of law, or some other specialty. In this connection, it is essential to differentiate between institutions in the sense of law (e.g., the German civil code) and institutions in the sense of rights (e.g., a concrete claim arising out of a labor contract)." (Ibid, p.3)

STROHBACH (2001) regroups the analytical tools, namely the theoretical basis, into three core elements – property rights, transaction costs and agency theory. The latter are to be complemented by a "public choice" theory, as Strohbach calls it, an approach dealing mostly with political and scientific issues and referred to as "new political economy", devoted to "researching and aggregating" priorities in the public sector.

According to STROHBACH, the property rights approach "follows both positive as well as normative goals", analyzing the behavior of individuals in conjunction with the existing institutional framework, and making assertions about the efficiency of property rights structures. He attempts to explain the change in property rights and researches how property rights structures need to be in order to achieve an optimum of aggregated economic results.

The term "property rights" complements the term "property" by resource utilization rights and also by the definition of behavioral norms to be adhered to by the owners. The property rights approach aims at internalizing the external effects by specifying the property rights per se. Thus, striving for the neo-classical goal of an unrestricted competitive market, where private utility maximization can occur, goods and factors can be transported to the location that guarantees their most efficient usage (ibid, p.205/6).

1.6 Reorganization of public tasks from the perspective of neo-institutionalism

New institutional economics and the state

The manner in which the public institutions of any given country function is directly related to the manner in which the state is organized, and its role in economic transactions.

In the historical work of North (1981; 1991) state evolution is defined in terms of an impersonal optimization that leads to configurations that minimize transaction costs. Many characterizations of the State exist in the NIE domain. North interprets state evolution mostly in terms of governance structure - public hierarchy.

The view of the state proposed by the new economics of organization, a field of study between economics and politics that applies the main concepts developed in the NIE to the political interaction, is less aggregated. MOE (1990) and WEINGAST (1995) have applied the principal agents and transaction costs theoretical framework to political institutions. They characterize all political and administrative activities in terms of contracts and analyze the effects of incomplete and asymmetrical information on political and administrative contracts. The result is that the action of parliament, government, and judges is never perfectly determined by rules. Moreover, political markets are not perfect, a fact which limits the direct expression of choices and proves the importance of political institutions (MOE, 1990). In such studies, FURUBOTN and RICHTER (1997) have proposed the following definition of the State:

"A state is understood ... as a network of relational principal-agent contracts between the constituents (the principals) and their representatives (their agents) with the objective of optimizing the public wealth through a suitable organization of the use of the force (coercion), that is, by the suitable allocation, administration, and transaction of political property rights. The governance structure (constitution) determines the flow of information and the methods that help make information credible (e.g., promises by the government or single politicians). Expressed in different terms, the constitution determines the country--specific property rights assignments of each constituent and indicates how these property rights can be used or transferred.." (FURUBOTN/RICHTER, 1997 p.277).

In a study about public firms in Germany, PICOT and WOLFF (1994) noted, "Generally there is no economic reason why all politically desired outputs should automatically be produced by public organizations or civil servants - even if those goods and services are demanded and paid for by the state. From an economic point of view, public firms and administrations are simply one organizational form of producing politically desired outputs, and compete with alternative forms of organization" (ibid, pp.213). They summarize the

range of possibilities for rendering individually or collectively those goods and services in Germany as follows:
- Civil servants or officials in public administrations
- Ordinary employees or clerks in public administrations
- Public employees in other public organizations, e.g. firms (such as public transportation or public savings banks) or social security etc.)
- All kinds of public and private non-profit organizations,
- "Private“ firms with a high share of government ownership, e.g. Deutsche Lufthansa,
  Deutsche Post, Deutsche Bahn
- Private firms with a low share of government ownership, but controlled by public supervisory authorities or politicians who are appointed to the supervisory boards of those companies, e.g. electric power-supply companies, such as RWE or VEW
- Private firms that are dependent on government orders, e.g. local garbage disposal and cleaning companies
- Private firms whose production is regulated by public restraints, e.g., environmental or data protection laws
- Private associations, which are not, recognized as non-profit organizations, e.g., associations of certain professional groups
- Independent private companies or individuals. (Ibid, pp.213/214).

Based on the above-mentioned range of different organizational possibilities, PICOT and WOLFF have developed an analytical framework showing how public tasks can be reorganized to minimize transaction costs, improve property rights, and avoid agent problems.

Transaction cost analysis

On the basis of the transaction costs' theory, they argue, "the allocation of different organizational forms should depend on the analysis of characteristics of the goods and services that are to be produced. When this classification is completed, the tasks can be allocated to the appropriate producer. Due to a better use of economies of scale, a reduction of organizational slack and the competitive forces of private markets, this method not only ensures a reduction of transaction costs but of overall production costs and an increase in adaptability to new demands and new frameworks as well".
They develop a purely economic framework demonstrating how a certain good or service can be produced most efficiently, thus ignoring cultural, political, and

other constraints. This is supposed to permit the definition of the "costs" considering non-economic arguments, so that the “taxpayer”, i.e. the voter, can decide if she or he is prepared to bear those costs. The procedure currently prevailing is invisible to the public because the allocation of public resources does not follow publicly discussed rules of efficiency, but nontransparent contingencies of bargaining between interest groups and politicians (ibid, p. 215).

PICOT and WOLFF classify the goods and services demanded under the terms of *specificity* and *strategic relevance.* A production process is highly specific if the required inputs can either not be used at all for the production of alternative products or only at high opportunity costs. From a practical point of view, specificity refers mainly to investments of the development of the design and quality of a product, human capital, machines and logistics. The fewer the alternative uses of an input resource, the higher the specificity of that resource. Strategic relevance refers to requirements which result from the competitive situation in particular markets, e.g., the observance of secrecy.

In order to develop guidelines for efficiency-oriented realization of public tasks, PICOT and WOLFF infer from transaction costs analysis that the following principle should be observed: “Goods and services that bear a high specificity and high strategic relevance demand a high degree of vertical integration, while goods and services with a high degree of specificity and strategic relevance can be easily outsourced”.

The degree of vertical integration of public tasks varies between the extreme of a total vertical integration ("make", i.e. *hierarchy)* and total disintegration ("buy", i.e. *market).* The "make" decision of a state means that a good or a service must be rendered exclusively by public servants working in the public domain, such as police services, for example. The "buy" decision means that a good or a service must be purchased externally, such as a pencil, which can be bought in an ordinary private stationery shop, for example.” (Ibid, p.216)

The two major alternatives of organization between civil service and private companies include *cooperation* as public private partnership and *public control* of private organizations by law and regulation.

As a result, they distinguish between four basic alternative forms of organizations for the production of politically desired goods and services that can be matched with specificity and strategic relevance.

“Unspecified tasks with low strategic relevance should be purchased from external partners in ordinary markets, e.g., stationery for public offices or cleaning and gardening services for public buildings. For specific tasks with low strategic relevance, e.g., public road planning and construction, we suggest cooperation between public organization and specialized private suppliers. Highly specific tasks, which at the same time are of high strategic relevance, can efficiently be performed by specialized public organizations, e.g., services in the fields of internal and external public security or jurisdiction. The accomplishment of unspecified, but strategically relevant tasks can be ensured by means of regulation, e.g., limits to exhaust emission or compulsory education” (ibid, pp.216/217).

As a conclusion of this classification, both authors are convinced that “once an agreement on the classification of tasks is reached - e.g. on the basis of elaborate questionnaires and interviews - there is hardly any need for discussion of the appropriate form of procurement” (ibid, p.217). This conviction seems overly optimistic, given the very difficult procedures and results of deregulatory approaches (see chapter 1.9), but is consistent with a viewpoint that excludes the above-mentioned cultural, political, and interest group-related aspects of this definition.

Property Rights analysis

Because of opportunistic and rational utility-maximizing behavior, individuals tend to cause external effects when dealing with resources allocated to third parties. If individuals do not have to bear the consequences of how they are dealing with scarce resources, they have no direct incentive to use the respective resources efficiently. In property rights terms: The more completely the rights regarding resources are communicated to the individual involved, the stronger the incentives to use and preserve the resources efficiently.

"Property rights assignments specify the behavioral norms with respect to rules that each and every person must observe in his or her interactions with other people, or bear the cost for nonobservance“ (FURUBOTN and PEJOVICH [1972, p. 391). There is an abundance of rights relevant to the economic theory of organization; these can be summarized into the following three categories:

a) The right to control a firm,
b) The right to be a residual claimant, and
c) The right to sell all rights that the ownership of a firm generates.

Following FURUBOTN and PEJOVICH, PICOT and WOLFF say that, "by the allocation of property rights, individual decisions are influenced and indirectly controlled: *The allocation of property rights defines the constitution of organizations."* They illustrate this presumption in the above table and refer to "historical evidence that some types of firms have been more successful than others, e.g., state-owner or worker-managed firms, for example, do not seem to have the same success as manager- or owner-led companies" (ibid, p.219).

The category "right to control" the firm comprises many different rights to make decisions and give instructions. These can be assigned individually. In addition, there are substitutes for personal ownership, such as performance-related pay, competition, or corporate culture, which can also be used as mechanisms to reinforce an individual responsibility for decision-makers. There is an entire set of different combinations that define different types of organizations. The different allocations of property rights, say, in an industrial holding or profit center organization and in a classical public bureaucracy allow for completely different incentive structures. Generally speaking, an allocation of property rights which internalizes a maximum of effects to the involved individuals will allow for the most efficient production process, in contrast to alternative settings.

In public enterprises and administrations, however, many of the organizational options are not available. Since property rights in state-owned firms and administrations are hardly transferable, options such as equity participation of managers and workers cannot be implemented. Incentive pay systems, e.g. in the form of profit participation, are difficult to introduce if performance cannot be measured. In addition, there is hardly any competitive pressure on public firms because the public owner guarantees their sales while their funding is guaranteed through the taxpayer. At the same time, civil servants and public employees are comparatively free of competitive pressure because their special legal status offers almost absolute job security and relatively safe career paths.

The definition and allocation of property rights or substitute mechanisms incurs transaction costs. These must be considered when deciding on the organizational design of a firm. There is a close correlation between transaction costs implications as described in the previous section and property rights.

Table 1.2 Allocations of Property Rights in Different Types of Firms

Perspective	Static			Dynamic
	Allocation of Property Rights			Trans-ferability of Property Rights
Type of Firm	Control	Residual Claim	Sale	
Enterprise with single owner-ship	Entrepreneur	Entrepreneur	Entrepreneur	Unlimitedly transferable
Corporation without wor-kers' codetermination	Management	Shareholders	Shareholders	Unlimitedly transferable
Corporation with sta-tutory co-determination	Management/ Employees	Shareholders	Shareholders	Limitedly transferable
Corporation with vol-untary co-determination	Management/ Employees	Shareholders	Shareholders	Unlimitedly transferable
Worker-managed firm (e.g., in Ex-Yugoslavia)	Workers/ Management	Workers	—	Non-transferable
Non-profit organization	Members, resp. Politicians (State)	—	—	Limitedly transferable
State-owned firm	Politicians (State)/ Management	State	State	Limitedly transferable
Public administration	Politicians (State)/Pub-lic Servants	—	—	Non-transferable

Source: PICOT; WOLFF 1994, p. 218

In order to secure maximum adaptability to environmental changes, e.g., new market requirements, it is important to choose an allocation of property rights, which allows for organizational changes by easily transferable property rights.

In order to change tasks, it is useful to choose an allocation of rights that can be changed at a low transaction cost. Keeping this fact in mind, publicly owned firms and government administrations have major disadvantages. Alternative settings are described in the column "Transferability of Property Rights" in the table presented above

As a conclusion and starting point for the reorganization of a specific public task the following must be considered: For an efficient procurement of politically desired goods or services, resources should be allocated to that organization which is defined by a transaction costs' minimizing allocation of property rights.

Principal-Agent Analysis

In addition to the transaction costs- and property rights-approaches, *risk aversion* of individuals and *information asymmetries* must be considered. In order to develop further principles of how organizations have to be structured to guarantee an efficient production of goods and services, PICOT and WOLFF concentrate on the problem of information asymmetry, while making the simplifying presumption that, in general, agents are more risk-averse than principals.

"If person P (principal) puts person A (agent) in charge of pursuing a certain goal on his behalf, an agency relationship is established. This means that P allocates resources to A, and A's decisions also affect P's utility. Wherever labor division or a task delegation occurs, asymmetric information is likely to arise. This means that P may lack environmental information, or information on A's qualification, efforts or intentions, or a combination of both. In any case, there is scope for opportunistic actions on the part of the agent A. This is very likely to happen if A's interests differ from P's, inevitably resulting in a conflict of interests. This is referred to as the "agency problem".

In the case of *hidden characteristics,* the principal lacks information as to the actual quality of the goods or services that are offered by the agent. The problem is that the principal cannot monitor and verify all characteristics of the agent's offer, making opportunistic behavior on part of the agent possible even before the contractual agreement takes effect. The principal must bear the risk of an *adverse selection* of his contractual partner. This is an essential threat to the principal's utility, especially when she or he is tied to a specific agent by a long-term contract, such as lifetime labor contracts in the public service. In addition, there is a dynamic aspect to be considered: The agent's characteristics might change *according* to his environment, even if the agent himself/herself does not change, but if his and her environment or the task does. In the case of *hidden action* or *hidden information,* the principal is unable to monitor or assess the efforts of the agent after the contractual agreement has been established.

This causes the risk of *moral hazard,* which becomes worse as the fungibility, "plasticity", resources and monitoring costs rise. The greater the degree of utilization to which a certain resource may be put, the higher its plasticity. In public administrations, the main inputs are human capital, office equipment, and money. All of this is fungible.

Simultaneously, there is a high risk of moral hazard in large bureaucratic organizations, such as public firms and administrations, because ownership (taxpayers) and control are completely separated from one another, and there are solid structures of hierarchy and delegation. There are also utility losses if, due to expert knowledge, senior employees cannot assess the jobs of subordinate employees. Although these problems also occur in large private organizations, the "plasticity of resources as well as monitoring costs tend to be somewhat higher in public firms and administrations" (ibid, p.222).

In the case of *hidden intention,* there is a dependency of the principal on the resources, which the agent contributes to the production process. The principal depends on a continuation of the agency relationship due to specific investments and lack of alternatives (GOLDBERG 1976, 439) call that type of risk "hold up". Even if it is possible to monitor the agent's effort and all external factors, the principal does not have the means to change the situation.

In general, there are two means of limiting the principal's disadvantages, either by a reduction of the information asymmetry or by a co-alignment of interests between principal and agent. PICOT and WOLFF conclude that signaling, screening, self-selection, and implementing of all contractual methods to co-align the interests of principal and agent should take place also in public firms and administrations, if they help reduce the costs resulting from opportunistic behavior and wasting of public resources.

1.7 Specific elements of the regulatory framework

On the basis of case studies in the telecom field, LEVY and SPILLER (1996) have attempted to show that core political and social institutions have an impact on regulatory structures and performance in the telecommunications industry. The study included Jamaica, the United Kingdom, Chile, Argentina, and the Philippines. The authors argue "the credibility and effectiveness of a regulatory framework and thus its ability to encourage private investment and support efficiency in the production and use of services, varies with a country's political and social institutions. Performance can be satisfactory under a wide range of regulatory procedures, so long as three complementary mechanisms are in place to restrain arbitrary administrative action: substantive restraints on discretionary actions by the regulator, formal or informal restraints on changing the regulatory system, and institutions to enforce the restraints".

According to the authors' findings, political and social institutions may have an independent effect on the type of regulation that can be implemented and therefore on the appropriate balance between commitment to a particular regulatory system and flexibility in response to technological change. They suggest that "credible commitment to a regulatory regime can be cultivated even in what appears to be a problematic environment and that without such a commitment, long-term investment will not result".

In some environments, solutions run counter to the prevailing wisdom: achieving commitment may require an inflexible regulatory regime, and sometimes public ownership of utilities may be the only feasible alternative. For example, regulatory schemes designed to maximize efficiency (price caps, incentive schemes, competition) usually require substantial discretion on the part of the regulator. But unless a country's institutions allow arbitrary behavior to be distinguished from useful regulatory discretion, a system that grants generous administrative discretion might not generate the high levels of investment and welfare expected from private ownership. Conversely, a regulatory regime that allows almost no flexibility, though seeming very inefficient, might still provide adequate incentives for investment if it corresponds to the country's institutional endowments.
The study focuses only on highly developed countries. However, the institutional and regulatory framework for utilities in general and public transport in particular differs substantially in these countries.

Three public transport characteristics provide the basis for this analysis. First, public transport services have important economies of scale and scope. Second, most public transport, especially rail transit assets, is specific and non-redeployable in other uses (although the extent of sunk investments varies with the application and the technology). And third, public transport services typically have a broad range of local users, sometimes representing important portions of the local voting population. Viewed through the lens of the new institutional economics, these characteristics create contracting problems that prohibit ordinary market mechanisms from delivering first-best performance (BARZEL 1989; GOLDBERG 1976; NORTH 1991; WILLIAMSON 1988).

Economies of scale and scope imply that the number of providers of rail transit services is going to be small. Because a large proportion of a utility's assets are s, a utility will be willing to operate even if it cannot recover its investments so long as it covers its operating costs. The social role of public transport and the sometimes wide base of local users implies that utility pricing will in many cases have a political component.

The combination of large investments in durable, specific assets and strong politicization have led to the responsibility of the state, the region or the municipality to finance and operate these systems. At a time where private management is intended to increase efficiency of existing systems and to replace public with private investments into existing or new systems, new ways of regulating private involvement have to be found.

The comparison's primary focus thus has to be on the regulatory framework for attracting private investment.

A common framework incorporating regulatory design and a country's institutional endowment guides the empirical analysis of how — and how well — each country has resolved its regulatory problems. The analysis also explains why the resolution took the form it did and demonstrates the relation between regulatory outcomes and the performance of private utilities.

To understand a country's ability to commit to particular regulatory processes and institutions, it is useful to look at regulation as a "design" problem with two components: regulatory governance and regulatory incentives. The governance structure incorporates the mechanisms a society uses to restrain the discretionary scope of regulators and to resolve the conflicts caused by these restraints. The regulatory incentive structure comprises the rules governing pricing, subsidies, competition and entry, and interconnection.

Regulatory governance and incentives are variables for policy makers. Yet the choices are constrained by the specific institutional endowment of the country, which determines the form and the severity of the country's regulatory problems and the range of options available to resolve these. Choices about regulatory incentives are further constrained by institutional endowment and by the governance features built into the regulatory system.

Following NORTH and others, five elements of a nation's institutional endowment are:

- Legislative and executive institutions — the formal mechanisms for appointing legislators and decision makers, for making and implementing laws and regulations, and for determining the relations between these two institutions
- Judicial institutions — the formal mechanisms for appointing judges and determining the internal structure of the judiciary and for impartially resolving disputes among private parties or between private parties and the state
- Custom and other informal, but broadly accepted norms that restrain the actions of individuals or institutions
- The character of the contending social interests within a society and the balance between them, including the influence of ideology
- The country's administrative capabilities.

None of these elements are entirely static, though changes in a particular country are often slow. Also, the "level" where institutional decisions are made and developments take place is not static. Furthermore, supranational levels may play an important part, such as in European countries, where the (de)regulation of public tasks is predominated more and more by the European level.

An independent judiciary with a reputation for impartiality, whose decisions are enforced, is a necessary prerequisite in order to make credible commitments. This prerequisite is fulfilled equally in each of the three countries and hence is to be neglected when analyzing both the approach and the impact of the regulatory structure.

The structure and organization of a country's legislative and executive institutions influence its regulatory options according to how well they restrain arbitrary government action. Formal institutional mechanisms for restraining government authority include explicit separation of legislative, executive, and judicial powers (GELY and SPILLER 1990), including a federal structure of power, with strong decentralization even down to the local level. Each of the countries involved has basically comparable stable democratic legislative and executive institutions. Basic distinctions are characterized through the strong legislative and executive role of the state level in the U.S. This is structurally comparable to Germany but not to Great Britain. The state level severely restrains the federal government's authority in areas of state responsibility. In the U.S. and Germany, this restraint applies especially to public transport

Countries may be distinguished between those whose political institutions allow them to make credible regulatory commitments through legislation and those that can best achieve such commitment by embedding their regulatory systems in the operating licenses of private companies. Legislation may provide regulatory credibility in a political system that does not generate a unified government, such as presidential systems with multi-chamber legislatures and different electoral cycles. Nevertheless, legislation must specify the process for making regulatory decisions; otherwise regulatory discretion will be unchecked. In two party parliamentary systems, with parties that alternate in government, legislation will not confer regulatory credibility. In this case a solution may be to embed the regulatory process in contract law rather than administrative law. The United States as well as Germany falls into the group of countries that can embed their regulatory systems in legislation, and the United Kingdom falls into the group that will find embedding its regulatory system in contracts more successful. A similarity within Anglo-Saxon countries that also is valid in Germany is that the institutional endowment includes informal norms or bodies of administrative law that restrains the arbitrary use of government power even in the absence of explicit legal restraints.

To promote welfare, the regulatory incentive structure should facilitate investment, allocatively efficient pricing, and the introduction of new services and infrastructures. Regulatory incentives, however, are not implemented in an institutional vacuum; they are affected by a country's institutional endowment, its distributive politics, and the nature of its regulatory governance.

Administrative capabilities such as the ability of the administrative professionals to handle complex regulatory concepts and processes smoothly and without triggering a proliferation of disputes and litigation are high in each of the countries involved, but they are not necessarily requested and stimulated. Thus, a potential lack of administrative capabilities in the case study countries does not restrain the implementation of regulatory incentives.

Distributive politics can interfere with the allocative efficiency that can be achieved by regulatory incentives. The social role of public transport may lead to "political prices" that have a strong impact on regulatory incentives. In fact, the existence and the aims of distributive politics lead to important distinctions of the degree and areas of privatization or private participation between the countries involved.

As a central hypothesis, three complementary sets of mechanisms for restraining arbitrary action must be in place and properly aligned with the specific characteristics of a country's background institutions for private performance to be satisfactory: substantive restraints on regulatory discretion, which can take the form of process regulation or specific substantive rules; restraints of either the legislative or licensing variety on changing the regulatory system; finally institutions that enforce the substantive restraints on changing the system.

The government systems of the case study countries as a prerequisite of the regulatory frame - similarities, differences

The U.S. and the United Kingdom have parliamentary government systems, a strong judiciary, and electoral rules that tend to support two strong parties. In UK the parliamentary system of the United Kingdom, the majority party invariably has an absolute majority in parliament and controls both the government and the legislature.

The formal institutions of government in the United Kingdom allow for substantial government discretion. That discretion can translate into important policy shifts, with the judiciary playing a minor role in restraining administrative discretion. In both countries as well as in Germany, informal rules of legislative decision making restrain the government's ability to shift policy without consulting with interest groups and building consensus beforehand. The need for consensus building arises as much from the imperative of legitimizing government decision making as from the need to maintain a solid front in the governing party to avoid losing the support of the legislature.

1.8 Regulatory systems and efficiency in case study countries

Successful regulatory policy encourages both private investment and efficient operation. It rests on the development of a regulatory governance structure that constrains arbitrary administrative action, thereby encouraging private investment, and on regulatory incentives promoting efficiency as well as investment. Institutional endowments and the requirements of regulatory governance influence which regulatory incentive structures are workable in individual country settings.

Competition

Competition can be a powerful spur to innovation as well as to technical and economic efficiency. The fact that major public transport companies in each of the case study countries failed to increase their market share for local transport for decades, despite continuously high and sometimes increasing public subsidies, led to calls for opening up the public transport sector to competition.

The first post-war privatization of a public rail network took place in the 1970s in the USA - the privatization of the freight rail network and the freight rail companies. Consequently, the market share of rail in freight transport increased and is presently substantially higher than in any European country. The fact that the success of this example has not been transferred to the local public transport market and to the long-distance passenger rail market (up to date) is a sign of significant political intervention, caused by the internal structure of Amtrak (long-distance rail), the social meaning of local public transport, as well as by the internal structure of the local and regional transport companies.

In the United Kingdom, Margaret Thatcher's deregulation policy of the late 1980s opened nearly every public utility sector to its competitors. The goal of this radical change to the strongly unionized public sector was to cut public subsidies and to have public tasks efficiently fulfilled by private companies. Results were mixed, but generally positive, thereby causing subsequent governments to continue and refine the deregulation policy even further. As a result of public procurement policies aimed at improving the efficiency of public investments, the "Private Finance Initiative" (PFI) was introduced in 1992 and improved in 1997 (PFI to be re-invigorated, BATES REPORT 1997). This not only led to reductions of public subsidies, but also to a powerful incentive to restructure public entities and administrations under the potential threat of private competition.

Price regulation

In most industrialized countries prices for the use of rail transport are regulated and determined at least partially by public authorities. The intervention of public authorities is even stronger with respect to urban rail transport. While the USA is among the most strictly intervening countries, the UK represents the liberal counterpart in this field. Inside the London transport system prices are regulated within the overall regulation of London City transport tariffs. Outside of the capital, though, only few restrictive regulations apply, such as price reductions for the handicapped, for students etc. The Public Transport Executive reimburses revenue losses. Germany's law system gives permission to the transit operator to determine economically viable user tariffs, but these are counterbalanced by the necessity of public permission.

Subsidies

Public transport systems are not profitable on their own. The goal of the private involvement is to reduce public subsidies to a minimum and not to generate public income. Both cases - inside and outside of London - are represented in the study. They do not deliver a clear indication of whether a liberal price setting mechanism is a factor that makes urban rail transit investment more attractive or not. In fact, the private share of the overall investment and operation costs is higher in the London project than those in the Manchester project. Investor-friendly public regulation of revenue streams may thus be as attractive or even more attractive as no regulation at all. The main question is who will carry the revenue risk. In both projects it was the private side that did. In the case of London Croydon, the risk is related to the passenger number to be realized - if lower than expected, the project would have substantial problems, if higher than expected, the profitability would increase beyond the projected level. In the case of Manchester, the risk is related to the achievable specified revenue per passenger. Increasing the number of passengers thus is an indirect goal.

1.9 Summary and introduction into the study structure

A very brief summary comes to the following, simplified conclusion:

In the USA, where public transport nowadays is considered purely a public task, no framework of cooperation between public transit agencies and private transit or real estate companies has been established and no clear definition of the character of the public versus the character of the potential private task exists. This will be shown in Chapters 2 and 3, in which the framework of public needs and activities in the field of public transport will be set.

Chapter 4 will describe the political, financial, as well as the urban and real estate development framework and the perspectives of the different types of public private partnerships in seven of the most transit-relevant North American Metropolitan Areas.

It will be shown that public agencies, which have nevertheless redefined these roles in order to achieve better results, were somewhat left alone. This resulted in very different, sometimes very creative, unorthodox and pragmatic but mostly financially non-optimal approaches.

Chapter 5 describes these approaches for so-called “turnkey-projects”, i.e. projects (Light Rail) that are at least built, mostly also operated and maintained, and sometimes financed by private companies. The lack of a clear PPP-framework has led to incomplete but still innovative and instructive solutions in the cases of New Jersey's transit's tendering of the Hudson-Bergen line and Tri-Met's cooperation with Bechtel to accelerate the Airport Light Rail connection in Portland/OR. The approach in New Jersey consisted of a very thorough preparation of the tendering, including a very sophisticated and actually over-defined project and performance specification as well as a short time frame of the contract, intent to regain total public control as soon as possible (which created very substantial bidding costs – only two bids were received). As a consequence, the project's public costs were very high. The approach in Portland/OR was very informal and consisted in accepting the cooperation offer of the local Bechtel-director, who happened to have been administrator of the Federal Transit Administration during the 1980s.

Both procedures have contributed to a substantial acceleration of the project delivery with financial conditions that do not rely on real market conditions.

The British cases, in contrast, were based on an increasing consensus about the share of public and private tasks in order to achieve best value for (public) money. Although in neither case had the PFI-model existed, both profited greatly from the methods and the knowledge that resulted from the privatization and deregulation policy of the 1980s and early 1990s. The procurement methods, applied to the Manchester Metrolink differed from those of the Tramlink in London-Croydon, but both were very instructive and led to very high value financial backing.

Both procedures provide guidelines according to which PPP's can be structured. They can either be acquired in cooperation with the private partners (Croydon) or the public partner can provide them before selecting the private organizations that are to be involved (Manchester). The cooperative method to define project specifications prior to tendering them may represent some legal obstacles, but seems to be the most adequate to respond to the recommendation quoted earlier of recognizing and exploiting the respective skills of the public and private sectors.

As will be reported and analyzed in more detail in chapters 6 und 7, the most creative PPP approaches in the US are transit joint development and transit oriented development. Unlike the financially burdensome contractual relationships of "turnkey"-projects, these approaches don't include private transit consortiums but real estate developers. The public as well as the private interest in these cases is generally motivated to the maximize the development impact of existing or future urban rail lines, not to their construction or financing.

The framework for these projects consists of a set of regulatory, real estate market, and policy conditions (described in chapter 4), that differs between states and local communities. The "spirit" on the regional and local level (e.g. the importance contributed to public transit and the readiness to take measures to steer the development within certain limits) is generally well reflected by the specific set of regulatory and policy conditions. The “spirit” within the transit company itself is of major importance to promote or set transit supportive development friendly regulations and commercial attitudes. And finally, the “spirit” of the private real estate development community and the existence of powerful individual private partners that are committed to public transit are factors that fill the framework set by the diverse authorities with life or can promote transit supportive developments on their own. It will be shown, that generally those committed investors can be found in areas with consensus about the need to promote transit. In a growing number of cases they contribute substantially to generate such a consensus.

Chapter 8 will summarize these findings and draw conclusions for the application of partnerships in all of these fields in Germany. The applicability of the tools and regulatory and organizational conditions investigated in this study under the German legal and political frame will be discussed. It will aso be estimated in how far they can contribute to reduce transaction costs, create a transit friendly set of property rights and optimize transit friendly principal-agent-relationship.

2. Urban Rail-transit in the US - Development-Trends, Federal Policy, Funding Limits

2.1 Urban sprawl and public transit in the US - a brief introduction

Since the 1920s, and more so since World War II, the mobility offered by automobiles has allowed development to spread out in patterns unsuitable for service by rail-transit. The strong suburban extension of many cities was politically supported, or at least tolerated, in order to increase home ownership for a large share of the population. Decreasing use of bus and rail lines has paralleled the steady decline of metropolitan development densities in the last half of the 20th century.

This policy contributed to an explosion in car ownership, creating the need for a dense, costly road system. The "Interstate Highway Program" was introduced through the Eisenhower administration in 1954. It represented for many decades the main element of the federal surface transportation policy.

As a result, bus and rail traffic make politicians, administrations, engineers and construction firms was to create investment schemes, tools and pilot cases. Unlike the co-financing of highways, very few studies have been undertaken to evaluate the conditions and possible results of public private partnerships for public transit investments.

Nevertheless – Universities (e.g. Massachusetts Institute of Technology or Rutgers University) have delivered some case descriptions about the financing of Light Rail Lines and new project delivery methods in the transit field. In 1998 the Federal Transit Administration published a systematical overview on Innovative Transit Financing that helped distinguish the diverse tools and to evaluate their potential results.

Only a small share of overall traffic in the United States. Public transportation is used for less than 2% of all trips in the whole nation. While these figures are a little higher in metropolitan regions, it can be assumed that the automobile dominates all other kinds of traffic within most urban areas.

The implementation of an extensive road network on the national, regional and local level led not only to high maintenance costs and the expense of further development but also to the deterioration of quality of life, especially in urban areas. Traffic and congestion increased, pedestrian safety and comfort declined, urban design and zoning standards yielded to the demands of cars, and environmental conditions became unhealthy.

This trend became apparent already at the beginning of the 1960s. It was President John F. Kennedy who established federal assistance of public transit. He also initiated a legal basis for public transit funding, the "Urban Mass Transportation Act", which was enacted in 1964. During the 1970s and 80's rail-transit systems were introduced in some metropolitan areas. This and the subsequent acceleration of rail system demands, contributed to the rediscovery of inner cities as investment targets.

Although the overwhelming trend of urban sprawl and geographical extension of urban areas continues, it seems now to be slowing down.

In the beginning of the 1990s the Federal Highway Administration held a series of workshops entitled "Searching for Solutions". Surprising new figures were discussed. Benjamin Chinitz, chairman of a conference entitled "Metropolitan America in Transition: Implications for Land-use and Transportation Planning", presented results of his analysis of trends relating to location and growth of population and employment within US metropolitan areas.

This data indicated the deceleration, during the 1980s, of the long-term trend favoring the strong growth of suburban areas. After four decades during which the suburban share of the US population increased from 15 percent in 1940 to 45 percent in 1980, the suburban share rose only slightly to 46 percent from 1980 to 1990. At the same time, the central cities of metropolitan areas modestly increased their share of the US population in the 1980s from 30 to 31 percent. Mr. Chinitz suggested that two factors underlie these trends. "Firstly, foreign immigrants, who accounted for one-third of the increase in US population during the 1980s, favor central cities in their initial location choices. The second factor involved the mix of household types. The number of so-called "non-family" households and one parent-families increased much more rapidly than the number of conventional two-parent family households" (US DOT, FHWA, Washington 1994, p. 3).

Every economic and demographic trend appears to point to a continuation of this move, which is naturally dependent on regional variations in different markets. For example, late in 1998, the Brookings Institute and the Fannie Mae Foundation Research Division issued a new study of 24 large American cities. This study showed that, in a reversal of a trend that began after the end of the Second World War, each of the cities forecast strong growth in the number of people living downtown.

In fact, by 2010, the study reported, downtown populations are expected to quadruple in Houston, more than triple in Cleveland, and to nearly triple in Denver, with additional growth in larger cities (FANNIE MAE 1999).

Brad Segal, an urban consultant serving on the board of the International Downtown Association, believes that demographics and accumulated wealth point to radical transformations in American downtowns in the coming decades. For example, by 2010, 52 percent of American households will not have children at home. These "empty nesters" have been discovered as a prime market for in-town housing in Dallas, Denver and many other cities.

As a consequence, many political initiatives on various levels are being undertaken to promote urban "livability", transit-friendliness, "smart growth", new urbanistic design patterns and so on. Although not very well coordinated until recently and far from being omnipresent throughout the country, they all try to encourage densification, diversification and identity-building of community centers, residential areas, cities and regions.

The most important common issue of these initiatives is to stop further sprawl-development in order to save existing open space within urbanized areas and to channel development along urban corridors, dense enough to allow mixed-use development and to be served by public transit.

The Clinton-Gore-Livability Agenda (AGENDA 1998) showed the recognition of these goals at the highest political levels. It also emphasized the interconnectivity of the involved government activities, such as environmental, economical, housing, urban development, transportation, social, labor, school and even crime prevention policy.

The Agenda was based on a wave of anti-sprawl and community-building initiatives throughout the country. The New York Times reported on June 9,

1998 that "in the previous two years more than 100 local and county governments across the country attempted to win voter approval for tax increases or bond referendums to help buy undeveloped land and curb suburban sprawl. This included a 7 cents per gallon increase in New Jersey's gasoline tax for the purpose of preserving one million acres of undeveloped land over the next ten years. In addition to buying undeveloped land, New Jersey, Maryland, Florida and other states are trying to improve their management of growth by seeking to direct new development away from now-rural areas to more established towns that already have roads and water and sewer lines".

Although these initiatives are certainly not shared by a large majority of mayors, they may soon become political mainstream. In a New York Times article about the "War on Sprawl" in Atlanta, Alan Ehrenhalt, a longtime urban development activist, pretends, "that public officials, citizen activists and chambers of commerce throughout the country have begun to talk about sprawl in terms they used to reserve for pornography or Communism. The dangers of uncontrolled real estate development are now taken for granted in almost every state legislature from Montpelier to Phoenix. And the national poll numbers against sprawl are so overwhelming that Vice President Al Gore took what was inherently a local issue and made it the focus of a Presidential campaign. He predicted that "the American people are coming to the conclusion that sprawl is to blame for a good deal of the discontent that attaches to end-of-century middle-class life. And this change of mind will shake up politics in many places in the first decade of the 21st century".

2.2 Development of Urban Rail-Transit-Systems and Transit Ridership in the USA

In the USA, three generations of urban rail-transit exist. The first generation consists of older subway, tram and commuter-rail systems from before World War II, many from before the turn of the century. Rapid transit or tram-service existed in almost all larger urban areas throughout the country, mainly in the New York – New Jersey region, Boston, Philadelphia, Chicago, Cleveland and New Orleans. Commuter-rail systems reaching far back into history still exist in all of these cities except New Orleans.

The cities' growth patterns of that time were closely integrated with the availability of transit.

The first explicitly transit-supportive developments in the United States were suburban projects built in the late 19th century along streetcar lines. Often, the developers themselves paid for extensions of electric railways to promote their pleasant secure neighborhoods where residents were within walking distance of transit stations.

The next wave, in the 1970s, was propelled by the immense population growth, the geographic expansion of metropolitan centers in North America and increasing congestion problems in major metropolitan areas that had never had urban rail-transit systems. Due to high costs, insufficient federal funding capacities and the lack of powerful lobbying, new urban rail systems were developed in only three regions: San Francisco (1973), Washington (1976) and Atlanta (1979). A little later and on a smaller scale, new systems were built in Baltimore (1987), Miami and Los Angeles. Prior to this, as a result of citizen campaigns against inner-city highway projects, comparable systems were built in Toronto (1954) and Montreal.

The third wave began in the early 1980s and grew in the 1990s. It consisted mostly of new Light Rail systems, above ground, operated on new lines in city centers and generally on existing freight tracks or based on existing rights-of-way outside of the city centers. These were San Diego (1981), Buffalo (1985), Pittsburgh (1985), Portland/OR (1986), Los Angeles (1990), Sacramento (1990), San Jose (1991), Baltimore LRT (1992), Detroit (1993), St. Louis (1993), Denver (1994) and Dallas (1996).

According to an internal project overview of the Federal Transit Administration (FTA), between 1964 and 1999, a total of 22 billion dollars (US) of federal money has been spent for 34 billion dollars worth of new rail systems or line extensions, or reintroduction of commuter rail service. This is relatively little by European standards but it permitted the start of new systems that expanded the basis of experience with urban rail-transit and created the desire to reinvent rail-transit as the basis of a real alternative for urban transportation.

As many of these systems were relatively successful, both in terms of cost-reduction (compared to the rapid-transit-development a decade before) and ridership attraction, the appeal for new rail-based transit systems developed. Besides the expansion of existing networks an impressive number of new systems are now planned, or under construction. Based on the requests for federal "New Starts" funding these are Ft. Lauderdale, Austin, Kansas City,

Las Vegas, Little Rock, Memphis, Orlando, Salt Lake City, Seattle and San Juan / Puerto Rico. New systems or system expansions revolve around Light Rail-transit (LRT).

In addition, in a growing number of cases the reactivation of commuter rail lines or the extension of commuter rail systems are now being planned. In many regions (e.g. San Diego) both systems have similar functions in suburban areas although mostly different operators and different technological and legal patterns (e.g. the reactivation of commuter rail lines often leads to a conflict with existing freight rail services).

WINSTON/SHIRLEY (1998) provide an overview about the system-expansions, as of October 1996 (table 2.1).

In addition to the existing 3162 mi long commuter rail network, 191 mi are under construction, almost 1300 mi in different planning and design phases and more than 700 mi were proposed (APTA 1999).

James Oberstar, member of Congress and ranking Democrat of the Committee on Transportation and Infrastructure explains the reasons for this demand: "The increasing congestion problems of American Metropolitan Areas cannot be resolved through car-related measures alone. Transportation alternatives are necessary, especially when substantial numbers of potential users can take advantage of it". In the case of his home state Minnesota he quotes the example of the reactivation of the commuter rail line between St. Cloud and Minneapolis.

This 70 mile long corridor, called the "Northstar Corridor", has a population of 2.5 million. According to the descriptions in the Environmental Impact Statement Project Scoping (July 1999) and the New Starts Funding Request for fiscal year 2000, the corridor represents the "third fastest-growing region in the nation". The commuter rail service is expected to attract more than 7000 passengers daily. This, says Oberstar, is equivalent to one highway-lane in each direction that doesn't need to be built as a consequence of the railway-line.

Table 2.1 Cities Planning to Build or extend Rail Systems, as of Oct. 1996[1]

CITY	CHARACTERISTICS AND STATUS
Building New Heavy Rail	
None	
Building New Light Rail	
Atlanta	14.5 miles proposed
Hartford	16.3 miles in planning phase, more than half expected to be open by 2000 (open)
Kansas City	15.2 miles in planning or design phases
Miami	9.6 miles in planning phase, some expected to be open by 2005
Milwaukee	22.0 miles in planning phase
New York	10.6 miles in planning or design phases, expected to be open by 2001
Norfolk	10.0 miles in planning phases
Oklahoma City	9.1 miles proposed or in planning phase, expected to be open by 2001
Orlando	24.0 miles in planning phase
Salt Lake City	15.8 miles in design phase, expected to be open by 2000 (open)
Tampa	2.3 miles in planning phase, expected to be open by 1999 (open)
Extending Heavy Rail	
Atlanta	12.6 miles in planning or design phases
Cleveland	3.0 miles in planning phases
Los Angeles	40.7 miles in planning, planned, design or construction phases, most expected to be open by 2003
Miami	37.6 miles in planning or design phases
New York	0.4 miles in construction phase
San Francisco	62.0 miles proposed, or in planning, design, or construction phases
Washington, D.C.	41.3 miles in planning or construction phases
Extending Light Rail	
Baltimore	7.3 miles in construction phase, expected to be open by 1997 (open)
Boston	2.1 miles proposed
Buffalo	28.6 miles proposed or in planning phase, most expected to be open after 2020
Cleveland	2.0 miles in planning phase
Dallas	48.8 miles proposed or in planning, design, or construction phases, most expected to be open by 2003
Denver	8.7 miles in design phase, expected to be open by 2000 (open)
Los Angeles	16.4 miles in planning or construction phases, most expected to he open by 2001
Memphis	4.4 miles in planning or construction phases, expected to open by 1999 (open)
New Orleans	7.9 miles proposed or in design phase, expected to open by 2002
New York (NJ Transit)	28.8 miles in planning or design phases (phase I open since 2000)
Pittsburgh	5.2 miles in planning phase
Portland	39.0 miles in design or construction phases, some expected to be open in 1998 (Westside MAX open)
Sacramento	36.6 miles in planning, design, or construction phases, some expected to be open in 1998 (phase I open)
St. Louis	66.6 miles proposed or in planning or design phases, most expected to be open by 2005
San Diego	21.8 miles in planning or construction phases, some expected to be open by 1997 (Orange line open)
San Francisco	34.0 miles in planning, design, or construction phases
San Jose	27.7 miles in planning, design, or construction phases, most expected to be open by 2003
Seattle	26.6 miles in planning phase, expected to be open by 2004

[1] *Source:* APTA, 1996 Transit Fixed Guideway Inventory (Washington, 1996), tables 13 and 19a. Projects without specific track mileage and commuter rail projects we excluded. Mileage is approximate one-way mileage.

APTA-president Bill Millar, at the opening of the Rail-Volution conference in September, 1999 in Dallas/TX, drew a very optimistic picture: “I am pleased to report the state of Rail-Volution is good. Rail Ridership is up. 5 new Rail Lines or extensions are opening in 1999. 37 new rail line segments or extensions are under construction. Nearly 200 new rail line segments or extensions are in the design or planning phase. Federal Funding is at its highest level in the history of the Federal Transit Program - $5.8 billion for fiscal year (FY) 2000 $407 million increase over fiscal year 99”.

2.3 Trends in Public Transportation Ridership

Public transportation ridership reflects the sequence of development, decline and redevelopment of transit systems throughout the nation. It “has gone through six major cycles of growth and decline during the twentieth century influenced by general social and economic forces. From 1900 to 1929 ridership grew steadily; first due to technical innovation and investment opportunities during the early development of street railways and then due to the economic boom of World War I and the post-war period. The Great Depression caused a steep decline in ridership between 1929 and 1939 as people made fewer work trips and often could not afford to take pleasure trips. A new federal law limiting utilities' ability to subsidize public transportation, as had been normal practice, led to a decline in public transportation capital facilities. World War II caused motor fuel rationing and an economic boom that led to a new rapid growth cycle in ridership. Ridership quickly declined from artificially high war levels as people fled to suburbs spurred on by cheap fuel and government policy favoring low-density suburban growth. In 1973, the ridership cycle reversed again and public transportation began a modest growth based on a partnership of local, state and federal government committed to improving American's transportation infrastructure” (APTA 2000, p.65).

The trend has been accelerating during the last five years and causes great pride within transit agencies and their representation. At the opening of the annual APTA conference in October 1999 in Orlando/FL president Bill Millar proudly presented the following figures about the development of public transportation in general: “In addition to federal funding increases, ridership is also skyrocketing. Ridership in the second quarter of this year is up 6.13% over the same period last year. Last year, 8.7 billion – that is “B” as in billion –

trips were taken annually. In the US this year we are on track for 9 billion trips. The most in 40 years--before there was a federal transit program. Since our last EXPO three years ago in Anaheim, 1.1 billion trips have been added to the U.S. public transportation annual total. Each day nearly 1 million more trips are taken on public transportation compared to one year ago".

As APTA announced on January 10, 2001 (*www.APTA.com*) "in the year 2000, more Americans decided to leave the driving to someone else. Last year, usage of U.S. public transportation systems grew by an estimated 320 million rides, to a total of 9.4 billion trips. This increase comes on the heels of record ridership the previous year when over 9 billion trips were made on the nation's transit systems. In the past five years, ridership on the nation's public transportation systems has grown by over 20 percent".

"Investments made in public transportation services offer the American people real opportunities and choices," said William W. Millar, President of the American Public Transportation Association, who made the latest ridership figures available. "When people are given a choice, they will ride easy-to-use quality public transportation."

The growth in public transportation ridership is attributed to the strong economy, higher levels of investment by federal, state and local sources and enhanced customer services by the nation's transit systems that meet the needs of today's traveling public.

2.4 Selected North American Study and European Study Areas

As shown in tables 2.2 and 2.3, based on 1990-1998/9 data (transportation indicators for major US and Canadian urbanized areas), the regions represent the largest population (**New York/New Jersey**), the densest urbanization (**Toronto**), the highest per capita daily vehicle miles traveled and, as a precondition of that, the lowest urban density (**Atlanta**). One even ranked among the lowest regional transit ridership rates with less than 20 yearly rides per person (**Dallas**), which may also be a consequence of the nation's densest specific roadway-network (6.3 mi or 10 km per 1000 persons (DUNPHY 1997, p.6). The selection finally includes the national capital **Washington D.C.** with its strong division between the dense transit-favorable regional core "inside the Beltway" and its opposite development patterns "outside the Beltway",

Portland, the only urban area with very decisive regional development restrictions (Urban Growth Boundary) and **San Diego** as California's economically strongest developing region with a history of freeway oriented urban development. Illustration 2-1 shows an overview of North American study areas.

The investigation focuses on North American cases but it was necessary to introduce several examples in Great Britain and Germany to improve the understanding of the respective North American cases. These reference cases are located in the Metropolitan Areas shown in Illustration 2-2. They include the Light Rail system in **Manchester** and in the **London** borough of **Croydon** as well as transit oriented developments in the **Berlin** area and in the area of **Düsseldorf.**

The comparisons with British and German cases will focus on four metropolitan areas that are presented in each of the two following tables:

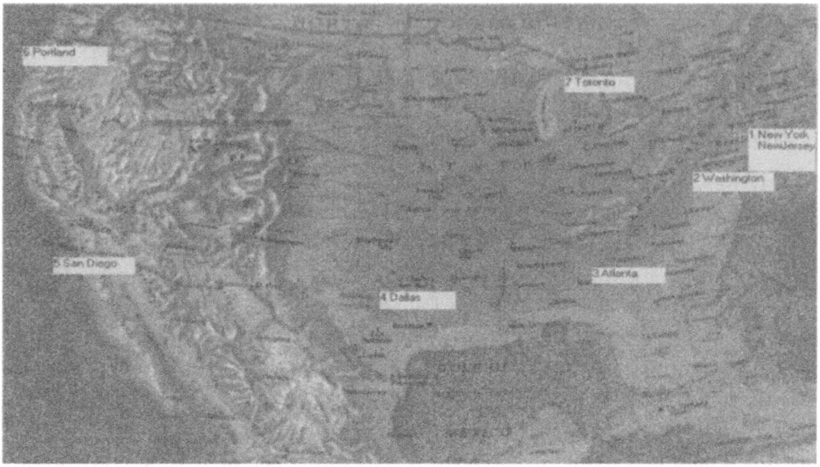

Illustration 2-1: Geographical Overview of North American study areas

Illustration 2-2: Geographical Overview of European case study areas

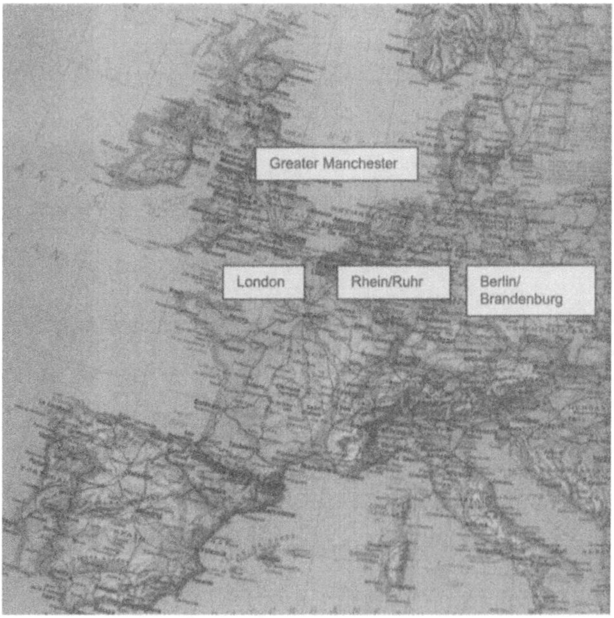

Table 2.2 Demographical Indicators for Metropolitan Areas in North America and Europe

	Population[1]			Density[1]	
	1990 (in 1000)	1990 - 1999[2] (%change)	Area (Sq. Miles)	Persons per (Sq.Mile)	(sqkm)
New York/Northeast New Jersey	**15,780**	**3.2**	**3,177**	**4,967**	**1,940**
Los Angeles/Long Beach	11,428	5.3	2,100	5,442	2,125
Chicago/Northwest Indiana	7,303	8.1	1,958	3,730	1,457
Philadelphia	4,216	0.6	1,086	3,882	1,516
Detroit	3,905	4.9	1,243	3,142	1,227
San Francisco/Oakland	3,676	8.7	816	4,505	1,760
Toronto	**3,667**		**572**	**6,409**	**2,503**
Washington, D.C.	**3,240**	**12.2**	**820**	**3,951**	**1,543**
Dallas/Fort Worth	**3,030**	**21.6**	**1,404**	**2,158**	**842**
Boston	2,803	2.2	1,033	2,713	1,060
Houston	2,798	20.7	1,549	1,806	705
Montreal	2,437		373	6,533	2,552
San Diego	**2,294**	**12.9**	**680**	**3,374**	**1,317**
Minneapolis/St. Paul	2,055	13.1	996	2,063	806
Baltimore	1,991	4.6	523	3,807	1,487
St. Louis	1,950	3.1	694	2,810	1,098
Phoenix	1,920	34.6	971	1,977	772
Atlanta	**1,860**	**30.3**	**1,198**	**1,553**	**606**
Miami	1,800	12.3	442	4,072	1,590
Cleveland	1,752	0.9	629	2,785	1,088
Seattle/Everett	1,730	14.8	645	2,682	1,048
Pittsburgh	1.708	- 2.7	713	2,396	935
Vancouver	1,632		1,017	1,605	626
Denver	1,540	21.9	433	3,557	1,389
San Jose	1,410	10.0	326	4,325	1,689
Kansas City	1,281	10.9	608	2,107	823
Milwaukee	1,220	2.1	550	2,218	866
Ft. Lauderdale/Hollywood	1,200	22.3	368	3,261	1,274
Portland	**1,196**	**21.8**	**416**	**2,875**	**1,123**
San Bernardino/Riverside	1,169	23.6	480	2,435	951
Cincinnati	1,136	6.6	564	2,014	787
Sacramento	1,096	16.1	340	3,224	1,259
New Orleans	1,080	1.6	361	2,992	1,169
Buffalo	1,064	- 4.0	405	2,627	1,026
Manchester/GB (Greater Manchester)[3]	**2,578**	**0.0**	**502**	**3,133**	**2.005**
London/GB (Greater London)[3]	**7,112**	**n/a**	**619**	**11,494**	**4.490**
Rhein-Ruhr/D (VRR)[4]	**7,315**	**0,5**	**1,960**	**3,725**	**1.455**
Berlin-Brandenburg/D (engerer Verflechtungsraum)[5]	**4,218**	**2.0**	**2,097**	**2,051**	**802**

[1] US-Census, United States Urbanized Areas, 1990, [2] US-Census, Metropolitan Area Population Estimates, 1.4.1990 - 1.7.1999, [3] Eurostat 2000: regions general indicators, Brussels 2000, [4] figures based on „Handbuch für Tarif und Vertrieb, VRR Gelsenkirchen 2001, author's calculations, [5] Branden-burgisches Landesamt für Datenverarbeitung und Statistik, Bevölkerungsprognose 2000

Table 2.3 Transportation Indicators for Metropolitan Areas in North-America and Europe

	Roads and Car-Use[1]				Transit Use [2]			
	Cars [6] per 1.000 inhabitants	Roadway Miles per 1.000 Persons	Daily Vehicle-Miles Traveled per Capita **1990**	Daily Vehicle-Miles Traveled per Capita **1999**	Total Trips (Millions)		Trips per Capita	
					1990	1998	1990	1998
New York/Northeast New Jersey	**709[7]**	**2.2**	**14,3**	**15,8**	**2,807.6**	**3,508.5**	**143**	**174**
Los Angeles/Long Beach	758	2.2	21.9	23.0	515.4	557.4	35	35
Chicago/Northwest Indiana	742[8]	2.6	16.9	20.0	697.2	561.3	85	63
Philadelphia	719	2.6	15.6	18.1	367.5	284.0	74	57
Detroit	801	3.2	20.0	21.9	94.9	65.9	22	15
San Francisco/Oakland	758	2.5	20.9	22.0	414.1	415.0	111	102
Toronto	**n/a**	**n/a**	**11.0**	**-**	**496.8**	**n/a**	**-**	**-**
Washington, D.C.	**762[9]**	**2.6**	**19.9**	**22.6**	**372.4**	**363.8**	**88**	**77**
Dallas/Fort Worth	**675**	**6.3**	**26.5**	**30.8**	**56.6**	**67.8**	**14**	**14**
Boston	829	3.3	18.3	20.4	323.7	340.1	11	10
Houston	675	6.1	25.6	26.4	90.7	95.1	25	20
Montreal	n/a	n/a	n/a	-	385.8	n/a	-	-
San Diego	**758**	**2.5**	**22.5**	**23.4**	**68.6**	**89.6**	**27**	**32**
Minneapolis/St. Paul	806	4.4	21.0	25.3	69.6	66.0	27	23
Baltimore	723	3.0	18.3	10.0	116.7	106.6	49	43
St. Louis	800	3.7	23.2	30.0	44.6	56.0	18	22
Phoenix	724	4.9	20.7	21.2	32.1	36.7	14	12
Atlanta	**856**	**5.2**	**34.9**	**40.4**	**149.6**	**160.9**	**50**	**41**
Miami	713	3.1	18.6	19.3	77.8	82.9	40	38
Cleveland	870	3.2	18.4	21.9	74.7	67.0	33	30
Seattle/Everett	808	3.7	23.6	26.0	100.3	120.6	49	51
Pittsburgh	71.9	4.4	19.0	10.8	89.3	77.2	37	33
Vancouver	n/a	n/a	n/a	-	104.2	n/a	-	-
Denver	913	3.9	17.6	25.1	55.5	72.6	34	36
San Jose	758	2.6	23.0	27.3	45.7	53.9	30	32

Kansas City	800	4.8	21.4	33.2	18.8	15.5	11	8
Milwaukee	776	3.9	23.5	25.9	66.3	73.6	41	44
Ft. Lauderdale/ Hollywood	713	3.5	20.2	22.9	18.6	26.7	12	20
Portland	**862**	**3.8**	**18.7**	**21.4**	**58.9**	**87.1**	**38**	**47**
San Bernardino/Riverside	758	3.2	21.4	27.7	9.8	20.9	-	-
San Antonio	675	5.8	21.7	22.6	42.1	42.0	31	27
Cincinnati	870	3.3	20.8	27.0	34.9	32.6	22	20
Sacramento	758	3.2	21.6	22.3	20.3	29.0	15	19
New Orleans	763	2.8	15.5	14.1	85.5	69.3	66	53
Buffalo	709	3.4	16.0	20.9	30.4	n/a	16	
Manchester/GB	375[5]	n/a	n/a	n/a				
London/GB	332[5]	n/a	n/a	n/a	1,713 [12]	2,223 [12]	241 [13]	305 [13]
Rhein-Ruhr/D	495 [4]	0.6 [4]	n/a	n/a	849 [10]	1,068 [10]	117 [14]	147 [14]
Berlin-Brandenburg/D	409 [4]	1.3 [4]	n/a	n/a	1,081 [10]	1,041 [11]	315 [15]	306 [15]

[1] = Federal Highway Statistics 1990 and 2000 ❖ [2] = APTA, Public Transportation Fact Books 1992 and 2000 ❖ [3] = author's calculations ❖ [4] = Eurostat, statistical yearbook 2000: regions-transportation infrastructure NUT-regions, i.e., administrative districts that don't correspond to Metropolitan Areas in Germany (generally: Regierungsbezirke) ❖ [5] = UK National Statistics, Motor cars currently licensed and new registrations, 1997, Regional-Trends Dataset, figures for Manchester are based on the statistical region "North-West" ❖ [6] = based on state-wide numbers (State Motor-Vehicle Registrations - 1999) ("all private an commercial motor vehicles" minus an estimated 3 % reduction for truck tractors and farm trucks) ❖ [7] = based on figures for New Jersey ❖ [8] = based on figures for Illinois ❖ [9] = based on figures for D.C., Maryland and Virginia ❖ [10] = based on BMVBW: Verkehr in Zahlen 2000 figures for Berlin-Brandenburg only for Berlin (West & East) ❖ [11] = author's calculation, based on total passenger journeys BVG plus S-Bahn GmbH ❖ [12] = based on London Transport Annual Reports 1989/1990 and 1999/2000, annual passenger journeys for Underground and buses ❖ [13] = author's calculation, based on figures of the "Transport statistics for London, 2000 ❖ [14] = author's calculation, based on figures of the Verkehrsverbund Rhein-Ruhr ❖ [15] = author´s calculation, based on population figures for the City of Berlin

3. Overview of areas and tools of public funding and private contribution

3.1 Federal Transportation Policy – Intermodality, Efficiency, Innovative Financing

ISTEA

The Intermodal System Transportation Equity Act (ISTEA) of 1991 introduced basic changes: Since 1954, the construction of the Interstate System had been the centerpiece of the national transportation policy. When this unique system, that Robert Cervero called the "worldwide largest public work project", was completed and its efficiency limits became clearer, transportation decision-makers, practitioners and stakeholders called for a more diversified, multi-modal and intermodal approach. ISTEA's central elements – strategic infrastructure investment, intermodalism, flexibility, intergovernmental partnership, a strong commitment to safety and the environment, and an inclusive decision-making process – provided the platform from which innumerable policies, programs and projects have been launched by State and local partners.

ISTEA loosened the once purely highway-related dedication of the gas-tax revenue based Highway Trust Fund and widened the financial and political frame for state governments to influence the priorities of federally funded transportation investments.

The US DOT (Department of Transportation) describes the path from ISTEA to TEA 21 as a longer process of discussions including all state governments as well as a series of non-governmental institutions: "In a series of 13 Regional Forums, plus over 100 focus groups in more than 40 States, held by each surface modal administration, the 1996 ISTEA reauthorization outreach effort provided invaluable ideas which were vital in shaping the Clinton Administration's ISTEA reauthorization proposal. This effort provided an opportunity to benefit from the insights of the stakeholders in the Nation's transportation system".

The $123 billion program for highway and mass transit was approved by a 91-7 margin. It was important for mass transit in two ways: 1) It called for spending an average of $620 million per year on new rail lines and extensions in two dozen cities across the nation. This amounted to a 50 percent increase over what the federal government had spent over the preceding five years. 2) The new legislation would give states like New Jersey, which violated the standards of the federal Clean Air Act, much more latitude to use federal highway aid to pay for mass transit projects.

ISTEA represents a groundbreaking, innovative approach to transportation policy in the US. This change has been strongly promoted by New York's former senator, the late Daniel Patrick Moynihan and the non-governmental organization "Surface Transportation Policy Project", whose director, Roy Kienitz, was the head of Moynihan's New York office for many years.

TEA 21

The Transportation Equity Act of 1998 (TEA-21) further promotes ISTEA's investment in both the transportation system and in people. TEA-21 ensures a guaranteed level of federal funds through 2003 for highways and transit. TEA-21 also guarantees that each state will receive a minimum of 90.5 percent of the amount each state contributes to the Highway Trust Fund. In addition to guaranteed investment levels, TEA-21 includes special programs to ensure mobility and access to jobs, health care, and recreational activities for all Americans.

The "Minimum Guarantee "was hailed at all of the listening sessions as one of the most important features of TEA-21. Numerous speakers and state DOTs in particular noted that the combination of guaranteed annual funding levels and minimum guarantees for each state will facilitate better long term planning, more certainty in the availability of funds, and better overall management of the transportation investment programs of states and Metropolitan Planning Organizations (MPOs).

TEA-21 also facilitates the attraction of private capital to transportation investments. The Transportation Infrastructure Finance and Innovation Act (TIFIA, explained in the next chapter) creates a mechanism through which DOT can provide credit assistance on flexible terms directly to public-private sponsors of major surface transportation projects to assist them in gaining access to capital markets. During the listening sessions, unanimous support was heard for the TIFIA program and requests for the expeditious release of implementing guidance and policies.

State Infrastructure Banks (SIBs, also explained in the next chapter) were also widely supported. Many State DOT representatives registered their disappointment that the SIB program under TEA-21 is limited to only four States" (US DOT 1999/1).

TIFIA as well as other innovative financing tools were strongly supported and pushed by John Chafee, the former Republican U.S. Senator from Rhode Island and Chair of the Committee on Environment and Public Works, who passed away at the end of October 1999. He is cited as saying, "TIFIA will stretch limited transportation funds for large, nationally significant transportation infrastructure projects. $500 million in TEA-21 will leverage $10.5 billion in additional investment." (US DOT 1999/1)

3.2 Operation versus Infrastructure-Financing; Federal versus local Funding

The following figures show the federal, state and local funding activities between 1989 and 2001. During this period two tendencies can be observed: a steady absolute increase of fare revenues, which was in average appr. 20 % beyond the inflation rate (see index under URL: www.bls.gov/cpi/home.htm#-overview) and strong absolute and relative increase of "other" sources, which are mostly local government subsidies but also revenues from bridge and tunnel tolls as well as parking lot funds.

Also the Capital funding sources have shifted from almost 100 % public subsidies to a relevant portion of internal funding sources, stemming from transit agencies fees and taxes and from their non-transit sectors (such as real estate). During the nineties this self generated funding sources has steadily increased.

Since the initial segments of the very cost-intensive heavy rail systems in the 1970s had very few beneficiaries, the government was obliged to re-think its public transportation funding policy. State governments had to react to the change of federal activities and then counterbalance them.

Table 3.1 Operating and Capital Funding Sources (million Dollars)[2]

Type of funding	1989	1991	1993	1995	1997	1999	2001
Operating Funding							
Fares (a)	5,420	6,037	6,351	6,479	7,126	7,504	8,133
Other (b)	837	767	764	2,622	3,091	3,624	3,727
Public	8,728	9,729	10,161	8.075	7,336	8,904	11,129
% of total Ope-rating funding							
Fares	36	37	37	38	40	37	35
Other	6	5	4	15	17	18	16
Public	58	58	59	47	41	44	48
Capital Funding							
Directly Generated (d)	118	1,075	1,002	1,900	1,627	2,797	1,857
Public	3,895	4,481	4,838	5,332	6,015	5,646	5,287
% of total Capital Funding							
Directly Generated	3	19	17	26	27	33	26
Public	97	81	83	74	73	67	74

While the federal government did not only try to reduce its operating contribution (which was already relatively low), but declared also parts of

[2] Source: APTA, Public Transportation Fact Book 2000, pp. 36, 52 and URL: www.apta.com/research/stats; author's calculations

(a) Includes fares retained by contractors; beginning 1991 includes fare subsidies formerly included in "other"

(b) Includes taxes levied directly by transit agency and other subsidies from local government such as bridge and tunnel tolls and non-transit parking lot funds.

(c) Preliminary

(d) Includes non-governmental funding, subsidies from non-transit sectors of a transit agency's operations, and, beginning in 1991, taxes levied directly by a transit agency and bridge and tunnel tolls former capital funding purposes (maintenance costs) as operating costs and withdrew thus from parts of its former capital funding obligation. Nevertheless - in absolute and relative terms the federal portion has only slightly been reduced from above 10 % to under 10 % during that period, while the total capital funding increased - clearly since the introduction of ISTEA.

Table 3.2 Operating and Capital Funding by Level of Government (million Dollars)[3]

Type of funding	1989	1991	1993	1995	1997	1999	2001 (c)
Operating Assistance							
Federal	937	956	967	817	647	872	1,130
State	2,796	3,200	3,704	3,830	3,919	4,879	5,701
Local	4,995	5,373	5,491	3,981	4,095	4,540	5,987
Percent							
Federal	11	10	10	8	6	8	9
State	32	34	36	38	37	47	44
Local	57	56	54	54	57	44	47
Capital Assistance							
Federal	2,427	2,774	2,432	3,422	4,276	3,960	5,769
State	666	695	1,326	1,020	1,037	912	1,067
Local	803	1,012	1,080	888	..899	1,128	1,304
Percent							
Federal	62	62	50	64	69	66	71
State	17	16	27	19	17	15	13
Local	21	23	22	17	15	19	16

Between 1993 and 1997, the amount of federal money increased by more than 75 %, the relative portion increased from 50 to 69 % during that time and

[3] Source: APTA, Public Transportation Fact Book 2000, pp. 36, 52; author's calculations
(c) Preliminary

remained at that portion ever since. Local communities and state governments have shared relatively equally the remaining one third. This underlines the decise role of federal policy for the development of public transit infrastructure and the strong investment push through ISTEA and TEA 21. It remains unclear whether TEA 21 will be followed up by a similar approach (see Bill Millar's remarks to the recent State of the Union adress of US-President Bush (apta.org, January 25th, 2004).

3.3 Public Funding Possibilities and Private Capital Needs

One of the major reasons why TEA 21 has so many supporters is that it guarantees transit funding at a high and increasing level. Although many projects are "earmarked" and will need specific congressional decisions (which may eventually be negative or lead to lower funding approbation), the "large picture" is reflected by the figures published in DOT's TEA 21 homepage: The total budget between 1998 and 2003 will include 198 billion dollars, of which 157 billion will be provided for highway-investments and 36 billion for transit investments. During this period the transit portion will increase by 50% from 4.8 billion in 1998 to 7.2 billion dollars in 2003. Highway funding is supposed to increase by 28% from 22.5 billion in 1998 to 28.9 billion dollars in 2003. So the transit share of the total surface transportation budget was suppposed to increase from 21% in 1998 to 25% in 2003.

These figures underline once more the growing political importance of public transit. Many of my interview subjects at the Federal Transit Administration as well as the Federal Highway Administration were convinced that this trend would continue independently from eventual political changes of the government. Despite the tax cut proposals from the Bush administration, the transit budget for 2002 was expected to increase substantially. In a press release from February 28, 2001, the American Public Transportation Association (APTA) applauded the Bush Administration's proposal to increase federal transit funding by 486 million, to 6.7 billion dollars in fiscal year 2002.

Gas taxes are the main revenue source of these expenditures. The gas tax revenues plus additional freight transportation related revenues are the basis of the Highway Trust Fund, which since 1956 has provided stable funding for highway programs. In 1996 the Highway Trust Fund had total receipts of almost 26 billion dollars. About 75% of that stems from gas taxes (US DOT,

FHWA 1998: Our Nation's Highways, selected facts and figures, Washington D.C. 1998, p. 37). The federal gas tax portion was 18.4 cents per gallon in 1996 and has not changed since then (Michelle Garland, STPP, 11/4 1999). The average additional state gas tax was 19.05 cents per gallon in 1997 (US DOT FHWA, highway statistics: State motor-fuel tax rates, 1983-97). That leads to an average total gas-tax of 37.5 cents per gallon (about 10 cents per liter, three to ten times less than in European Countries!). Due to relatively high gas consumption per car and relatively long average travel distances, federal and state gas taxes together generate remarkably high total surface transportation funding sources of almost 50 billion dollars (1996).

The possibilities for funding public transportation with this money are nevertheless limited. Whereas on the federal level it is legally possible to use gas-tax-income for transit projects, many states (38 out of 50 US states) prohibit by law the use of car-related income for anything other than car-related purposes (MANVEL 1998). Even in the opposite case the political readiness to use portions of this money for transit instead of highways is limited (New Jersey with a portion of 50% for transit is exceptionally high).

Despite these public funding sources that contributed to a record federal transportation budget in 1999 of over 50 billion dolalrs, the gap between (national) transportation tasks and federal funding possibilities is large. In a speech at a conference on "Public-Private Ventures" before the American Road and Transport Builders Association at the beginning of November 1999 in Washington D.C., Jack Basso, the Assistant Secretary for Budget and Programs at the US Department of Transportation tried to address this gap:

"As we come into the new millennium and enter the new century, we are faced with economic trends that are global. We in the US are also enjoying an unparalleled economic expansion and vitality. Transportation and effective logistics are vital to our economic survival as we compete in the global market.

Transportation today is 11 percent of our GDP and therefore, how we meet the needs for a transportation system that is intermodal, international in reach, and inclusive in its service, is the major challenge and critical to the economy and thus our well being as a nation. We must also realize that the population of the United States will grow by an additional 60 million persons over the next 30 years adding substantially to the stress on our transportation system. ...

All forms of transportation are growing. Passenger miles on domestic flights have doubled by over 60 percent and ton-miles of freight have grown by 25 percent. With the economy expected to grow almost 30 percent by 2010, we expect these growth trends in transportation to continue. Against this growth are studies that show the need for total public investments in airport and air traffic infrastructure to be about $ 9 billion annually. The highway system will require an annual investment of about $ 46 billion by all levels of government just to maintain current conditions and performance. Our maritime, transit and rail infrastructure will require billions more. Today, public investment in all transportation infrastructure totals just a little over $ 60 billion a year. Even with a record level of investment at the federal and state level we will fall substantially short of the projected need."

He then mentions innovative financing techniques, described more in detail in the following chapter. These new credit and bonding possibilities (except TIFIA (see next chapter), that has been applied only since 1999) "have enabled over 12 billion dollars in infrastructure projects to move forward.... It is a change from the Fed's as a primary source of cash as was the case in the Interstate System to the Fed's as a flexible junior investor and enabler. It is clearly an era of public-private-partnerships that bring new capital to the table and allow mega-projects that are needed to be put in place."

This is particularly true for public transit. As an inevitable result of the successful rail system extensions, the current demand exceeds very strongly the federal funding possibilities for the expansion or new construction of rail-transit systems. Only seven of the 50 projects late in the planning stage that applied for funding for 2000 through the New Starts Program could be given start funding. A summary of the fiscal year 2001 New Starts Application, including 9 projects in the "Final Design" phase and 39 in the "Preliminary Engineering" phase (see attachment 3), shows that the total cost of the realization of all of the applied projects would be more than 22 billion dollars. This is substantially more than APTA estimates suggest. On the APTA home page a total need of 14 billion until 2015 was estimated. That included not only new investments but also maintenance costs.

Both numbers seem to be substantially lower than the real investment needs if the new rail infrastructure demand that APTA-president Bill Millar mentioned (200 new lines or line-extensions) will ever be realized. Despite all of the funding increases, only a little more than 1 billion dollars on the federal level is provided for New Starts projects each year.

What ever the exact amount of uncovered costs will be – any additional funding source will be necessary to maintain the current re-introduction of rail-transit systems throughout the country. The following chapter explains which type of cooperation with the private sector is being considered and which tools to attract private investment have been developed.

3.4 Leverage private capital through project related bonds

Bonds are one of the most important instruments of public investment funding in the USA. They can also be used to finance private investments. The most important bond types are US treasury bonds, corporate bonds and municipal bonds. Treasury bonds are generated by the national government to provide the flow of capital. Private corporations generate corporate bonds. Therefore these two bond-types are not relevant in the context of this study.

Municipal Bonds are issued by individual US states and their political subdivisions, which include counties, cities and public agencies. The interest received on municipal bonds is exempt from federal income tax. It may be subject to state and local taxes. Most states will exempt bonds issued by political entities within their state from state and local taxes.

Two types of Municipal bonds exist:

A *General Obligation Bond* (GO Bond) is secured by the "full faith, credit, and taxing power of the issuer" (Securities Training Corporation, New York 1998, p.11-8). Only those issuers possessing the ability to levy and collect taxes may issue general obligation bonds.

State general obligation bonds are usually secured by income, sales, gasoline and other taxes collected on the state level. For local jurisdictions such as counties and cities, the most common taxing power is on property or sales. The value of the specific GO bond depends on economic development of the bond issuer, population growth, per capita debt and other factors.

Revenue bonds are issued for either projects, or enterprise financings in which the bond issuers pledge to the bondholders the revenues generated by the financing projects. Revenue bonds can be used to finance airports, water systems, bridges, road rail transportation projects and many more. The revenue bond is secured by specific sources of project-related revenues, including gas tax, highway tolls, airport landing fees, passenger fees and others.

Example 1: Part of the measures undertaken in the context of the aforementioned “Livability Agenda” is a five-year, 700 million dollar program that will allow state and local governments to issue low-interest "Better America Bonds" to lenders, who would claim a tax credit for the life of the bond rather than receive high interest rates. “The characteristics that sets municipal securities apart from all other securities is the tax exemption”, i.e. the interest on municipal bonds is exempt from Federal income tax. “Local issues are usually exempted from state tax in their own states as well, although states generally tax the interest income from securities of other states” (Public Securities Association, 1982, p. 7) Tax-exempt municipal bonds may attract investors in return for a very low yield rate. It is common that high- rated bonds may have yields one or more percent under the short or long-term US-treasury rate.

Example 2: In March 2000, the 30-year treasury yield was about 6.1%, the 10-year yield at 6.4%. Tax-exempt bonds may have had yield rates of 4.5%. The credit worthiness of the bond-issuer or the project itself is “rated” through specialized rating agencies, including Moody’s Investor Service, Fitch IBCA and Standard & Poor (S&P). Depending on the bond category mentioned below, these companies evaluate the reimbursement risk for a bondholder or of the project revenue. The rating may range between triple A and triple B (“investment-grade”) or below this (“junk” bonds with higher investment risk but higher potential gains). To offer an investor higher safety, bonds are usually insured. Difficulties in finding insurers ready to secure the given project may result in higher risks and higher yields.

The large majority of public projects are now being financed through bonds. Not only is the local portion of federally funded projects financed through bonds, but increasingly the federal funding portion is being pre-financed by bonds (see GARVEE).

Example 3: Fare box revenue bonds involve the issuance of debt by a transit agency, which is secured by a pledge of the revenues collected by operation of the Transit system. Fare box revenue bonds are rare due to the simple fact that most transit systems operate at substantial deficits. Transit riders on average pay less than 40 percent of transit operating costs. Federal, state, and local subsidies are necessary to maintain operations[4].

---

[4] For a traditional revenue bond, such as one for a water or sewer system, an issuer covenants to charge rates that will produce revenues sufficient to cover operating and maintenance costs and debt service. Such a covenant is called a "rate covenant." A "coverage factor" is also commonly desired in which the issuer will create a covenant to maintain revenues in excess of operations and maintenance expenses by a certain multiple of the annual debt service owed on its outstanding obligations. "Transit systems are different: Because a transit system does not produce sufficient net fare box revenues to cover debt service, a gross revenue pledge is employed. A gross revenue pledge measures gross revenues to debt service and requires substantial coverage (3 or 4 times debt service).

To evaluate the potential transaction, the viability of the system is analyzed to determine how creditworthy it is. The essentiality of the system to the local economy may be more important to a credit analysis than an impractical rate covenant. It will not be desirable to require an increase in rates by way of a rate covenant if the result of such increase is fewer riders and ultimately less revenue. What percentage of total commutes are provided by the transit system?

...

Rate increases may also lead to less public and political support for subsidy payments. What is the elasticity of the demand for the transit service? What are the alternatives to the transit system and the relative cost of the alternatives? Large metropolitan systems with well-developed routes and consistent ridership levels are most appropriate for fare box revenue borrowing. Even with such a transit system, other dedicated subsidy sources such as sales taxes or bridge tolls may be essential in order to obtain an investment grade rating on debt.

...

Key Legal Issue: Are fare box revenues sufficient security for a financing and does the transit agency have the authority to issue fare box revenue bonds? The first part of this issue is a credit determination ultimately made by the ability to sell the bonds in the capital markets. The latter legal issue is governed by state law" (Collins/McDaniel 1999, p. 26).

In a *case study* including the Metropolitan Transportation Authority of New York, MTA issued more than $ 300 million in principal amount of its Transit Facilities Revenue Bonds. The bonds were issued to refund other bonds issued to fund the capital needs of the Transit Authority.

The financing agreement obligates the Transit Authority to fix or adjust the rates of fares, fees, rentals, and other charges for the use of the system if this is necessary to pay debt service.

"Pledged revenues amounted to approximately $3.36 billion in 1998 (representing 21 times aggregate bond service for such year). Revenues derived from fares charged to users of the system in 1995 aggregated approximately $2.0 billion, or approximately 68 percent of operating disbursements.

The rate or fares charged to users of the system are determined by the Transit Authority ... after reviewing and adopting operating expense budgets. After assessing the availability of governmental subsidies, the Transit Authority ... makes a determination of the level of fares needed to operate on a self-sustaining cash basis.

Due to the impact of fares on users of the system and on the regional economy, it is the policy of the Transit Authority to attempt to reduce costs or obtain additional revenues from other sources prior to increasing fares. Consequently, the amount and timing of fare increases are affected by the federal, state, and city financial conditions and budgetary and legislative processes.

Fee or tax-based forms of financial contribution

Direct investment can be related to the building of the new system (generally for the costs of new stations) or to the cost of maintaining it. The investment can be voluntary or the result of a local government decision. In some cases the public share of the costs is financed through an increase in real estate sales tax (incurred by transit improvements).
The following forms of private involvement regarding the funding rail stations and other parts of the rail-transit infrastructure were observed:

Voluntary or Obligatory Fees through Property Owners

Benefit assessment districts

Property owners who are expected to profit from new or improved transportation infrastructure pay a portion of the value increase expected from public investment. This financial contribution relies in certain cases on the acceptance of the measure by a majority of property owners near a future station. In other cases, the assessment may be imposed by the decision of the municipal council. The share to be paid by each property owner depends on the expected advantages and, for example, is greater when the property lies closer to a station.

Setting up a benefit assessment district requires a legal foundation and very few states have instigated specific laws. The instrument is seldom used because of the necessary majority vote and level of administrative action, or,

---

The Authority relies on a mixture of federal, state, and local subsidies; operating surpluses; and dedicated special taxes to make up the operating deficit and fund capital costs. There is an inherent tension between the desires of the credit markets for a secure revenue bond ... and the reality of transit operations, which is one of providing a public service that, while in part is user-based through fee collections, is also subsidized as part of the Transportation District's infrastructure. ... A traditional revenue bond would require net revenues sufficient to cover debt service" (Collins/McDaniel 1999, p. 28). Two particularities have permitted the issuance of these bonds - the inability to declare bankruptcy and the state's appropriation of MTA's capital improvement debt service. These are reasons why, in size, rail-transit bonds can become very important. As mentioned in chapter 5.1, the most recent bond issuance for MTA's capital improvement program may lead to the largest municipal bond ever issued in the United States ($22 billion). But - due to these guarantees and due to the inherent risk of such revenue bonds for the state budget, certain bond issues need voter approval. The fact that the last new bond issue was defeated shows one of the limits of this debt-based capital funding system.

in case of mandatory assessments, because of the lack of acceptance by the concerned landowners.

Despite this there are several successful projects. In financing the first 4.4-mile segment of the Southern California Rapid Transit District's Metrorail in Los Angeles, value-increase based fees brought in $130 million representing a 10% share of the total costs. However, a ruling by the California Supreme Court in the early 1990s suspended this system. Based on resulting legislation, owners of residential property are explicitly exempt from district fees.

CERVERO (1993: 42- 44) describes cases in Minneapolis, Seattle and Denver, where bus systems were financed in this way to offer transportation to shopping centers in these cities. A further example of using this instrument is classified in Denver, where a separate bus lane along the main shopping street was financed and maintained with fees from property owners. The fees are based on proximity to the bus route.

Voluntary agreements to split costs

This instrument deals with the costs incurred by both parties that can be reduced by coordinated action, for example reducing the necessary Park and Ride capacities by double-usage (i.e. transit use / shopping use) or the sharing of ventilation, heating and cooling systems. Joint purchasing and splitting of property can also reduce costs.

Examples of this can be found in many regions in the USA, regardless of the type of rail-transit. In New York, agreements were made on the ventilation, heating and cooling systems. In New Jersey, and many metropolitan outskirts, double-use of parking lots is in practice. The financial value of these agreements is difficult to assess and none of the public transportation institutions could give specific estimates.

Transit impact fees

Developers in a certain area are required to pay a one-time fee into a revolving fund for the financing of new transit infrastructure and services. San Francisco is the only example of this instrument to date. It was used to raise a substantial amount of the local government contribution toward inner city BART stations.

Tax increment financing

Tax Increment Finance (TIF) districts are set up in many municipalities to finance the local portion of new infrastructure systems or the necessary improvements to maximize the benefits of these infrastructures. In a growing number of cases they serve as a substantial instrument for the financing of new rail-transit systems and new rail stations or to the improvement of areas around existing stations. Property or sales tax is frozen in a certain area delineated by the local government around (future) stations. All property (or – depending on the respective state law – sales) tax earnings above a set level contribute towards infrastructure financing. The distribution of these funds is a matter of the local government.

3.5 Leverage private capital through new financing tools[5]

"**Certificates of Participation**" (COP) as well as so called "**Cross-Border Leases**" or "**Domestic Leases**" are new financing instruments based on the interest of vehicle suppliers or their home-countries to sell their products and to create a long term relationship with the transit agencies. For the more important cases of Cross Border and Domestic leases, most backing is accomplished by expected future grant payments through federal or regional governments. They are exclusively focused on the purchase of new or treplacement vehicles.

State Infrastructure Banks have not yet been introduced as nationwide new funding sources for transit and other transportation projects, so that they are still pilot projects in only few states. State Infrastructure Banks (SIBs) are infrastructure investment funds that are created at the state or multi-state level. Designed to provide states with a new financing capability, they are intended to complement other parts of the US Department of Transportation Program. SIBs are created with Federal seed money (also known as capitalization grants), offer a menu of loan and credit enhancement assistance (such as lines of credit), and give states/locals maximum flexibility regarding selection and financial management. States may choose to establish a revolving loan fund (RLF), or they may choose to leverage their federal and local deposits through credit enhancement or bond issuance.

[5]The majority of this chapter (exception: TIFIA) is based on an FTA publication, describing: "Innovative financing techniques for American transit systems" (FTA 1998)

A broad variety of financial assistance might be available from SIBs, including low interest loans for all or part of the project, loans with interest-only periods in early years. Public entities at the county or local level, transportation authorities as well as private projects sponsors were entitled to seek these loans or grants. "SIBs were intended to support transportation infrastructure projects that had a strong income base from which to repay loans. At first, it appeared that toll roads and bridges, and possibly ferryboats, would be the primary clients of SIBs. However, as implementation of the SIBs progressed, it became evident, that potential benefits were sufficient to attract other projects, including transit rolling stock and facilities acquisitions or reconstructions. While transit systems do not charge fares sufficient to cover all operating expenses, much less contribute toward capital costs, they may have access to other sources of funding. These may include benefit assessment districts, special appropriations, dedicated tax increments of various kinds, and joint development revenues (all described below more in detail). Real cost savings from project acceleration and project finance justify the use of these sources of funding to repay SIB support" (FTA 1998, p 68). The most significant SIB-loan co-financed transit project is the "Gateway Multimodal Transportation Center" in St. Louis.

As no case studies were available for this innovation due to its recent introduction, Collins/McDaniel (1999) could only explain the structure of a State Infrastructure Bank Transaction: According to their explanation "an SIB is an infrastructure investment fund established to facilitate and encourage investment in eligible transportation infrastructure projects sponsored by public and/or private entities. Through an SIB, a state can use its initial capital, provided by its federal-aid highway apportionment, federal transit allocations and nonfederal monies to make loans, provide credit enhancement, serve as a capital reserve for bond or debt financing, subsidize interest rates, issue letters of credit, finance purchase and lease agreements, provide debt financing security, or provide other forms of financial assistance for construction of projects qualified under the federal-aid highway program and transit capital projects.

The revolving loan fund allows pooled vehicle purchases that may help reduce acquisition costs. In addition, it provides a mechanism for states to make loans (with interest) or leases to transit operators who might not be able to finance transactions on their own. Because the interest and lease payments returned to a state's fund are considered "program income" they need not be returned to the US. Treasury. The SIB can make new financial assistance available to other eligible projects, continually recycling the initial monies, thus leveraging the initial funds available. Local grantees can use subsequent years rural or urban grant funds to make loan or lease payments, including reasonable interest.

The SIB was expressly designed to provide states with new levels of financial flexibility to advance needed projects. There are numerous potential approaches to implementing an SIB under the Pilot Program. The chosen approach in each case will be influenced by state laws, the desire to employ capital markets for additional financing, the type of financial assistance the state seeks to provide the projects, the needs of the individual projects to be financed, and a variety of other factors" (Collins/McDaniel 1999, p. 31/32).

The authors of the study suggest, "Transit agencies in states where they have been authorized or established under prior legislation should explore the potential offered by these programs" (Collins/McDaniel 1999, p. 32).

Grant Anticipation Revenue Vehicle (GARVEE) bonds, named after the former deputy administrator of the Federal Highway Administration (and now head of the Federal Aviation Administration) – Jane Garvee, are revenue bonds based on "grant anticipation notes". These notes are issued on the local level. They have long-term validity of up until 12 or 15 years. Grant Anticipation Notes are declarations of the local government about the probability to obtain the requested portion of federal (and state) funding. The background is not so much based on the reliability of federal investment programs as such but the so called "firewall", raised by Congress, through which transportation revenue (Highway Trust Fund) may only be used for transportation investments.

The **Transportation Infrastructure Finance and Innovation Act** of 1998 (**TIFIA**) program, under the Transportation Equity Act for the 21stCentury (TEA-21), will accelerate new business opportunities for not-for-profit corporations and public and private partnerships, as well as investment opportunities for bond investors in surface transportation projects. The federal government estimates that TIFIA could provide up to $10.6 billion in leveraged credit assistance for new transportation projects over the next five years, from a total budget authority of $ 530 million. This assistance will come in the form of loans, loan guarantees, and lines of credit. Since TIFIA assistance covers no more than 33% of eligible project construction costs, total project financing over this period could exceed $30 billion, depending on the mix of TIFIA loans, loan guarantees, or lines of credit to other sources of public or private sector funding.

While the TIFIA assistance is small in comparison to the national gap between funds needed and funds available for surface transportation projects, it represents an innovative approach to transportation financing, a significant increase in available funding for this purpose, and a potentially wide range of new debt transactions. In some cases, TIFIA assistance will provide the incremental protection to senior project debt to achieve a Fitch IBCA investment-grade rating, However, an important consideration for investors is that TIFIA assistance cushions, but does not eliminate project finance risks.

In September1999, the first five projects to benefit from TIFIA funding were selected. These include the Pennsylvania Station Redevelopment Project in New York (Farley building of the Central Post Office), the Miami Intermodal Center in Miami, State Route 125 toll road in San Diego, Tren Urbano in greater San Juan, Puerto Rico, and Washington Metropolitan Area Transit Authority (WMATA) Capital Program in Washington, D.C. These have a total estimated construction cost of $6.6 billion, and have been approved to receive up to $1.6 billion in TIFIA assistance.

However, actual funding will not be provided until the projects have received their environmental records of decision (RODs), executed their TIFIA term sheets and credit agreements, and received a formal investment grade rating on their senior debt. DOT's TIFIA consulting agency Fitch IBCA expects these initial projects to be financed in 2000, with new projects also being selected annually through 2003. Thus, the TIFIA project selection list serves as a forward supply list for a portion of U.S. surface transportation project transactions.

The TIFIA-program is managed by the Federal Highway Administration (FHWA) and funded through the FHWA budget. It is interesting to note though, that four out of the five selected projects are non-automobile projects. The monorail at Miami-Airport, the new Penn station in New York, the capital program for WMATA, and the Tren Urbano in San Juan are projects serving directly or indirectly urban rail transportation.

3.6 Location-efficient mortgages

It has been shown in many studies that real estate values are higher the closer they are to transit stations than at a distance. This is not only the case in Europe but also in the US, despite the lower importance of public transportation in its regional passenger transportation markets. As a consequence, the housing costs for people living closer to transit stations will be higher than for people living further away from them. (This is a major obstacle for transit-oriented residential development (at least in Germany and many other European countries).

On the other hand, the lower housing costs for non-transit locations may be neutralized through higher transportation costs. Homeowner-households further away from transit stations usually need more cars and will use their cars more often than households in areas with better access to public transportation. This leads to a different ability of both household-types to pay their housing mortgages.

In order to calculate these differences and to draw credit market consequences of it, a research team, formed in spring 1996 by three non-profit organizations, began to work on an innovative mortgage product called the Location Efficient Mortgage (LEM). They created the “LEM Advisor Map and Legend” as an instrument to calculate the “Location Efficiency Value (LEV)”. The LEV is the additional monthly rate that a homebuyer and loan borrower is able to pay for a home close to a transit station (compared to a home of the same value in a car dependent area. The LEV is used to offset the enhanced value of the “location efficient” property. It allows the bank to accept a higher debt-ratio for transit friendly homebuyers, than without taking the location factor into account.

The LEM recognizes that when families rely on public transit rather than automobiles for their travel needs, they spend less on transportation. Similarly, the LEM acknowledges that families save money when they "live locally." Those who shop, work, recreate, socialize, learn, and participate in the resources of their local community don't need to travel because their more densely populated, urban area is pedestrian friendly and amenity-accessible. The LEM Program enables banks to grant households living in close proximity to transit service a higher loan-to-debt ratio. The lower transportation costs of “station” households are subtracted from principal, interest, taxes, and insurance when calculating mortgage. This procedure would create a significant "stretch" in borrowing capacity.

One example: Research in Chicago showed that residents near a major facility were likely to own just one car per household and drive fewer than 900 miles per month. The research has also found, that monthly transportation costs were just $ 380 Dollars per month for residents near stations compared to about $ 660 Dollars per month for a typical suburban dweller.

Illustration 3.1: LEM zones Chicago

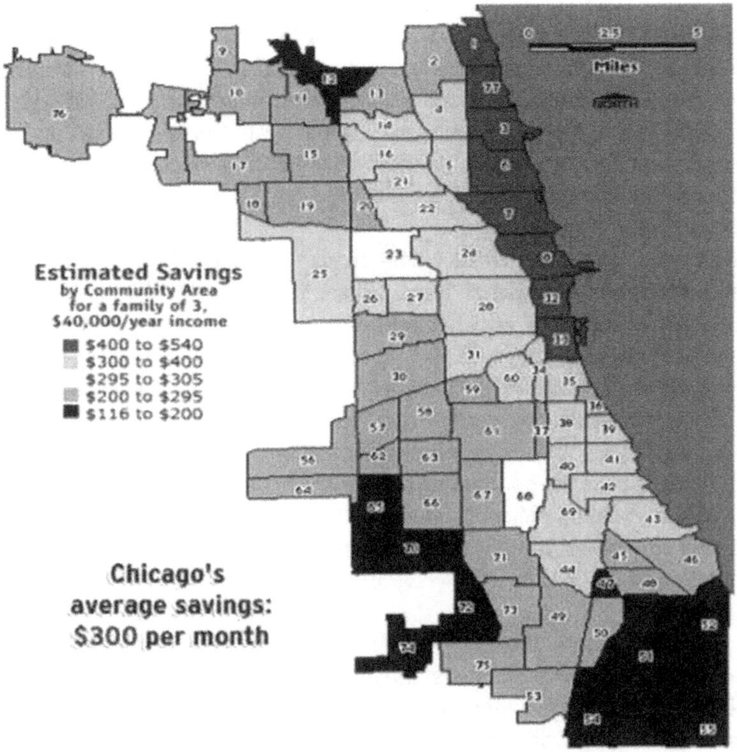

In accordance with different real estate market situations, the LEV differs between metropolitan regions; the calculation has to be based on a specific regional LEM Advisor Map. As a pilot-model these calculation models have been worked out in three Metropolitan Areas: Chicago, San Francisco and Seattle. The LEM Advisor is based in the GIS program MapInfo and uses several data sets including household density, transit stops, and the TIGER street network. The program runs as a new menu item in MapInfo; the user can input geographical data as well as the usual financial information needed in the mortgage underwriting process. The program then uses all the information to evaluate the value in reduced transportation cost relative to the share of all household that drive the most in the region. The user is then able to print both a spreadsheet mortgage qualification analysis and a map of the homebuyer's area.

The LEM partnerships offer the following LEM Advisor demo. The demo takes you through the process of the evaluation a house on the south side of Chicago in a very transit friendly location where the potential home buyer is using a 5% down payment and getting an 8%, 30 year mortgage.
The costs of such a commuter program are $ 100.000 to $200.000, which for these regions has been funded by "Fannie Mae", a short name for the Federal National Mortgage Association.

After negotiations, Fannie Mae was convinced that LEM would be an interesting innovative mortgage product that could help it achieve its "One Trillion Dollar Commitment" to expand home-ownership opportunities for low- and moderate-income neighborhoods. Fannie Mae agreed to buy $125 million worth of mortgages, based on the LEM-model.

As this agreement is very recent, location efficient mortgages have not yet been fully concluded. But, according to the "Center for Neighborhood Technology" in Chicago, which is the leading advocacy group for this product in the country and the LEM advisor for Chicago, many homebuyers are interested and local banks are ready to close on such contracts. The immediate realization of the LEM- program is to be expected.

Through direct grants, wealthy communities can reduce the home-buying costs in proximity to a transit station: In San Matteo/CA every home-buyer is eligible for a $2000 grant per bedroom constructed in a CalTrain-corridor. Conditions are a maximum distance of 1/3rd of a mile from the railway station and housing density of at least 40 housing-unities per acre (equal to 100 units/ha). (see article in the San Jose Mercury News, August 31st 1999).

3.7 Public risk and cost reduction and project acceleration through new project delivery methods (Design-Build, Operate, Maintain, Finance, Transfer etc.)

The “conventional” method of contracting for public works calls for the owner to engage a consultant to provide complete plans and specifications, to obtain competitive bids from the contracting community based on those plans and specifications and to award the construction contract to the bidder. The design-bid-build approach is in many cases not the most efficient or the most cost-effective way to deliver a particular project. In fact, design-build (or “turnkey”) may be the only feasible means of completing certain projects, particularly where schedule is an important concern.

Therefore more and more specific projects are contracted on a “turnkey” basis, tying the project design with the project-realization. There are many types of turnkey contracts in use today, but the underlying rationale in each type is to allocate risk to that party that can better manage the risk. The simplest contract is called "Build/ Transfer." As the name implies, the contractor builds a facility, then transfers it to the owner. The term "turnkey" refers to the delivery of a building in finished condition, so that the owner may take possession by turning the key (as in a lock or control panel).

The contractor is usually in charge of the scheduling, equipment, construction and assembly, hiring of sub-contractors, and securing of necessary permits and inspections. The transit authority undertakes to review and approve architecture and engineering plans, to ensure making regular payments on time, and to assist the contractor in acquiring the necessary permits and inspections. The contract specifies the total dollar cost of the project, as well as the settlement of delays, change orders, and early completion. Once the project is completed, the owner inspects it, makes change orders and/or accepts it. This usually ends the relationship between owner and turnkey manager.

A "Build/Operate/Transfer" contract is somewhat more complex. The builder is contracted to operate the facility for a time after construction, then to transfer it to its owner. This mechanism has been used particularly with new Light Rail and rapid rail-transit system construction. New rail-transit systems tend to be unique, and they may take a decade or more to complete the first operable portion. The turnkey manager is most often the designer of the transit equipment (vehicles, control systems, etc.). By agreeing to operate the system for a time after its completion, the turnkey manager demonstrates that the system can operate within the parameters specified in the turnkey contract.

Contracts known as "Super Turnkey" involve the initial design, construction, operation, and transfer, but they may also include maintenance, financing, or a lease. In a structure known as DBOM (Design/ Build/Operate/ Maintain) the turnkey manager will in fact become a permanent contractor to the transit operator, undertaking to operate and maintain the new transit system, possibly for all of its useful life. In a super turnkey project, the manager may:

a) Maintain the equipment for a specific time. This is often because the equipment or project is state-of-the-art, and requires significant time for the owner's maintenance and operations staff to learn how to properly maintain the equipment or system.

b) Finance: The project owner may not be able to finance the project with its own resources. Most transit providers are in this position, as they must depend upon annual appropriations to buy rolling stock, facilities, and whole new systems. In such a case, the turnkey manager may be able to use its own credit rating to seek financing for the project. The transit operator may defray the cost of financing in part through progress payments (as it is able to obligate grant funds or other funds year by year), or through a bond issue of its city or State. The local bond issue acts as "take-out" financing.

c) Lease: This variant on vendor financing provides a mechanism for the turnkey manager to lease the completed facility to its eventual owner. Generally, the turnkey manager is granted a nontransferable ownership interest in the project, once it is completed. The cost of construction may have been met with a combination of vendor debt and owner capital. The turnkey manager then leases the new system to the transit operator for a time, and at a cost, sufficient to cover the financing cost and provide a profit. This is a very flexible mechanism, which allows other factors to be addressed such as ongoing maintenance, fleet replacements and system expansions. At the end of the lease term, the turnkey manager is "bought out" by the transit operator, which then takes full possession of the system. This may take 10, 20 or even 30 years from beginning to end.

This procurement method has several different benefits, depending upon the owner's situation. For most U.S. transit operators, the benefit comes from executing one contract with one entity at a pre-determined price. The transit operator avoids negotiations with subsidiary contractors, and it avoids the risk of labor and raw materials price changes. Of course, the fee paid to the turnkey manager includes a return for assuming these risks. However, the fixed price contract avoids another risk - that of price inflation.

Most rail-transit projects today involve non-U.S. systems and equipment. Some of the major providers in recent years have included Siemens/Duewag of Germany, Breda of Italy, and GEC-Alsthom of France. Thus, project costs may be affected by foreign exchange fluctuations. Few transit operations in the U.S. are adept at managing foreign exchange risk. These risks also may be mitigated through a turnkey-contract.

Finally, the turnkey manager may help in putting together a financing package for the project.

The U.S. Environmental Protection Agency has long promoted public/ private turnkey arrangements for such projects as solid waste management, wastewater treatment plants, and drinking water supplies. Case studies of these projects identify the benefits as follows:

- Lower capital and operating costs
- More rapid project completion
- Better or more comprehensive product performance guarantees (i.e., fewer opportunities for multiple contractors to "pass the buck"
- Access to sophisticated technology and methods
- Flexible financing
- Risk sharing
- Fixed Price contracting

The parallel between EPA and public transit projects is that of the public utility. Water works are often regulated by a local public utility board, which sets rates, geographic boundaries and operating practices. Public transit service is usually governed by a locally elected or appointed board, which sets rates, defines geographic boundaries, and sets operating policies. The biggest difference between EPA and public transit projects is that water works are integrally linked to the land, and to development, which provides a predictable, long-term revenue source through development fees and property taxes. Public transit is usually maintained in operation through grants and local tax initiatives that are rarely long-term. Very few communities link the provision of transit service with the establishment or improvement of local communities. It is this kind of link that will make possible the broader use of turnkey procurement for public transit in the U.S.

3.8 Private financial contribution to the use of transit assets

Investment experience by property owners who directly profit from the new local transit service is very valuable. Indirect private co-financing is more closely linked to the marketing of public transportation company properties and/or the density of development at train stations and the siting of apartments, stores etc. This is meant to draw more train passengers, increase earnings, and improve the financing capability of the transportation companies for the necessary investments.

Both forms of co-financing are being considered in an intense ongoing discussion under the terms 'Transit joint development' (when train company properties are used) and 'Transit-oriented development'. Existing institutional, financial and organizational experiences in 'Transit-oriented development' are of special interest for the rail-oriented urban and regional development in Europe because transit companies generally do not own property there.

The term "Transit-oriented joint development" refers to a joint real estate development project undertaken in concert with an existing or new transit facility. The overlaps and distinctions between Transit Joint and Transit-oriented Development are indicated in the graph next page.

In the US, the ownership of land-property until the late 1990s has never been primarily related to urban development purposes. CERVERO, HALL, LANDIS suggest "at least four reasons why joint development has never been a high priority for most of the nation's transit agencies:

The first relates to the agency mission. Most transit agencies are organized around the central purpose of providing rail and bus service. To most, real estate operations have traditionally meant the leasing out of small station spaces to concessions. Until just recently, real estate operations as property development were rarely recognized as a legitimate function for a publicly chartered agency.

Second, transit agencies, like most public service providers, are usually organized bureaucratically into function-specific divisions. This organizational form is at odds with the entrepreneurial character of most real estate development companies. And as public entities, transit agencies are unaccustomed to assessing or taking the types of risks inherent in real estate development. Keeping the trains and buses running are their primary charge.

Illustration 3.2:
Relationships between transit oriented development, transit joint development and livable

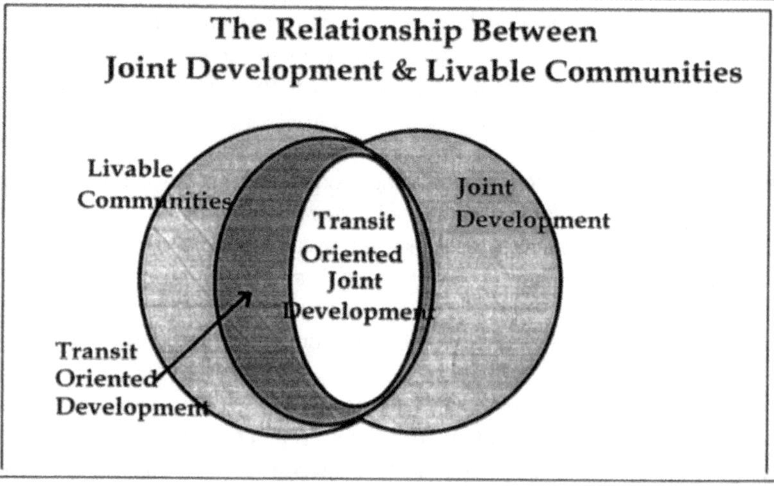

Third, until the late 1970s, transit agencies didn‘t necessarily see themselves as having anything to bring to the development-negotiating table. Land, the most important ingredient to the development process, was typically in short supply. Most transit facilities were either underground (in the case of heavy rail), along public rights-of-way (buses and light-rail facilities), or limited to dedicated rights-of-way (commuter rail systems). Existing transit systems were usually in "cold“ real estate markets, places where relatively little development was occurring. State and local charter restrictions made it difficult for those transit agencies developing new systems to acquire the excess land parcels, which might later be used for development or for leveraging real estate deals.

Mostly, however, the vast majority of new real estate development was occurring in suburban areas, and at low densities – precisely the types of places that transit agencies found it difficult to serve, as well as to compete with the private automobile.

Fourth and finally, real estate development in general, and joint development in particular, had never been viewed as particularly lucrative. As operating costs steadily rose throughout the post-WWII period, transit agencies turned either to fare increases or federal assistance to help cover deficits; *given* the rising size of such deficits, the cash potential of non-farebox revenue sources was seen as minimal. With a ready cache of federal and state subsidy bailouts, few transit managers felt any pressure to go after real estate money".

According to their 1992 study, things have turned around since the 1980s. "The nation's abrupt economic downturn in the early 1980s, combined with the pro-marketplace philosophy of the Reagan Administration", obliged transit agencies to reorganize their (financial) management. They also point out that in the beginning in the mid-1970s (and strongly accelerated during the 1990s), "once-moribund central-city real estate markets" began to boom across America. Suddenly what had been largely worthless excess land holdings became valuable. Finally, the private development community came to see that it could in fact "do deals" with public agencies. Public-private partnerships became fashionable and profitable.

It would, however, be a mistake to see these latter trends as universal. Except perhaps in Washington, D.C., joint development has not yet been adopted *as a major element or centerpiece of transit agency policy.* If anything, in the cities in which joint development has occurred, it has occurred in different ways and for different reasons, often through the leadership of individuals who were not employees or officials of a transit authority." (CERVERO, HALL, LANDIS, 1992, p. 55/56)

The three commuter-rail systems built in the 1970s in San Francisco, Washington and Atlanta each have very different conditions for joint development. Although all three were built with the understanding that they would have a great impact on growth and economic development in the region, and that these effects would be the greatest around the stations, each dealt with the development of stations and train stops in a different way. The Bay Area Transit system (BART) in San Francisco was planned primarily as a modern commuter-rail system to transport employees from the suburbs to the inner city of San Francisco and Oakland. As a consequence the areas around the stations were cleared and set up as Park and Ride facilities. This decision drastically inhibited urban development around the stations.

The Metropolitan Area Rapid Transit Authority (MARTA) in Atlanta was planned to serve as a commuter system (with similar effects as in San Francisco) but also to improve connections between the three central business districts (Buckhead, Midtown and Downtown). Private investment in the stations and the areas near them was planned primarily for downtown, and proved successful. Even the design choice of these areas was left mainly to the investors.

Washington's urban structural conditions are dominated by the fact that it is no longer possible to increase density downtown. In all of the District of Columbia, building heights are limited to ten stories in regard to the importance of Capitol Hill as the dominant topographical feature. Because the economic development of the Washington region has been very dynamic since the 1980s the network of the Washington Metropolitan Area Transit Authority (WMATA) has been able to have an influence on the urban patterns in many areas outside of the city.

In light of this more land has been attained than actually necessary for operating systems and Park and Ride facilities. Construction of tunnels required vast areas of land for maneuvering. All of this resulted in large land holdings by the WMATA, which can now be used to increase density around stations and as an additional form of income.

The question of the influence of new rail systems on urban patterns also played an important role in the planning of the new Light Rail systems of the 1980s. But because Light Rail construction requires less logistic effort, there was not the operational necessity for large areas of land around the stations. Park and Ride facilities were limited in size in comparison to those of earlier commuter-rail systems.

Legislative restrictions on the purchasing of (condemnable) land and the government funding of such purchases were also much tighter at that time. (They have since been recognized as counter productive to the goal of influencing urban development patterns with rail projects and in the framework of ISTEA weakened through amendments in the 1990s, (see the description of the new Federal Transit Joint Guidelines below[6].) All of this creates a difficult basis for joint development policy in these places but does not affect the necessity of partnerships with private developers in developing available property near stations (transit-oriented development).

---

[6] Policy on Transit Joint Development, AGENCY: Federal Transit Administration (FTA), US. Department of Transportation.

SUMMARY: FTA is revising and clarifying its Joint Development policies with respect to program income in relation to real estate acquired with funds under Federal transit law, 49 U.S.C. 5301 et seq. This Notice supplements the guidance contained in Appendix B of FTA Circular 9300.1 '"Joint Development Projects." All joint development projects undertaken in conformance with this policy will be considered "mass transportation projects" eligible for funding under FTA capital programs. This policy is applicable to development of properties acquired wider previous grants as well as new grants, as specified in the FTA Master Agreement dated October 1, 1996. All such projects must generate a one-time payment or revenue stream for transit use, the present value of which equals or exceeds the fair market value of the property. In determining the fair market value, FTA will consider appraisal methods that factor in the "highest and best transit use" of the property as defined in the body of this notice. Where the grantee retains continuing control and use of the joint development for mass transportation purposes. all proceeds will be considered program income. Proposals that meet the criteria described below may be submitted any time to the appropriate FTA regional office, listed in Attachment A.

DATE: Effective March 14, 1997. FOR FURTHER INFORMATION CONTACT: Richard Steinmann. Director, Office of Policy Development on (202) 366-4060 or Paul Marx, Economist, on (202) 366-1675.

Policy on Transit Joint Development, AGENCY: Federal Transit Administration (FTA), US. Department of Transportation.

SUMMARY: FTA is revising and clarifying its Joint Development policies with respect to program income in relation to real estate acquired with funds under Federal transit law, 49 U.S.C. 5301 et seq. This Notice supplements the guidance contained in Appendix B of FTA Circular 9300.1 '"Joint Development Projects." All joint development projects undertaken in conformance with this policy will be considered "mass transportation projects" eligible for funding under FTA capital programs. This policy is applicable to development of properties acquired wider previous grants as well as new grants, as specified in the FTA Master Agreement dated October 1, 1996. All such projects must generate a one-time payment or revenue stream for transit use, the present value of which equals or exceeds the fair market value of the property. In determining the fair market value, FTA will consider appraisal methods that factor in the "highest and best transit use" of the property as defined in the body of this notice. Where the grantee retains continuing control and use of the joint development for mass transportation purposes. all proceeds will be considered program income. Proposals that meet the criteria described below may be submitted any time to the appropriate FTA regional office, listed in Attachment A.

DATE: Effective March 14, 1997. FOR FURTHER INFORMATION CONTACT: Richard Steinmann. Director, Office of Policy Development on (202) 366-4060 or Paul Marx, Economist, on (202) 366-1675.

3.9 Overview of private contribution forms and their application in study areas

Table 3.2: Private Contribution Forms

Topic / Region	voluntary agreements, station-(co)financing	developer fees	tax increment finance	real estate lease	Location efficient mortgage	Benefit assessment districts	GARVEE	TIFIA	DBOM	BFO
USA										
New York/NY				x				x		
New Jersey/NJ									x	
Washington D.C.	x		x	x				x		
Atlanta/GA				x						
Dallas/TX			x		x					
San Diego/CA	x	x	x	x						
Portland/OR	x		x			x	x		x	
Canada										
Toronto/ON					x	x	x			

4. Trends of transit-development, infrastructure funding, urban and real estate development and perspectives of public-private partnerships in Study Areas

4.1 New York/ New Jersey: city and suburbia are re-focusing on transit, but weak regional coherence limits project-related private financial contribution

The **New York / Northern New Jersey** area has the most complex transit system in the country. An investigation of public transit in the US without New York would leave aside the only entirely transit-oriented city in the US. The Greater New York City region has a relatively dense urbanization with a clear regional core in Manhattan. However, as in every region of the US and also Europe, statistically the growth rates are higher outside of the core area. The New York area is unique but due to its relatively low growth rates and the regional development patterns, it has more in common with large European Metropolitan areas (such as London and Paris) than most other regions.

The Tri-State Area of New York – New Jersey – Connecticut is by far the most important public transportation market in the United States with one of the world's densest and most extended railroad-networks.

The region is served by a variety of transportation providers, including **the Metropolitan Trans-portation Authority (MTA)**, **New Jersey Transit (NJ Transit**, 200 million trips in 1997 or 700,000 per day) and the Port-Authority Trans-Hudson Corporation (PATH, 70 million trips 1997 or 240,000 per day). MTA consists of five subsidiaries of which three are rail-transit providers – the New York City Transit Authority (NYCTA, 2,200 million trips in 1997 or 7.4 million per day, Metro North Commuter Railroad (Metro North, 65 million trips in 1997 or 220,000 per day) and the Long Island Rail Road Company (LIRR, 100 million trips in 1997 or 340,000 per day) (APTA).

Even though MTA and, Metro North in particular, serve the Connecticut parts of the Tri-State Area, the transportation policies of the State of Connecticut do not influence the regional public transportation development as much as those of New York and New Jersey. Thus, the transportation companies and policies of Connecticut will not be treated in this summary. **MTA** subways, buses and railroads move **1.7 billion New Yorkers a year,** that is about one in every four users of mass transit in the United States and two-thirds of the nation's rail riders. MTA has over 2,000 miles of subway and railroad track, NJ Transit, 470 miles.

Illustration 4.1:

Commuter Rail System of the Tri State Area New York – New Jersey – Connecticut

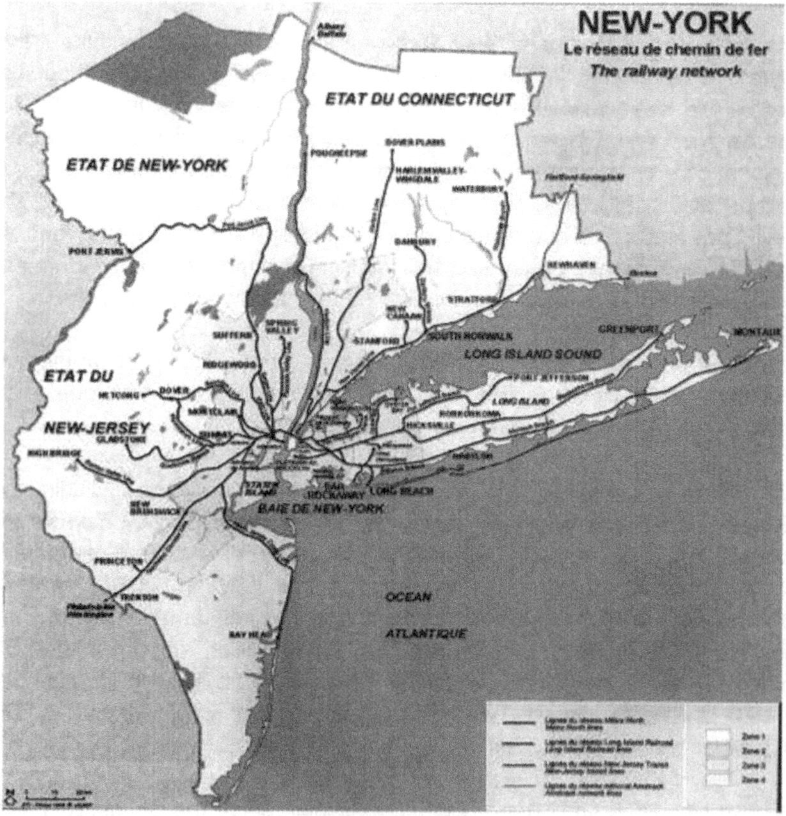

The railway-infrastructure in both New York and New Jersey has gone through major restructuring during the last 15-20 years, including 32 billion dollars of track-and station-renewal and vehicle purchases in New York between 1982-

1999 (see e.g. NYCT capital budgets 1982-1999) and 6 billion dollars of development in New Jersey.

Despite the fact that no common fare system and in many cases no technical connection between the region's major transit providers has been created yet, the ridership of each of the major transportation companies increased steadily during the last years. In only one year – between March 1998 and March 1999 – New York's subways had 7.5% more riders, PATH 2.5% more, LIRR 1.3% more, Metro North 2.9% more and NJ Transit 6.3% more (3). Apart from a favorite economic context with high employment rates, a slight regional population growth and probably an increasing congestion-fatigue, there are specific reasons for the strong increases of NYCTA and NJ Transit ridership numbers. In the case of New York, it is the introduction of the weekly or monthly Metro-pass, ending the era in which every single ride had to be paid with a "token". In the case of New Jersey, it is the introduction of the "Midtown-Direct"-trains on several rail-lines, that ended the inconvenient obligation for commuters to transfer to other trains or ferries in Hoboken.

Between 1990 and 1996 the **Tri-State Area, by far the largest populated metropolitan area of the United States**, grew slowly from 19.5 million to 19.9 million inhabitants. According to the data and predictions of the Regional Plan Association, the area has now more than 20 million inhabitants. 8.6 million of them live in New York City, 2.6 million outside of the city in Long Island, 6 million in the northern part of New Jersey and the rest either in the southern parts of New Jersey, the northern counties of New York or in the area's share of Connecticut. The region continues to grow, although at a slower pace than the metropolitan areas of the Pacific Coast and the Sunbelt. As in all the United States, the region becomes ethnically more diversified through a strong influx of Hispanic and Asian immigrants. High housing costs in the city of New York are cited for a continuous movement to suburban areas "but total population is bolstered by the **more than 110,000 immigrants arriving in the city each year**" (PRICE WATERHOUSE 1999, p.145). The city has one of highest concentrations of households earning over $100,000 in the nation.

Northern New Jersey's population increased at the average regional pace of 3% between 1990 and 1998. Significant apartment construction along the Hudson River waterfront is reversing population declines in Hudson County, the most densely populated county of the most densely populated state. It remains, though, the county with the lowest median household income.

New York City is a major national and international center of commerce and culture, employing 3.5 million people. Employment growth between 1997 and 1998 was 1.6 percent, the strongest in over a decade. The city's heavy involvement and participation in financial and international export markets, traditionally seen as plusses, have come to be seen as threads as the global economy continues its downward slide. Locally, the growing entertainment, multimedia, and high-tech industries, as well as a soaring tourist industries, cast positive, though cautious, hopes for the city's future economic development.

Northern New Jersey's economy emerged from a recession in 1993 and completed its fifth year of recovery and its second year of significant strength in 1998. The region's economy has an unemployment rate below 5% (as of 1999) and even experienced labor shortages in the high tech sector. The southwestern parts are being established as the region's premiere high tech areas, with some of the nation's leading companies in electronics and high definition television development.

The real estate markets in New York and New Jersey are obviously very different although similar trends are to be seen.

The **housing market** in New York is **dominated by renter-occupied multi-family units** with 71 percent of the city's housing stock being rented and 82 percent located in multi-family buildings. In 1998 10,000 housing-unit permits have been issued, 2,000 more than in 1997. The **housing construction is strongly focused on Manhattan**. In **New Jersey** "the residential market continues to be dominated by **single family cluster** development" (WELSH ET AL.1999, p.160). **Prices** for such housing types have **increased within one year about $25,000 to between $250,000 and $300,000 in 1998**. The number of building permits increased by almost 2,000 and reached 17,300 in 1998.

Northern New Jersey has the second largest retail market in the country. But despite the fact that the disposable household income has significantly increased, no new large regional mall has been constructed since 1992. Due to lawsuits by environmentalists groups, the largest mall had to reduce its surface and, through 1998, there was no significant regional mall renovation. Meanwhile "the New York City retail market remained strong through 1998, with demand keeping rents at their highest level in several years" (PRICE WATERHOUSE 1999, p. 149).

Office space in New York City totals approximately 347.6 million square feet, strongly concentrated on Manhattan. "The past several years have seen limited construction with **no completions since 1992**. A few new projects, started in the past 18 months, will add about 1 million square feet to the market by year's end 1999" (PRICE WATERHOUSE, p. 151). These **projects are located almost exclusively in Manhattan.** The situation in **New Jersey** is far more dynamic. "Since January 1995, nearly 8 million square feet of office inventory has been absorbed". By far the **most vibrant activities** occur **on the Hudson Riverfront**. Two large office projects in Jersey City alone will total 6.5 million square feet, attracting large companies who will move here from downtown Manhattan.

The **policy framework** is at first glance characterized by **weak regional coherency**. The very fragmented political power of the Tri-State area led to a split of the original Tri-State-MPO. The area of New York's Metropolitan Transportation Commission (NYMTC) includes 12 million inhabitants within the city of New York and five of the 31 counties of the Tri-State area. As a consequence NYMTC faces the dominance of the City of New York, which, by fear of losing taxpayers, has a strongly competitive position with its neighbors and seems to be not very interested in contributing to the regional context. The transit initiatives of New York City do not strongly take into account the city's, and in particular, Manhattan's role as the center of a much larger area. This may cause future problems because New York is a strongly transit-oriented city, mostly due to the very high density of Manhattan, the amount of time necessary to get to it by car, and the significant lack of (affordable) parking space in its central business districts. Accessibility by transit from all parts of the Tri-State Area is of vital interest to the city's economy. However, it seems as though major players of the city's industry, politics and administration do not share this view.

New Jersey is very car-dependent. Driving through the High Tech Corridor on Route 1 for instance gives a very strong impression of the degree of this dependency. It seems almost irreversible in some parts of the state. But, due to the unique amount of urban sprawl, the State is forced to take action to improve life quality and to promote transportation alternatives to the car wherever this is possible. As a consequence, just after her re-election,

Governor Christine Todd Whitman released a "**Transportation Vision for the 21st century**" which sets a fairly transit-friendly policy framework for the coming years. Light Rail, transit villages, Airport Access, a regional transit fare card (together with PATH) as well as the preservation of remaining open spaces, play an important role in this framework.

Table 4.1:
List of "Circle of Mobility" Projects as amended in New Jersey legislation

	The "Secaucus Transfer"
II.	The "Kearny Connection"
III.	The "Waterfront Connection"
IV.	The "Northeast Corridor Signal System"
V.	The "Hudson River Waterfront Transportation System"
VI.	The "Newark-Newark International Airport-Elizabeth Transit Link"
VII.	A "Rail connection between Penn Station Newark and Broad Street Station, Newark"
VIII.	The "New York Penn Station Concourse"
IX.	The "modification and restoration of the West Shore line in Bergen County connected to the Allied Junction/Secaucus Transfer Meadowlands Rail Center"
X.	The "construction of a rail station and associated components at the Meadowlands Sports Complex"
XI.	The modification and reconstruction of the Susquehanna and Western Railway" from western New Jersey to Hoboken
XII.	And, the "modification and reconstruction of the Lackawanna Cut-off Commuter Rail Line connecting Morris, Sussex and Warren Counties to the North Jersey Transportation Rail Center"

The groundwork for this transit-policy was laid in the late eighties under the (republican) governor Kean and, despite some differences between democratic and republican governors, permanently renewed ever since. The "Mobility Circle" projects presented in 1994 through the newly elected governor Whitman are very similar to today's priorities.

The **Northern New Jersey Real Estate Market Report** is the only report in which these policy elements are highlighted as significant policy conditions for the market development: "New Jersey voters approved record funding for open space acquisition financed by bonds and sales taxes. In addition, local voters approved the dedication of property tax increases for municipal open space acquisition. Governor Whitman continues to place emphasis on the State Plan, which is in the final stages of cross-acceptance and guides the location of public infrastructure improvements. ... Large-scale mass transportation projects continued in 1998 as the region is heavily investing in its infrastructure via New Jersey's Urban Core Program. Construction of the Allied Junction, which will allow all the region's rail lines to connect without the need to transfer to Manhattan, continues in the Meadowlands and should be completed in two years. The Port Authority, which will make over $ 1 billion in capital improvements to Newark Airport, is extending an interior monorail to Amtrak's Northeast Corridor line" (WELSH ET AL. 1999, p.159).

In view of the existing regional differences, it is currently very difficult to establish a coherent transit-oriented policy framework between the state and the major city governments of New York and New Jersey. One major approach though seems to be common throughout the entire region: the improvement and extension of the rail-systems.

In New York, the increase in ridership goes along with a growing acceptance of long overdue systems expansions. For the first time in 75 years, significant new infrastructure elements are under consideration, in a concrete planning phase or under construction. The **63rd street connection** consists basically of a rail-tunnel under the East River. On the basis of a "full-funding-agreement", FTA will fund 50% of the total 645 million dollars in costs. The project will be completed in 2001. 15 trains per hour will then improve the connection between Queens and Manhattan. The tunnel will also be used for the **"East-Side-Access"**. This 2 billion dollar project, which is in a concrete planning phase, will allow LIRR-riders to have direct access to Manhattan's East Side (service currently terminates on the West Side in Penn Station). After 150 million dollars of planning studies and preliminary engineering, 1.5 billion dollars are the costs now foreseen in the new MTA capital program draft 2000-2004 (which stills needs approval from the State of New York). The **Second Avenue subway** is a strongly debated new subway-line, created to improve mass transportation on the same East Side of Manhattan. Although the final size of the project is not clear, the MTA capital program draft provides $700 million for planning, engineering and construction-preparation of the segment between 125th street and 63rd street. The project-start will also receive planning and implementation funding from FTA. The "**Secaucus-Transfer**" between New York and New Jersey is under construction (see description below). From 2001 on, it will allow future direct access into Manhattan from the northern New Jersey Railway lines. The expected or yet-to-be realized increase through these improvements of the NJ Transit Commuter Rail system requires a better "**Access to the Region's core**". This project should permit a better link between NJ Transit and Manhattan through a new railway-tunnel under the Hudson and a connection between Penn Station New York and Grand Central Terminal. Details aren't clear, and a reduced version, linking Penn Station and Grand Central Terminal is more likely to gain support in New York.

Other long-debated improvements may now find at least intermediate solutions. This is the case for the railway-link to the region's biggest airport, John F. Kennedy, in Queens. Whereas the Port Authority of New York and New Jersey, as the airport-owner, refused to dedicate parts of the revenues from the airport-passenger fees to the financing of the initially proposed airport-rail-link, it agreed on financing a reduced version of the original concept, that is currently under construction: the monorail-connection between the various JFK-terminals and the connection of this monorail with the existing subway-system.

The **most radical long-term concept** to improve the regional commuter-rail-transportation situation has been developed by the **Regional Plan Association (RPA)** under the name of **Regional-Express-Rail – Rx** (see graph). The costs to implement this system are estimated at $21 billion over a 20 years period. These necessary investments almost all exceed existing capital programs. Their financing would require substantial additional funds, based on either car-user-fees ("2 cents on each mile traveled by motor vehicle in this region") or a payroll tax (half percent) similar to the example of Paris ("versement transport"). RPA also suggests considering new public-private partnerships, the privatization of the East-River-bridges or "value-capture"-taxes along new lines (e.g. t.i.f., see chapter 7).

Illustration 4.2: Regional Express Rail – Rx

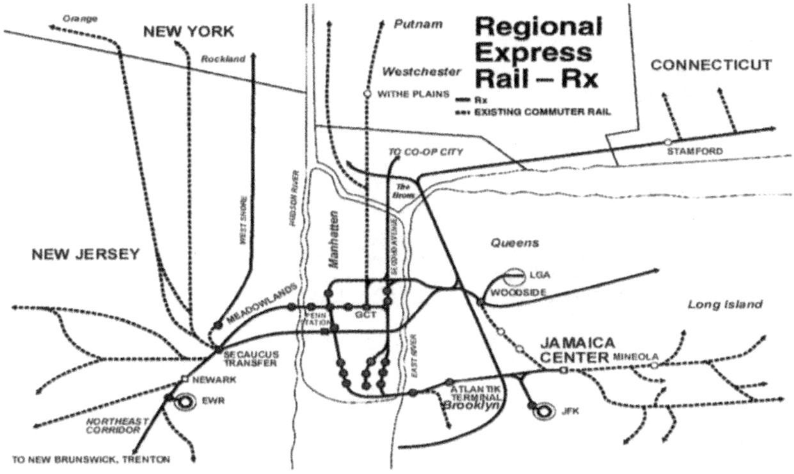

Now opinions seem to be changing. The funding needs as such are acceptable, although project priorities differ, but the suggested (private) financing sources still are not. **MTA's** 2000 **five-year capital plan** calculates a necessary capital budget over the next five years of **17 billion dollars**. This amount is supposed to be financed through an increase of state funding, possible through an important state budget surplus and mostly a huge bond issue, "the largest sale of municipal bonds in history, 22 billion over five years" (New York Times, May 1st, 2000). This amount is necessary to refinance existing bonds. In the eyes of the New York Times, "the MTA is taking a calculated risk that by putting forward an ambitious and much needed plan it will generate sufficient pressure on city and state elected leaders to plug a 2.4 billion dollar hole in the MTA's budget over the next five years with 850 million dollars in new funds. They also authorized a 3.8 billion dollar bond issue on the ballot in November (7th, election day), with 40% of it earmarked for the MTA" (New York Times May 4th, 2000). State voters in fact accepted this bond issue and must now be aware of potential transit fee increases that will be necessary if the debt service will not be covered by increased state funding.[7]

[7] All of the above does not take into account the major additional projects after 9/11, that led to a $ 50 billion vision together with the projects mentioned above. The new projects include a „Super-Shuttle" connecting Downtowm with airports and regional transport, a new PATH-hub underneath the World Trade Center site, the „Fulton Street Transit Center" and, in view of new York's Olympics 2012

Illustration 4.3: Major NJ Transit Investment Projects

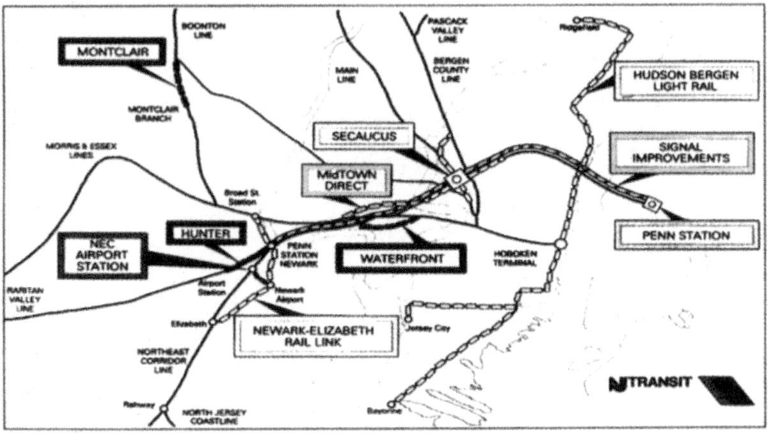

Apart from these major projects, each relevant for hundreds of thousands passengers daily, smaller projects, improving the intra-regional transportation situation are under way or concretely planned. It is interesting to see that they are only occurring on the New Jersey side in the construction or design phase.

As in other American Metropolitan Areas, these are mostly Light Rail Projects. The following projects are either on the way or in different planning phases:

A one mile Light Rail extension of the of the 4.2 mile long **Newark City Subway** at the State House Area between Penn Station and Newark Broad Street Station as a separate part of the Hudson-Bergen Design-Built-Operate-Maintain (DBOM) contract with a private consortium, the first segment of which to be completed by mid 2000

The 8.8 mile 640 million dollar **Newark – Elizabeth – Rail-link**, consisting of two parts, Newark (Penn Station) to the Newark Airport and Newark Airport to Elizabeth (LUCZAK 1999, p.58, see map 3), to be completed by 2004; a third and even fourth part are under consideration: Elizabeth – Cranford and Cranford – Plainfield.

application, the prolongation of subway line 7 westwards to Penn Station and to the 11th Avenue vacant land.

The **Hudson-Bergen-Light Rail-transit**, already mentioned in chapter 4.1 of this report. It's a 20.5 mile, 36 station Light Rail line, running from Bayonne through Jersey City, Hoboken and Weehawken to a New Jersey Turnpike's park & ride facility (Vince Lombardi Park). In 1996, NJ Transit awarded the 1.1 billion dollar DBOM "super turnkey" (LUCZAK 1999, p. 58) contract to 21st Century Rail Corporation. Phase 1, a 6.5-mile section from Bayonne to Jersey City has opened service in March 2000 (see map). This project is one of the most innovative US transportation projects in terms of delivery methods. The DBOM contract is the first of its kind for Light Rail in America. The project history and existing experience will be examined and analyzed in detail in chapter 5.

The 4.5 mile **automated monorail serving Newark International Airport** will have a 1.1-mile, 415 million dollar extension to an intermodal station at the North East Corridor (Amtrak and NJ Transit). The extension is under construction and will be completed in January 2001. NJ Transit will serve the station every 15 minutes (LUCZAK 1999, p.58, see map 3).

The 53-mile **South Jersey Rail Line between Camden and Trenton**, in the southern part of New Jersey, along the Delaware-River, opposite to Philadelphia, a 700 million dollar DBOM project, entirely financed by the State of New Jersey. The line will have 30 stations. It is supposed to help revitalize the towns along the former freight rail-line, passing at huge former industrial sites in the economically most distressed area of the State. The Light Rail "right-of-way" will be shared with the freight-rail company Conrail LLC. Passenger trains will run every day from 6 a.m. to 10 p.m.; freight will operate during the remaining eight hours, six days a week.

In addition to the Light Rail Projects, the connection improvement or extension of some **commuter lines** is under consideration. Two lines in Bergen County, New Jersey, one in the New Brunswick Area (no further information), one in West Trenton, NJ, and one in Duchess County, New York are planned.
A **Montclair Connection** project will link NJ Transit's Montclair and Boonton lines into a single, more efficient system by early 2001 (see illustration 4.3).

West Shore line restoration: The project, currently in the major investment study phase, is "looking at three separate alignments – two Light Rail and one commuter. The commuter line would operate over a rehabilitated West Shore line and connect with a new line through the "Meadowlands", the Secaucus

Transfer and Hoboken. It could extend as far north as Nyack or Haverstraw, N.Y. A Light Rail option would offer a northern terminal on the Hudson-Bergen line with a termination point in the Teaneck area" (LUCZAK 1999, p.59). Another option would connect the Bergen-Hudson line and extend to abandoned railway line mentioned below.

Reopening of the abandoned **New York – Susquehanna – Western Line** in Bergen County is also being considered. A major investment study exists already.

A 25-mile long **northern extension of the Hudson-line** between Poughkeepsie and the remote village of Tivoli is under planning. The publication of a feasibility study has nevertheless led to very hostile reactions through the inhabitants of this village. They fear that the line may lead to an extension of the New York's sprawl area towards this location, 100 miles north of the city (see New York Times, October 12th 1999, B1).

In New Jersey these investments are supposed to be financed through the state transportation fund. "Former Governor Kean, a Republican, began the transportation fund in 1984 and said it was intended to operate on a pay as you go basis. His successors, governor Florio and Whitman, have borrowed to finance many transportation projects, and the fund is now 4 billion dollars in debt" (NY Times, December 29th). Despite an important budget surplus, governor Whitman now intends to raise the gasoline tax portion, currently one of the lowest in the nation (14 cents per gallon compared to 30.4 cents in New York and 35.1 cents in Connecticut). This increase should allow refinancing the transportation fund and thus create healthy conditions for additional publicly financed transportation solutions. The possibility of private co-financing has not been discussed as a feasible alternative.

Some conclusions may permit to establish or explain the link between the regional development, the role of rail-transit (infrastructure) and the perspective of private financing:

As in many, if not most American metropolitan areas, the New York area is characterized by a bipolar development: On the one hand, this is a continuing geographical extension of every urban function. Places to live, to work and to buy continue to spread out in a "diffuse" way. Main factors include the search of affordable real estate property (home buyers), and the optimization of car accessibility in a geographical subdivision (commercial and office centers). On the other hand concentration and sometimes city building processes, occur in the regional core and at locations with a relatively easy access to the regional core. The strong attraction of the southern part of Manhattan (between downtown and midtown) is a particularity of the New York Area. In Metropolitan Areas like Atlanta, Georgia or Dallas/, Texas, the urban center has never been strong enough or has been so extensively monostructured, emptied and devastated, that concentration and diversification are more decentralized.

Both developments are real estate market driven. Quantitatively, the extension-process is still dominant, although growth rates for many real estate segments are stronger in central areas. Qualitatively a more important change seems to occur: Many people and businesses want to get closer to the city then during almost the entire post WW II period: they want either to be in the city center (such as High End entertainment or High End Commerce), or they want to be closer to the city (regional) center, both in terms of time and geographical proximity.

As a result, the development chances for the riversides in and facing Manhattan get better. They offer development opportunities for both: residential and business. The most strongly developing part is now the Hudson county riverfront.

As another result, railway service on the local and regional level becomes increasingly important. Thus, it seems surprising that financial support for new or improved rail infrastructure through developers or real estate owners is so rare. It's in fact limited to very few stations where development depends very strongly on the construction or improvement of commuter or subway stations (this will be described more in detail in chapters 7 and 8).

As will be shown through the comparison with other metropolitan areas, various reasons cause this reserve: the high price level reduces the financial scope for additional access-modes, the still dominant estimation of many suburban developers that the only relevant transportation vehicle is the automobile, the feeling of urban developers that subway and commuter rail is a given service (i.e. exists anyway as a public task), the fact that until recently the transportation policy on the state and local level underestimated the strong importance of a fast and reliable railway network, the fact that until now political and economical leaders don't seem to be willing to accept the mutual dependence on the regional level, and so on.

The level of trust between private and public partners seems to be particularly low. This may have contributed to a culture of individual fights to defend corporate or group interests.

As a consequence private financing of new railway infrastructure doesn't exist (with the rare exceptions of transit-oriented development, presented in chapter 7). On the other hand, a great variety of public financing tools have been applied.

Due to the large gap between infrastructure needs and public funding sources, most of these tools are debt-based. Chapter 4 makes clear that even debt based instruments (especially bond-issues) may add to existing public financing tools in Germany and most other European countries – they may very well contribute to project acceleration. Project acceleration is also the goal of innovative contracting forms with construction firms. The Design-Build-Operate-Maintain contract between New Jersey Transit and a consortium of rail-infrastructure and rail vehicle production firm is so important that it will be described in detail in the following chapter about new project delivery forms. The example of the Hudson Bergen line will also serve to examine more closely the project development and project funding conditions in the Tri State Area.

4.2 Washington D.C.: Further improving WMATA's land-use impacts inside the Beltway and building new connections outside it

The **Washington, D.C.** area has had a very efficient, modern and clean heavy rail system since the nineteen seventies. The major transportation provider of the region is the **Washington Metropolitan Area Transit Authority (WMATA),** serving the Washington Area with Metrorail and Bus-service. In addition, two commuter-railroad companies, the Virginia Railway Express (VRE) and the Maryland Railway Company (MARC), Baltimore's Mass Transit Administration with its Light Rail, Subway and Commuter Rail System as well as several smaller private companies, are operating in the region. This summary will concentrate on WMATA, due its dominance in the relevant area of Washington itself.

Illustration 4.4: Metrorail system map

The Authority began building its rail system in 1969, acquired the four area bus systems in 1973 and began operating the first phase of Metrorail in 1976.

Metrorail currently operates 92.4 miles of lines, with a fleet of 764 rail cars serving 78 stations; system extensions to achieve a 103-mile network are under construction. The system consists of four lines, designed to follow existing or planned higher-density development corridors in the various jurisdictions (see illustration 4.4). Many lines are routes along major road and highway corridors, although some follow railroad rights-of-way for all or part of their length. Stations were located at existing and future activity nodes. Much of the system in the District and close-in jurisdictions is underground.

The transit zone includes the District of Columbia, Montgomery and Prince George's Counties in Maryland, the counties of Arlington, Fairfax and Loudoun in Virginia as well as the cities of Alexandria, Fairfax, and Falls Church.

Between 1976 and 1998, $8 billion was invested to build 93.7 miles of rail lines. $6.5 billion of these capital investments have been provided by the federal government “via special legislation outside the structure of routine transit assistance”, including substantial use of the “Interstate Transfer” (table New and Expanded Rail-transit lines and systems, 1964-1999).

The **Area served comprises 1,500 square miles (appr. 3880 sqkm) with 3.4 million people**. The total ridership on an average weekday from July 1998 through April 1999 was 753,000 passengers, 383,000 rail, 214,000 bus, and 156,000 combined bus/rail trips (WMATA web-site). Metrorail ridership slowly increased after 1998 by 1.4 % (APTA transit statistics)

The **Metropolitan Area**, such as it is defined by the National Census, comprises an area far larger than described above. It includes for example, the entire state of Maryland with its capital, Baltimore, which has its own Heavy and Light Rail System. The economic and population growth is one of the most dynamic of the United States. This growth concentrates on the area of Washington D.C., where during this period 340,000 more people added up to a total number of 4.6 million inhabitants.

The Washington metropolitan area includes 13 counties in Virginia and Maryland plus the District of Columbia. This area alone is the nation's eighth largest metropolitan area. Within 6 years between 1990 and 1996, the region grew by 340.000 people to 4.6 million. In prior decades, it had achieved growth rates of up 21 percent a decade. Until World War II, although Washington was the nation's capital, it was a rather unprepossessing small city outside the downtown concentration of federal buildings and monuments. Its explosive development began in the 1940s, and since then development has expanded into the counties surrounding the District of Columbia, creating bedroom communities and suburban business centers.

Illustration 4.5: Technology Centers in the Washington, D.C. Area

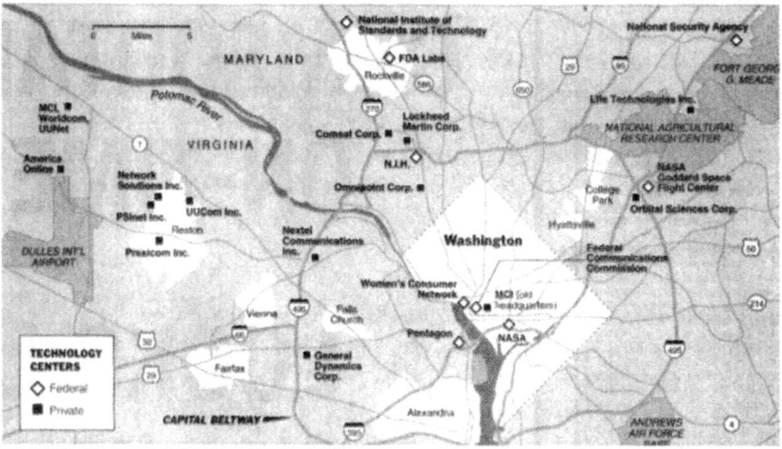

The **profound change of the Washington D.C. area** from a pure government city **into a vast High-Tech region** was recently analyzed in a New York Times front page article (October 12th 1999): " Anyone trying to understand who holds power in the nation's capital need only look in one place: the owner's box at Jack Kent Cooke Stadium, home of the Washington Redskins (the local football-team). For as long as anyone can remember, prominent government officials and media stars have dominated the owner's box guest list. But when the Redskins played the archrival Dallas Cowboys last month (September 1999), a new figure joined the Washington elite, reflecting a cultural change for this city: Seated next to the team owner, Dan Snyder, was the leader of a local business, Stephen M. Case, the (former) billionaire chief executive of America Online, which has its headquarters in suburban Virginia.

For its entire history, most Americans have viewed Washington as a swampy den of political intrigue. The capital's culture, sometimes derisively called "inside the Beltway", is seen as a narrow world of bureaucrats and politicians, lawyers and lobbyists, feeding off the Federal Government. But quietly over the last several years a new, outside-the-Beltway culture has grown up in and around the city – so quietly, in fact, that even longtime residents are generally unaware of the change. Now Washington and its suburbs are home to far more entrepreneurs and other businesspeople than Federal workers and assorted private companies and institutions connected to the Government. In fact, by at least one measure, Washington is now the technological capital of the United States.

Over the last several years, vast high-tech corridors with thousands of businesses and hundreds of thousands of employees have grown up in the city and its Virginia and Maryland suburbs (see illustration 4.5). Now these Internet, computer services, telecommunications, aerospace and bio-technology companies employ more than 470,000 people, easily outnumbered the roughly 350,000 people employed by the Federal government, for two centuries the base of the city's work force.

With **one of the nation's lowest unemployment rates** (below 3 percent, as of 2000), it is the role of real estate executives "to wonder about the long-term effects of federal government downsizing (minus 54,000 employees projected by 2002) on the area's economy". According to a REAL ESTATE (1999, p.305) market report, "ongoing government relocations from office space continue to raise concerns for the long-term among some area landlords and developers. Navy-BRAC will be vacating 2.15 million square feet in Crystal City and another 600.000 square feet of Navy-owned space in Ballston/Columbia Pike".

The same report points out though, "despite its efforts to downsize, the federal government will continue to be the biggest single source of development contracts in the region. The Pentagon is undergoing a $1.1 billion renovation; the department of Agriculture has announced a new Center for Food Safety and Applied Nutrition to be built in Prince George's County..." (p.312). The Department of Transportation is considering building a new headquarters near Union Station, and so on.

The housing market is characterized by a 22 percent increase of building permits in 1998. The **single family housing market is stronger** (plus 26 percent) **than the multi-family market** (plus 11 percent), which remains though an important share of residential construction.

"The availability of less expensive land at the edges of the inner suburban jurisdictions and in the outer suburbs continues to be the driving force determining the geographic concentration of the metropolitan area's residential growth. These areas are also close to the expanding business bases as development increase at a rapid pace in the outer suburbs" (REAL ESTATE 1999, p. 307).

So the **Real Estate Market remains divided**. As can also be seen in map 2, the growth occurs in two different sections of the region – one close to the city, very often in proximity to the existing rail network, one far outside in areas in which no Metrorail- or commuter-rail service exists at the moment.

Unlike many urban regions in the United States, **the Washington metropolitan area is made up of relatively few jurisdictions**. In both Virginia and Maryland, **counties are the key units of government** for most of the area around Washington, except for the District of Columbia, the city of Alexandria, and a few relatively small suburban cities and towns. **County officials possess authority to guide development over considerable expanses of territory**. Officials in Maryland counties have tended to wield that power with considerable force to channel development into designated areas and regulate its quality and timing. Montgomery County is known nationally for its aggressive growth management program, and other Maryland counties routinely follow rigorous planning and zoning practices.

By contrast, officials in most Virginia counties have felt bound by state restraints on their planning and zoning, and have made relatively timid moves to guide urban growth.

The third component in the region's governmental structure, the District of Columbia, was not granted self-government until after Metrorail was planned and under construction. Congress continues to restrict its exercise of municipal powers, although after the election of the former chief financial officer Anthony Williams as the new major in November 1998 many restrictions were aleviated. Like many other metropolitan centers, the District has a large share of the region's minority population, a problem-ridden school system, a higher crime rate than in the suburbs and many other problems which nonetheless did not prevent the strong redevelopment efforts of the last years. This was clearly supported by WMATA's transit joint development policy, mentioned below and described more in detail in chapter 7.

According to PARSONS BRINCKERHOFF 1996 "**regional coordination of development policies and regulations has been quite weak**; the District and the urban counties are jealous of their powers and feel inclined to go their individual ways unencumbered by actions of adjoining jurisdictions. The Metropolitan Washington Council of Governments has played a role as facilitator and consensus-builder on regional issues but has refrained from crafting a regional growth strategy that would link the development aims of the various local jurisdictions. Its transportation arm, which acts as the metropolitan planning organization for the region, suffers from similar problems in surmounting jurisdictional rivalries" (p. 41).

Some regional planning guidance for area jurisdictions was provided in earlier decades by the National Capital Planning Commission, a federal agency that produced a plan in 1960 ("A Policies Plan for the Year 2000") calling for development organized in a system of radial corridors, supported by highway and transit lines, separated by green "wedges" of open space and low-density development. This planning concept found its way into many of the local governmental plans since the 1960s, thus introducing to local development policies the role of transit in shaping urban form.

The perception of **Rail-transit as an element of development policy** has a long tradition in the D.C area. The U.S. Congress enacted the National Capital Planning Act in 1952, mandating preparation of regional plans for transportation systems, which was followed in 1954 by establishment of an interjurisdictional commission. In 1960, the National Capital Transportation Act created an agency to plan a rapid-rail system. Upon completion of a plan for a 25-mile system, capable of being expanded into the region, the Washington Metropolitan Area Transit Authority (WMATA) was established by Congressional action. An interstate contract was signed in 1966 by the states of Maryland and Virginia and the District of Columbia.

The rapid transit system envisioned by the contract was designed to serve radial corridors extending from downtown Washington into the suburbs, thus becoming a key component of planned metropolitan growth patterns laid down by the National Capital Planning Commission. In fact, joint development or transit-oriented development has taken place at many of the stations, especially those in the District's downtown area and in certain suburban centers.

When planning for the rail-transit system was initiated, the potential relationships between rail-transit and development were understood differently among the jurisdictions involved. The jurisdictions most immediately affected by the construction schedule for the transit system were the District of Columbia, Montgomery and Prince George's counties in Maryland, Arlington County in Virginia, and the city of Alexandria. These jurisdictions were highly receptive to the potential advantages of rail-transit in promoting and directing development, particularly economic development.

By contrast, jurisdictions scheduled for Metrorail service at a later time (some of which are still waiting for completion of the system) have been considerably less enthusiastic about transit-supportive development. Fairfax County, to which service was extended in the mid1980s (with another extension still planned), was unable to reach consensus on station area development opportunities, in part because so much business development was taking place in areas not served by rail-transit, including the Tyson's Corner megacenter. Prince George's County, whose expectations for development around its first transit extension proved overblown, has found communities along the line planned for the late 1990s extremely reluctant to respond to growth opportunities. Also, although ideas for additional lines and extensions have been explored, the jurisdictions most affected by them have remained decidedly cool about their potential impacts. In addition, in this fiscally conscious age, all Washington-area jurisdictions are greatly troubled by potential costs of such extensions.

As a consequence of both, these weak regional planning conditions and the geographically dispersed economic development, described above, "transportation continues to be the region's primary public issue" (REAL ESTATE 1999, p.305). In the outer parts of the region these problems have so far been approached by road construction alone, although lately this has faced some difficulties. Outside the Beltway, "Virginia is studying the feasibility of a western bypass linking I-95 and Route 7, but a northern bypass proposal in Montgomery has been killed. The 14-mile Dulles Greenway (toll road) between Dulles International Airport and Leesburg, Virginia, has continued to suffer from low use and is on the verge of bankruptcy. Construction has begun in Springfield on reconstructing the "mixing bowl", the interchange between the Beltway and I-395. This ten-year project is expected to cause significant gridlock unless 2,500 commuters switch to public transportation permanently." (As one reaction the Virginia Railway Express saw a 23% passenger increase in only one year). Inside the Beltway, the Metrorail-system is seen as the predominant strategic transportation element. This view is underlined by the fact that from the very first day forward, a newly opened WMATA-station drew 10,000 riders a day.

After completion of the originally planned 103 mile Metrorail network, relatively **few new rail lines** or extensions are under consideration, either as part of the Metrorail system or as separate entities. WMATA's "Transit Service Expansion Plan" is focusing on improving service to double ridership by the year 2025. Approved by the WMATA Board of Directors in March 1999, the plan calls for "expanding access to Metrorail through station improvements, more feeder bus service and additional parking, new stations and extensions to the Metrorail system, more metrobus service to under-served and expansion into unserved areas" (URL: wmata.com/expansion/expansion/htm). Three major regional rail projects in the Virginian part of the metropolitan area are in different phases; two of them in early planning phases:

In 1997, the Virginia Department of Transportation (VDOT) completed a Major Investment Study (MIS) for **the entire Capital Beltway Corridor (I-495)** to address problems of existing and projected congestion. The recommended strategy package included highway improvements and express bus planning. The study further recommended that an in-depth study of rail-transit be conducted from an area-wide or regional perspective. The Capital Beltway Rail Study will satisfy both the legislative mandate from the General Assembly and the recommendation made by VDOT's MIS.

The I-66 – corridor proves that "outside the beltway" transportation problems may no longer be resolved with highway extensions alone. The corridor is an area with a "projected growth in population and jobs in the I-66 corridor outside the beltway - an almost 100% increase by 2020 – that clearly calls for improvements in capacity. However, any highway improvements on I-66 outside the Beltway are constrained by the intersection of I-66 and I-495, limited capacity inside the Beltway on I-66, and potential impacts of any highway widening on adjacent properties in the central Fairfax area. As a result, the Policy Advisory Committee is urging that major improvements in the I-66 corridor begin with the extension of Metrorail to Centreville" (Mayor Mason (Fairfax City), Chairman of the Policy Advisory committee of the Major Investment Study currently undertaken to examine possible improvements).

The study, conducted by the Virginia Department of Rail and Public Transportation (DRPT) and the Virginia Department of Transportation (VDOT) suggested that a first priority should be a Metrorail extension in the I-66 corridor. It also pointed out the necessity of rebuilding the I-66 and I-495 interchange and the need for the building of barrier-separated high occupancy vehicle (HOV) lanes similar to those on I-95/I-395. The MIS policy advisory committee recommended "that the strategy adopted for the corridor be fast-tracked by beginning the environmental studies called for in the National Environmental Policy Act (NEPA/EIS) so that affected property owners are aware of potential impacts as soon as possible". Right-of-way issues weighed heavily in their concerns. They urged VDOT and VDRPT to "take a long term view, as much as 50 years in the future, in considering any potential right of-way acquisitions. This approach will allow the local governments and property owners to plan more effectively for the long term needs of the area".

The I-66 Corridor Major Investment Study Summary Report concluded that a multi-modal transportation investment strategy is required to accommodate projected travel demand in the study area in the year 2020. The recommendations include an extension of the Metrorail Orange Line from the Vienna Station to the Centreville area; construction of a two-lane, reversible, barrier separated HOV facility between I-495 and the vicinity of the proposed Route 28 Bypass; one general purpose travel lane in each direction between Route 50 and I-495; expansion of bus transit, VRE and Metrorail services; and continuing coordination with other major projects that might affect the efficient functioning of the I-66 corridor. (See PB Farradyne: Major Investment Study I-66, summary, Rockville, MD, 2000). The project financing and the question of how to introduce private capital has not been clarified yet.

For the Dulles corridor project (between Washington D.C. and Dulles International Airport and Tyson's Corner, the country's largest "edge city ") the financing issues have been predominant. The project has a longer history and is apparently in a stronger need of transportation improvements. After a very long preceding planning and discussion period a bus rapid transit system is currently under way. The Virginia Department of Rail & Public Transportation (VDRPT) describes the project as follows:

"This BRT project is part of a multi-year, multi-phased effort to bring Metrorail rapid transit to the rapidly growing 22-mile Dulles corridor. The Bus Rapid Transit (BRT) project will operate on the uncongested lanes of the Dulles Airport Access Road, stopping at three stations that ultimately will connect to a planned extension of Metrorail. Both the project and the rapid transit extension are expected to generate extensive high-density land development." In March 2000, the FTA approved the start of preliminary engineering for the BRT phase of this project.

Illustration 4.6: Dulles corridor Bus Rapid Transit

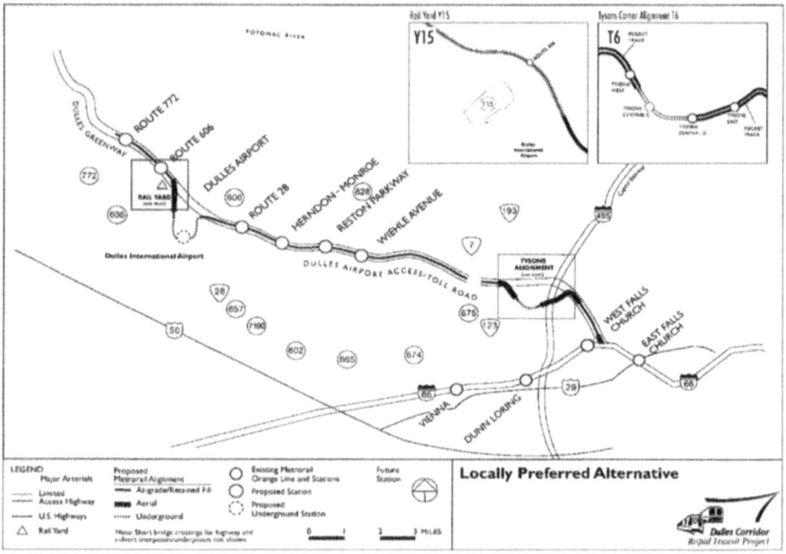

Phase I Express Bus: Phase I, implemented in July 1999, provides new and expanded Fairfax Connector and Metrobus service, including express, reverse commutes, collector-distributor, feeder, local and regional routes. Buses use the Dulles Airport Access Road (DAAR) to deliver significant time savings.

Phase II Enhanced Express Bus: Starting in 2001, 18 more bus routes will serve eastern Loudoun County and Fairfax County to Tyson's Corner and the West Falls Church Metro station. The method of operation will be similar to Phase I.

Phase III Bus Rapid Transit: Starting in 2003, four BRT routes will operate on the Dulles Greenway and Dulles Airport Access Road (DAAR) with up to four stations in the DAAR median. Three of these stations will be readily convertible to rail stations. A fifth station at the West Falls Church Metrorail station will permit transfers from BRT to existing Metrorail service. BRT will be similar to rail: high quality, frequent service, timed transfers, and a unique identity.

(BRT on-line stations in the median of the Dulles Access Road will be designed so that they can be easily converted to rail use. This design alternative uses removable platforms).

Phase IV A Rail and BRT: Starting in 2006, new rail service will operate from the East Falls Church Metrorail station through Tyson's Corner. BRT will continue to operate west of Tyson's Corner via the DAAR and Dulles Greenway to Reston/Herndon, Dulles Airport, and eastern Loudoun County.

Phase IV B Rail and Feeder Bus: Starting in 2010, rail service will be extended west from Tyson's Corner via track in the DAAR and Dulles Greenway median.

Private contribution to the financing of this line has been an issue since the mid eighties:

In 1985 the Urban Mass Transportation Administration (now the FTA) sponsored the Dulles Corridor Transit Development Feasibility Study of private sector strategies for transit improvements in the Corridor. The study concluded that rail was financially feasible using: (1) farebox revenues, (2) benefit-assessments applied to airport passengers and Toll Road users, (3) leases and development of federally owned land around the airport, and (4) special benefit assessment districts around proposed stations.

Between 1985 and 1992 DartRAIL Dulles Access Rapid Transit, Inc. (DartRAIL) proposed raising funds from assessments and donations from interested parties (i.e. property owners and Dulles Airport), plus surplus Toll Road revenues and WMATA to build rail from Metro's West Falls Church Station to Dulles Airport.

Through a series of four resolutions in 1992 and 1993 the Commonwealth Transportation Board called for a rail service implementation plan using surplus funds from the Dulles Toll Road, directed development of financial plan using $6 million in federal funds, and several times expressed strong support for the establishment of rail service at the earliest possible date.

Finally, as a result of the Dulles Major Investment Study (1996-1998), which suggested the multi-step BRT solution, the Virginia Department of Rail & Public Transportation (VDRPT) received two proposals pursuant to the Public-private Transportation Act (the Act) from Raytheon Infrastructure Inc. and

Bechtel for the Dulles Corridor Transportation System. But, because the decision-making process has been so strongly slowed down, both private companies stepped out of these plans.

This information permits **some conclusions** about the particular rail infrastructure situation in Washington D.C. and the reality and possibilities of involving private money into the system or into system expansions.

The financing of the WMATA rail system has been different from most other systems, due to the city's role as the national capital. The federal funding portion exceeded the maximum of 80% and in absolute numbers the Metrorail system has received by far the most substantial federal support of any urban rail system in the country. (In total more than 30% of the nationwide federal support for rail-transit since the beginning of federal assistance for urban mass transportation in 1964). As a result, Washington could build up the only very substantial postwar urban rail system in the US. As the "Transit Service Expansion Plan" shows, the system is practically completed in the inner part of the region "inside the beltway". It may now serve as the basis for further substantial growth of passenger numbers.

Despite the low portion to be paid by local authorities, the absolute amount of local money has been very high. But as the funding did not require additional local tax it was possible for every county outside the District of Columbia to participate in the system financing. Local Improvement Districts, described more in detail in chapter 7, permitted the concentration of incremental local tax for the financing of the local portion of the system itself and in many cases of the preparation of un- or underused areas around the Metrorail-stations for "transit-oriented development".

Now it becomes clear, that the local contribution was a very solid long-term investment. The first reason is the fact that the excess land, necessary for the subway-construction-preparation on the swampy ground the capital and the area is mostly close to the stations, opening thus the possibility to offer some of the most precious real estate of the entire WMATA served area. The second reason is the fact that the Metrorail-system may serve as the basis to improve the local and regional situation in the national competition to deal with gridlock and congestion.

The latter is the most important reason why system extensions far into the suburban area are now switching from discussion into action. This is necessary for the concerned areas but also for the sustainability of the existing system. If these outer growth centers, which, as described, play also a growing role for the regional identity and culture, will not be linked with the existing rail-system, the long-term success of the mass transportation system in the regional core might be endangered.

It is both – the success of Metrorail and the lack of comparably comfortable federal funding sources, that contributes to the necessity and potential feasibility of private financial contribution to build these new rail lines. The fact that this has not yet happened has a lot to do with a lack of regional consensus about local financial contributions, details of the rail corridor, connection with land-use planning and so on. This is the reason why the Dulles rapid bus and rail corridor was for a long time a very significant example of missed opportunities, and it is still not clear whether the planned rail connection will ever be realized.

4.3 Atlanta/GA: Planning to stop highway-extension and to build up various layers of rail service and concentrating development at subway-rail stations

Atlanta's Metropolitan Area Rapid Transit Authority (MARTA) system incorporates north-south and east-west lines with 38.2 miles of double track and 33 stations, which was opened between 1979 and 1986. MARTA opened a 7.1-mile northern extension in mid-1995 and other extensions are planned. This extension, plus the Olympic Games, brought high ridership increases of more than 26% between 1995 and 1996. After a decrease in the post-Olympic years, 1997 and 1998, ridership increased recently by almost 10%, compared to 1998. It has now reached the level of 1996 with an average daily ridership of almost 250,000 riders.

Compared with the technical performance of the system, its length and its convenience in terms of frequency, reliability, waiting convenience etc., this number seems relatively low. Apart from the generally strongly car-oriented travel behavior, already mentioned above, reasons for that are the fact that the system serves only a small portion of the region (i.e. two of the 13 or according to the National Census even 20 counties) and the fact that Atlanta is served by

a very dense road-network including three Interstate highways going directly into downtown Atlanta.
The system was planned in the late sixties and early seventies to serve the denser urban areas of the metropolitan region. It was financed through a high federal contribution of up to 75%. The local matching portion was financed through a half percent sales tax in the two member counties: Fulton (including the city of Atlanta) and De Kalb. This tax was later used to cover the system service costs.

As shown in the infrared aerial photos however (next page), already in 1972, four counties had relatively high densities: Fulton, De Kalb, Cobb and Gwinnet-County.

The 1993 aerial photo makes clear how extremely dynamic the development since then has been, especially in these two last counties. That shows that the whole system has been planned for too small a portion of the region. This contributes also to the fact that the existing system is far underused, both in terms of urban development and ridership-potential.

Demographic and Economic Trends and Real Estate Development

Since the 1980s, Atlanta has evolved from a regional service center to a center of national and international importance.

According to the chamber of commerce's deputy director this development is based on Atlanta's role as a national and international transportation hub. In 1998 the 20 county metropolitan area of Atlanta had 3.75 million inhabitants, three times more than 1960. This development spread out into a metropolitan area of more than 6000 square miles (approximately 16500 square-kilometers or half the size of Berlin/Brandenburg, which in contrast, is in its core has an area with approximately 5 million inhabitants). Up to 1990, the development was disconnected from the existing urban core in downtown Atlanta. Atlanta's regional growth has historically moved northward, radiating outward along I-75 to the northwest and I-85 to the northeast. These patterns slightly changed over the last years. As shown in the map of the "Atlanta Market Area" office development and some sectors of residential development concentrated in three areas – downtown, Buckhead and the so called Perimeter Center or GA-400 Corridor.

Illustration 4.7: MARTA Metrorail system

"Encouraged by the success of the 1996 Olympics, planners and business leaders are working to stimulate growth in downtown Atlanta, in the residential base, expand retail and entertainment opportunities, and retain existing businesses. Since 1990, over 3300 residential units have been developed in downtown, either renovations or new construction, and most of them are occupied. Originally offered as rentals, many of these units have been converted to condominiums." (ANDERSEN 1998,p. 3)

But these figures are minimal, compared to the overall growth. As a result of the population boom, Atlanta has been among the top housing markets for many years. Nearly 200,000 new housing units were permitted between 1990 and 1995, with single-family detached homes being the dominant and preferred housing style in the region. Growth rates are still strong. Over 40,000 construction permits have been issued in 1998, 5.3 percent more than one year before. Almost 20% of this growth concentrated on Gwinnet County at the northwestern edge of the region, far away from any existing transit line (according to ANDERSEN 1998, the historically transit resistant county recently approved a county bus system that would include routes into downtown Atlanta). Atlanta's retail market also remains one of the largest in the United States, with increased in development in all sectors of the market.

Illustration 4.8:
Infrared aerial photo of Fulton, DeKalb, Cobb and Gwinnet County

1972

Illustration 4.9:
Same area 21 years later

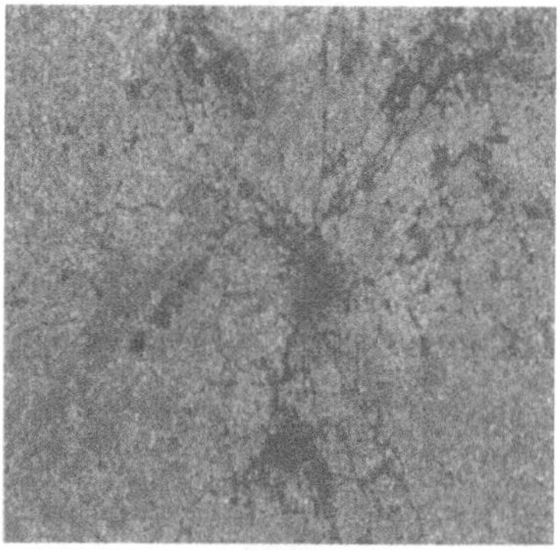

1993

The office vacancy rate has dropped nearly 20% between 1985 and 1990, to a low of only 11% in 1995. This led to high market absorption of new offices. The construction in 1997 and 1998 was about 6 million sq foot, spread over the entire region. Offices in downtown and midtown represent about 25% of the overall market. Atlanta's downtown has become a major entertainment center, including many new restaurants and cafes. Meanwhile large numbers of "power center" developments have occurred on the outskirts of Atlanta in recent years, focusing on the northern areas described below. The development in the southern part of the region, especially in the "Southern Crescent" three county area (Henry, Fayette and Clayton) is spurred by the access to Hartsfield International Airport. Locating corporations "tend to be manufacturing- and distribution-oriented". (ANDERSEN 1998, p.5).

Due to its economic success, the region has increasingly tight labor markets with unemployment rates so low (3% and lower), that job shortages may prevent companies from considering the area although, according to ANDERSEN 1998 (p.3), "no evidence of that [is] yet happening."

Atlanta, being the region with the longest average daily car-trips, 35 miles per day and driver, has to face car-related environmental problems, in particular a high degree of ozone pollution. Since 1980, the Atlanta metropolitan area has exceeded federal standards for ground-level ozone and after failing air pollution limits, defined in the Clean Air Act of 1990, it was classified as a "serious non-attainment-area".

As the region shared this status with many others, particularly in America's Eastern States, no sufficient consequences to improve air quality followed. In January 1998, the regional transportation plan which included a number of highway-projects, some of which had already received federal funding promises, was declared as non-compliant with EPA's Regional Air Quality Plan, set up by the state Environmental Protection Division (EPD). This led to the designation as a "severe non-attainment area". Highway projects had to be stopped and several investors reduced their investments in the region. In 2003, when the regional transportation plan had to be reviewed no compliance with air quality goals has been achieved. As a consequence of this crisis, the region's leading institutions saw the need for a very fast and strong regional management solution.

Policy context

Here is how Atlanta's Chamber of Commerce reflected on it in its "Strategic Directions":

"It was during the years leading up to 1996, metropolitan Atlanta focused on the Centennial Olympic Games...when the eyes of the world would be on Atlanta.

The Games left an incredible legacy for our city, making Atlanta as well known across the globe as New York, London, Hong Kong and our other great business centers.

Immediately following the Games, Atlanta was faced with the challenge of sustaining the resulting momentum and explosive economic growth into the new millennium. The time had come for bold change and a new strategic vision.

So the Metro Atlanta Chamber of Commerce – allied with the DeKalb and South Fulton chambers – turned to its most valuable asset, the brain trust of its membership. The group assembled was called the Dream Team – 30 CEOs, academic and civic leaders who, with the help of Andersen Consulting, seized the opportunity to reposition the Chamber for the future.

Illustration 4.10: Atlanta postcard

What resulted was a new "value system" for the Metro Atlanta Chamber, including delivering quality jobs to the region, improving quality of life, promoting balanced growth and providing valuable services to our more than 8,600 members across metro Atlanta.

Economic development – expanding the job base – remains the Chamber's major raison d'être. The way we reach that goal, however, has changed. We are focusing on growing select target industries – "industries of the mind" – to offer metro Atlanta the most promising opportunity for quality job. To be able to attract high-tech companies and talent, we are addressing the issues threatening the highly desirable quality of life for which Atlanta is known across the nation. Topping our list are regional transportation and its impact on air quality; public education (K-12); and metro area governance.

Illustration 4.11: Atlanta Highway Interchange (Morland)

Chambers of Commerce do not typically do this kind of work. They do not typically speak openly of the challenges facing their communities. They do not typically stride confidently into the forum of public policy. We are no longer simply a marketing operation for job creation. We are now working to directly sustain and improve the product being marketed - the quality of life of metro Atlanta. This is the bold change." (URL, Atlanta Chamber of Commerce, strategic directions, 2000/1)

As a consequence, the Metro Atlanta Chamber of Commerce actively supports a "balanced" regional transportation plan. In June 1998, the chamber announced the Metro Atlanta Transportation Initiative, called MATI.

In fact the MATI effort was the precursor to Governor Roy Barnes' proposal to create a new statewide authority to oversee regional transportation planning, the Georgia Regional Transportation Authority (GRTA) which only nine months after the new governor's election, was approved by the State House and Senate, and started working.

During this very short time, the Regional Transportation Act passed the Georgia Legislature "amid desultory debate that belied its profound implications. To fight sprawl in metropolitan Atlanta, the state has effectively given Gov. Roy Barnes powers that none of his 49 counterparts in America possess" (EHRENHALT 1999).

The law places Governor Barnes at the head of the GRTA, as a "sprawl-fighting superagency that can practically dictate land-use decisions all over the metropolitan area. It can tell the state Transportation Department not to build a highway. It can tell a county not to allow a new shopping mall within its borders. If it wants to, it can build and operate a mass transit system in any of the jurisdictions surrounding Atlanta. It can then force those jurisdictions to pay for it by threatening to take away their state financing" (EHRENHALT 1999).
The GRTA area is built by the city of Atlanta and the 13 non-attainment-counties. Its toolbox includes

- the approval of the transportation improvement program,
- the right to negotiate adjustments to MPO- and DOT-plans and to adopt a regional development plan,

- the approval of any road funding (negative decisions can be local overridden by a ¾ vote but in that case no state- or federal money will be granted)

Illustration 4.12: MARTA skyway

The GRTA also has the right to issue bonds up to $2 billion worth to finance the necessary regional investments.

Illustration 4.13:
Real Estate Developer John Williams, President of the Atlanta Chamber of Industry and Commerce

All of a sudden a strong push to reduce car dependence came from the real estate sector itself, the State government and the national Environmental Protection Agency. Alan EHRENHALT, executive editor of Governing magazine and the author of "The Lost City", tried to cap-ture the mind-change in a New York Times article in on April 13th, 1999, before the agency was even created:

"Talk to John Williams for five minutes, and he will begin preaching to you about the importance of sidewalks. 'We have to interconnect people again', he says. 'We have to go back and re-create the neighborhood, all the things that humans feel comfortable in. We can't keep putting shopping centers in the middle of cornfields. We need sidewalks, and we need to get people out on those sidewalks'."

There's nothing startling about those ideas. Lots of people talk that way these days: architects, environmentalists, and urban planners, even vice presidents seeking promotion. But John Williams is none of those things, not even close. He's a suburban Atlanta real estate developer who has accumulated a large fortune in the past 20 years by building garden apartments along freeways all over the Sunbelt and enticing affluent young professionals to live in them.

He isn't giving back the money, but he is repenting, at least in a way. Having profited mightily from sprawl, he has declared war on it. Williams is a born-again New Urbanist, and everything he builds nowadays comes straight out of the New Urbanist tool kit -- high-density, mixed-useprojects with stores on the ground floor, apartments above, transit stops as close as possible and sidewalks to stroll on.

Illustration 4.14:
Williams' (PostProperties) early and recent development locations

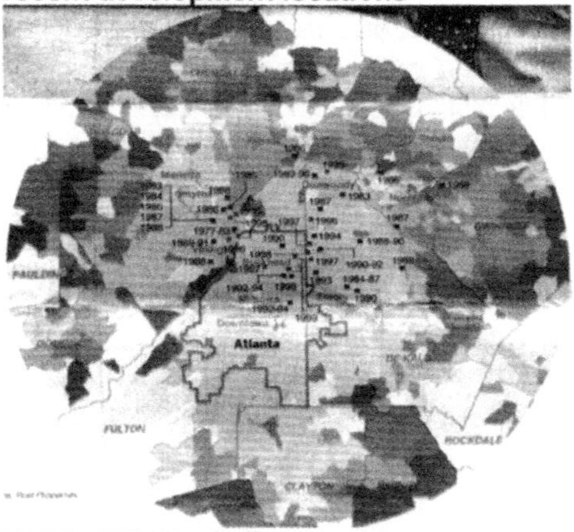

One big-time developer turning against sprawl in one city is a small piece of news. The big news is that Williams is no maverick, bucking the local real estate establishment. In Atlanta, he is the real estate establishment. He is the chairman of the Metropolitan Atlanta Chamber of Commerce.

When he talks wistfully about the need to re-create the European town square in urban America, he is expressing sentiments that have spread through his entire business community with remarkable speed and intensity.

Everybody in Atlanta seems to be against sprawl now – developers, bankers, utility companies – all the interests that have profited from it for five decades. Highways and mega-malls and parking lots have become politically incorrect, and this has happened so fast that those who have long argued against them can hardly believe the change. "You think back two years," says John Sibley, chairman of the environmentalist Georgia Conservancy, "and the change in the mindset is stunning."

Among those still trying to come to terms with this extraordinary development is the Governor himself. He campaigned against sprawl when he won the office last fall, and he wrote the bill that created his new powers. But he still seems a little shocked to have been granted them. "If two years ago you had told me you would have a governor who would propose something like this, I'd have said no governor would be that foolish," he says. "But that's what we've done. What I underestimated was that sprawl can be a pretty good political issue. You had a public that was ready."

But what made the public ready? What persuaded a freeway-loving, edge-city-building boomtown like Atlanta to impose the equivalent of martial law on its transportation policies?

One answer is dirty air. Atlanta's smog, most of it caused by automobiles, has placed the entire 13-county metropolitan region out of compliance with the Federal Clean Air Act, and until a plan is drawn up for dealing with that problem, all Federal money for new highway projects is frozen. That's no small issue. But by itself, it could not have created the G.R.T.A. – land-use planning and New Urbanism won't have a dramatic impact on the region's air quality, especially in the short run.

A better explanation is traffic. The residents of metro Atlanta currently drive an average of 35 miles a day to and from work – more than their counterparts in any other big city on the planet. Their median commuting time is 31 minutes, far above the national average, and the projection for two decades from now is 45 minutes. As Governor Barnes puts it, "People in Atlanta are just tired of sitting in cars."

The Chamber of Commerce also worries that once Atlanta develops a national reputation for gridlock, businesses won't want to locate there anymore. Existing companies won't want to expand. The whole engine of metropolitan prosperity, built to a large extent on real estate itself, will sputter. As Yogi Berra might say, Atlanta will become so crowded that nobody will go there.

What it will mean in the end nobody knows, not even the Governor. It is widely assumed that Mr. Barnes and his Council of 15 will decree an expansion of mass transit, discourage new residential subdivisions in some outer suburban counties and smile on pedestrian-friendly, mixed-use development of the sort that Mr. Williams and many of his colleagues now specialize in. Whether the physical environment of freeways, shopping malls, smog and gridlock will change noticeably as a result is another question. The whole Atlanta region, like its counterparts throughout much of the United States, was essentially built for the automobile; how to redesign it in accordance with other values, even gradually, is still a puzzle".

It is a puzzle to which also the Atlanta Regional Commission (ARC, the regional MPO, responsible for the region's core area of 10 inner counties) wants to contribute pieces. ARC'S 25-Year Regional Transportation Plan

(RTP) will be opened to public comments at the end of January 2000. The current draft provides $37 billion of transportation investments to meet air quality standards and mobility targets through the year 2025. The findings of intensive computer modeling and testing of the proposed plan were released for the first time Thursday, October 14, 1999 at a meeting of the ARC Board's Transportation and Air Quality Committee.

The RTP, scheduled for adoption by the ARC Board in March 2000, represents a dramatic shift in investment to include a vast selection of new transportation options, from additional rail and bus systems to extensive sidewalks and bike lanes.

The plan is supposed to meet air quality standards by the Region's target date of 2003 and, according to ARC's own description "it maintains and further enhances air quality through 2025. This improvement in air quality occurs despite the projected 40 percent increase in population over the 25-year planning period. ARC projects that the 10-county Atlanta Region will gain a million new residents by 2025, for a total of 4.4 million people".
The RTP key elements are described as follows:

- Unprecedented investment in transit facilities (57% of total)
- A 300% increase in HOV lane mileage throughout the region, with 232 new lane miles added by 2025
- A 447% increase in passenger rail mileage throughout the region, with 202 new rail miles added by 2025
- A Light Rail Line between Arts Center Station and Town Center Mall
- MARTA extensions to Windward Parkway, Hapeville, and Six Flags incorporating both express and local service
- A Regional Bus Network incorporating both express and local service, representing a 69% increase in miles of bus service
- More than $500 million expansion of regional Bicycle and Pedestrian system
- $250 million expansion of Transportation Demand Management programs
- A $50 million Alternative Fuel Programs
- Stricter Emissions Control and Inspection and Maintenance (I/M) Programs

It is difficult to draw **some conclusions** about the future role of private rail infrastructure investment at this moment. The mind-change is so recent that currently no realization of new projects can be analyzed.

The city spreads out so fast, that the planned 20 billion dollar system extensions and commuter rail re-developments are needed as quickly as possible. Each of these systems will have significant, up until now underestimated, development possibilities. But it will be necessary to accelerate their construction through strong local public contributions. The hope that the transit infrastructure program provided through the Regional Transportation Plan will be basically funded through federal subsidies is unrealistic.

The role of the private sector will be a) to help the public accept increases of local taxes or fees necessary to match federal infrastructure funding or only local funding and b) to contribute actively to achieve adequate ridership numbers, that will justify these investments.

It is evident that the private sector already plays a crucial role in demanding and also actively pursuing the redirection of regional development towards the inner parts of the enormous Atlanta region. “Inner parts” is not only downtown Atlanta. It means the orientation towards a stronger concentration and multifunctional development at existing regional economic centers, preferably those that are connected with the MARTA-system or that may be connected with this system in the future.

It is unclear whether and under which conditions private developers or construction firms may be ready to directly co-finance specific rail extensions. That is not to be expected in this decade. But as the development in other metropolitan areas show – if the current transit friendly mind-set continues and the rail system will actually be extended at the pace the Regional Transportation Plan prescribes, chances are that even in the Atlanta region private co-financing of the infrastructure itself may not be impossible. In summary, the current projects of important regional employers to increase ridership in the existing corridors, are fairly encouraging signs.

4.4 Dallas/TX: Local sales tax pays for the start of a new Light Rail system that follows and strongly spurs development

The **Dallas Area Rapid Transit (DART)** is the (exclusive) regional transit provider, serving an area of 700 square miles (more than 1800 sq.km – two times the area of Berlin) with 13 communities and 2 million inhabitants. It operates bus, Light Rail, commuter rail, paratransit and trolley bus service with more than 800 buses, 56 Light Rail cars, 13 rail diesel cars, and 178 lift-equipped vans. It is also partnering with the Texas Department of Transportation to expand and maintain the HOV-lane-network, currently 37 miles long. It has an annual operating budget of 229.6 million dollars(1999) and occupies 2,750 full- and part-time employees.

Ridership is increasing. In 1999, it had reached the level of 91 million passenger trips, relatively few compared to other American metropolitan areas, but already significantly higher than in 1990. (43 rides per year instead of 20 nine years before).

The 20-year DART **Transit system plan**, adopted in 1989, called for a 58-mile Light Rail system, a 37-mile commuter rail system, 98 miles of High Occupancy Vehicle lanes as well as regional rideshare- and telecommuting concepts. These projects are primarily funded through a one-percent regional sales tax, decided as early as 1983.
Due to the unexpected success of the system, in particular the rail-transit lines, this plan will be added to by a stronger increase of Light Rail and commuter rail infrastructure.

Bus service is the backbone of DART. More than 47 million customers rode a DART bus in the past year, driving bus ridership three percent higher. According to DART's home-page (www.dart.org) "much of the increase is due to the introduction of more customer-friendly route information tools and a growing, high-tech bus fleet. DART is rolling out more than 500 new buses equipped with wheelchair lifts, a convenient kneeling feature for those who have difficulty boarding, and audio and digital display systems that announce key points along the route in English and Spanish. ... Demonstrating a commitment to cleaner fuels, DART's bus replacement program includes new natural gas-powered city coaches and 20 natural gas-powered Trolley Buses that operate circulator routes in Addison, Irving, Richardson, Dallas and South Oak Cliff. "

The 20-mile Light Rail system in Dallas consists of two "starter"-lines. The first 12 milw of the system was opened in June 1996 and the following 8 miles in 1997. The system has 21 stations. Two extensions with 13 new stations into the most vibrantly developing northern parts of the city are currently under construction. The completion of the rail extension to Richardson is scheduled in 2002 and to Plano in 2003. These extensions will be funded through a federal full funding grant agreement of 333 million dollars. Local sales tax proceeds are funding a second northeast extension to White Rock Lake, opening in fall 2001, and to downtown Garland, opening in fall 2002.

In addition, Dallas and Fort Worth jointly purchased a freight rail line that connects the two cities. Commuter rail operations began in 1996 with the opening of three stations. At the Fort Worth end of the commuter rail line, the city is developing an intermodal center in downtown that will link commuter rail service with the Amtrak station and two interstate highways. At the Dallas end of the commuter line, commuter service will connect to the Light Rail line at Union Station in downtown Dallas. Including the 20-mile Light Rail starter system and the 10-mile Trinity Railway Express line to Irving, DART plans to build nearly 115 miles of rail serving the area's busiest corridors. DART and the Fort Worth Transportation Authority are working together to expand the Trinity Railway Express to serve Tarrant County in fall 2000. Commuter rail service will link downtown Fort Worth and downtown Dallas in mid-2001. Additionally, DART is working with the North Central Texas Council of Governments to examine possible east/west rail alignments to link Addison, Carrollton, Plano, Richardson and Dallas/Fort Worth International Airport

Strong economic growth contributes to strong demographic development. The Dallas area is characterized by a large central city, surrounded by an extensive network of low-density suburbs in eight counties. Together with the Fort Worth area they create the largely sprawled Dallas – Fort Worth Metropolitan Area with 4.7 million inhabitants. Economic growth has been strong during the last few decades. It was fueled mainly by a boom

As a result, between 1960 and 1990 the area grew by about 50% and has an annual growth rate of over 2.5% since the 1980s. The development of the city of Dallas itself was even stronger. Within the last 40 years the number of inhabitants doubled and is now over 1.2 million inhabitants. Downtown Dallas holds 39 million square feet of office space, one forth of the total office space in the area.

But meanwhile suburban office space was approaching full occupancy and the downtown area had high vacancy rates in the early nineties (up to 33%).

Now a reverse trend is taking place. It seems to be linked to the introduction of the DART Light Rail system in 1996. For several years, the totally mono-functional office districts of the downtown area, dead, sad and unsafe during off-office hours, have been slowly diversified. The most visible signs are the redevelopment of old warehouses for entertainment purposes in the historic Westend district and residential developments, partly as a rehabilitation and reutilization of old industrial buildings, partly as new multi-family housing projects.

Illustration 4.15: DART rail system map

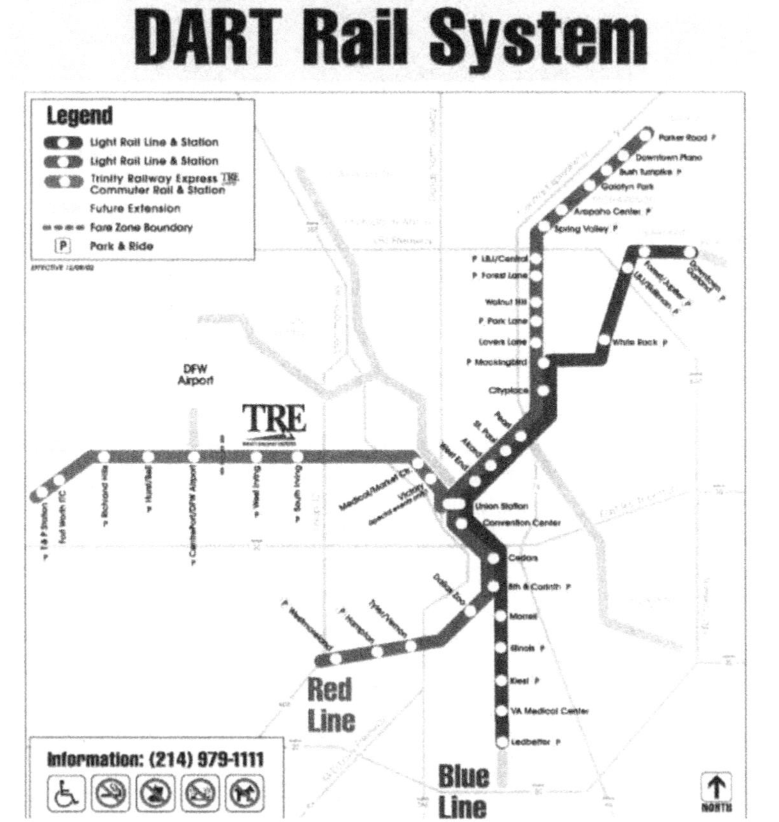

According to DART-sources ("In Motion", the official newsletter of the DART, Fall 1999, Special Rail-Volution-Edition) the downtown residential population grew from only 250 at the end of the 1980s to now nearly 13,000 (p.2).

A detailed review of the **development of real estate values** (WEINSTEIN 1999) shows that during the period of 1994 and 1998, real estate values in all categories (retail, office, residential) began to rise at a significantly higher increase rate (+ 25%) in areas close to (future) DART stations than far away from them. This is remarkable also because the increase started almost two years before the line was actually in service. The study has also shown that the vacancy rate in all categories decreased much faster in station areas, including the entire downtown area.

The Central Business District of Dallas is currently experiencing its strongest growth and development in more than 20 years. The trend that started in 1996, the same time DART opened its first rail operations, has seen the renovation of a number of empty buildings. But for the first time, many of the renovations are for residential uses. A recent survey by M/PF Research, Inc. showed that the in-town apartment market grew from 4,300 units in mid-1997 to 6,900 units in mid-1999. Loft condominium construction is also in full swing.

Downtown Dallas is rapidly becoming a mixed-use area that will enjoy improved livability, property values and attractiveness to newcomers.

All these changes were partially caused by the rail line. The North Central Texas Council of Governments, the regional planning agency that performs MPO functions for the Dallas area, has adopted no policies that specifically promote transit-oriented development (TOD). The most recent transportation plan - Mobility 2010: The Regional Transportation Plan for North Central Texas - contains only the most general references to linking land-use with transportation. The city has adopted no incentives for development around DART stations.

DART has adopted no specific policies supporting TOD, although its 1995 official mission and goal statement refers to the desirability of the DART system stimulating economic development. However, the transit agency is conducting a study to determine ways to link its stations with the extensive pedestrian network below much of downtown Dallas.

The impacts of DART on land-use could be higher than they are. Developers, asked what they liked and disliked about DART, said that they found the trains fast and the stations clean and attractive and even that DART rail creates "big city" flair in Dallas. But they miss more DART incentives to communicate and cooperate with the real estate community. They also think that DART should acquire more land and prepare master plans for joint development around rail stations. There seems also to be consensus in the real estate community that a redevelopment agency should be created in order to bring housing, retail, entertainment and a pedestrian mall into the CBD. These developments in turn would help DART because of the higher densities and limited parking. For a long time it seemed as if the real estate development community in Dallas was the strongest supporter of a closer link between transit and land-use.

All of the above mentioned local and regional institutions have only very recently discovered **the development impact of transit corridors.**

Just recently DART remembered "transit-oriented development is not new to Texas. The powerful rail incentive that seeded and developed our towns and cities at the turn of the century is again stimulating growth. This time rail is attracting greater residential and commercial density around existing DART stations near downtown, and also spurring renovation and new development near future stations in suburban cities. Reflecting an emerging trend in many southwestern and western cities to curb urban sprawl, developers and city planners in DART's member cities are working with the agency to maximize opportunities for citizens to move from work to home to neighborhood services and entertainment without driving a car. While nobody imagines the private automobile is likely to disappear from the scene, an increasing number of folks clearly want to avoid the rush-hour driving experience – and they'll pay for the option."

The spring 2000 edition of the DART magazine "InMotion" presents the current view of the future cooperation between the transit agency and real estate developers:

A **Northwest Corridor** 18-mile Light Rail line is planned from downtown Dallas through Farmers Branch to Carrollton – and a 14-mile segment will branch from the Northwest Highway/Webbs Chapel area, past Texas Stadium, to the University of Dallas and Las Colinas in Irving. DART planners **estimate the $1.4 billion line with 18 stations will carry more than 25,000 riders a**

day. Although the final dates for service won't be set until after preliminary engineering, environ-mental and financial planning studies, planners estimate the first trains could arrive in Carrollton and Farmers Branch as early as 2007, and Irving as early as 2008. An extension from State Highway 161 could reach the north end of D/FW International Airport by 2012.

Illustration 4.16: DART magazin

Although a different, technically-preferred route originally emerged from the major investment study, Irving officials believe the Texas Stadium/University of Dallas alignment has the greater potential for economic development. To support its preferred alignment, the city agreed to enter into an interlocal agreement with DART to provide $60 million through contributions or cost savings.

"We can't lose on this route," DART Board Chairman Jesse Oliver said. "The overall benefits not only to Irving, but to the DART Service Area in general, can be immeasurable. There's great potential for development in that area." In addition to Light Rail service in the Northwest Corridor, High Occupancy Vehicle (HOV) lanes and additional main lanes are planned for part of Interstate 35E and State Highway 114.

The **Southeast Corridor** Light Rail will stretch east along Bryan Street from DART's Pearl Station, turning south along Good Latimer Expressway, then east at Gaston Avenue, following the old Union Pacific rail line to the northwest corner of Fair Park where it will turn south to Parry Avenue. The route crosses R. B. Cullum Boulevard, and then follows the former Southern Pacific Railroad alignment southeast to Pleasant Grove. DART projects **the line with nine stations will cost $450 million and carry 19,500 riders a day**. Planners estimate the line could be operational as early as 2008.

The role of private investors for the development of the rail-transit system is crucial but it is unlikely that they will soon be ready to co-finance system expansions.

The various rail line extensions under planning or construction in Dallas are financed through traditional public financing tools. The most important is a 1% sales tax in the 13 DART communities. This tax was introduced through a vote in 1989. The decision is valid until 2009. By then an important part of the rail infrastructure program will be completed, so that in case it should be lowered, the regional network will be able to function nevertheless. The percentage of federal funding for the construction of the DART Light Rail system was relatively low, about 25% according to DART sources. Only few of the upcoming new lines or system extensions will have federal support, one though is the first rail-transit case of a full funding agreement.

No line has so far been built as a design-build project. Also no innovative project financing or delivery methods are being considered.

Although questions about private financial contributions are rarely raised, it is very evident that the private real estate community is strongly interested in an extension of the rail system. The transit-oriented real estate market is still not dominant in the Dallas/Fort Worth area but it is increasing. New transit corridors are prime real estate markets. Once the rail network becomes denser and capable of delivering a substantial solution to transportation problems in the inner parts (the future transit corridors) of the Dallas/Fort Worth area, the possibility of a private investor to participate financially in transit investments will increase. Instruments and results of a closer relation between transit investments will be presented and analyzed in chapter 8 (TOD).

4.5 San Diego, CA: the country's first new Light Rail system attracts development interest and prepares developer co-financing of new lines through transit villages

The **Metropolitan Transit Development Board (MTDB)** serves as the policy-setting and overall coordinating agency for public transportation in the San Diego metropolitan area. The fixed-route operating entities have banded together to form a "federation" of transit service providers called the Metropolitan Transit System (MTS). The purpose of this Metropolitan Transit System, and the related MTS symbol, is to identify this unified transit system to the public. In this way, riders can be aware that a coordinated route, fare, transfer, and information system is available to them. MTDB created the Metropolitan Transit System in July 1985, as part of several actions, including consolidation of San Diego Transit Corporation within MTDB.

The Metropolitan Transit Development Board (MTDB) oversees the planning, design, and operation of transit services in the San Diego metropolitan area. It operates the San Diego Trolley, a Light Rail system, on three lines, one of which connects downtown to the international border at Tijuana, Mexico. Its two lines total 47 miles and have 34 stations (see system map). Service began between 1981 and 1995. Both lines are on former railroad rights-of-way. An 86-mile Light Rail network will be completed by MTDB in 2010 and the North County Transit District (NCTD) is planning a 22-mile Light Rail line to be completed by 2000. Other Light Rail extensions and lines are under study, being planned or under construction. Details are explained below. Transit ridership has risen 60% since 1981. In 1998, the San Diego Trolley carried an average of 75,000 passengers daily. Still, the transit system is used only by a small percentage of San Diego resident for work trips. The MTDB hoped to capture a greater share of that market through different forms of transit-oriented development.

Illustration 4.17: San Diego trolley

The San Diego Association of Governments (SANDAG), in conjunction with the Metropolitan Transit Development Board (MTDB), and the North County Transit District (NCTD) developed the Regional Transportation Plan (RTP). The RTP indicates the corridors with existing and future rail services as well as the corridors under study to determine what form of transit would be most appropriate in the future. The facts and projects described below are presented in the RTP. The **Blue line** was the first modern Light Rail line in the USA - 25.7 miles (41.1 km) with 25 stations from the international border with Mexico to Rancho Mission Road in Mission Valley. There is 15-minute service most of the day (7.5 minute service during morning and afternoon rush hours between Old Town and San Ysidro).

In July 1981, revenue service began on 15.9-mile (25.4 km) line from the border to downtown San Diego. The 116.6 million dollar cost included right-of-way, second phase improvements, 24 Light Rail vehicles (LRVS) and 18 stations. In July 1992 revenue service began on 0.5-mile (0.8 km) segment from Santa Fe Depot to Cedar Street. In June 1996 revenue service began on 3.2-mile (5.1 km) segment from Cedar Street to Taylor Street in Old Town. The 114 million dollar cost included 4 stations, 4 grade separations, and 4 LRVS. In In November 1997 revenue service began on the 6.1-mile segment between the Old Town Transit Center and Rancho Mission Road. The220 million dollar cost included 7 stations, 10 grade separations, 11 LRVS, and a 25+ acre wildlife preserve for wetlands mitigation.

The Orange line is now 21.6 miles (35.8 km) long with 24 stations from downtown to Santee. 1.2 miles and 6 stations are shared with Blue Line in downtown. It includes15-minute service most of the day and 30-minute service between El Cajon and Santee.

In March 1986, revenue service began on 4.5 mile (7.2 km) line from downtown San Diego to Euclid Avenue. The 33.6 million dollar cost included 4 stations and 6 LRVS. In June 1989 revenue service began on 11.3-mile (18.1 km) segment from Euclid Avenue to El Cajon Transit Center. The 108 million dollar cost included 8 stations, 15 LRVS, and one grade separation. In June 1990 revenue service began on 1.5-mile (2.4 km) Convention Center segment from America Plaza Transfer Station to Imperial & 12th Transfer Station. The 48 million dollar cost included 3 stations and 5 LRVS. In August 1995 revenue service began on 3.6-mile (5.7 km) segment from El Cajon Transit Center to Santee Town Center. The109 million dollar cost included 3 stations, 7 LRVs and two grade separations.

In February, 1995 **Commuter Rail** - revenue service began on the 43-mile (68.8 km) line from Oceanside to downtown San Diego. The line has 8 stations (3 served by AMTRAK and two served by the San Diego Trolley's Blue Line). One-way travel is 55 minutes. NCTD is the lead agency with assistance from MTDB and SANDAG. NCTD is also planning a 22-mile Rail-transit project for Oceanside and Escondido. Parking and other improvements are planned for the Sorrento Valley Coaster Station, and a new Coaster station is planned for University City.

Illustration 4.18: San Diego trolley 2

To finance the existing infrastructure MTDB had the following revenue sources:

- Local Sales Tax: From 1988 to 2008, the region will collect a 1/2 percent sales tax, a third of which, by 2008, will have generated over one billion dollars for public transit capital and service improvements.
- Short-Range Planning, Fund Administration, Regional Services: Administration, short-range planning expenses, and regional service operating subsidies are primarily funded by Transit Development Act (TDA) and State Transit Assistance (STA) monies.

In 1997, MTDB carried 66 million passengers over 19.3 revenue miles with 51.3 percent farebox recovery. The recovery is lower now then after the opening of the first Light Rail line in 1981 (blue line) because of increasing investment costs for the following lines, and also because of the stable transit fees. Fares to pay are prorated in clear steps, based on distance: They vary between 1 dollar (one station) and $2.25 dollars for more than 20 stations.
As in most southwestern cities, the **economic and demographic development** has been very strong **and the Real Estate Market** strongly encourages urban sprawl.

San Diego, located just north of the Mexico border has grown to almost 3 million inhabitants. A major Pacific coast port, San Diego saw a dramatic population growth of 142% from 1960-1990, and another 13 percent by mid 1999. Population densities are still relatively low, at an estimate count of 1,309 persons per square kilometer according to 1990 figures, due to the fact that the population is spread over a large area of San Diego County. San Diego is California's fastest growing region; it even "surpassed full employment". Its largest industries - manufacturing (aerospace, electrical machinery), defense, tourism (e.g. golf equipment companies), telecommunications, electronics (Sony, Hewlett Packard, TRW) and software development – continued strong growth throughout the 1990s. (COLLIERS 1999, p. 255).

Illustration 4.19: San Diego Skyline

San Diego's city policy reputation has very much improved since the beginning of the 1990s. It's now considered the "second-safest city in the USA"(FBI), "the second-best US city for achieving global business success" (World Trade Magazine) and the city with an AAA bond rating, the highest of any big city in California (COLLIERS 1999, p. 258). Real estate markets, after suffering under the overbuilding and bad economy of the 1980s are now very strong. Vacancy rates have fallen far below the national average. In 1998, they were substantially below 1%. Especially in the residential market "all measures of prices showed tremendous gains over previous years, many exceeding 20 percent in 12 months" (COLLIERS 1999, p. 258). Although the growth also affected the downtown area, new developments are still occurring primarily in the suburban area. In the retail market much of the new development consists of large-scale (big-box) retailers and suburban centers. (see San Diego Market Area map).

This contributes to a strong real estate development that creates new locations or offers opportunities to densify existing locations. As a consequence, several Light Rail extensions are being planned.

The **Mid-coast-extension**, a 10.7 mile route (17.1 km) from Old Town to North University City will be developed in stages. Preliminary engineering/final environmental impact statement is near completion for the first segment, the 3.4-mile (5.5 km) Phase 1 Balboa Extension. Alignment refinement studies are being conducted for selected segments of the Phase 2 University City Extension.

The **Mission Valley East extension** with_5.8 miles (9.4 km) of new tracks plus 1.0 mile (0.6 km) of shared existing tracks from the Mission San Diego Station in Mission Valley to the Grossmont Center Station in the City of La Mesa will close the gap between the existing Blue and Orange Lines. The route planning and environmental impact analysis phase of the project is complete. Final design is underway with construction scheduled to begin in late 2000. Service is scheduled to start in late 2004. (431 million dollars, according to SANDAG's regional transportation plan 2000).

The **I-15 corridor** line with approximately 30 miles between North County Fair and the Pacific Fleet trolley station on the Blue Line would connect with the Blue Line at the Stadium and Pacific Fleet stations, the Orange Line at a new station, the proposed Mira Mesa Line, and the North County Transit District's (NCTD) proposed Oceanside-Escondido Line at North County Fair.

The Phase 2 report (Short-to Mid-Term Plan) was adopted in November 1998, outlining development of a Bus Rapid Transit (BRT) system that utilizes an expanded system of High Occupancy Vehicle (HOV) lanes along I-15 to maintain highspeed operations. MTDB is currently working with CALTRANS on environmental studies for the BRT/HOV improvements in the I-15 corridor. Construction was supposed to begin in 2002. The Phase 3 analysis will develop a long-term plan for the corridor. Alternatives will include Light Rail and bus rapid transit, including hybrid combination rail-bus options.

Other future LRT (or other technology) extensions such as the Beach Area, Airport, and South Bay extensions are planned. But they would require additional study and funding sources and cannot be realized or even started before the end of the 20-year sales tax period in 2007, described below.

Illustration 4.20: MTDB transit corridor plan

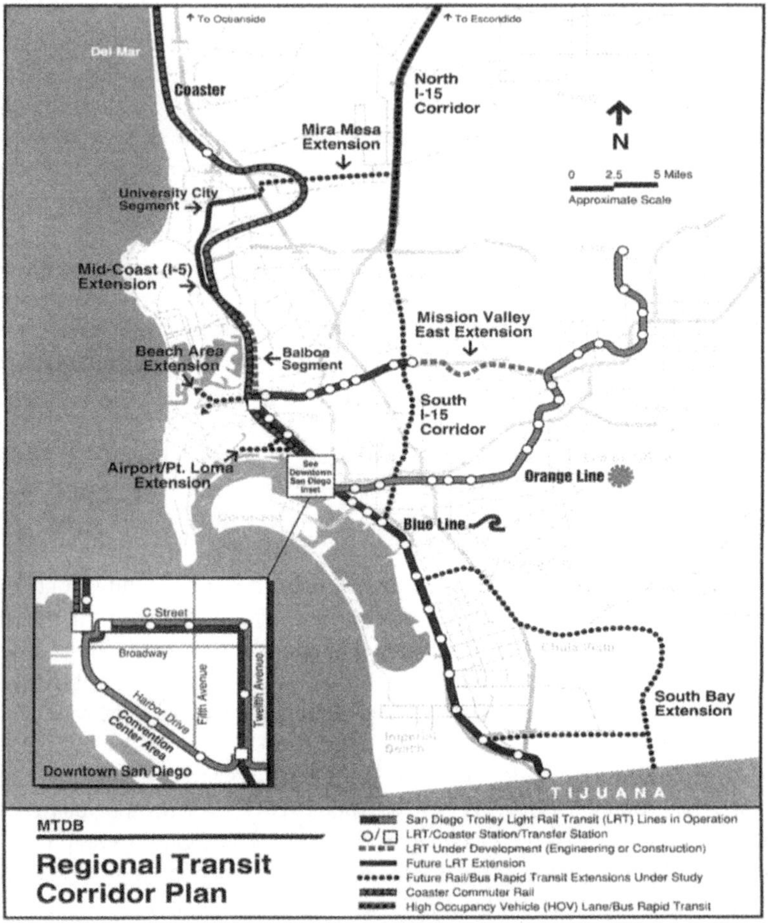

By the year 2010, if funding permits, a 70-mile LRT network and a 43-mile commuter rail line would serve the San Diego region. This network is incorporated in the RTP and is revised every two years by SANDAG. Several other types of rapid transit alternatives, tailored to meet specific community, passenger, and environmental needs, may also be in place. All Metropolitan

Transit System and NCTD rail services would be coordinated with bus services operating as one system.

As federal and state capital and operating support only covers a limited amount of the overall costs, additional local funding sources are crucial for the extension and operation of the system. Robert Dunphy (1997, p.133-135) describes how carefully local tax initiatives to finance transit have to be managed to be accepted by voters: "Completed on time and under budget, the Original south line of the *first* new US Light Rail line in many decades was constructed at a bargain basement price of $7.3 million per mile. Ridership reached 30,000 per day in the mid-1980s, a level that initially had been projected for 1995.18 Fares covered as much as 95 percent of the operating expenses until a second, 16-mile line opened. By 1995, fares were covering 66 percent of operating expenses". The trolley's capital costs translate into an investment per weekday roundtrip rider of less than $8,000, extremely low by American standards, only comparable with the most competitive European projects (see chapter 7).

The MTDB's design philosophy – keep it simple and functional – has kept down costs. The agency has developed a reputation as a lean and mean construction manager that pays close attention to the bottom line. The trolley corridor is located in an especially strong transit market. Tourists and travelers between San Diego and Tijuana make up 14 percent of the riders, and military personnel are frequent riders. The trolley captures the highest share of by-choice riders among all the San Diego transit systems: over 40 percent of its riders have an automobile that they could use for the trip.

Despite the MTDB's good record in operating transit service, transit use in San Diego faces impediments. Some of these reflect prevailing development patterns. In 1993, the MTDB produced a manual, *Designing for Transit,* and joined the regional dialogue to reshape development patterns to better support transit.

The integration of transit services, the construction of the trolley, and the shifting of growth to developed areas all helped San Diego deal with transportation and growth. However, the need for road investment and financing mechanisms was still large. The impacts of growth were on the minds of everyone, with the most prominent issue being traffic congestion. Although they complained a lot about traffic, residents were still surprised by a study from the Texas Transportation Institute that showed the growth of congestion in San Diego to be the highest among 60 regions studied. The San Diego region was hardly alone in its transportation-funding crisis, as a 1984 survey by the County Supervisors Association of California of county road needs and financial deficiencies throughout California made clear.

The 1984 regional transportation plan was developed by SANDAG, CALTRANS (the state transportation agency), MTDB, and local agencies. It identified projects and financial resources for the next 20 years. The price tag came to 9.9 billion dollars, about equally dividedamong local streets and roads, state highways, and transit. Not surprisingly, anticipated resources were estimated to account for only 60 percent of the needs. If San Diegans were to be spared a future of gridlock, it was essential to find new money to carry out the plan.

The primary source of funding for local and state roads in San Diego is the state gasoline tax. Of revenues spent on state highways in 1983, 88 percent came from state and federal user fees. Most of the expenses on city and county streets are for maintenance, and state and federal gas taxes (in 1983) paid only 40 percent of the costs. In the 1980s, California had one of the lowest gasoline tax rates of any state and not enough revenue to sustain the state highway program.

To obtain enough money from a gas tax to carry out the San Diego region's transportation plan would have required a tax hike of $0.20 per gallon. A proposed $0.02 gas tax increase had been defeated in a 1982 election, and voters were not likely to support this much larger increase. Moreover, the transportation plan called for both highway and transit money, and Californians, like others, resist the allocation of road-user fees to pay for anything but roads. Less than 1 percent of California's highway tax revenue goes to subsidize public transportation. Furthermore, fuel taxes in California are collected at the refinery, not the gas pump, making a local gas tax assessment administratively difficult.

The transportation planners set their sights on a sales tax increase. A 0.5 percent increase in the sales tax would raise 2.25 billion dollars over 20 years, enough to meet the funding shortfall, and it would be much more politically palatable. Of course, a higher gas tax would have been a financial incentive to reduce driving, encouraging the use of transit. However, the primary goal was to raise money, not to shape demand. The SANDAG board sought state authority to create the San Diego County Regional Transportation Commission, with the SANDAG board serving as the commission. In 1985 the commission was authorized to determine a transportation sales tax of up to 1 percent, subject to the approval of a majority of voters.

In making the case for funding, it was important to communicate the message that the solution to growing congestion was transportation improvements, and not no-growth. The one-third each allocation to transit, state highways, and local streets and roads appeared to be roughly in line with the needs and, more importantly, opinion polls showed that the public approved. The one-third portion for city streets and county roads was an attempt to deal with their severe disrepair, which had severely cut into local tax revenues. According to William Lorenz, an engineer for San Diego County: "Nobody got as much as they wanted," but the formula was about right. In fact, this allocation set a pattern for other California counties, according to Arthur Bauer, who heads Californians for Better Transportation.

Building support for the vote involved the creation of the private Foundation for Quality San Diego to help publicize the campaign, through presentations to community groups and other organizations. "Prop A was designed to pass," according to campaign chairman James R. Mills, who had formerly served in the California senate. "We put together enough support for a majority. We left out projects with substantial opposition, which would cost votes."

The most popular part of the package, according to Mills, was the lowering of senior transit fares by 25 percent of the normal rate. (Senior passes were available at half price.) Rail was generally more popular than highways, except in North County, where the spread-out population is more dependent on highways. Devoting 1 percent of revenues to bicycle projects was a popular idea.

Some needed highway projects were left out of the package because local pockets of opposition to them could have cost votes. Local Sierra Club members opposed one included project, the center section of SR-56. However, supporters of the transit package, arguing that opposition to the highway might hurt transit, persuaded the state organization to not take a position, leaving the local chapter unable to oppose the measure. Funding for transit operating subsidies, which continues to be a big issue, was left out because it lacked voter support.

Developers and contractors provided much of the financing of the $500,000 campaign to pass Proposition A. To include a growth management element in the projects package would have lost their support, if not the support of the voters. The campaign was targeted through mailers. Voters in Chula Vista saw their local projects, and voters in Escondido saw theirs. The campaign also targeted seniors. The focus on mailings surprised skeptics. The campaign avoided TV ads not only because of the expense, but also because advocates did not want to offer a platform to no-growthers, some of whom were skilled at manipulating the media. The campaign obtained the support of virtually every elected official in the county. Official support was not publicized, because of citizen cynicism toward officials but having it immobilized another potential source of opposition.

Proposition A passed in November of 1987, with a 54 percent majority. It allowed the imposition of the tax for a 20-year period. Some people were surprised that the vote ran best in minority communities not served by projects. This is, however, a common pattern in California (and probably elsewhere): the more conservative the area, the less the support for a tax initiative. James Mills feels that if one or two controversial projects had been included, 4 percent of the voters would have gone the other way - enough to defeat the tax. Unlike a similar campaign the neighboring Orange County that lost at the polls, the San Diego campaign "took polls and responded," according to the campaign chairman James R. Mills.

Many counties in California have adopted sales taxes to fund transportation improvements. San Diego added its own twist by giving oversight responsibility to the existing regional association of governments, SANDAG, rather than creating a separate county transportation commission. SANDAG is also the region's designated metropolitan planning organization for federal transportation planning. SANDAG administers the funding through a regular meeting process. One-third of the revenue is allocated to projects in each of the three categories - state highways, public transit, and local streets and roads - that were specifically identified on the ballot.

The city and regional planning agencies and the transit agencies in San Diego County have taken impressive steps to establish a policy framework for transit-oriented development. The SANDAG regional growth strategy, found in its 1993 Blueprint for the San Diego Region, exposes changes in land-use patterns to result in better use of transit and increasing development intensities within walking distance of transit stations and major bus routes.

SANDAG's 1995 Land-use Distribution Element of the Regional Growth Management Strategy incorporates land-use policies calling for higher-density, mixed-use development in transit access areas and for local governments' adoption of design guidelines and consideration of local zoning and subdivision revisions that would encourage such development. These initiatives are based on a tradition already established in 1989, as a network for regional cooperation on transportation and land-use (LERNER-LAM 1989, pp. 92-96).

Some conclusions: San Diego's initial Light Rail lines were built along existing railroad rights-of-way, with much of their length through older neighborhoods or industrial areas - not prime area for real estate activity. Also, since these are pre-existing developments, the scope of any new TOD will depend on the city's willingness to redevelop the area. Cities like Chula Vista, El Cajon, Lemon Grove, and National City already have major developments near existing stations and they continue these developments. Finally, in some cases land-use along pre-existing rights-of-way are not considered conducive to residential use because of pre-existing freight rail. Market conditions and fiscal and economic incentives are also important factors in implementing successful TOD. Voter approved sales tax revenues are available for another 10 years, but securing funding for planned rail extensions remains difficult.

As the map of ongoing development projects shows, a very large percentage of developments still seem to have no relation at all with the existing and future railway network.

This might change in the future, as San Diego has an elaborate public policy framework in place to encourage transit-oriented development and the transit agencies have positive experiences on which to build future projects. The one future development to watch for is the Mission Valley Line. Together with the Santle extension, this line is the only line that does not use a pre-existing freight rights-of way, but instead is placed on a high growth corridor to the north of downtown. Along with pre-existing developments like shopping malls, hotels, commercial and residential complexes, the corridor is still growing and has developable land. Therefore, the Mission Valley Line must be considered as particularly suitable for future TOD outside the City center of San Diego.

Another promising area for current and future TOD is Otay Ranch in Chula Vista. This line is a promising candidate for private co-financing: "As part of an agreement with the county and the city of Chula Vista, the developer (Baldwin) agreed to contribute right-of-way for the line and stations and a fair share contribution to the construction costs. Construction costs have not been required of any other property along the corridor. Baldwin successfully argued that it should not be singled out. The transit agency is looking for additional contributions to assist in construction, possibly through broad based benefit assessment districts. The developer has estimated that its land contribution amounts to 26 percent of the cost of the line, which is well above MTDB's rule of thumb that 20 percent of costs need to be borne locally" (DUNPHY 1997, p.139).

Similar to Portland, Oregon, although under less favorable regional planning conditions, the development of these lines are important indicators of TOD-possibilities in other parts of the country, especially in other growth areas.

4.6 Portland, OR: a long and expensive phase to reverse strong car dependence, spur development through Light Rail-transit and attract developers' financial interest to expand the system

The **Tri-County Metropolitan Transportation District (Tri-Met)** covers 592 square miles of urbanized area, including the city of Portland and parts of Clackamas, Columbia, Washington, Multnomah, and Yamhill Counties in Oregon. Originally created to operate the bus system, which now includes 80 routes extending over 760 route miles, Tri-Met completed its first Light Rail line in 1986.

Known as **MAX (metropolitan area express)**, the 15.1-mile eastside line has 30 stations and serves a steadily growing ridership on an average weekday. It was constructed between March 1982 and September 1986. The U.S. Department of Transportation funded 83 percent of the 214 million dollars (in 1983 dollars) project; state and local funds paid the remaining 17 per-cent. Federal fun-ding for the project came largely from trading in funds for an urban freeway and investing in transit and smaller road projects.

Tri-Met began construction of a second line, the **Westside MAX**, in 1993 and completed it in September 1998. This 18-mile line, which has a three-mile long underground segment, including the deepest station (260 feet/ 80 meters) in North America at Washington Park, opened in September of 1998 with a total of 21 stations. The line led to an increase in Light Rail ridership to 63,700 in July 1999 (TRIMET 1999). The federal government funded 73 percent of the 963.5 million dolalr project; state and local funds paid the remaining 27%. 113 millions dollars came from lottery funds, 21 million dollars from local governments and in 1990 Portland area voters approved 125 million dollars of property tax bonds (by a 74 percent margin).

Illustration 4.21: Tri-Met system (present and future)

Priority number one for Tri-Met's future planning is the extension of this existing East-West line through north south elements.

A 5.5-mile long **airport extension (AirportMAX)** of the Eastside MAX is under construction. It is scheduled to operate in 2001. Airport MAX is a 125 million dollar, 5.5-mile extension developed through an innovative public/private venture involving the Port of Portland, Tri-Met, the city of Portland, Portland Development Commission and Bechtel Enterprises. Because of this private/public venture, Airport MAX requires no additional property tax dollars, state general funds or federal new starts monies. The participation of the construction company Bechtel (headquartered in San Francisco) to achieve this 125 million dollar piece of infrastructure has been described previously. 28.3 million Port Authority (through a portion of the Airport-passenger-fee),

45.5 million Tri-Met, 23 million city of Portland (through tax increment from the Urban Renewal District) and 28.2 million from the Bechtel development arm "Cascade Station Development Company". In return, Bechtel, in partnership with Trammell Crow Company, will develop a 120-acre (50 ha), transit-oriented development at the entrance to the airport. Around 11,000 jobs and 400 million dollars worth of investment for hotels, entertainment, retail and office space will be built at the site, called Cascade Station, when it is completed in 2015.

As the following picture, presented in Tri-Met's "strategic plan 2003" shows, the most important system extension being planned is the North-South MAX. This line should create a connection between the northern extension of the Portland metropolitan area, north of the Columbia-river in Vancouver, in the state of Washington and the strongly growing southern part of the region in Clackamas. The entire estimated costs are 2 billion dollars. But so far public approval of the financing of the entire line has been refused.

Illustration 4.22: Interstate MAX alignment

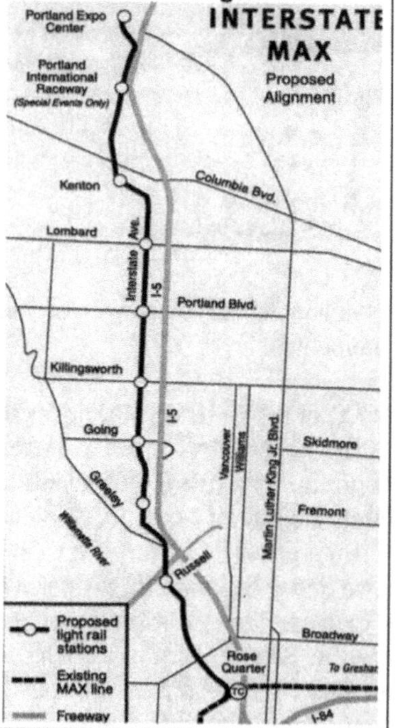

The city of Vancouver refused to participate, and the local match financing (10%) in the Oregon-branch of the line (through a property tax) was defeated by the voters in November of 1998.

A scaled back North line is now in planning, called Interstate MAX. The **Interstate MAX** is a $350 million, 5.6-mile extension connecting MAX to the Expo Center along North Interstate Avenue. A renewed streetscape through MAX construction and an enterprise zone under the Portland Development Commission (PDC) will encourage redevelopment oppor-tunities to this onetime main gateway to Portland. If adequate federal funds are appropriated, construction of this extension could begin in 2001, with opening set for Fall, 2004. To finance the local contribution, a tax increment financing district was created. The additional property tax expected on this part of the North-South-line is approximately 150 million dollars in a 20-year period, according to PDC estimations. 30 million dollars of this expected additional tax would be issued as project related bonds to finance the local portion.

Also, construction has started on 2.4-mile track of a new City Streetcar, linking in phase 1 Portland State University with the commercial parts of Portland's Downtown district, contributing to the development of high-density residential renewal areas. Streetcar service will begin in 2001. This first streetcar-element has a capital budget of 42 million dollars. Only 5 million dollars of that are federal grants, 8 million dollars are provided by the private sector (in the context of the Local Improvement District).

The bus system still plays the predominant role in Portland's public transit, carrying about 75% of the combined 249,400 daily rides. But the bus ridership figures seem to be linked with the success of the Light Rail System. After the opening of the Westside MAX, the combined bus and Light Rail ridership rose 137 percent. The Eastside bus ridership rose 35 percent since East-side MAX opened.

Altogether, Tri-Met estimates that the city's transit system eliminates 164,000 car trips inside the Tri-Met-area (TRI-MET 1999). This and additional measures to increase bicycle use, carpooling incentives and the application of Telework Guidelines to encourage (2000) city employees to work at home are mentioned as very positive cases for local Climate Protection (ICLEI 1997).

Despite the success of the Tri-Met-system, its operation costs are only covered to a very low degree through farebox-revenues. 65% of the operating revenue sources for fiscal year 1999 stemmed from payroll taxes (138 million), 19% from passenger fares (41 million), 13% from other sources including property-lease (27 million), 2% from interests ($ 5 million) and 1% from cigarette taxes. Payroll taxes are $6.17 per $1000 growth payroll.

The **Portland Metropolitan Area** goes beyond the Tri-Met area and includes Clark County in Washington. The population of this area **rose an average 2.1 percent yearly from 1991** to 1.8 million in 1998. The area's job growth during that time was even stronger, averaging 4 percent between 1990 and 1997. The regional government, predicts 700,000 more people until 2017. As these new residents must be accommodated within the "**Urban Growth Boundary**"

(UGB), developable land becomes more expensive. But despite the fact that the National Home Builders Association ranked the area the second least affordable housing market in the nation, "the median price of a single-family home is considerably lower than other West Coast cities" (ULI 1999, p.213). Although big-box retailers still expand their facilities in the suburban areas (Salmon Creek, Battleground, southern Clackamas County and the Sunset corridor) important developments are occurring in Downtown Portland (including a 150,000 square foot addition to Pioneer Place). Office construction has been concentrated in the downtown area.

Illustration 4.23: Willamette River Road before ...

Illustration 4.24: ...and after removal

"As in other North American cities, it was the threat of a freeway that galvanized public support for upgrading transit. In the early 1970s, the region needed a transit project to absorb federal funds from **the withdrawn Mount Hood Freeway project**. **Light Rail** was favored over busways because it was widely viewed as providing superior services and a more modern image. This **proved to be a monumental decision**, for it completely redirected how the region would evolve for decades to come." (CERVERO 1998, p. 416).

The Portland region provides now a unique policy context for transit-oriented development. Driven by the change of opinion during the heated freeway-debate, Oregon's 1973 state land-use growth management law called for local governments to plan for development in conformance with state objectives, including establishment of urban growth boundaries.

The state Land Conservation and Development Commission (LCDC) set statewide goals. Cities and counties are responsible for writing and implementing land-use plans that must comply with statewide goals. Over time, LCDC has refined and added to the list of statewide goals. When this occurs local plans must be revised to comply with the new rules.

One of the original statewide goals required that every city and the Portland metropolitan area have an urban growth boundary identifying where urban activities would be located in the next 20 years. The Metro Council adopted the Portland metropolitan area urban growth boundary in 1979 and has made only minor revisions in the boundary since then.

Metro, the regional government, that has also the role of an MPO, was created in 1978 and unites strategic planning for regional development and transportation systems. The 1991 state/regional adoption of a '"**Transportation Rule**" refined the transportation goal to require changes in land-use and transportation planning to reduce per-capita vehicle miles traveled (VMT) by 20 percent in 30 years.

The revised goal, generally known as the Transportation Planning Rule, aims to reduce reliance on the automobile; avoid the air pollution, traffic and the livability problems faced by other growing areas; and provide better planning for transit, walking, and bicycling. Local jurisdictions are currently changing their land-use standards for building access, parking lots, pedestrian and bicycle networks, transit stations, and other aspects of the built environment to comply with this rule (BRODY, 1994; MOORE and THORSNES, 1994).

Metro's 1995 **Region 2040 plan** contains future growth through development and redevelopment of compact centers and corridors served by high-capacity rail and bus systems. The plan calls for concentrating one-third of new residential develop-ment, and two-thirds of new jobs in transit corridors and station areas.

Tri-Met participated with regional and local jurisdictions in a cooperative program of station-area planning and adopted a strategic plan in 1993 that incorporated a goal to locate the majority of new housing and jobs within a five-minute walk of the primary transit network (high capacity rail and bus network).

Illustration 4.25: Portland City Center view of Mount Hood

Metro has worked with local governments and citizens to develop a consensus conceptual statement on future settlement patterns in the region in a process known as Region 2040. The adopted growth concept accommodates future growth with limited expansions of the urban area by concentrating growth in existing and new regional and town centers that are connected by multi-modal arterials and transit. Now that the urban growth concept has been adopted, local governments are required to adopt plans to comply with the Region 2040 growth concept.

In a joint effort with Metro and other government-institutions, **Tri-Met influences Land-use Planning.**

Tri-Met first became involved in land-use planning when it worked with local jurisdictions to put in place transit-supportive zoning around the eastside Light Rail stations. To promote station related local plan-ning on the westside, the Agency supported the communities to hire an experienced planning consulting team for this purpose.

Tri-Met has also developed guidelines for transit supportive development that identify potential markets, present planning and design principles, and identify steps the public and private sector needs to take so this type of development can become a reality. Tri-Met's planning and design guidelines contain recommendations on locating transit stops, configuring streets and sidewalks, placing facilities in commercial areas, mixing housing types, providing parks and community buildings, integrating with existing neighborhoods, and designing different types of station area neighborhoods. A model zoning code has also been developed (Tri-Met 1993b).

Non-Profit Groups advocate Transportation and Land-use Alternatives.

One of the reasons Oregon's planning system has worked well is due to the efforts of **1 000 Friends of Oregon**, an independent monitoring group supported by its members. 1,000 Friends of Oregon has provided education and advocacy on land-use planning since 1975. It has litigated when it believed local governments were not complying with the state's land-use laws. Recently it has put together a demonstration project on alternatives to traditional suburban development called “Making the Land-use, Transportation, Air Quality Connection (LUTRAQ)”. LUTRAQ addresses transportation problems using land-use and design changes coupled with transit improvements instead of more highways.

LUTRAQ demonstrated that 65 percent of new homes and 78 percent of new jobs in suburban Washington County could be located within walking distance of transit without increasing the currently planned density of the county (1000 Friends, 1992). This advocacy work has played an important role in shaping public opinion about alternative transportation and land-use policies.

The fact that transit-oriented development in the Portland region is supported by strong state and regional policies, and very prestigious non-governmental institutions contributed to a change of modal split, unique in the US, and very rare in European countries.

In a recent publication Tri-Met points out, that “thanks to the Portland region's land-use policies, transit is starting to do the unthinkable – win the war with automobile dependency. In central Portland, transit-related development was encouraged by a downtown plan adopted by the city in 1972. Major features of the plan were a bus mall on two one-way streets through the heart of downtown and limits on development of new parking spaces, one result being that 40 percent of work trips to downtown occur by transit. **Between 1990 and 1996, Tri-Met's ridership grew 20 percent faster than the growth in vehicle miles traveled**, 41 percent faster than the growth in transit service and nearly 150 percent faster than the growth in population" (TRI-MET 1998, p.2).

The statement of these unexpected successes underlines Portland's role amongst transportation and urban planners as a national laboratory of the feasibility of a less car-dependant development pattern for American cities. But as this debate is politically and ideologically very charged, it provokes many adverse or at least less enthusiastic opinions. The most drastic counter-opinion has recently been expressed by a Harvard University Researcher Jonathan Richmond, who is quoted in an article (The Oregonian, July 8, 1998) saying, that Portland's Light Rail system, as well as the rail systems in Baltimore, Buffalo, New York, Dallas, Denver, Los Angeles, Miami, San Diego, San Jose, CA and St. Louis "worsen the financial performance of transit agencies and produce little or no gains in transit ridership". He and many others (such as O'TOOLE 1999: The Vanishing Automobile) are convinced that a bus-only service would have the same or better ridership-impact at much lower costs.

Some conclusions: Portland, OR represents one of the most inspiring examples of the attempt to recreate a city and metropolitan area that is not held together by the car as the only link between uses, neighborhoods and open spaces. Rather, there are visible links, by a growing diversity of uses within walking distance and a growing diversity of travel choices between regional destinations, including bike and hike trails. The Light Rail plays a very important role as a new backbone of metropolitan growth and development.

The secret of the feasibility and success of the Portland model is wise leadership, including the former mayor Neil Goldsmith and successors, who endorsed a basic agreement about major regional development goals, the possibility of reliable project-agreements within the regional political and economic leaders and a very preservation-oriented civic movement. This includes many of the farmers on the city's edge, who are normally highly interested in realizing land values through future urban development. The "Urban Growth Boundary" is basically accepted by a growing part of the regional population and by growing parts of the development community. For all of my interview partners, the growth boundary represents investment-security more than development-limitation.

An energetic and devoted development staff at Tri-Met, city and regional agencies and the regional government, have facilitated development of a number of small projects that have boosted rail ridership. The projects have required significant assistance from Tri-Met in suggesting development strategies, securing financial assistance, and clearing regulatory hurdles. Many of them have involved complex financial and construction procedures.

The organizational and financial support for private developers on many of the small-scaled Eastside projects was and is necessary to spur the required transit friendly development. It contributes to the benefit of increasing ridership and creating attractive, safe and inviting station environments.

It creates examples that contribute to the way development happens in each of the station areas and to the making of station area communities.

The Westside MAX extension shows that Light Rail can also spur bold development projects that are entirely based on private money. The Orenco station development is the largest suburban residential transit-oriented development project in the entire nation. Only a few suburban heavy rail stations in Washington, Atlanta, San Francisco and other Metropolitan areas have the potential to match Orenco and other possible large residential developments along the Westside MAX. (It is probable though that other new Light Rail lines in other metropolitan areas may generate comparable project sizes. This will most probably occur in San Diego and other Sunbelt cities).

As Tri-Met doesn't own significant land-property, this development potential can only be realized through the active application of the entire planning toolbox on the local level. This is achieved through the participation of local and regional public development agencies (although the large number of parties and agencies involved plus the variety of issues raised, may have in some cases complicated the process for reaching agreement on project details), and through the willingness of large land landowners to contribute to this process.

It is **not surprising that Portland, OR is the first US community with a private company ready to co-finance a non-touristic rail extension** just because of its value to attract investors to this easily accessible site.

If ridership numbers continue to grow faster than the population, and faster than the number of car trips, even more developers will be attracted, and the many demands of "smart growth", "livability" and transit-friendliness could be well enough fulfilled to further justify Portland's ambitions as a "national urban laboratory". This laboratory will also be good to test a broad variety of TOD tools.

4.7 Toronto, ON: North America's only postwar transit-oriented city is increasingly disconnected from a car-dominated region and from a car-oriented development community

The **Toronto Transit Commission (TTC)** operates three rapid transit lines reaching from downtown to suburban areas. The U-shaped Yonge-Spadina subway opened in 1954, has been growing ever since (last extension 1996 to Downsview), and serves as a backbone of the **34.2-mile long system with 60 stations**. The Bloor-Danforth-line opened in 1966 and was extended 1980. At the eastern end of this line, the Scarborough RT-line was opened 1985. The subway lines carried 568,000 passengers on an average weekday in 1991. The subway lines are **supplemented by a 223.7-mile long network of seven commuter rail lines** (operated by GO Transit), used by more than 120,000 passengers. It is a 51.3-mile network of nine streetcar lines, with approximately 200,000 riders every day and many bus lines.

In 1994, the Metropolitan Council authorized construction of two new subway lines. Construction was begun, but current economic difficulties in Canada and the Toronto region have partially postponed construction.

The **Greater Toronto metropolitan area** includes the municipality of metropolitan Toronto (Metro Toronto) and the five surrounding suburban regions Peel, York, Hamilton-Wentworth and portions of Halton and Durham. In 1996, the area **had almost 5 million inhabi-tants**. After the amalgamation with the surrounding municipalities, the city of Toronto has 2.3 million inhabitants, of which the modestly growing central city has only 600,000. The region is considered Canada's economic center. It was strongly hit by a recession in 1990/91 and has since been slowly recovering. As a result, office vacancy rates began to decrease. Downtown Toronto has now the highest occupancy rates.

Toronto is considered "**Canada's corporate capital**; roughly 40 percent of the top 500 Canadian companies are headquartered in the area. In addition, Toronto is Canada's largest employment center, accounting for over **one-sixth of the nation's workforce**. It is **the second largest automotive center in North America after Detroit**. The Toronto Stock Exchange is ranked as North America's third largest exchange and is a major engine of the local economy. Toronto's strong manufacturing and financial services has attracted other industries to the area, making the local economy both diverse and dynamic" (ROYAL LEPAGE 1999, p.321). 2.35 million people were employed in 1998, 4.4 percent more than the year before. The unemployment rate dropped down to 7.4 percent, 1.5 percent lower than Canada's average.

Since 1995, encouraged by low interest rates after a recession-related halt, **Toronto's housing market strongly increased**. In 1998, 27,100 building permits were issued, 5.9 percent more than the previous year, almost 10,000 of them (city) condominiums, the rest single-family housing in Toronto's suburbs, "where large tracts of undeveloped land are available". ROYAL/LEPAGE (1999, p. 323) point out, that "**municipalities with readily accessible public transit and sufficient regional road infrastructures are expected to provide excellent opportunities for new development**".

Whereas the residential and also the office market (with the strongest development in inner city areas) seem to be partly or largely transit based, the retail market creates new centers, based on car access, that will have negative impacts on future possibilities to channel urban and regional growth along transit corridors. "The expansion of US-based retailers into Canada has meant an influx of big-box retailers and category killers (i.e. specialty superstores, warehouse clubs, discount superstores) that are challenging traditional department stores. Between 1990 and 1997, the market saw the addition of more than 11 million square feet of big-box space, an increase of 450 percent. Of late, retail development in the Toronto area has taken on a character with the emergence of urban entertainment centers, which include movie theaters, restaurants, bookstores, cafes, arcade games, and billiards" (ROYAL LEPAGE 1999, p.324).

Two major decisions in favor of public transportation were taken in the 1950s and created the basis of what Alan Wulkan and Gregg Snyder call "a European city set in North America" (WULKAN/SNYDER 1997, p.23): The cancellation of the planned Spadina Expressway (and its replacement by a subway line) and the decision to retain the street car system. Ever since then, the importance of city planning and zoning policy to shape the city and to influence regional land-use development has been very high.

The Metropolitan Toronto City Plan of 1976 (Metroplan) designates areas along the transit lines as suburban major or intermediate city centers. Once they conform to the plan, the local municipalities develop more detailed plans for the city centers. North York City and Scarborough Center were designated as major Centers, whereas the area between Kipling and Islington Stations in Toronto is designated as Intermediate Center.

According to DEAKIN 1997 (p.92) "Toronto's rapid transit system has played a tremendous role in steering the location of new development". A TTC study (Metro-politan Toronto: The Transit- Development Connection, TTC 1987) points out that during the 30-year period between 1954 and 1984 "**half of all new apartment construction was put in place within walking distance of rapid transit**. In the same period **90% of all new office construction** occurred **adjacent to downtown subway stations** and at stations located at Bloor, St. Clair and at Eglinton" (p.1). These calculations were based upon surveys of building permits issued in municipalities in Metropolitan Toronto. All together 30 billion Canadian dollars were invested in proximity of transit stations. The study expected a continuation of this location role of the subway, estimating that until 2001 another 20 billion dollars will be used for the existing and planned new lines.

Metro's 1994 plan, "The Livable Metropolis," stresses "re-urbanization," or redevelopment and reinvestment in the existing urbanized area. The plan proposes that local plans and zoning facilitate the concentration of housing and employment in centers and corridors served by and supportive of transit. Development plans are intended to physically integrate stations with surrounding development and produce a high quality of design for pedestrian access, the streetscape, and the built environment. (The provincial government, however, has deferred approval of Policy 30 pending possible revisions.) Also in 1994, the Metropolitan Council approved the initiation of a study and demonstration project of the most effective means of encouraging development at rapid transit stations.

Toronto's "Network 2011" tries to encourage the continuation of the polycentric system through a consistent zoning policy, permitting high-rise and other forms of transit-friendly developments only in an area of 1500 feet (500 m) around transit stations.

Consequently, ever since the 1970s, the City of Toronto also enacted maximum and minimum-parking requirements in the Central Area, along with higher all-day parking rates for publicly supported lots, to encourage greater use of public transportation. Its 1994 "Main Streets Initiative" reduced parking and loading requirements. The planning initiative has encountered opposition from neighborhood groups concerned about parking issues, however.

Illustration 4.26: Toronto Commuter Rail Network

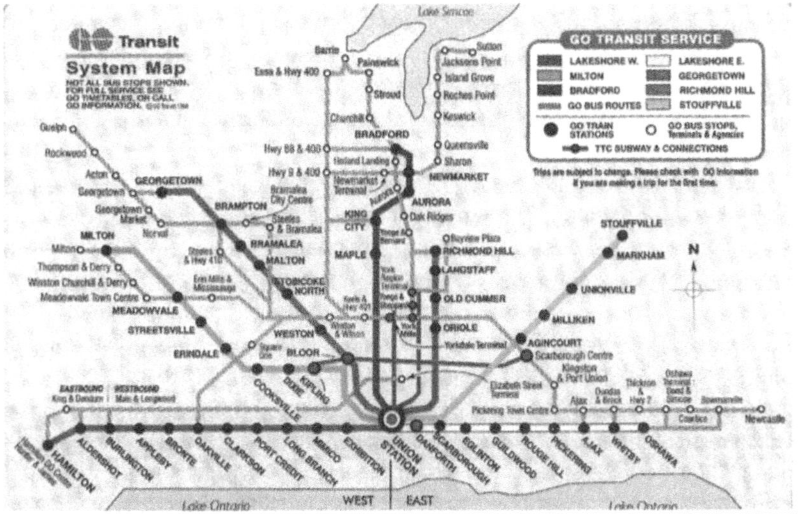

Despite that, the City planning commission isn't satisfied with the land-use effects of the 17 new stations opened since 1978. They "include 10 stations with densities less than 75 inhabitants plus employees/ha and 9 with modal splits with less than 20%. None of the new stations outside the old city has achieved densities and transit modal splits comparable to that achieved in areas served by surface transit alone in the older parts of the city" (TTC, Service Planning, April 30, 1999). This represents a large gap compared to the goals of the Metro Plan, which called for 350 workers and residents per hectare close to rapid transit stations, "which, if implemented in conjunction with parking restrictions, should allow modal splits of 50%, or more, to be achieved" (TTC 1999).

The lowest modal shares of the TTC-area are much higher as in most other North-American metropolitan regions. WEINSTEIN (1999) points out that from the many studies about the impact of public transportation on real estate values, "the only evidence that consistently supports the notion that rail transportation improvements positively impact property values comes from two studies of Toronto's rail-transit system…" (DeWees 1976 and Bajic 1983 p.6). However, he doubts the relevance of the experiences made in one "of the most modern infrastructure of any metropolitan area in the western hemisphere" (TTC 1987, p.2) to urban areas in the United States. "First, Toronto has strong development controls for which there is no counterpart in the US, as well as an almost complete absence of suburban highways. Moreover, Toronto encouraged a broad range of public policies to encourage rail-ridership, including restraints on automobile use" (p.7).

In 1991, GO Transit, the Ministry of Transportation, and Metropolitan Toronto directed a Metropolitan Toronto Commuter Rail Station Location Study to determine future land-use and transit relationships. As stated in the study's final report, "The location of stations needs to be cognizant of operational considerations, but must relate primarily to two goals: the improvement of the total transit network; and the development of transit supportive land-use patterns." The parties involved in the study focused on encouraging and - increasing total transit usage, while taking advantage of existing and proposed facilities on both TTC and GO Transit networks. Wherever possible, connections between TTC and other local surface transit routes would be maximized. An important consideration in determining transit station locations is the potential for development opportunities and intensity. At locations where high densities are not permitted, shuttle bus services have been considered. The study recognizes that the ability to either walk or take a short, direct bus ride to a transit station enhances the attractiveness of transit as the preferred commuting mode. GO Transit planners have ultimately hoped that the transit system would serve both outbound and inbound commuting trips. "The combination of transit-oriented development at the origin of a trip and transit-oriented development at the destination would provide the best possible attractiveness for transit usage."

Despite these studies and goals, the GO-transit ridership often does not exceed a 1% level in the concerned communities, which shows once more the split of development patterns between the inner and outer parts of the Toronto Area.

"Perhaps the greatest public policy issue facing Toronto centers around the consolidation and management of the new megacity, which was created on January 1, 1998, through the amalgamation of the metropolitan Toronto municipalities (to the "Municipality of Metropolitan Toronto", now the "City of Toronto"). The new municipal government, the largest of its type in North America, must confront issues such as growth management, cost allocation, restructuring of services, and property tax reform" (ROYAL LEPAGE 1999, p.321). This unification was ordered in1997 by the Province of Ontario, and took part despite the protest of large parts of the concerned municipalities.

Some conclusions: Toronto's development in close relationship to its transit system has been strongly supported by public policies and actions, as well as its residents' propensity for living and working in high-density urban environments. However, the regional government's firm control over transit-related development patterns has been diminished by extensive growth outside its jurisdiction in regions more tolerant of automobile-dependent development patterns. In addition, although development within the Metro area continues to focus on transit service, and Metro has continued to plan for transit-related development, current economic difficulties have severely restricted plan implementation. The consequence is that most new development taking place in the larger region is not strongly oriented to transit service.

The effects of the city amalgamation, and its political domination by more suburban-styled citizens on the future of public transportation, are not clear at the moment. But, as the first common conference of the UITP, CUTA and APTA in May 1999 showed, the city's pride in the transit system did not linger. It is more likely that the conflict of interests between the current City of Toronto and the suburban area beyond its city limits will have a stronger pro-transit advocate through Toronto's growing weight in the decision making process within the Greater Toronto Area.

5. Design/Build - Turnkey Projects

5.1 Privately Initiated and Financed Turnkey-Projects - the Las Vegas Monorail

In some cases, private developers or property owners have financed lines alone. In contrast to large-scale rail-transit investors of the last century in America and Europe and in other practices in modern day Japan and South-East Asia, these projects are generally limited to people-movers servicing sites of very high tourist interest, including Harbor Bay in Tampa and the connection between Park and Ride facilities and Disney World. Also the State Government of Colorado plans a new Light Rail line to link the Park & Ride facilities at the entrances of the Grand Canyon. The line financing will be entirely covered through parking and user fees.

Illustration 5.1:
Prospectus picture of the MGM Grand Bally's Monorail extension

The most spectacular current and future project is the **monorail in Las Vegas** (see picture). In 1993, the entertainment and hotel companies MGM Grand and Bally's conducted an international competition among transit suppliers for a monorail system. The selection criteria required the system to shuttle between the two resorts, and then eventually expand into a public transportation system for Las Vegas, connecting the Strip to the Convention Center and Downtown.

To reduce initial costs and accelerate the system's opening, MGM and Bally's bought and refurbished two monorail trains that were previously in service at the Disney World Resort in Orlando/FL. In its first year of operation the system carried 5.1 million passengers, a number, comparable to many other conventional Light Rail Systems (e.g. New Orleans, Newark/NJ, Denver/CO).

MGM Grand-Bally's Monorail LLC, the system managing and operating company, has now achieved a franchise agreement from the County Administration to expand this system. In several areas, the LLC has been able to negotiate with private property owners to relocate the monorail route out of public right-of-ways and onto private property.

The franchise provides for the first privately financed, constructed and operated public urban transit monorail system in the US, according to Bob Broadbent, who heads the LLC management team and is president of Broadbent & Walker, Inc. The monorail is expected to reduce traffic congestion in the Las Vegas Strip area that hosts some 30 million visitors each year and includes 67 percent of local employment.

Illustration 5.2:
Alignment of the Vegas Monorail

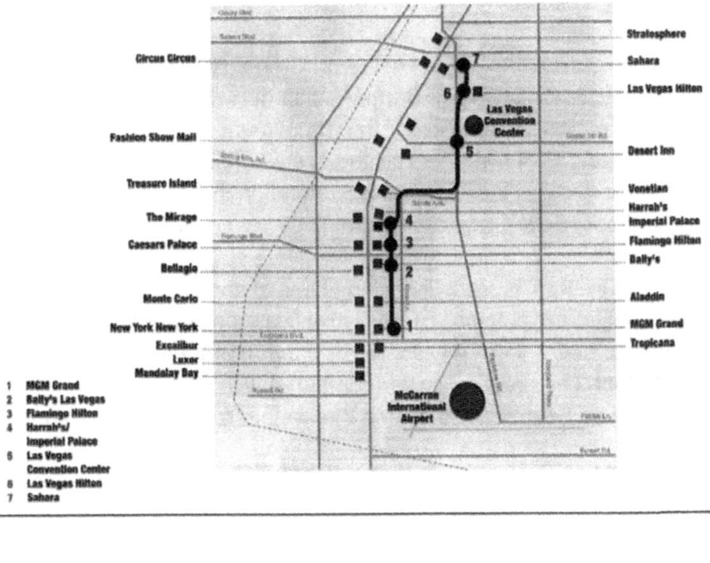

The approximately $600 million project will be fully financed by a combination of the sale of revenue bonds, ridership fares and resort station investment, with no commitment or obligation by county, state or federal governments, according to Broad-bent. "Thanks to Las Vegas' healthy and growing economy, preliminary ridership studies are very positive, showing nearly 20 million riders in the first year alone" (on the basis of a daily "20 hour-peak period" (Geoffrey Yarema, LLC's legal consultant).

The 3.3-mile extension, due for completion in Fall 2003, will include the construction of new passenger stations at Flamingo Hilton, Harrah's and Imperial Palace, the Las Vegas Convention Center, the Las Vegas Hilton and the Sahara (see alignment-map).

A "Super-Turnkey" Plan includes the design, building, financing, operation and maintenance of the entire system. The Las Vegas Monorail Team includes Bombardier Transportation Inc., Granite Construction Company, Carter & Burgess, Inc., Gensler of Nevada and Salomon Smith Barney.

The technology chosen, Bombardier M-VI, meets all Regional Transportation Commission standards for a true urban transportation system. The M-VI has the smallest footprint of any elevated transit system, is the most cost effective and most attractive, according to Broadbent.

URS Greiner is conducting an Investment Grade Ridership and Revenue Study. On its side, Salomon Smith Barney will underwrite the issuance of non-recourse revenue bonds that limits the repayment to the monorail's net revenues. The State of Nevada will be the likely conduit issuer of the bonds, on behalf of a non-profit, special purpose corporation that will be formed by the LLC to own and operate the monorail system.

The Las Vegas system is very inspiring. Due to the very specific tourism aspects it will not, in my opinion, be easily replicated elsewhere. According to Geoffrey Yarema, LLC's legal advisor, the system has a daily "20 hour peak" period. Due to high construction costs (compared with conventional Light Rail Systems) it will even be difficult to extend the system to the airport nearby (see map).

5.2 Privately built and co-financed projects - the MAX Airport-extension in Portland/OR

Because of the potentially higher shares of public transportation in Europe, there are more examples of private co-investment in the development of rail lines, especially along attractive development corridors. These examples are generally lines serving airports (Great Britain, Sweden, Norway) and new inner-city transportation systems (Great Britain).

In the USA, there are several projects of this nature being planned (for example a Light Rail line in New Jersey co-financed by the train builder Raytheon). However, it is still too early to include them in this case study.

Illustration 5.3: Alignment of the AirportMAX

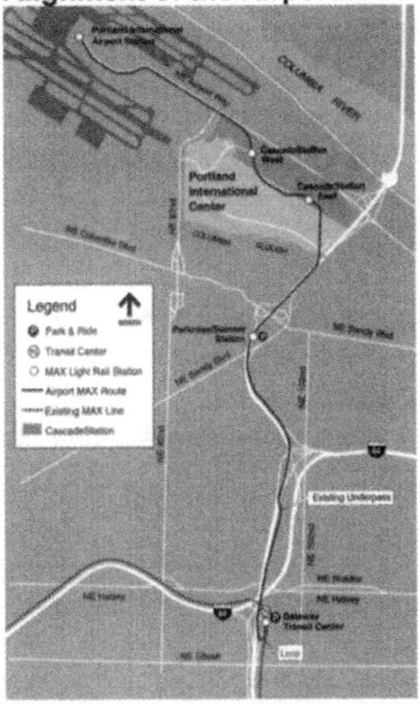

The most inspiring new project of the commuter rail type is currently under construction in Portland, Oregon, **'Air Max'**, an approximately 5.5 mile (9 kilometer) long Light Rail line connecting downtown to the airport. Bechtel Enterprises, an American construction company, which was, in 1998, the largest construction company (ENR 1999) worldwide, will invest a 25 million dollar share in the project. Besides the financing role, Bechtel is responsible for the planning and construction management.

The first notice of the project was given in 1997, when Tri-Met and port authority joined with Bechtel Enterprises to announce their plan for a public-private venture to fund the Light Rail extension. The December 1997 front page article of Public Works Financing, an "international business guide to public-private partnerships and innovative finance" described project details: "Three public entities would each assume responsibility for specific components using a variety of business taxes and benefit assessment credits. Bechtel, teamed with Trammell Crow Co., proposed advancing profits from a $400 million, 15-year build-out of leased public land near the airport to raise the last $30 million needed to complete the line."

"If successful", according to the magazine, "the venture would be the first in the U.S. to use a cost-sharing approach with the private sector to fund a public Light Rail project. The public agencies and Bechtel have agreed that the final package will not seek new federal appropriations, use state general funds, or go to the voters for a new citywide property tax."

On that basis, a memorandum of understanding (MOU) for the Airport Metropolitan Area Express (MAX) program and intergovernmental agreement was approved by the Port of Portland Commission, the airport owner/operator, on December 10, and the Tri-County MetropolitanTransportation District Board on December 17. The City of Portland Council followed their lead on Dec. 31.

Each has agreed to contribute $500,000 to the cost of preliminary engineering studies by Bechtel. The privately held firm will match the $1.5 million in public funds in hopes of winning the right for Bechtel Infrastructure to negotiate a fixed-price, design-build contract with Tri-Met. The transit agency and its public partners have agreed in the MOU to seek authority to bypass competitive bidding requirements.

The MAX extension would be jointly owned by the Port and Tri-Met, which will operate the line. Bechtel will firm up rough construction cost estimates of $130 million to $170 million up in the eight-month, $3 million study. The goal is to have environmental studies, detailed cost estimates, land-use plans and other issues resolved and construction started in 1999.

Tri-Met's General Manager, Thomas Walsh, a former contractor, was hired a few years ago to deal with large cost overruns, including an $80-million tunnel claim, on the city's West Side transit line. That experience, plus voters' rejection of funds for a South-North line last year, set the stage for the transit agency's test of alternative contracting with Bechtel. In addition, the funds advanced for the public-private project are expected to count as the local matching share for future federal funds to expand Portland's transit system.

The airport extension will use the I-205 right-of-way owned by the Oregon Department of Transportation that has been reserved for transit. Near the airport, the Light Rail line will run west through the Port of Portland's

International Center with the terminus at the southern end of the airport terminal. Airport planners made accommodations for a Light Rail line 15 years ago.

The Port would fund construction of an in-terminal Light Rail station at the south end of the airport's baggage claim area and a 1.2-mile segment from the terminal to 82nd Avenue. Funding will come from Passenger Facility Charges (PFCs), pending approval by the Federal Aviation Administration.

Tri-Met and the City of Portland would be responsible for developing a funding package to cover the cost of a 2.9-mile segment along Interstate 205 between Airport Way and the Gateway Transit Center downtown.

In the MOU negotiated for Bechtel by Senior Vice President Ralph Stanley, Bechtel would bear the cost of a 1.4-mile segment in the middle, from 82nd Avenue to Interstate 205. In return, it would get development rights to the Cascade Station development site in the Portland International Center, the Port's 450-acre commercial and industrial development on the east side of the airport.

The proposed terms of a lease between the Portland Bechtel include:

- A lease of 120 acres along Airport Way.
- Initial term of 85 years.
- Option period of 14 years.
- Rent during the initial term will be used for payment of the International Center section of Light Rail and construction of an overpass.
- Option period rent will include fair market value times 10%, adjusted every three years. Bechtel will be responsible for constructing a $ 14 million overpass of Airport Way. The Port's contribution will be limited to $ 7 million."

The following rough financial overview of the each partners' shares, recently presented on Tri-Met's home page, shows that the initial plan has been realized:

Key funding sources include:

1) Port of Portland: $28.3 million through Passenger Facility Charges (PFCs): The Port is using the three dollar per passenger PFCs, a locally generated fee dedicated to airport-related improvements
2) Tri-Met: $45.5 million general funds
3) City of Portland: $23.0 million Airport Way Urban Renewal Funds managed by the Portland Development Commission
4) Private funding: $28.2 million. Cascade Station Development Co., LLC provide roughly 20% of total project cost in return for a long-term lease hold (85 years + 14-year option) for 120 acres at Cascade Station.

The Cascade Station site, located within the Port's 458-acre Portland International Center, is adjacent to I-205. Cascade Station Development Co. proposes a high-density development and transit-oriented design to create a busy employment center anchored by two rail station plazas. The proposal emphasizes a pedestrian-friendly park block environment with open spaces and views of Mt. Hood. Full build-out is expected to take 15 years, creating up to 10,800 new jobs.

The site is the largest assembled, commercially zoned tract available within Portland's urban growth boundary, a locally revered Maginot line for halting sprawl. "It's a very valuable piece of land in a constrained market," says John Stirek, who heads Trammell Crow Co.'s development investment for the Western U.S.

The Light Rail extension is expected to serve 4,000-5,000 riders per day during its first year of operation. In 2015, the ridership is expected to grow to 7,500 passengers a day. These (Tri-Met) estimates seem to be cautious. About 35,000 passengers and 8,000 employees travel to PDX (Portland airport) each day now. Annual air passenger numbers rose from 6 million in 1991 to 12.6 million in 1999. By 2020, passenger traffic is projected to more than double to 29 million.

Actual passenger operation began in September 2000.

This project, more than any other US Light Rail project, shows that a long-term transit-oriented planning policy, accompanied by regional planning restrictions outside of the "Urban Growth Boundary", and a very proactive city/regional administration and transit agency can "make a change". Under these circumstances three differences to the "usual" procedures and results are possible:

- Private investors, confident in the administration's ability to steer the regional development and to accelerate the particular project, are ready to take a development-risk and share parts of the expected revenue in order to take advantage of possible project-related extra profits.
- If rights-of-way exist, the project planning and development period can be reduced to a minimum of approximately three years.
- Due to private project planning and management, project-acceleration and private financial participation, project costs and the public cost-share can be strongly reduced.

Illustration 5.4: Cascade Station Masterplan

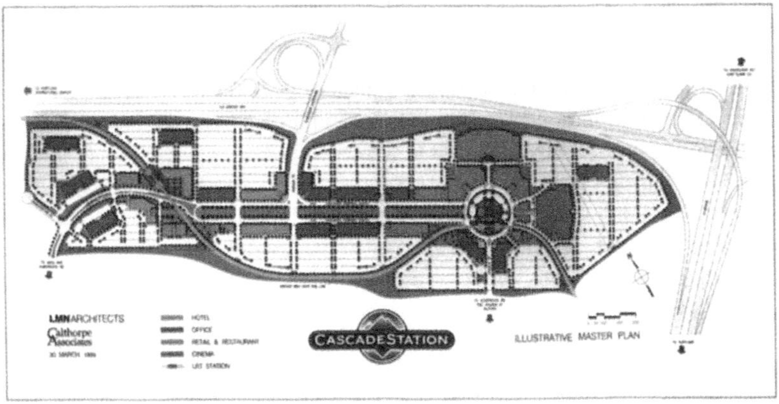

Due to the proximity of the airport, the expected passenger development of this airport and the favorable lease-conditions, the private contribution to AirMAX is very lucrative and cannot easily be copied. But the spirit of the project and the financial results can. In so far, AirMAX is the first complete American example of public-private partnerships for Light Rail. It is the only example that can be compared to the British examples, described below. It is interesting to note that the project "inventor", Ralph Stanley, Bechtel's Vice President served during the Reagan presidency as the head of the former Urban Mass Transit Administration. This may be an advantage in promoting the project as a national showcase of how, and under which conditions, private investors are ready to participate in urban rail projects.

5.3 Build Operate Maintain - the Hudson-Bergen Light Rail Line in New Jersey

Projects in which train lines were planned and built and in a growing number of cases later run by private consortiums are gaining interest. The most important example at the national level is the "Bergen-Hudson-Line“ a 20.5-mile (37 km) Light Rail line with 33 stations parallel to Manhattan in New Jersey. Another important example in the US-influenced arena is the so-called Tren Urbano in San Juan, Puerto Rico, planned by a consortium led by Siemens.

New Light Rail projects offer unique opportunities to comprehensively integrate development at the stations. In response to legal requirements within the framework of TEA 21 (Transportation Equity Act), the Federal Transit Administration closely assesses how well the specific projects meet the demand to serve as a catalyst for transit-oriented urban development and to include neighborhood development at future stations.

The following case study about the Hudson Bergen line will describe in detail the entire process of this particular DBOM-procurement process. It will especially emphasize the land-use development aspect of this particular new Light Rail project.

Background

During the late nineteenth and early twentieth centuries, the landscape of New Jersey's Hudson River waterfront was dominated by vast spans of railroad, numerous ports, port-related warehousing facilities, and heavy manufacturing plants (see the aerial photo of the Weehawken area). Freight and wares from the entire country, aiming at the markets and the population of New York City, arrived here to be shipped over the Hudson River. As the northeast's economy reeled from industrial decline, changes in the transportation industry forced the bankruptcy and retreat of many railroad companies and steamship operators. As a result, thousands of previously unavailable riverfront acres were sold to developers during the late 1970s and early 1980s.

This disposition of property created enormous opportunities for both the public and private sectors to create new commercial and housing developments close to Manhattan, but without the prohibitive costs of New York City.

In April 1984, Governor Kean directed the New Jersey Department of Transportation to conduct a transportation study to analyze the transportation implications of waterfront redevelopment and define a possible course of action, which could facilitate this redevelopment. The study was undertaken by the state because the area of waterfront redevelopment transcended both municipal and county boundaries. The study called for widespread public discussion and judgments by municipalities, counties, developers and a number of transportation agencies. While the study-report identified a preferred course of action, officials acknowledged that the recommendations must be fully understood, scrutinized and ultimately accepted in their proposed or revised form. The NJ DOT hoped that if the reports' recommendations received widespread public support, it would work to ready elements necessary for implementation.

The Hudson River redevelopment area spans 18 miles of coastline from Bayonne to Edgewater. It encompassed eight municipalities with a population of over 450,000 people. Most of the redevelopment area is in Hudson County, with a small portion in Bergen County. The study found that residential developments were widely dispersed along the waterfront, while commercial development was mainly confined to the south near the PATH (Port Authority Trans Hudson) subway system. The study found that development was stymied between Hoboken and Edgewater due to limited access and the absence of infrastructure. Development was occurring in a "piecemeal" fashion, with no apparent provision for future adjoining development. Thus, the report concluded, absence of an overall transportation plan would be a serious stumbling block for continued rational development. (NJ Transit, "Hudson River Waterfront Study: Draft Transportation Plan," November 1985)

The report recommended a series of transportation improvements including: expansion of existing bus and heavy commuter rail service; construction of Light Rail and "people mover" systems; and, establishment of park-and-ride lots with improvements to the existing roadway network. It finally recommended a variety of funding sources including the federal and state governments, the Port Authority of New York and New Jersey, the NJ Turnpike

Authority, and private developers through the creation of a special district to assess development impact fees.
Parallel to the Waterfront Development Committee's efforts, in 1982, NJ Transit selected Parsons Brinckerhoff to make a study about the necessity of easements for specific transit systems and system alignments. In 1986, NJ Transit set up an office to organize the planning process, the office of New Rail Construction.

Two subsequent reports issued in 1986 and 1987, developed financing strategies and continued the engineering design. The proposals called for much of the funding to come from private developers whose office and commercial projects were straining the local roads and bus systems and who would benefit from the major transportation improvements. By 1987, the original $800 million price tag had climbed to $1.2 billion. However, softening commercial real estate markets, and staggering time and cost estimates made developers unwilling to pay for more than just a fraction of the elaborate plan. The plan was also hampered by lack of an agreement on routing by local officials, and longer than expected negotiations for right-of-way (ROW) acquisition. In addition, competition among state and local governments for scarce public transit dollars during the Reagan era made the plan appear even more elusive. (NJ Transit, "Hudson River Waterfront Study: Draft Transportation Plan Technical Report," April 1986)

Acquiring Conrail Right-of-way "ROW"

In June, 1989 after almost four years of negotiations, the Kean administration and the Conrail Railroad Corporation signed an agreement that the state of New Jersey would acquire Conrail's 5.5-mile "River Line" running along the Hudson River from North Bergen to Jersey City, which included a rail tunnel through the Palisades in Weehawken. According to the agreement, Conrail, which owned and used the line for freight movement, would move its operations to a parallel line called the "Northern Branch" on the western side of the Palisades. Under the conditions, the State would have to upgrade the Northern Branch, which it hoped to complete by 1993.

The federal Urban Mass Transit Administration (UMTA, since 1992: FTA, Federal Transit Administration) had awarded a $20 million grant for the acquisition of the Northern Branch right-of-way. However, the cost of upgrading the Northern Branch for Conrail's use was estimated between $40 million and $42 million, with additional items to be determined through a contracted arbitration procedure. In addition, the Port Authority of New York and New Jersey had committed $50 million towards the cost of the rehabilitation work. The bi-state Port Authority's rationale for contributing $50 million to help relocate Conrail to the Northern Branch was to help improve the movement of goods and people as well as helping maintain the region's economic competitiveness.

Illustration 5.5: Weehawken Terminal, beginning of the 20th century

The long road from DEIS to the final alignment decision

The "Alternatives Analysis/Draft Environmental Impact Statement" (AA/DEIS) was a requirement of the National Environmental Policy Act of 1969 (NEPA), which called for a thorough review before the investment of federal funds into large public works projects. It was estimated that the "AA/DEIS" study would take 18 to 24 months to complete. Parsons Brinckerhoff, who had already conducted the preliminary planning for Kean's 1985 proposal, conducted the study and the firm was supposed to provide an opportunity for local officials, developers and private citizens to participate.

The study explored seven alternative plans for the corridor including: a "no-build" scenario; making small improvements to the existing network of streets, bus-lanes and PATH (Port Authority Trans Hudson subway system); building a system of busways for the exclusive use of buses; the original 1985 proposal which included a combination of trolley lines, busways and park and ride lots; constructing monorails on elevated tracks; building a north-south roadway for automobiles; and an option that would blend two or more of the alternatives (DEIS 1992).

Illustration 5.6:

End of the 20th century: View from the HBLRT to the World Trade Center on the other side of the Hudson

The possibility of achieving any plan depended not only on the chosen technical and alignment alternative but also on the number of competing projects, in particular the planned Light Rail connection between Newark and Elizabeth, a project that had been carefully studied and planned parallel to the Hudson-Bergen line.

To reduce financing problems, Martin Robins, director of the NJ Transit Waterfront Development Office suggested that the Port Authority (of New York and New Jersey) would have to be tapped, and Hudson County officials would have to form a "Transportation Development District" under state legislation pending in Trenton. The spe-cial district would have po-wer to impose uniform fees on developers to pay for transportation improve-ments that would benefit the district. These pro-posals were rejected and have never been picked up again.

In December 1990, the waterfront transit project received an important endorsement when Gover-nor Florio's "Transportation Executive Council" relea-sed a list of highway and transit projects for northeastern New Jersey totaling 3.6 billion dollars. The Council, together with the new State-Transportation Commissioner Tom Downs limited the number of transportation projects to those that could reasonably win environmental approval and be paid for with state, federal and authority funds.

The Council split the plans into projects which could be completed within five years, and longer-term projects. The Council also selected five urban areas, ripe for revitalization, to be supported by new infrastructure investments. Among the projects that received an endorsement from the council were: the waterfront Light Rail, a waterfront busway and the "Secaucus Transfer" with its Bergen Arches component. A key part of the plan called for the state legislature to raise the cap on spending from the state's Transportation Trust Fund (TTF) from $365 million a year to $565 million a year. Doing so would allow the state to draw additional federal funds and spend in excess of $1 billion annually for NJ DOT and NJ Transit capital projects over the following four years (Star-Ledger 12/13/1990).

The FTA approved NJ Transit's Draft Environmental Impact Statement (DEIS) in November 1992. The action came 2½ years after the study first began by NJ Transit. However, by that date, the NJ Transit Board had still not adopted the Locally Preferred Alternative, and had postponed its consideration from the October board meeting to sometime in January.

Despite a consensus by transit and local officials, federal guidelines required that the transit agency conduct a series of meetings and hearings for the public. The first four public meetings were briefings by transit officials where they distributed executive summary copies of the DEIS and answered questions about the Alternatives Analysis report. The four town meetings were held in the municipal buildings in Bayonne, Jersey City, Weehawken and West New York. The final two sessions were formal public hearings recorded for public comment, held in the county administration building in Jersey City and at the Hoboken City Hall. Upon the conclusion of the meetings, the public comment period was officially over.

Illustration 5.7:
HBLRT Final Alignment and construction segments

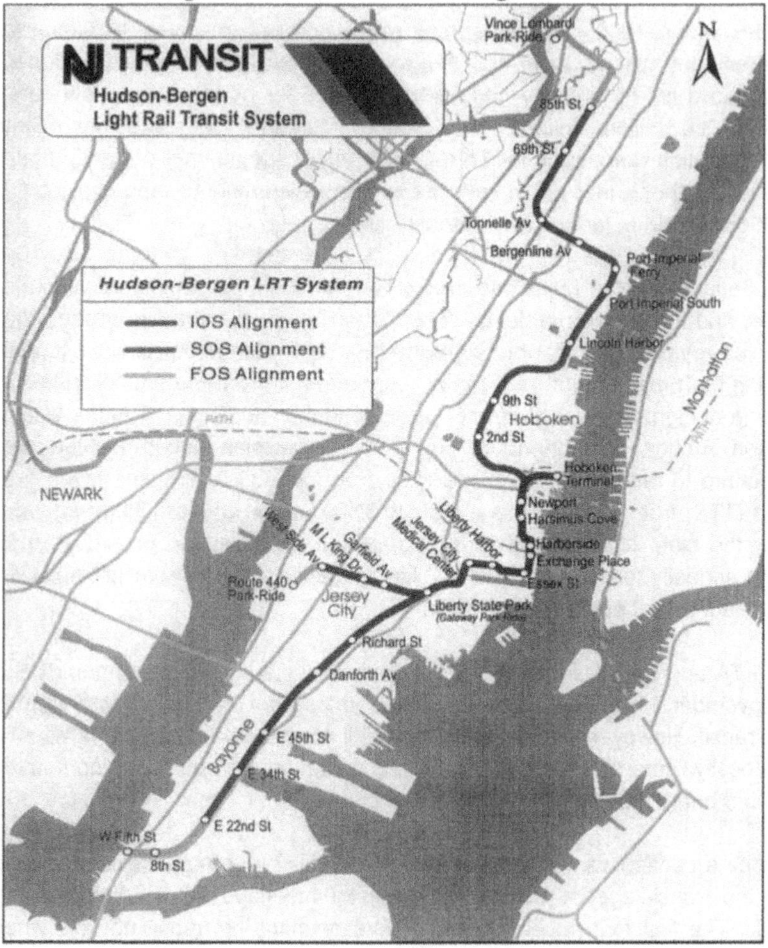

At the first public hearing held in the county administration building in Jersey City, the Light Rail plan won strong support from a wide array of government officials, business leaders, and environmental advocates. Immediately before the hearing, all 12 Hudson mayors formally signed a 10-page "Intergovernmental Consensus Agreement" (FEIS II, A11). Shaping the "consensus" plan for the proposal to win unanimous support of all 12 municipalities was not easy, but essential for the project's success. Given the very different socio-economic background and political context of each community, the signing of such a consensus was a unique expression of mutual commitment. In February 1993, after 43 months of planning and negotiations, the NJ Transit Board finally adopted the Locally Preferred Alternative (LPA) for the Light Rail. Nevertheless there were five contentious issues left un-resolved. NJ Transit had formally agreed to study the cost effectiveness of a southern extension into Bayonne; to analyze downtown Jersey City and make a determination on the best possible alignment; and to study the feasibility of constructing a station in Union City above the Weehawken Tunnel. Officials informally agreed to address a Hoboken routing issue, and investigate the possibility of a northern extension into Bergen County.

Illustration 5.8:
LRT alignment through historic neighborhoods in Jersey City

The Bayonne extension had the greatest political support, the best cost-benefit ratio and was the least controversial. In the spring of 1993, Mr. Robins released preliminary findings, which showed that the Bayonne extension was feasible. Officials reported that constructing the Light Rail line 5.2 miles south to the tip of the Bayonne peninsula would boost potential ridership by about 15 percent, or by more than 8,350 passengers per day.

NJ Transit officials preparing the Supplemental Draft Environmental Impact Statement (SDEIS) said the extension turned out to be much more cost-efficient than transit planners had originally anticipated. Mr. Robins said that the key turned out to be extending the project's terminus further south to the tip of Bayonne. The study showed that if existing rail rights-of-way were used for the extension instead of on-street routes, commuters could make the 5.2-mile trip from Fifth Street in Bayonne to Liberty State Park in just 12 minutes. And, by ad-ding a 1,500-space park-and-ride lot commuters would be attracted from both Bayonne and Staten Island.

It was estimated that the cost of the extension would be 119 million dollars. However, half of that cost would be offset by potential savings if the extension turned out to reduce parking demand at the planned park-and-ride lot near Liberty State Park. While the original plan called for a 5,000 space parking garage near the park, much of the demand was anticipated from Bayonne and Staten Island residents. If those commuters were to use the extension, than the Liberty State Park lot could be reduced to 1,500 surface level parking spaces. By avoiding the construction costs of a parking garage, agency officials planned to recapture $58 million.

In 1994, there were a number of significant administrative changes at NJ Transit affecting the Light Rail project. First, came the departure of NJ Transit Waterfront Development Office Director Martin Robins. Mr. Robins had served as director of the office since 1987. Under Mr. Robbins and his predecessors, the director of the waterfront office was on par with the Executive Director of NJ Transit and reported directly to the Commissioner of NJ DOT, chairman of the NJ Transit Board. The office in Jersey City had been created in 1985 to replace the Governor's "Hudson River Waterfront Development Office."

Under the Whitman administration, the waterfront office was closed and the operations were relocated to NJ Transit's corporate offices in Newark, and renamed "New Rail Construction." Mr. Robins was eventually replaced by Frank Russo, an engineer who had followed NJ DOT Commissioner Frank Wilson from San Francisco's BART (Bay Area Rapid Transit) authority. These two changes had an important impact on the DBOM-approach.

The Jersey City Supplemental Environmental Impact Statement (SEIS) was the result of a controversy, which pitted two separate historic districts against one another, and local merchants against well-heeled developers. Specifically, the proposed "City Center" alignment would split the historic Van Vorst neighborhood, while the proposed "City South" route would impact the historic Paulus Hook community. Local merchants favored the "City Center" route because it would better serve their patrons and businesses. Transit planners, developers and many local officials supported the "City South" alignment because the line would allow access to a 34-acre parcel of waterfront property ready for major commercial development. After a long and controversial debate, the "City South" route was selected.

The DBOM-concept

NJ Transit had expected to construct the Light Rail project using the conventional design-bid-build procedure. An initial project schedule would have had the construction under way in 1995 and trains running by the end of 1999. However, the plan was delayed due to routing problems and delays in funding by the FTA. A revised schedule based upon a delayed start and reduced annual funding suggested that it might take until 2016 to complete the full project. Projected inflation over the extended period would substantially increase the total cost of the work, and the extended schedule would diminish the ridership, which was necessary for the continued redevelopment of the waterfront.

NJ Transit was under enormous pressure to reduce costs while bringing at least some of the project on line as originally scheduled. The agency opted for a design-build approach and decided to shift some of the project financing to the contractor. This was done to prevent cash-flow shortages, caused by limited annual FTA grants. The additional costs associated with financing the project were also expected to be substantially less than the cost of inflation for the project, if it was delayed.

There were many obstacles and issues that NJ Transit officials and newly appointed members of the Whitman administration had to overcome in 1994. "We had a project that was probably 15 years away from being done, we were facing two more years of environmental work and maybe three years of engineering work, about a year to determine the site, and maybe eight to ten years of construction. We had the funding coming from the federal government and from the state and from other sources. It was at that time that we decided we needed to change our deadline. That's when we focused on turnkey," explained Dan Censullo, Senior Director of New Rail Construction at NJ Transit.

In June 1995, NJ Transit issued a "Request for Expressions of Interests." The agency began evaluating prospective DBOM teams based upon their technical qualifications and financial capacity. Five teams were found to be in competitive range and were pre-qualified for the project. Over a six-month period, NJ Transit and Parsons Brinckerhoff, its general engineering consultant, worked out issues for the final "Request for Proposals" (RFP).

NJ Transit issued the "RFP" in November 1995 with an initial submission from the teams scheduled for February 1996. Bidders would be evaluated on the basis of their financial and organizational proposals, and technical considerations including their management plans, facilities, systems, vehicles, and benefits to the state. Officials later met separately with each team to discuss how their proposals could be improved for final submittal.

The HBLRT-RFP is an extraordinarily large document with a core element, the two volumes (several hundred pages) contract-draft (Book III) and all together 60 additional volumes, categorized in 16 books of engineering details, environmental requirements, business documentation etc. The contract includes the following aspects: Design/Build of IOS and SOS; Design/Build of vehicles for the three segments, Operation/Maintenance of IOS and SOS for a 15 year period.

Some examples: According to the contract, the contractor "shall obtain and pay the cost of obtaining all Governmental approvals required in connection with the project"; The contractor "shall achieve Revenue Ready Status of the IOS (and the SOS) on or before 40 months after issuance of the IOS "Notice to Proceed" and shall achieve final acceptance of the IOS project within 180 days after achieving the Revenue Ready Status"; the owner "shall have no obligation to extend a Guaranteed Completion date" (except as otherwise specifically provided – as a consequence of differing site conditions and utilities, force majeure events, hazardous substances etc.) and the contractor "shall not be relieved of its obligation to achieve Revenue Ready Status by the applicable Guaranteed Completion Date, for any reason".

Additional duties of the contractor include the necessity to insure LRT-vehicle payment bonds. The acquisition of the right-of-way remained a task for the owner.

DBOM contract for designing, constructing and equipping the system was a fixed price contract. In addition, it contained an opportunity for cost extras and change orders only for unforeseen circumstances including wetlands mitigation, environmental remediation, utilities relocation and "political risks." While the contract was for the Initial Operating Segment (IOS), it was designed to be compatible with later contracts for the Subsequent Operating Segments (SOS) and final completion of the 20.5-mile line.

Illustration 5.9: HBLRT in service, May 2000

The Initial Operating Segment (IOS – see illustration 5.8) in phase 1 consists of 9.5 mi of double track, 16 stations, 3 major intermodal transfer sites, 5 regional park & Ride lots, with 3,750 spaces, a storage yard and maintenance shop as well as 45 Light Rail vehicles. This first phase has created a connection between the primarily residential neighborhoods of Bayonne, through Jersey City to Hoboken along the Hudson River. This so-called "Gold Coast" has been strongly transformed in the last 20 years, attracting high-profile firms Merrill Lynch, Dean Witter, Paine Webber, Bankers Trust and Goldman Sachs. Phase 1 of the project was scheduled to open in March 2000 and was expected to serve 25,000 daily customers in the first operations year.

Illustration 5.10: HBLRT, Initial Operating Segment

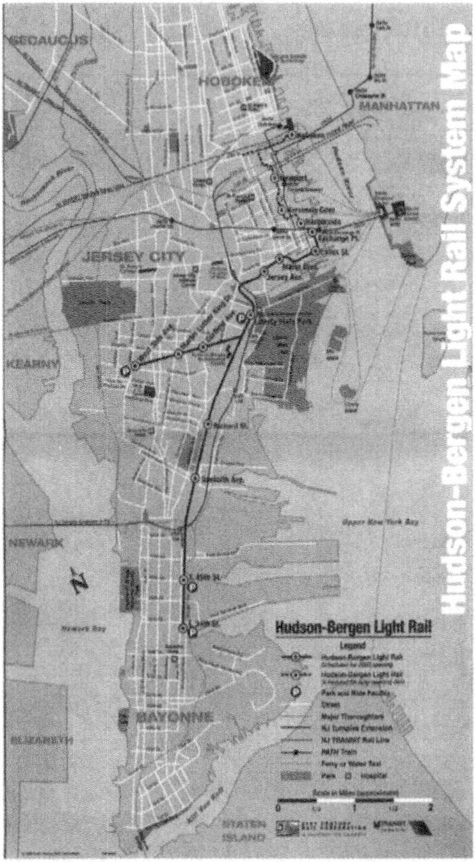

In Phase 2 (see illustration 5.7) the subsequent operating segment (SOS) will run between Hoboken, the ferry in Weehawken and routes 1 and 9 at Tonelle Avenue. It includes 7 stations, 3 of them intermodal, 4 Park &Ride facilities, a 4000 foot long tunnel in Weehawken and 14 additional Light Rail vehicles. The expected ridership on this segment is 32,000 passengers by 2010.

The final operating segment (FOS, see illustration 5.6, p.83) will add another 9 stations and complete the total system of 20.5 miles.

After phase 3, 100,000 riders a day are expected on the entire line (DUFFY 1998, p.2), almost 20,000 more than initially projected (see below).

The operations and maintenance component of the contract included funding for capital asset replacement as well as track and vehicle re-habilitation. This provision was inserted to insure that NJ Transit would have a system in a state of good repair at the end of the 15-year operation and main-tenance period. At that point, NJ Transit could ex-tend the original contract, rebid it, or conduct the operation and maintenance itself.

In addition, NJ Transit inserted a "service quality index." The index included such performance measu-rements as trains running on time, low noise, passenger comfort, and insu-rance liability. If the con-tractor did not perform to the desired standards, NJ Transit could monetarily penalize it. Conversely, the contractor could also re-ceive a small bonus for exceeding the index.

The final bids were submitted in May 1996 with separate sealed price and financial proposals. By the final round, two teams had dropped out and the proposal by a third team was found to be technically "non-responsive" and therefore not evaluated. The final two proposals were then evaluated against the project criteria on a numerical basis. Following the technical evaluation, NJ Transit publicly opened and scored the sealed bids. A weight of 40 percent was given to the technical proposals and a weight of 60 percent was given to the price proposal.

Twenty-First Century Rail Corporation, a consortium headed by Raytheon Infrastructure Services, Inc., a subsidiary of Raytheon Engineers and Constructors submitted the lowest bid. Other members of the consortium included Itochu Rail Car and Kinki Sharyo (USA), Inc. The total value of the contract was approximately 1.082 billion dollars over the full contract period. This was significantly lower than the 1.433 billion dollar proposal submitted by the second bidder, Siemens Corp.

In August 1996 the Board of Directors for NJ Transit gave final approval and awarded the DBOM contract to the Twenty First Century Rail Corporation. The consortium's proposal included a three-year period for construction of the IOS and a 15-year period for operation and maintenance. Specifically, the contract included 476 million dollars for system-design, construction and facility equipment; 434 million dollars for maintenance and operations of the system; 93 million dollars for vehicles; and, 100 million dollars for separate work related to the Newark City Subway (DUFFY 1998, p.8).

Financing through FTA subsidies and additional state and local matching funds would have required at least 10 years until an initial line-segment would have been completed. As a non-obligatory requirement of the RFP, the idea was to get a "bridge loan" through the private contractor. Both DBOM teams proposed full financing plans for the work. The contractor offered a bridge loan with interest rates of 9.5%. Despite this offer, and the importance that it had for the DBOM decision, it was finally not accepted. Instead, the state of New

Jersey selected a far cheaper alternative to finance the project. This was accomplished through the issuance of tax-exempt "grant anticipation notes," borrowed against the state's Transportation Trust Fund (TTF), to finance the gap between project spending and the flow of annual FTA grants. NJ Transit anticipated receiving a total of 605 million dollars from the FTA. The contract called for the DBOM team to be responsible for the short term financing of the Light Rail vehicles, with NJ Transit only issuing payment when the cars entered service.

As a result, "in April 1997, NJ Transit issued 351.6 million dollars of capital grant anticipation notes bearing interest rates between 4.625 percent and 5.500 percent and maturing on September 1, of the year 2000 through 2003, inclusive" (NJ Transit Annual Report 1999, p. 39)

Under the terms developed by NJ Transit, the contractor would be responsible for completing the project design, construction, supply of systems equipment, and operation of the completed system. The basic bid for the design, construction and equipment was a "fixed price contract" with allowances for some variation for the operations and maintenance portion of the agreement depending upon actual ridership.

The contract was the single largest public works contract ever awarded in New Jersey, and the first largest DBOM contract for a new rail system in North America. Thus, the design-build "turnkey" contract became the nation's first design-build-operate-maintain (and finance) "DBOM" contract, or "super turnkey" project for a mass transit system.

Factors influencing ridership

The Business Documentation in Book XI of the Request for Proposals (RFP XI 1995) summarizes the ridership number forecast as follows: The market for the proposed service includes commuters going from New Jersey into New York City, as well as travelers within the Waterfront area. This area has a complex mix of existing transit service, which the proposed LRT system would complement.

The total ridership numbers have been mentioned above. Interestingly, ridership expectations after completion of the entire system have increased since the initial forecast was made. Instead of 81,400, mentioned in the RFP, a total of 100,000 daily passengers appears to be more realistic now. This increase is even more significant than the numbers suggest, because the western alignment that was finally chosen in Hoboken is supposed to generate less ridership than the waterfront alignment. One of the reasons for this change is the amount of development that has already taken place on the Hudson River Waterfront. The forecasts suggests that of the total number of system riders after completion of the final segment, approximately 30%, will have destinations along the Waterfront, 42% will head to Manhattan locations, and the remaining 28% will end elsewhere in the study region, primarily areas west of the Hudson River. Among all areas west of the Hudson, including the Waterfront, roughly 40% or 30,000 are supposed to be local, intra Hudson County LRT trips.

The majority of LRT trips to the Waterfront will originate south of Hoboken, while most of the Manhattan trips will begin north of Hoboken. Staten Island, Bayonne, southern Jersey City and Waterfront residents represent 65% of the trips to Waterfront locations. Remaining areas within and outside Hudson County represent the balance of LRT trips into the Waterfront.

Northern Hudson County and Bergen County residents combined account for 48% of the LRT trips into Manhattan. In smaller percentages, all other LRT trips into Manhattan will originate elsewhere, primarily in Hudson County and other New Jersey areas.

According to the forecast, the ridership development depends on the following factors:

Employment growth is the most critical factor affecting projected Hudson-Bergen Light Rail-transit. A model run, which assumed 1990 employment and population, generated more than 30,000 fewer LRT riders than one which assumed 2010 economic conditions, roughly one third fewer potential riders.

Three other policy variables which are important in projecting LRT ridership and fare levels are, in order of importance:

LRT fare – according to the forecast sensitivity test, a $1.00 increase in a flat $1.00 LRT fare produced a 12% decrease in LRT riders. However, the annual revenue under these conditions may increase by approximately 76%.

LRT runtime - An increase in downtown Jersey City LRT runtime by approximately 8 minutes, to simulate additional street congestion for the LRT resulted in a 10% decrease in ridership.

LRT frequency - An increase in the LRT headway from 9 minutes to 12 minutes generated a 9% decrease in LRT riders.

All sensitivity tests for fares, frequencies, travel time, parking pricing and development demonstrate that elasticities moved in the expected direction and are consistent with historical local/regional experience.

An effective LRT feeder bus system enhances patronage of the system. The ability to control and influence the feeder service will affect the degree and consistency to which this can be accomplished.

Expected farebox-recovery:

The current average farebox recovery at NJ Transit achieves an average of 55%, with a rail service recovery rate of 57% and a bus-service recovery-rate of 52%. Despite the fact that the fares have not been changed for 10 years, the farebox-recovery increased over the last years. This is related to the strong ridership-increase of 27% during that time.

The Hudson-Bergen line, if the forecasted ridership numbers come to pass, is expected to cover 30% of the operation costs of the first segment (IOS) and to break even (= 100% recovery) after completion of the rest of the line (WEDEL).

Expected maintenance and operation costs:

Also in Book XI (RFP XI 1995) the expected maintenance and operation costs are discussed with estimates based on the analysis of Booz, Allen & Hamilton:

Because actual ridership may vary significantly, operations and maintenance costs have been calculated for a range of ridership levels. Ridership for the IOS was assumed to be in the range of 20,000 to 50,000 daily one-way trips. For the FOS system, it was assumed to be 60,000 to 120,000.

a. Estimates of the annual operations and maintenance costs for the IOS range from 12.5 million dollarws at 20,000 daily riders to 14.9 million dolalrs at 50,000 daily riders. These estimates assume that peak headways are either six or nine minutes on each route, depending upon the ridership scenario.

b. Estimates of the annual operations and maintenance costs for the SOS range from 19.7 million dollars at 50,000 daily riders to 26.8 million dollars at 110,000 daily riders. These estimates assume that peak headways are either six or nine minutes on each route, depending upon the ridership scenario.

c. Estimates of the annual operations and maintenance costs for the FOS range from 26.3 million dollars at 60,000 daily riders to 31.7 million dollars at 120,000 daily riders. These estimates assume that peak headways are either six or nine minutes on each route, depending upon the ridership scenario

d. The costs stated in points a, b and c above can be reduced through reductions in service levels (i.e. increasing headway). However, a preliminary analysis indicates that the resulting loss in fare revenue would be greater than the savings in operations, maintenance, and incremental capital costs. This is due to the elasticity of ridership demand with respect to headway, which NJ Transit estimates to be -0.25 percent ridership change per percent headway change.

e. A preliminary estimate of the net present value (NPV) at start-up of capital asset replacement costs over the 15-year operating and maintenance phase of the DBOM contract is approximately 40 million dollars for the IOS. An additional 45 million dollars is required for the FOS at its start-up.

f. Labor is clearly a major cost driver. There may be additional opportunities for savings in staffing levels and costs. The assumed staffing levels are based on a traditional transit environment, with some moderate reductions for the DBOM environment. The DBOM contractor may actually be able to make further reductions to achieve a leaner, more efficient, and less costly organization.

The cost per rider steadily decreases with increasing ridership. It is estimated that the cost per rider ranges from over $2.00 at 20,000 daily riders to about $1.00 at 50,000 daily riders. It is estimated that the FOS cost per rider ranges from about $1.50 at 60,000 daily riders to about $0.90 at 120,000 daily riders.

h. Preliminary analysis indicates that running a West branch off-peak shuttle service, rather than running no-turn-back during off-peak, reduces annual costs by approximately $1 million per year for the IOS, and approximately $2 million per year for the FOS System. However, analysis of the net impact on operating costs and revenues for the shuttle have not yet been completed.

Transit Joint/ Station Area Development Opportunities:

Since ISTEA, the FTA put a strong emphasis on the need for revised community design, land-use and parking policies to reinforce transit use. The effort was part of the FTA's "Livable Communities" initiative, which essentially rewarded jurisdictions, which used mass transit to reduce suburban sprawl, improve neighborhoods, expand employment opportunities, and provide better access to the community for those who could not, or would not drive. The initiative came after disappointing results in some cities in which new transit lines failed to spark significant development, or where it took years for the new line to attract the ridership, economic development and other benefits promised by local proponents.

Light Rail advocates in New Jersey believed that a three-pronged approach would lead to a successful mass transit system. The first prong was the actual establishment and operation of the Light Rail system. The second was corresponding land-use design to support ridership. And, the third ingredient was providing pedestrian amenities (JENNINGS 1997).

The most difficult part of this equation is the fact that each prong is supported by a different entity. Mass transit planning and financing are the domain of federal, state and regional agencies. On the other hand, in New Jersey, municipalities have nearly sole discretion over local land-use and zoning regulations through the adoption of municipal master plans. Thirdly, pedestrian amenities, when they are considered at all, are frequently left to the discretion of the developers.

The possibilities for station area development activities have been investigated through a study of the Regional Plan Association/NY together with the National Transit Center in Berkeley/CA, quoted here as BERNICK, the main author. The study aimed at incorporating Station Area Development requirements into the Request for Proposals (RFP).

According to this study, the promotion of station area development was complicated by four factors:

1. NJ TRANSIT owns no land at the stations.

2. Under current New Jersey state law, Code sections 27:25-13b, NJ TRANSIT is only able to condemn land "reasonably necessary for the purposes of the corporation..." These "purposes" are likely to be interpreted narrowly, and past NJ TRANSIT activities have not included joint development or station area development.

3. Under current New Jersey state law for redevelopment and economic development, public sector entities are empowered to purchase and/or condemn land within legislatively determined bounds. The NJ Economic Development Authority Act of 1974 which created the EDA (NJSA 34: IB-I et seq.) limits condemnation authority to job-creating industrial and commercial development contingent to municipal approval. The NJ Housing Mortgage and Financing Agency can also purchase and/or condemn property as well as grant loans for project "primarily residential in character..." or "provide services to the residents of an area or project which is primarily residential in character, (NJSA 55:14K-3e)."

4. The station area that NJ TRANSIT has promoted most enthusiastically, and for which it has commissioned a station-area plan, the Martin Luther King Blvd. station in Jersey City, probably does not hold major revenue potential for the Proposer". (BERNICK 1995, p. 43).
Despite these inconveniences, it is very interesting to see what the effect of station area development as a requirement of the RFP was: The authors quote the example of the RFP of the planned Light Rail line for Honolulu/Hawaii[8].

[8] "The Honolulu Light Rail system, actively pursued by the City of Honolulu through the late 1980s and early 1990s, was a $1.7 billion Light Rail project consisting of 17.3 miles of track from the Waiwa Station near Leeward Community College to the University of Hawaii/Metcalf station. The system included 24 stations.

The project was structured as a design-build contract, with the system scheduled to open in 1997. As part of the RFP, bidding teams were asked to include a joint development plan: a plan of financial contributions that could be expected from joint development, to offset the project cost to the City.

The team that was selected, the Oahu Transit Group (Morrison Knudsen, AEG Westinghouse, E.E. Black) presented an aggressive joint development plan that the team claimed could yield near $1 billion to the City over a twenty-five year period.

It is worth looking at in some detail, as indicating possibilities for joint development.

The OTG joint development plan focuses on developing the station areas at eight of the stations: Concert Galleria, Dillingham Plaza, University/King, Lowers, Kaiulani, Aloha Stadium, Piikoi/Pensacola and Nimitz/Fort. The OTG, combined with the local development firm of the Myers Corporation, would be the master developer for these station areas.

The largest scale development is Concert Galleria, envisioned as a large-scale retail, commercial and residential center at the Ward Avenue station near downtown. Concert Galleria is to include a regional shopping center, two office towers, and three residential towers. The development is projected to total over 5.5 million square feet. Dillingham Plaza is the other high-rise development, a mixed use development consisting of apartment buildings and retail/office complexes on both sides of Dillingham Boulevard. Reflecting on these two developments and others, the OTG proposer writes:

"What we have learned from our intensive effort at Concert Galleria, is that value can be created from real estate at transit stations and this value can be used to finance the transit system. This value can be captured only by careful planning. Such planning balances a creative design process and careful attention to market realities with the need to create revenues from transit and the business reality of attracting qualified financial partners."

The Oahu Transit Group (OTG) currently owns little or no land at the station. The OTG proposal does not ask the City to obtain and convey the land. Instead, the City's contribution is to come through: 1. creating Transit Improvement Districts (TID) at all of the stations; 2. as part of the TID providing OTG with condemnation authority at all of the stations; 3. as part of the TID providing OTG with exemption from industrial, affordable housing and public facilities requirements of the city; 4. master-developer rights on concessions.

The OTG, thus, is empowered as a form of transit-redevelopment district: with power to obtain land through condemnation and payment of fair market value, and with power to develop without going through the same City planning process as other projects. The TID is similar to the redevelopment district concept, in utilizing tax increment financing. The tax increment is to be placed in a Transit Development Fund for 25 years and used for capital costs and then for system operations and maintenance.

In return for these City actions, OTG's joint development will generate revenue to the City in four main forms:

Shared Profits: 20% of the net profit from Concert Galleria, a flat profit sharing at Dillingham Plaza and a 60% sharing for the concession revenues. The other sites are at 20% of net profit similar to Concert Galleria. Identified shared profits are estimated at $418.9 million.

Contributions from projects upon planning and zoning approvals: Developer fees from the eight sites are estimated at over $l 00 million.

In-Kind Contributions: The OTG offered to build the Ward, NBC and Pearl Highlands stations, valued at $5 million per station.

Real Estate Property Tax Revenues: The added real estate property tax revenues are estimated to be over $600 million over a twenty-five year period.

The OTG did not commit to the City the $1 billion in the joint development plan. What it did pledge was $5 million up front, and a $100 million premium for development at eight stations to be paid upon financing and issuance of building permits and fulfillment of conditions.

The OTG invested significant time and effort in its joint development proposal, and team members saw it as an important component of the proposal. Whether or not it was realistic is difficult to determine as it was never implemented. Even before negotiations could start on the joint

Despite the failure of the Honolulu-LRT project itself, the idea of introducing aggressive private sector ideas into the planning of the development of stations proved to bring positive results in this and other cases (such as the Los Angeles Airport Express, LAX). And independently from the RFP no legal tool to generate money for public activities to improve station access and other public investments was ever used. This is also surprising as developers actively suggest the use of instruments as the designation of transit improvement districts or tax increment financing.

Development Impact of the Light Rail Line

The redevelopment of the Jersey City Waterfront started before the Light Rail was put in place (which, as shown later, proved to be a technical and legal burden for the LRT right-of-way). The best example for the dynamic development along the Jersey Waterfront is Exchange Place, which was impossible without transit, but it was the PATH train that spurred it.

The Port Authority Trans-Hudson Corporation (PATH) connects Manhattan with the New Jersey cities and suburbs - Newark, Hoboken, Jersey City. The trans-Hudson service has been in operation since 1908, but by the late 1950s was nearly financially insolvent.

The system was overhauled and re-opened in 1962, now owned and operated by the Port Authority of New York and New Jersey: the old rail cars replaced by a fully air-conditioned transit fleet. Before September 11, 2001, the trip from Newark to the World Trade Center was only 22 minutes, 11 minutes from Hoboken to the World Trade Center, and 14 minutes between Hoboken and 33rd Street station in Midtown Manhattan.

"PATH has served and continues to serve primarily as a means of moving commuters living in New Jersey to jobs in Manhattan. However, during the past decade, the Exchange Place PATH station in New Jersey has emerged as a transit business center, with nearly 4 million square feet of office space developed since the mid-1980s" (BERNICK 1995, p. 34/35). PATH carries over 200,000 passengers each weekday, more than two-thirds of these during the morning and evening peak hours. Ridership has increased for many years

---

development approach, the entire rail project was questioned by the City Council. In 1992, just one year after approving the project, the City Council voted 5 to 4 not to proceed on rail. Since that time the project has not been revived". (BERNICK 1995, p.4/5)

and has attained pre-war levels. According to information at Rutgers University (Martin Robins at a meeting on May 4th, 2000) PATH ridership in 1999 was as high as in 1929. This increase is a clear indicator of the strong economic development of the Jersey City Waterfront area.

The Exchange Place station served for the first part of the twentieth century "as an "exchange place" for passengers to transfer from the railroad lines and streetcar lines in New Jersey to ferries and subsequently railroads traveling into Manhattan. By the early 1980s, the station area had deteriorated into an area of empty warehouses, decaying small commercial buildings, and abandoned railroad equipment.

The City of Jersey City launched an aggressive policy of property-tax deferrals to lure office construction into New Jersey. This policy coincided with the heated New York-New Jersey office market of the mid1980s, as well as the movement of back office jobs out of Manhattan, to produce an office building boom at Exchange Place.

During the 1980s, four major office complexes were built among the former warehouses of Exchange Place: the 1.7 million square feet Harborside, the 1 million square feet Colgate, the 660,000 square feet Exchange Place Center and the 324,000 square feet Evertrust. Additionally, on the drawing boards were plans for an additional nearly 7 million square feet of office, including 5 million square feet on the Colgate complex, and an additional 1 million square feet on the Evertrust II development. Exchange Place was envisioned as a business center larger than the nearby World Trade Center. With the downturn in the local office real estate market, these office development plans have been in abeyance. Similarly, the proposed residential complexes for Exchange Place have been in abeyance. During the 1980s, the Evertrust H development was to include a 470-unit residential high-rise as well as a hotel, and the Harborside development was to include a 650-unit residential high-rise. Neither of these have been built due to the inability to obtain private financing.

Still, Exchange Place today is a major office center, built on the transit link-primarily PATH, but also bus lines that spread throughout the region. It reflects mainly the private sector office boom of the 1980s in New York-New Jersey, but also benefited from the property tax deferrals offered by Jersey City. The transit agency, PATH, recently has assumed a more aggressive development role in building a transit mall, to better connect the office complexes and the transit station". (BERNICK 1995, p. 34/35).

Exchange Place has since been added to by additional office buildings and is still expanding. The development of the former Colgate factory immediately south of it will start soon. It's difficult to say in how far the LRT will generate additional development at places that are already served with the PATH. It certainly serves as an internal connector of a total amount of office space that will soon be comparable to Downtown Manhattan.

It adds value in every case and in many cases it generates development of places that would not have been developed otherwise. This is the case at every station that was not transit accessible without the LRT, at locations far away from the PATH. In Hoboken for example, some developers are waiting to start their projects until the LRT will have a clear building and operation schedule. Some of them would also be ready to participate financially to accelerate the realization of the LRT.

Jeffrey A. Warsh, NJ Transit's current executive director, expressed the hopes related to the Light Rail line: "In addition to providing congestion relief, Governor Whitman intended the Hudson-Bergen Light Rail to be an economic generator. The governor's vision is now a burgeoning reality. Already, the skyline along the Hudson River shows evidence of growth and development. Between 1996 and 1999 1.4 million square feet of office space has been developed and occupied. Another 1.4 million square feet of office space is now under construction, totaling 4,200 jobs. Developers cite the impact of the Hudson-Bergen Light Rail as one of the reasons for this construction boom. Additionally, residents of Bayonne and Jersey City see the arrival of the Light Rail not only as a boost to economic development, but also to higher property values". (HBLRT-Newsletter, Vol. 1, No. 2, 1/2000)

So what did developers and land-users at the existing LRT-segment do to accelerate or co-finance the Light Rail?

(Non-)Participation through developers

Only one form of participation was planned: the donation of the necessary easement at places where the LRT had to leave the existing right-of-way of the former Conrail tracks and go through developable property. This was mostly the case along the Hudson Waterfront and on the southern connection between the former Conrail tracks and the Waterfront.

The Waterfront developers were obliged to donate the part of their property needed for the LRT-easement, not those on the southern connection to the former Conrail tracks. The reason was a requirement of an "agreement for the grant of easement" as part of the construction permit for Waterfront developments, issued in the late eighties, in a period where the precise LRT-alignment was far from being decided.

One example is the agreement from August 27th, 1986 between the New Jersey Transit Corporation (NJ Transit) and the New Port City Development Company (NCDC). The agreement shows how difficult a (forced) donation is when the benefiting partner doesn't know precisely where he needs the land. In Article 1.01 point c) of the agreement "the parties acknowledge that insufficient design work has been performed as of the date hereof to permit a detailed description of the property over which the easement shall be granted". A 100 to 150 feet large corridor of a "preliminary easement path" is nevertheless fixed. This corridor fixes a "review zone" in which "the locations and plans and specifications for any development ... shall be subject to the review and approval of NJT". Article 1.01 point g) specifies, "within three years of the date hereof NJ Transit shall precisely define the actual easement necessary for the Public Transportation System..."

As the final alignment could only be specified eight years instead of the mentioned three years after the completion of the agreement and as this agreement and analogous agreements for other Waterfront properties had no precedent within New Jersey, the real estate acquisition for the LRT-Waterfront alignment was facing two major problems: 1) A straight corridor was no longer available because three years after the agreement NJ Transit had no right to review the preliminary transit corridor and could not prevent it from being overbuilt and 2) The legal insecurity on behalf of the requested easement grant weakened the negotiating position of NJ Transit. As a consequence, many months of negotiations with the developers were lost. This was the major reason for the delay for the beginning of operating services on parts of the initial segment and the even longer delay for the completion of the first segment.

And still, in addition to the 40 million dollars for the acquisition of the (20 miles long) former Conrail tracks, 48.6 million dollars had to be spent for land acquisition for the Maintenance Facility and the southern connection between the Waterfront and the Conrail tracks. No land owner/developer who was not obliged to do so was ready to grant the necessary land for the transit easement.

Also NJ Transit's costs for preliminary engineering, the investigation of hazardous materials and for legal advice totaling 118 million dollarshad to be added. Theoretically, it would also be necessary to add another approximately 120 million dollars, that NJ Transit will have to spend to reconstruct bridges on the new western Conrail-corridor. These bridges need to be replaced to allow future freight traffic on this alternate line. As the latter represents a specific problem, not directly related to the LRT-infrastructure, the total infrastructure costs of the initial operating segment will be 685 million dollars. The costs of the purchase of 45 vehicles need to be added, to represent the total costs before operation and maintenance. These costs are 93 million dollars, according to the contract and 151.7 million dollars, according to information through NJ Transit.

Even these high costs of $778 million dollars (or 837 million dolalrs) for 9.5 miles of Light Rail are lower than the additional real estate value created through the line. Once again, the proposal for the Honolulu Light Rail counted on a total, real estate related gain of the (unrealized) LRT line of more than 1 billion dollars over a ten-year period.

If one takes into consideration that the specific costs for the future operating segment (SOS and FOS) will be lower than the initial segment, it is not impossible that the relation between costs and (real estate) gains in the case of the Hudson-Bergen-line is much more favorable than expected in Honolulu. None of this could be captured under the current DBOM-conditions. The disconnection between land development and line development doesn't reflect the real gains that the line will produce for the landowners.

Disconnection between farebox recovery and Light Rail operation:

A potential, not yet visible problem is related to the disconnection between the operating system and the farebox-revenue. NJ Transit has the full farebox-risk, 21st century has the full operation cost risk. This leads to a potentially dangerous conflict of interests: Theoretically 21st century can optimize its maintenance costs through a minimization of passenger numbers: the less passengers, the less damage, the less weight, the less staff. Although it will also be in the general interest of a 21st century rail corporation that the line succeeds regarding passenger numbers; this may lead to a future conflict about marketing aggression and public appearance.

Conclusions:

After more than 20 years of planning and more than 5 years of building activities, the first part of the Hudson-Bergen line started operating service on April 15th, 2000. It will certainly be a very important tool for the development of one the most densely populated counties in the country and one of the poorest counties in New Jersey. It will contribute to the rededication of one of the most valuable parts of New Jersey – the part directly opposite Manhattan. The former function– serving as a delivery point into Manhattan-- has turned into a destination on its own, with high quality offices (including headquarters and a decreasing percentage of back-offices) and very desirable housing locations, for brokers as well as for families. At some points, the Hudson Riverfront has changed its industrial attitude, it's inaccessibility, into a relaxing leisure zone.

The Hudson-Bergen Light Rail will accentuate these developments and extend it into communities that have not yet been touched by these changes. The southern part of Jersey City and its waterfront, as well as Bayonne, are the first examples. The Light Rail there, although massively disturbed through the eastern branch of the New Jersey turnpike, will continue to create a corridor of future growth.

In the light of the Hudson-Bergen Light Rail as the first new transit system in New Jersey and in the entire Tri-State Area will prove to be an important development factor for the corridor through which it runs. The relatively high investment costs of the Light Rail of about 30,000 dollars per daily rider on the initial operating segment (if the forecasted ridership of 25,000 per day will be achieved) will thus be justified.

As for many major public infrastructure projects, the time between the first concrete planning steps and the project start was very long. This was caused by the following factors:

- The long decision-finding procedure on the state and local level.
- The strong political interference into the planning and project development process.
- The legal requirements of the planning procedure; in particular the Environmental Impact Statement (EIS – now Major Investment Study, MIS) and the authorization procedures for any environmental project aspect.
- The refusal of necessary approvals through the Department of Environmental Protection that contributed to permanent time-consuming detours of the alignment, and a substantial disadvantage in the competition with the private car.
- The very complicated land negotiations with real estate developers along the line.
- The extremely detailed conditions of the DBOM request for proposals and the DBOM contract, which might be related to the lack of experience with this new project delivery method.

Illustration 5.11:

HBLRT final alignment as a result of influences and compromises

5.4 Design Build Operate Maintain (DBOM) projects in the UK as elements of the national Public Private Partnership strategy

Two brief case descriptions of British Light Rails systems may contribute to understand the decisive role of the legal and administrative framework to encourage public private partnerships. The two systems, taken into consideration, are not as spectacular as the famous example of the Dockland Light Rail. But the more ordinary setting makes it a little easier to draw conclusions from procedures, investor risks taken, and results.

The British examples need to be studied to get a better understanding of the broader question of how to involve private investment into the development or improvement of urban rail systems. It is also necessary to investigate these British cases to contrast with the role of the private sector in American rail investment.

The former conservative British government developed a radical strategy to redefine the role of government and the role of private enterprise to fulfill government tasks. This policy change took place in a weak economic as well as budgetary situation and was supposed to reinvigorate the economy as a whole. A very advanced public-private partnership policy was developed which proved to be so successful that the Labour government welcomed it, continued it and developed it further.

Since the beginning of the eighties the use of private funding had to be systematically tested against publicly funded alternatives, and preferred to the public solution, if shown to be more cost-effective ("Ryrie-Rules"). These rules, although initially criticized as being too restrictive for public entities seeking private investments, have been refined over a decade and on the basis of case examples. These examples included starter lines of new Light Rail systems, such as the Manchester Metrolink, described below.

Many local authorities have then established successful partnerships with the private sector. "Nevertheless, following case-studies and consultations carried out by the Department of Environment and the Chancellor's Private Finance Panel, it became clear that changes in the framework of financial controls within local authorities operating would be needed." (HM Treasury 1995, p. 8). Necessary changes included "fewer controls on the participation by local authorities in companies led by the private sector" as well as "measures to facilitate the transfer of assets to companies into the private sector" (ibid, p. 8).

The resulting new policy – the "Private Finance Initiative (PFI)" – was introduced in the autumn of 1992. While publicly co funded private projects still needed to be compared with the public sector comparator, "self-financing projects undertaken by the private sector would no longer need to be compared with theoretical public sector alternatives" and "the government would encourage the private sector to take the lead in joint ventures with the public sector" (HM Treasury, 1995, p. 6).

Even after overhauling the initiative in 1997, the initial definition, goals and challenges remain the same: "The public sector contracts to purchase quality services, with defined outputs, on a long-term basis from the private sector, and including maintaining or constructing the necessary infrastructure. The term also covers financially free-standing projects where the private sector supplier designs, builds, finances and then operates an asset and covers the costs entirely through direct charges on the private users of the asset, with public sector involvement limited to enabling the project to go ahead through assistance with planning, licensing and other statutory procedures." (HMTreasury 2000, p. 47).

The goal is to "benefit from private sector innovation, to generate radical new synergies between the design and operation of assets, and to take advantage of private sector commercial discipline, so helping to modernize public services and obtain better value." (ibid)

In order to achieve these goals, the public side had to set up clear "requirements on the private sector partner from the start (for example through a robust performance regime), and to ensure there is a proper and appropriate allocation of risks between the public and private sectors, so as to deliver real improvements in the quality of service provided, and value for money for the taxpayer."(ibid)

The current approach of the Labour government is broader and includes all types of partnerships with the private sector. "Public private partner-ships (PPPs) are key element in the Govern-ment's strategy for delivering modern, high quality public services and promoting the UK's competitive-ness. They cover the entire range of business structures and partnership arrange-ments, from the Private Finance Initiative (PFI) to joint ventures and concessions, to outsourcing, and to the sale of equity stakes in state-owned businesses". (HM Treasury 2000, p. 8).

Illustration 5.12: PFI-fields 1992-1998

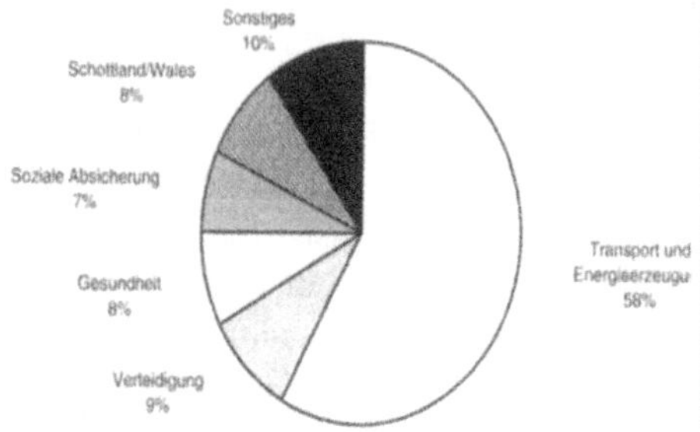

Bild 1: Prozentuale Aufteilung des PFI-Investitionsvolumens

[80] Siehe Expertengespräche: Male, S. (1998)
[81] Siehe Internetadressen: UK Progress Report (1998)

Despite this widened approach, PFI remains the most prominent and most complex method to generate public private partnerships. While PFI started with transportation projects, other government departments became interested in applying the same rules, so that since 1995, the Treasury "would not approve any capital projects unless private finance options have been explored". As a consequence, PFI projects were very diverse, and appeared in the sectors of transport, health, defense, accommodation, urban re-generation, information systems, prisons, higher and further education, water and sewerage and others (see also Illustration 5.12). In 2001, the National Audit office estimated that "there are over 400 PFI contracts currently in force committing (government) departments to future expenditure of around £ 100 billion." (NAO 2001, p. 1).

One of them is the Croydon Tramlink project, presented below in chapter 5.6. The project was mentioned as one of the most prominent PFI examples in the 1995 Treasury report (HM Treasury 1995).

5.5 DBOM limited contract - the Greater Manchester Metrolink

The agglomeration of Manchester represents a typical northern European region with former heavy industries, strong structural changes over the past decades, slow development pace and an urban and transportation pattern, that reflects the same trends as in the US, but with different quantitative levels. The densities are still so much higher and the regional core (city of Manchester) as well as the regional sub centers (mentioned below and shown in the map) remained so much more mixed and economically important, that these quantitative differences are a sign of a qualitative difference. This different quality was a precondition of the enormous success of the Light Rail system, reintroduced decades after the prewar-system was closed down.

The most important regional development features and their transportation implications are described in the Greater Manchester Local Transport Plan (GMLTP). A provisional version of this plan was published in July 1999 (GMLTP 1999). Some extracts introduce development trends, well known from the US: parallelism of increasing car-owner-ship and urban sprawl. The regional development and transportation policy tries to alter this trend through the strengthening city-centers and the creation of interconnections with a privately financed and operated Light Rail system.

"...Greater Manchester is a complex polycentric conurbation. The Regional Center, which lies at the heart of the county and is the focus of road and rail networks contains the largest concentration of employment, retailing, entertainment and educational facilities in the (British) Northwest. Its continued well being depends on its accessibility being maintained and enhanced and our transport strategy gives emphasis to achieving this objective.

Good accessibility is also of critical importance to the other major town centers in the county. Wigan, Bolton, Bury, Rochdale, Oldham, Ashton, Stock-port, Eccles and Altrincham are all major retail and employment centers which generate significant numbers of trips and are the focus of local road and public transport networks (see map).

The road pattern associated with the growth of Greater Manchester comprises major radial routes extending from Manchester City Center to and through each of the satellite towns. A secondary network of routes radiates from each of the larger towns. Some of these link the satellite towns together and form orbital routes around the county. This radial/orbital pattern was echoed in the tramway network until the 1940s, and the railway network, which is centered on Manchester City Center. The exception to this pattern is in Wigan, which is characterized by sinuous routes connecting small towns and villages – and by the north-south axis formed by the West Coast Mainline and more latterly the M 6 motorway.

The location of economic activity reflected the transport network. Initially concentrated in the inner parts of the industrial towns, industry expanded along the rail routes and spine roads. Housing developed near industry. Later, residential areas expanded along commuter rail lines, especially towards south Manchester, Trafford and Stockport. Until the post-war period the dominant means of travel to work were walking, cycling and public transport along the radial routes.

Illustration 5.13: Greater Manchester Metropolitan Area

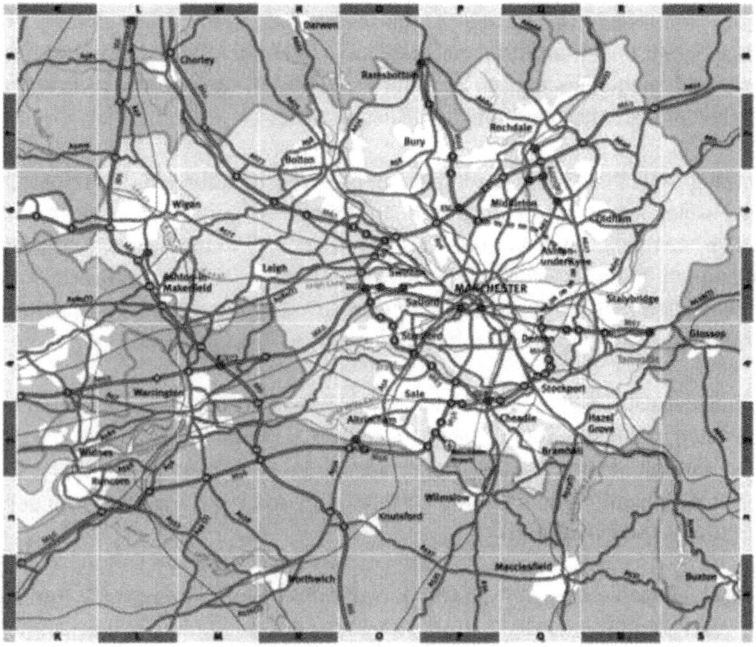

Problems

Increasing car ownership has led to the decentralization of activity. The movement of offices and modern manufacturing businesses to suburban business parks and other peripheral areas, was the first wave of decentralization. This has been matched by dispersal of other activities particularly shopping and leisure. An increasing proportion of shopping now takes place at large out of center food stores and retail parks. The same is true of leisure activities such as multi-screen cinemas and bowling alleys, hotels and restaurants. Housing has also moved further away from traditional radial transport routes and, in doing so, has become more difficult to serve by public transport.

The single most important transport feature of this decentralization of activity is the greater reliance that it places on the private car. Public transport works best where there are concentrated flows of people, but a widely dispersed network of employment, shopping or leisure facilities cannot create sufficient demand for high frequency public transport services.

More recent developments such as 24-hour call centers and late night shopping have created new patterns of travel demand, which again are difficult to serve by public transport. Decentralization, reinforced by the resultant increase in traffic, has also resulted in less walking and cycling as the means to access employment, services and facilities.
The challenge is to seek to contain and reverse the process of decentralization. The Greater Manchester Local Transport Plan (GMLTP). concentrates on an urban regeneration strategy to support existing centers, prevent further dispersal and encourage more mixed use developments which reduce the need to travel other than short local journeys by foot or by bicycle. For those journeys where public transport can offer a good alternative, measures to create a virtuous circle of improved quality leading to increased use, thus enabling further investment in improved quality, are being pursued.

Travel patterns

In developing the transport strategy that underpinned previous package bids, a detailed analysis of travel patterns in the county was carried out and it was looked at how these had changed over recent years. Detailed data existed for 1976 and for 1991/92. While we recognize that these data are in need of updating we are confident that the trends which they exhibited and the information on journey patterns contained within them provide a sound foundation for the package bids and are still relevant for the development of the Provisional Local Transport Plan. The key points are:

- between 1976 and 1991, car ownership increased by 30%, but car use increased by 70%;
- in 1976 the car accounted for 45% of all trips, by 1991 this had grown to 60%;

- by contrast, the bus accounted for 21% of all trips in 1976 but had fallen to 14% by 1991;
- the share of trips made by walking and cycling also fell between 1976 and 1991;
- the share of trips made by rail, although small, remained fairly constant between 1976 and 1991.

The analysis of movement patterns demonstrates that the overall share of trips to and from the City Center and other major centers declined slightly over the period. The proportion of short trips not to centers also declined slightly whereas there was a significant increase in the number of trips that were neither short nor to centers. These data emphasize the trend to greater decentralization, which has occurred in the county.

In the 1996/97-package bid it was advised that, taking into account a fairly tight boundary around each "major center" and noting that the next tier of centers such as Hyde and Leigh, are not included as "major centers", estimations were that

- 20% of travel in Greater Manchester was to or from the City Center, town centers and major concentrations of employment
- public transport can often compete with cars for these trips
- 35% of travel in Greater Manchester was short and local - walking and cycling can often compete with cars for these trips,
- the remaining 45 % of trips were neither short nor to centers - cars dominate these trips." (GMPTL 1999, p.9/10)

On the basis of this analysis the Greater Manchester Passenger Transportation Authority (GMPTA), a public entity on the regional level with local politicians as board members and an administrative body (Greater Manchester Passenger Transportation Executive) as the planning and organizing institution for public transport in the Manchester Area, developed a counter-strategy emphasizing the potential impact of urban rail transportation.

The most important tool to stimulate change was the introduction of a Light Rail starter line. The **Greater Manchester Metrolink** opened in 1992. A design, build, operate and maintain contract refurbished two run-down suburban rail lines and linked them by a short section of track across Manchester City Center with a spur to Piccadilly, the main rail station.

The majority of the 31 km (19 miles) Bury to Altrincham Metrolink line is on segregated lines connected by on-street running in Manchester City Center. Trams run from early in the morning to late at night, seven days a week - usually with a tram every six minutes. They are clean, quiet, and comfortable and there is level access throughout the system. This combination makes for a transport option that is drawing people out of their cars.

Each tram can carry a total of 206 passengers, with seats for 86. They operate at up to 80 km/h (50 mph) along former rail lines and at a maximum of 50 km/h (30mph) on street.

The net cost of the first phase of Metrolink was £145 million. This came from the following sources:

- £69m Greater Manchester Passenger Transport Authority
- £48m Department of Transport Section 56 grant
- £15m European Investment Bank
- £ 13 m European Regional Development Fund

The net cost is calculated after deducting a contribution of £5m from the operator by way of a concession fee and contributions of £4m from other bodies.

Metrolink had reached 13.9 million passengers a year in 1999 and was increasing after six years of operation. This compares to the forecast maximum patronage of 12 million, and the 7.5 million annual trips made on the two heavy rail lines before conversion to Metrolink. Detailed monitoring studies have revealed that 65% of Metrolink passengers have a car, which they could have used instead of Metrolink and that within the prime target area (within 2km of the line) between 14% and 50% of car trips to destinations served by Metrolink have switched to Metrolink. These alone are stunning successes in a conurbation with cheap and often free car parking for commuters, and little car restraint. Even better are the benefits that come from full wheelchair accessibility to many other groups, such as parents with baby carriages or older people. Some completely new public transport markets have appeared such as short trips within the city center, and journeys within the corridor rather than to the major centers of Manchester, Bury and Altrincham. The latest Metrolink figures (http://www.-metrolink.co.uk) in-dicate that after the completion of phase 2 the daily patronage has risen to 47,000 passenger-journeys, which lead to an annual ridership of 17.2 million in 2001.

Geoff Inskip, the GMPTE director of Finance and Corporate Planning, explains the planning and tender process and the important role of private participation for this project: "The government made private involvement a condition of any grant for the first phase of Metrolink. Accordingly, tenders were invited to design, build, operate and maintain (DBOM) the system. In September, 1989 the GMPTA/PTE resolved to award the contract to the GMA group, a consortium made up of GEC, Mowlem and AMEC. The DBOM contract was the first of its kind for a public transport system in the UK. A new private company, Greater Manchester Metro Limited (GMML), was set up by the GMA group to operate and maintain the system. GMML is jointly owned by GEC Alsthom, Mowlem, AMEC and by the Greater Manchester Roadcar company (a subsidiary of GMPTA) and GMPTE.

Essentially the DBOM contract was one where the public sector promoter (GMPTE) defined the primary requirements and features of the system and retained ownership, and the successful private sector consortium was awarded the contract to carry out the detailed construction and the concession to operate and maintain the system" (INSKIP 1996, p.21). Extracts of the contract between GMPTE and GMML are presented in **attachment 10.2**.
Inskip describes "some of the more complex issues which had to be negotiated and which were the subject of lengthy debate between the DOT and GMPTA/PTE and the contractor."

Term of Concession: While the British government wanted a long-term concession of 30 years, the regional Authority (GMPTA/PTE) "did not feel that full value would be received by the public sector for such a period". They wanted a short-term contract of only 3 years, after which the contract may become tradable. The tender was finally allowed for a 15 year term, which for the private sector would have allowed to maximize the concession value.

Risk Transfer: The British government "wished to see a full risk transfer option explored. Thus, the private sector guaranteed to remain operating the system throughout the operating period, come what may, i.e. even in the event of legislation changing. The PTA/PTE felt this option would be, firstly, extremely costly and, secondly, felt that in principle, any private sector company had a right to "close down" its operations in the event of continuing losses. The

PTA/PTE preferred option was to limit the guarantee period to 3 years. This period was chosen as it coincided with both the warranty period for the system and the "settling in" period, i.e. the period when patronage would build up to a steady level and all the niggling faults could be ironed out". The Minister of State finally agreed that the full-risk transfer option could not be financially justified, so that the shorter period was agreed on.

Illustration 5.14:
Manchester Metrolink, phase 1, Inner-City

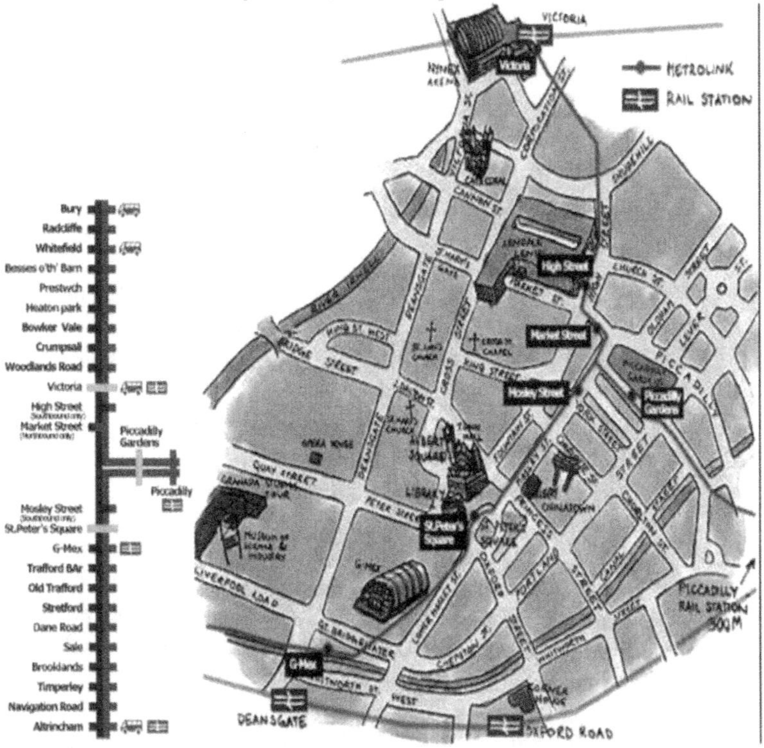

Super benefits: "It became evident at an early stage that all bidding parties had different expectations of revenues/patronage. Consequently, the idea of "super-profits" was considered. It was only right to allow the operator a "fair" reward for his efforts but, once he had obtained this, then the PTA/PTE wanted to share the surpluses. The PTA/PTE will therefore receive 50 % of any profits earned on the system" (ibid).

Network Expansion: "Because the operator had to guarantee the financial viability of the concession company for the first three years, he was also given certain rights to negotiate tenders for both the design and construction and operation and maintenance of any extensions which may be built during that time. After that time the PTE had the right to go to competition for the design and construction".

A very important difference between the GMPTE concession contract and similar contracts in the US, as well in Germany, is the possibility of the concessionaire in Manchester, to "be free to determine all fares and fare structures for the system and to retain all revenues therefrom"! As a consequence, the fares presented further down are thus relatively high, compared to German or US standards

The termination clause permitting an interruption on either side after three years of operation was actually used for phase 2, a 6.4 km (4 mile) long Light

Rail extension on new tracks to Eccles via Salford Quays[9] (see map).

The extension should be built by the future operator, who should also take over the operation of the existing Metrolink line. Therefore GMPTE started another tendering-process in 1996. Four consortia were invited to submit proposals: Altram (comprised of Serco, Laing Civil Engineering and Ansaldo Trasporti), Eurotrans (comprised of British Bus, Christine Nelson, Morrison Construction, Taylor Woodrow and Vevey technologies), MGA (comprised of John Mowlem Construction, GEC Alsthom Transportation and Amec Civil Engineering Limited), and Greater Manchester Metro Limited (GMML), the phase 1 DBOM-consortium.

"The tender documentation included both draft documentation and a reference specification which set out the performance and other minimum criteria.

[9] Background: the Salford Metropolitan Borough Council (MBC) had to take action against the quays falling into dereliction because dockyard activities had ceased or relocated to Merseyside; re-development was needed and the MBC took the lead in pressing ahead with Metrolink Eccles extension as a PHASE 2 project in favour of other possible extensions

However, alternative solutions to those proposed by the PTE were also encouraged. In addition, a number of pricing options were requested" (ibid). The PTE expected the bidder to pay half of the infrastructure costs. The assumption was that the winner would be receiving the profits not only from the extension but also from the (very profitable) Phase 1 of the system. The evaluation of the bids was highly complex with basically two aspects – financial, commercial, legal and construction, technical. The evaluation process took almost 4 months - between July and November 1996.

Illustration 5.15:

Manchester Metrolink, phase 2, Salford Quays extension

Due to the success of Phase 1, bidders were ready to pay an even higher share of private contribution than originally calculated by the GMPTE (two thirds, see table below). As a result of the process, GMPTE chose a different consortium than the operators of phase 1. An agreement between the initial operator GMML and the PTE regulated such matters as the transfer of employees and assets, and the payment of compensation. The contract between GMPTE and Altram included not only these matters, but also matters such as the financial and organizational tasks and responsibilities of the main contractor (Altram), their subcontractors and the complex financing structure. It provides that the private financial portion is "being financed through equity and subordinated debt from John Laing, Ansaldo, Serco, and 3i's with the primary lending from Bank of America. In return, to meet their financing and equity returns, Altram has the benefit of the net revenues from the extension for the next seventeen years[10]. A brief summary of important contract features is presented below:

[10] Relevant Legislation

The contract was signed by the Altram consortium in April 1997.
The net cost of the second phase of Metrolink, for the extension to Eccles via Salford Quays is estimated at £160 million. Construction is underway and funding is coming from the following sources:

- £95m Altram
- £43m Greater Manchester Passenger Transport Authority/Central Government
- £12m Developers
- £10m European Regional Development Fund

The extension is expected to bring at least £70 million in benefits to the area, including reduced pollution, congestion and noise, and it is estimated to remove a further one million car trips from the local road network.

Financial Contribution of Real Estate Developers

One of the most significant elements of the extension is the conceptual and financial participation of real estate investors in the Salford Quays area. Developers, whose projects depended on the tramline being built, contributed £12 Mio. Of that 50% consisted of land donations and 50% of cash payments. Cash payments came from: *Property Exchange Trust*, developers of Exchange Quay, provided about £3 million over 10 years towards financing the public sector investment; another £3 million were contributed by *Pier Holdings – Manchester Shipping Canal Company.* The reason for both companies was that significant contributions from the developers were required from the government for granting the order under the Traffic and Works Act. contribution agreements thus formed part of the final funding package that was put before the government and the European Commission[11].

PHASE 1: Section 56 of 1968 Transport Act: enables the Secretary of State for Transport to give capital grants to large, new public transport infrastructure projects where there are exceptional reasons for spreading the cost beyond users and local charge payers

Route to the Broadway stop had obtained parliamentary powers through a private members bill in the British Parliament (pre-PFI procedure), the section between the Quays and Eccles obtained powers under the Transport and Works Act (see also Croydon Tram Link) through public enquiry (Transport and Works Act order); Order, once given, conveys the right to construct and operate the system and also the right to acquire properties through compulsory purchase order if necessary

4 For better understanding GAFRON et al. (2002, attachment 2) describe the planning process of the project as follows:

Further Metrolink Extensions

Greater Manchester Passenger Transport Authority is developing a countywide, high quality, fully integrated transport network to promote modal switch from cars to buses, trains and trams.

The countywide strategy involves investment in all modes of public transport including bus, guided bus, heavy and Light Rail. Metrolink forms the central spine of this strategy, which will help to deliver seamless journeys, by ensuring that interchange between modes takes place in a safe, reliable and convenient way.

The Authority plans to extend the system to:

For the Transport and Works Act Order, GMPTE has to draw up a proposal/application detailing the proposed scheme including route, stops, purpose and demand forecast; people can then comment and should enough people object in writing, a public enquiry is held by Secretary of State;

a so called Enterprise Zone was created at Salford Quays; the tool is used to encourage the arrival of businesses; thus the layout of the building plots is structured to serve the car (parking, access roads etc.); though a route alignment for a possible Metrolink extension was protected as the possibility of it being built was reasonably strong, the route is not direct, quite tortuous and therefore relatively slow "the tram goes in between the buildings rather than the other way round" (GMPTE)

In the early 90's the route was decided in consultation between traffic planners of GMPTE and Salford City Council; at the time The Lowry (a new cultural center) and the Designer outlet location had not been decided, otherwise the route might have been different; route was decided by what was there and was known to come

The developers / investors determined land uses through their own feasibility studies to a certain extent; therefore Salford MBC feels they could not have been too prescriptive in selecting proposals for land uses as they generally wanted to see redevelopment in general and did not want to put off prospective investors through too many demands;

In 1995 the process of "procuring" the extension was set in motion with the intention that the new concession holder would also take over operation of existing system;

In September 1995 the "capital challenge money" (GMPTE contribution) was allocated to the scheme, which was when all public funding was in place and Phase Two became a relative certainty; but actual building still depended on receiving bids with pricing, which was more or less in line with the forecasts of the GMPTE;

The deadline for bids was July 1996; they were in line with the forecasts and degree of certainty increased; by this time major office blocks with large car parks were already completed at the Quays as up to the opening of the Metrolink, public transport to the area was poor and it was difficult to get to other than by car

The contract for the Phase 2 Extension (and take over of phase 1 operation) was signed with the ALTRAM consortium in May 1997, operation of existing lines was taken over at the end of that month

The work on line through Salford Quays to Eccles started in July 1997, a first section (Cornbrook to Broadway) opened in December 1999, the second section (Broadway to Eccles) opened in July 2000 (official Royal Opening in January 2001)

- Oldham and Rochdale – the top priority scheme
- Ashton-under-Lyne – to serve the Commonwealth Gaines Stadium and the Velodrome
- South Manchester and Manchester Airport
- Trafford Park – provided the private sector pay for the line

These extensions would almost treble the size of the system and all have been carefully planned to create maximum regeneration within the corridors they serve. It is anticipated that they will bring extensive benefits to the county and increase the total patronage to over 50 million passengers per year which is over three times the number of passengers carried on the county's more extensive rail network.

In addition, right-of-ways exist for extension to the Lowry Center and to East Didsbury. Public consultation recently took place into the extension of the East Didsbury line to Stockport. "This consultation was very successful and Greater Manchester Passenger Transport Authority will decide later this year, whether they wish to apply for a Transport and Works Act" (Metrolink 2000/1).

The requirements of the Manchester Metrolink Phase 3 project are the design, construction and operation of three defined extensions to the current network (together with the requirements for integration with and upgrade of the Phase 1 and 2 Metrolink system), there are also a number of additional "optional" extension lines the Greater Manchester Passenger Transport Executive would like bidders to review and offer-up proposals for their inclusion.

The Authority estimated that the completion of this extension program will

- take "a further 6 million car journeys off the road annually"
- create "a further 6,000 jobs within 10 years and boost Greater Manchester's economy".

The question was whether the Oldham/Rochdale lineeach extension should be sequentially built until the network is complete, or whether the whole network should be built under a single contract. To maximize private contribution and to avoid future operator changes, the single contract approach became the preferred alternative.

"The single contract approach is supposed to minimize public sector cost, optimize funding for Metrolink from the private sector, and complement the government's national strategy for a sustainable, integrated transport system, by combining: economies of scale – capital costs are estimated to be reduced by over £32 million network benefits – each succeeding extension feeds more passengers into the network and this is estimated to add about 1 million extra journeys per year, compared to "stand alone" patronage forecasts

- a reduction in the risk profile due to the increased size of the project
- operating efficiencies
- maximized job creation
- public transport integration
- decrease in the number of car trips accident saving and pollution reduction" (Metrolink 2000,1).

According to information provided by the GMPTE website (http://www.gmpte.com) the preferred bidder will be announced in Autumn 2002, followed by negotiation with this bidder. The contract and commencement of design and construction contract will take place 2003.

In 2007/8 the construction will be completed: "A construction programme has not been outlined at this stage, it is anticipated that the construction period will be in the region of five or six years. It is not yet possible to foresee how the concessionaire will want to progress the works – either simultaneously or in sequence, line by line" (ibid).

Some conclusions:

The success of the Light Rail system in Manchester since 1992 is very impressive. It has achieved many of the goals of the Greater Manchester Local Transport Plan quoted initially. It takes cars from the road, stimulates the economical development of Manchester's inner city, as well as its regional subcenters, and creates very encouraging examples of public-private cooperation to achieve these goals.

The success is self-reinforcing. Since the alternative to car-traffic into the city-center has proven to be accepted by a significant share of the regional population, and since it has also be proven to be a field of private entrepreneurship, more initiatives are being undertaken, that will serve both private and public financial interest and attract more passengers to public transportation.

The best example is the future management of the formerly public free-of-charge inner city parking facilities through a Joint Venture between the City Council and the private company NCP. Public parking spaces and structures made up the majority of parking spaces in this area. In the future free parking will no longer be possible in the inner city of Manchester. That will increase Light Rail patronage but also free developable land in this area which once used, will attract further riders.

Private real estate owners generally benefited from the Light Rail lines. But their financial contribution was relatively low. This is due to the lack of instruments to resemble private participation, but also to a lack of policy-focus on this issue. Nevertheless, in the context of the Metrolink extension to Eccles, private real estate owners were involved in the private financial portion of the project. Landowners had to donate the necessary land and pay a cash contribution to the new operating consortium. The total value of the real estate contribution was £12 million. This is a substantial contribution to the total private portion of £107 million and the total costs of £160 million for this extension. The contribution was voluntary. It was only possible because the realization of the line depended on private money and the line had a positive impact on the real estate value.[12]

Despite the steady ridership-increase, patronage of public transit in Manchester is generally still relatively low, compared with Croydon's 28 km system. A further surge in usage is needed. The potential success of the new Rail System may be limited by the fare structure. A single one way ride in Zone 1 (equaling 4 stations) costs £ 0.90 ($ 1.50), a ride in zone 4, i.e. the entire line, costs £2.60 ($4.00). A round trip is a bit less than twice this price, off peak trips are 20% cheaper and the yearly fee of £850 (almost $1500) is relatively the lowest price. The percentage of season tickets is low with single tickets are dominating. One third of those are off-peak tickets and 60% of all rides happen during that time. This guarantees relatively stable rail utilization over the entire day and justifies 6-minute intervals during the entire day.

---

[12] The argument was that the government made it a condition for granting the order under the Traffic and Works Act that significant contributions from the developers, who would benefit from the scheme would be attracted; thus giving the money (contingent upon the scheme commencing and becoming operational) makes it more likely to go forward; contribution agreements thus formed part of the final funding package that was put before the government and to the European Commission.

But even if these relatively high fares may limit patronage of people who need fast access but can't afford it (the deregulated public transport market permits parallel cheaper bus transit), the flexible pricing policy contributes significantly to private financial interest – patronage gains translate directly into a higher profit margin. As a consequence, the system extension can be realized much faster than in a more regulated frame - as is also the case of London-Croydon, described below.

Illustration 5.16: Metrolink system extensions

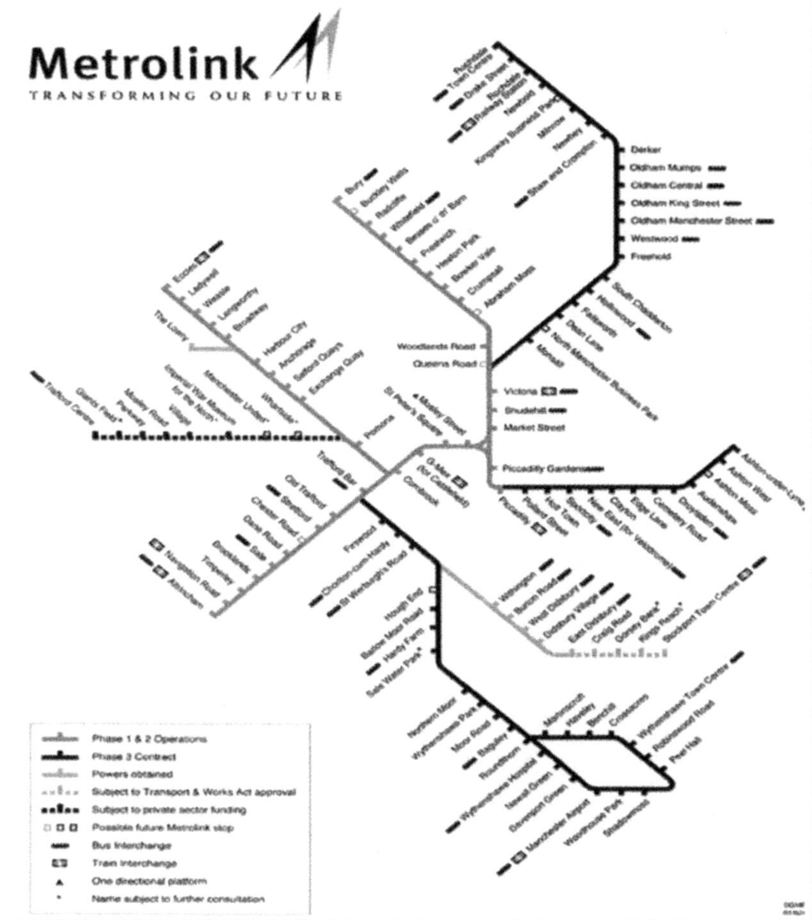

Table 5.1: Metrolink Extensions - Facts and Figures, as of 14. February 2000

Route	Length km (miles)	Approx cost in £millions (Out-turn prices)	Est. required Central Government funding d (£millions)	Other Public Sector (£ millions)	Private Sector (£ millions)	Jobs created	Patronage (millions p.a.)	Car journeys taken off the road (millions p.a.)	GDP in-crease (£ mil-lions per annum)
Bury - Altrincham	31(19)	155	133	17	*5*	200	13	2.6	Not available
Eccles via Salford Quays	6(4)	160	17	*35*	108	3,300	6	09	70
Oldham/Roch-dale	24(15)	185	156	-	29	2,750	10	1.5	102
Ashton-under-Lyne	10 (6)	155	108	-	47	2,250	6	2.2	67
SouthManchester & Airport	22(14)	209	138	-	71		8	22	
Single Contract	56 (35)	**514**	327	-	**187**	**5,000**	25	5.9	**169**
Trafford Park	*5 (3)*	72	0	-	72	1,000	*5*	Not available	Not available
East Didsbury	4 *(2.5)*	*33*	31	-	2	n/a	3	Not available	Not available
All Powers Option subtotal	65 (40.5)	619	358	-	**261**	**6,000 ±**	33	5.91-	169±
Total Network following All Powers option	102 (63.5)	934	508	52	374	9,300 ±	52	9.4+	239±

This is underlined by the spectacular interest of the private sector in participating in the tendering for the phase-3-extension. At the opening of this procedure, in November 2000, 23 companies and consortia formally expressed their interest in the contract to construct and operate the new extensions and to take on the existing Metrolink operations.

They include the European "Who's Who" of construction, rail vehicle producing and public transit providing firms: Alstom Transport ; John Mowlem & Co PLC; Stagecoach Holdings (operator of Greater Manchester Buses South Ltd. (trading as Stagecoach Manchester)); Altram (Manchester) Ltd; Amey Ventures Ltd; Arriva Passenger Services Ltd; Ansaldo Trasporti SPA; Gibb Ltd; Jarvis Facilities Ltd; Astaldi SPA; Balfour Beatty Capital Projects Ltd; Bechtel Ltd; Bus Shelters Ltd; Cobra Instalaciones y Servicios, SA ; Connex Transport UK Ltd (also bidding for the Trans-Pennine rail franchise through Manchester); Construcciones y Auxiliar de Ferrocarriles, SA ; Daimler Chrysler Rail Systems (UK) Ltd; Greater Manchester Rapid Transport Consortium, including Amec Project Investments Ltd, Bombardier Transportation and First Group PLC (operate First Manchester Buses); John Laing Investments Ltd; Manchester Tram Company, including SERCO Ltd (current operator of Metrolink) and SNC Lavalin; Racal Communication Services Ltd ; RATP International Investissement, including BEFEC Price Waterhouse ; Siemens Transportation Systems ; Sir Robert McAlpine Ltd ; Transdev PLC (the Nottingham Light Rail company) ; Travel West Midlands Ltd, including Ashurst Morris Crisp, Ernst & Young, HSBC and Travel West Midlands Ltd (operator of Midland Metro); Via GTI; W S Atkins Rail Ltd.

5.6 DBOM long term contract - Tramtrack Croydon Limited

Croydon is one of the largest boroughs of Greater London (see map) and has 325,000 inhabitants. It is the center of an area of more than half a million inhabitants. It is the largest commercial center in the south of England outside central London (Dorey, 1998). Central Croydon was suffering from huge increases in motor traffic, and for many years it was obvious that extended areas were poorly served by public transport.

In 1986, London Transport (LT – now Transport for London, TfL) and British Rail (BR) produced a study of Light Rail schemes for London, which included modifying existing rail infrastructure to make it more effective in satisfying local demand. One of the proposals considered was a Light Rail scheme centered on Croydon with branches to Beckenham, Wimbledon and New Addington. This coincided with the growing realization that the future economic development of the London Borough of Croydon (LBC), and the quality of life of its residents, required radical improvements to be made in transport provision. It also indicates that future growth of car traffic in the town center was unacceptable.

In 1990 the Croydon Council and London Transport began working together to promote a Light Rail network, the so-called Tramlink project. Extensive public consultation during 1991 showed considerable support for the idea, with over 80% of respondents in favor of Tramlink. Encouraged by this positive response, the Croydon Council and London Transport promoted a Bill in Parliament seeking the provision of public funds to realize the idea.

In November 1991, the Croydon Tramlink Bill was deposited in Parliament. After a series of amendments the House of Lords Select Committee cleared the way for the Bill to proceed. The Croydon Tramlink Act received Royal Assent on 21 July, 1994, allowing London Regional Transport to facilitate construction of Tramlink.

Similar to the Manchester Metrolink concept, the government decided that it would only permit LT to seek Parliamentary Powers on the basis that the scheme should attract substantial private funds and be led by the private sector.

The Tramlink Project Development Group, consisting of the Croydon Council, London Transport and 3 private sector companies: Tarmac, AEG and Transdev, was established in 1992. The private companies were interested in building and operating the future tramlink system. But instead of tendering the DBFO (Design-Build-Finance-Operate) – project from the beginning on, LT and LBC wanted to prepare a detailed performance specification, not only to optimize bidding results but also to convince the government of the innovative private finance approach. The group of private companies, interested in an engineering task during an economically weak period, agreed on being paid on a normal engineering revenue basis, and was disbanded in 1995, after not winning the tender, which was advertised across Europe.

Illustration 5.17: Croydon – a City inside of Greater London

In March, 1995, LT started the preselection process, which resulted in four groups preparing tenders over the period from October, 1995 to January, 1996 for a concession to finance, design, build and operate the system. Given the Government's approach, the tenders were effectively bids for the minimum amount of public sector grant required. All bids were considered by LT to require too much public sector funding, but LT and LBC worked with Tramtrack Croydon Limited (TCL), as the group who required the least grant (preferred bidder), to find ways to make the project affordable to the Government. This process was concluded in April 1996, when TCL was selected as preferred bidder. The Concession Agreement was executed and TCL achieved financial close in November 1996. The Concession Agreement is for a period of 99 years, a time frame requested by both – government and tender preparation group.

System-design, costs and financing:

Croydon Tramlink serves the four London Boroughs of Croydon (LBC), Bromley, Merton and Sutton. It is based on street-running round Croydon town center with three radial branches running west, east and south. The system consists of 28 kilometers of route with 38 stops. Stops are close in the on-street section in the town center and generally widely spaced on the reserved track right-of-way. This should combine convenience of access for short journeys with fast journey times on the branches.

About ninety per cent of the route is segregated from other traffic, and trams will have priority at road crossings. When they run on the highway they are generally in lanes reserved for buses and trams, and other traffic is permitted on only a short section. Bombardier Transportation has delivered the 24 trams required for the service. They are based on the K4000 cars successfully operating in Köln and are of low-floor design, providing easy access for the mobility-impaired at all doors (see DOREY 1998, p. 15-18).

Of the 28 km (17.5 miles), more than 50% are new construction (15 km), and less than 50% (13km) are existing British Rail tracks. The total investment cost was £200 million ($320 million), of which £80 million (40%) are private, and £120 million (60%) are public (London Transport/DOT). The original public contribution plan was £20 million higher (which would have had a design impact rather than an impact on essential technical standards). The private portion is a mixture of lease (2/3, Tramtrack-lease and Rolling stock), risk capital (3i £20 million, subordinate debt), and a small portion of shareholders equity (£ 3 million).

Illustration 5.18: Croydon Tramlink network as of May 2000

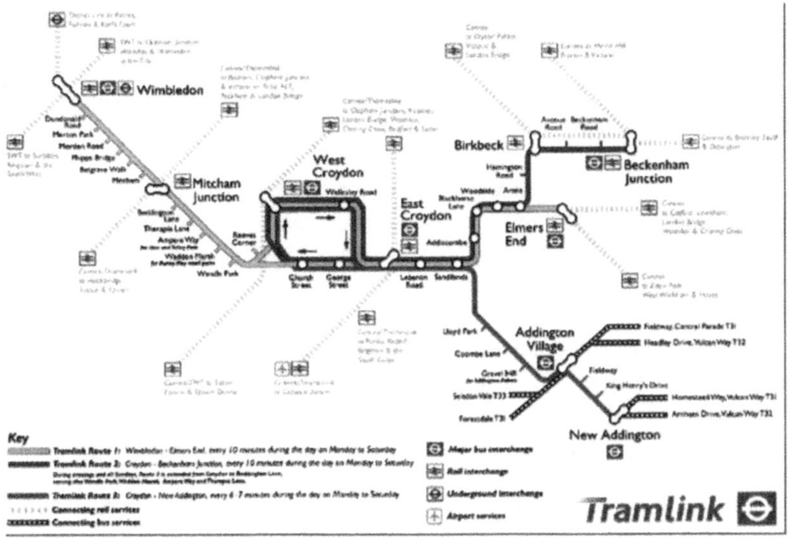

The system map shows that the branch to the West serves Wimbledon mostly along the previously wider-utilized rail corridor. Additional stops are being provided to improve access to residential areas, and to serve important industrial and retail areas. This branch also includes the depot and operational control room for the system. The branch to the East will link Croydon to Elmers End and Beckenham Junction, partly on disused railway formation, partly on new construction arid partly alongside continuing railway services. The branch to the South will link Croydon to New Addington. It will use some existing cuttings and tunnels of a derelict railway alignment, but will consist primarily of new segregated rights-of-way alongside existing roads.

Economic risks and political context:

Unlike other cities in the UK, transport in London is still regulated. In particular, LT (TfL) has a statutory duty to determine fares and service levels on the Underground and on bus services. This creates a relatively stable environment in which services, ticketing and information can be planned together, but it also imposes constraints on the commercial freedom of the tram consortium (TCL).

There is, of course, no certainty that this environment will always prevail. At the time of bidding for the concession there appeared to be a real possibility of deregulation of buses in London. This possibility has now receded, but the decision to elect a Mayor for London, with the powers formerly exercised by the Secretary of State, arguably creates a much more volatile situation for the future.

The risk TCL takes, is based on their "strongly held belief that Croydon Tramlink has a certain and important future as part of the transport network for London whatever the political and institutional changes may be" (Dorey 1998, p. 20).

LT retained the management and financial risk of the utility diversions and some limited and specific public policy risks. TCL has taken all other risks, including

Design and construction
Planning and approvals
Property acquisition
Economic risk
Financing and inflation
General changes in law and taxation
Operation and maintenance
TCL has sought to optimize its management of the patronage and revenue risk through appropriate contract arrangements and, in so far as it is possible, insurance of residual risks. A key part of this approach has been the placing of contracts with single point responsibility for project delivery (with the Construction Joint Venture of Amey/Sir Robert McAlpine) and for operations and maintenance (with Tram Operations Limited). Nevertheless, the main commercial risks continue to reside with TCL.

Concession Agreement:

The Concession Agreement reflects the risk-sharing and responsibilities described above. It also contains commitments from LT to fund part of the construction of Tramlink and to operate specified feeder bus services for a limited period. The funding is a fixed contribution of approximately fifty per cent of TCL's total development costs, paid upon achievement of specific milestones. There is no continuing public payment during the operational period, unless a low fares policy is imposed, or there are discriminatory changes in public policy. Within these limits, TCL is entirely responsible for the financial and operational success of Tramlink.

The concession is believed to be the longest of any awarded under the Government's Private Finance Initiative, recognizing that Tramlink is an operational business rather than a construction project. The length of the concession ensures that TCL is motivated to maintain the system to a high standard, and to replace assets at the optimum time to meet its long-term objectives. The fact that TCL will receive no operational subsidy, and needs high levels of net revenue to service debt and reward investors, ensures that it is well-motivated to deliver and market a high quality service.

The concession and other agreements, nevertheless, incorporate a wide range of controls. At the heart of these is the fact that Tramlink remains a service for which LT is responsible under the 1984 London Regional Transport Act, and both service levels and fares are subject to LT's control. Throughout operations, TCL is required to comply with a Performance Specification which is extremely detailed in its requirements, including such matters as approval of timetables, service disruptions, service and equipment reliability, cleaning of stops and vehicles, customer charter and so on.

Operational success and transport integration

Tramlink has to achieve high levels of patronage if it is to deliver the public benefits sought by LT and LBC, and meet the objectives of TCL. The System must carry more than 20,000 passengers in every peak period of three hours and more than 20 million passengers every year, if it is to meet its financial targets. The system capacity is 75,000 passengers per day, i.e. 27 million per year (maximum frequency of 6-7 minutes in peak periods), the prediction was for approximately 24 million passengers per annum after three years of service. It is economically essential for Tramtrack to achieve the forecasted ridership numbers.

Tram service started six months later than originally planned between May and July 2000 after over 12 years of development and construction. After a few months of operation, 45,000 passengers per day were estimated (on the basis of the number of sold cash tickets and an estimation of the user-share of month-pass owners), equaling approximately 15 million passengers per year.

The ridership-numbers actually achieved after the first year of operation reached over 16 Mio. passenger trips (http://www.tfl.gov.uk/trams/initiatives/ini_index_tlext.shtml), proving the success in its initial phase. This success is has already led to growing demands to extend the system, as mentioned in the concluding remarks on the following page.

Tramlink makes a major contribution to improving integrated transport in its area and beyond. It has good interchange with rail services at Wimbledon, Mitcham Junction, West Croydon, East Croydon, Birkbeck, Beckenham Junction and Elmers End. It thus connects with the services of the Underground, South West Trains, Connex South Central and Southeast and Thameslink, providing excellent journey opportunities to most of South and South East England as well as to London and beyond. Bus services are being re-designed to be complementary to the Tram System and in particular feeder buses will be provided in the New Addington and Selsdon areas.

The Tramlink fare system is part of the London Travelcard and Concessionary fares schemes, and a new bus-tram ticket is being introduced. Opportunities are also being sought to develop other forms of through ticketing with the Train Operating Companies and London Underground. New transport area guides have been produced, real-time information feeds into LT's London-wide travel information service and a new rail map for South London is prepared.

The tramlink system is expected to reduce car journeys by more than two million each year.

Potential extensions:

Consideration is already being given to possible enhancements and extensions to the system. A study of relatively minor interchange and access improvements has been completed. Additional stops may be provided to assist in regeneration or redevelopment. Extensions to the system may be a long way off, and they will only be built if they make economic sense as part of an integrated transport solution. However, extensions to Tramlink offer the possibility of providing good-value public transport at a lower cost than starting from scratch. In the meantime, TCL will concentrate on delivering and operating a reliable and high quality system that will provide the best possible argument for its extension.

Since the opening of the system in May 2000, passenger demand continues to rise and local authorities and residents are keen to see Tramlink extended to other areas.

The "unofficial Croydon Tramlink website" (www.croydontramlink.co.uk) reports that at a Sustainable Transport Conference in Croydon in September 2000 the TfL representative Scott McIntosh suggested a number of potential extensions (Harrington Road - Crystal Palace, New Addington - Biggin Hill, West Croydon - Norbury – Streatham, Croydon - Purley – Coulsdon, Merton, Colliers Wood, Tooting, Richmond, Rosehill – Sutton, Morden). If they were realized, the Croydon Light Rail network would expand at least at the pace of Manchester.

Although no precise plans have yet been made, some extensions are very likely to happen. This and the available data about the current Light Rail operations in London proves

- that Light Rail is also in London the strongest expanding part of the entire transport network (since the opening of the Dockland Light Rail in 1987 almost 60 km (35 miles) of Light Rail lines were built)
- that Light Rail attracts private investment more than other rail transport modes
- that it is possible to operate urban rail lines without operational subsidies
- that if TCL will become an economic success, chances are, that the current Tramtrack investors and others will also be ready to participate at the financing of future extensions.

Some conclusions:

Some insiders think that TCL had to face cost overruns in the construction phase. This seems to be realistic. It is very likely that the initial private group, which prepared the performance specification, did not submit the cheapest bid because it was more aware of the real construction costs than the preferred bidder. Construction cost overruns may not touch the long-term project profitability. But it may cause the minimization of service and maintenance costs and potentially affect the system's appeal.

But despite these dangers, the system seems to be more attractive than originally hoped. According to McIntosh (TfL) the predicted maximum passenger numbers may be achieved one year prior to the 3-year period. Ridership seems to be increasing. On Sundays (while shops are open) ridership is so high, that the numbers of trains in service had to be doubled to one train every 15 minutes. It may be necessary to lease or buy additional vehicles.

Unlike the contract conditions in Manchester, the TCL 99-year concession agreement has no break clause. As a consequence, potential extension may be tendered, but the tender cannot include the take-over of the existing system, which makes it so much less attractive for private investors, that TfL is not sure whether extensions will be tendered. It is possible that the tender may focus only on the construction and track ownership, but not on system operation.

It is surprising to notice that the Light Rail line needed no objective or contract term in order to attract real estate investment along the line, and in so far maximize the potential ridership. There is also no obligation for the borough of Croydon to concentrate administrative efforts on attracting developers to existing or future stations. Developers can be asked to pay for equipment costs (including transport access) in case of a major development, but the potential financial share is very low.

5.7 New procurement methods for Light Rail Projects in the UK and the US - summary with special attention to the role of the principal agent relationship

Each Light Rail project as well as each large infrastructure project has its own and sometimes decade-long history. Many project particularities can only be explained through this history or through a very specific local situation. In order to draw conclusions, it is important to ask

- what is a successful project,
- which role did the institutional setting play to achieve positive results?

Due to the differences of the project-settings it is difficult to measure the success of a project. Many different aspects of this have been evoked and investigated. From a public sector standpoint, the most significant one is the ability to achieve maximum value for public money and to reduce public financial risk. Others include the impact of the Light Rail project in shaping the urban and regional land use structure, the impact of the Light Rail line to generate and spur economic development, and the ability of the project to release hidden (real estate) assets. The cases investigated in this chapter have substantial, although strongly diverging successes to offer. The differences are partly due to the specific urban and economic context but mostly due to the institutional setting in which the projects are realized.

In the discussion about possible partnerships in the field of urban rail transit in the USA, new light rail systems play a prominent role. The reason is the large financial gap between the strongly expanding demand for new systems and the very slowly expanding federal funds for this purpose. However, until now only very few partnerships have been started. This may, at least partly, be caused by the fact that public transportation companies in the USA are still being seen as a branch of the transportation economy that is reserved for purely public management. This is comparable to the current situation in Germany, where publicly owned companies monopolize the market of their "home"-area.

Public monopolies offer specific PPP possibilities, including transit focused real estate policies, which will be described in the next two chapters. In most cases though they make it more difficult to generate partnerships with the private sector to build, maintain and, most of all, operate new rail lines. In so far, they hinder those types of partnerships that are financially most attractive to the taxpayer.

This has to do with the specific principal-agent relationship in these cases. Principal, agent, and service provider are so close that they become indistinguishable. The service provider is its own agent and its own principal.

In the public transport sector of the US, the two new light rail projects in New Jersey and Portland/OR are nationally closely-surveyed new approaches of sharing the task with the private sector and thus of generating new principal-agent-relationships. They will soon be followed by other examples, including the very well known "Tren Urbano" project in San Juan, Puerto Rico. (As already mentioned - the monorail project in Las Vegas, though highly inspiring in itself, is regarded as too costly and too specific to be transferred to ordinary public transport settings in other parts of the country and will therefore not be commented in this summary.) Each of these projects are major investments, and rank among the most important surface transportation projects nationwide.

In short - the US has relevant turnkey-projects and initial experience with this new type of cooperation. Their sheer existence and the role of the existing public transit agency are relevant from a German perspective, although design-wise and financially, they might not be transferable to transportation tasks in Germany.

The two investigated US projects have very different issues and approaches:

The AirportMAX, an extension of an existing, publicly operated system, is comparable to current extension projects for Light Rail systems in Germany. The contract with the construction firm Bechtel to design and build the extension, has financial and organizational advantages, which might be applicable in the German context. Construction costs are clearly defined; the private side has to carry the risk of cost excess and the period between the project decision and the project realization can be minimized. The additional element of realizing a public real estate asset through a long-term lease to the construction firm is very instructive. It is on the one hand, a specific form of commercialization of a public asset, and, on the other hand, an intelligent and innovative transit-land-use-connection.

The initiation, negotiation and content of the contract with Bechtel are the result of "typical" local particularities, i.e. circumstances which can be found in different appearances in other US and European regions. In the given case, they include the local economic importance of the construction company Bechtel, the fact that Bechtel's regional Chief Executive Officer was administrator of the Federal Transit Authority under Reagan's presidency, the proactive role of Portland's mayor, the innovative spirit of the transit agency and the coincidence of developable public land in proximity of the airport.

The role of the transit agency did actually not differ very much from its usual role as an organic and relatively indistinguishable part of the public side, i.e. a prolonged arm of the municipal/regional administration. While it accepted to give up tasks, that would normally be genuine tasks of the agency itself, it acted as a willing agent of the mayor. The type of untendered procurement that took place would, under the German and EU-wide regulatory framework, not be allowed by law. The complicated legal requirements of tendering public tasks in Germany (less than in other European countries, see chapter 8) may in so far have an adverse effect to their original sense, which is to create fair conditions for private competition. They may very well discourage the transfer of public tasks to the private sector and thus prevent any role of the private side.

The Hudson-Bergen Light Rail system has not only been built and equipped through a private consortium, but is also operated by this consortium. This is a completely new approach to the US transportation sector. No comparable project exists so far in Germany. Through a costly and time-consuming procedure, the tendering has been very carefully prepared. Due to an extensive planning period before the turnkey decision (more than a decade), political influence led to an alignment with so many obstacles, that a technically smooth result will not be achievable. The per-rider amount of public investment for this line is so high, that neither the procedure nor the result looks very tempting from a German perspective.

Nevertheless – here is why North America's first turnkey contract in the public transportation field is an important showcase:

- it has strongly accelerated the project implementation,
- it has reduced costs compared with the public realization and operation of the same project,
- it has reduced the risk of system deterioration through clear and ambitious clauses to define the technical state of the system at the time of re-transferring it, after 15 years of operation, to the New Jersey Transit, and, finally,
- it has contributed to a substantial gain of experience in dealing with Build-Operate-Transfer (BOT) contracts in the transit field.

If the turnkey contract for this line will not remain a single or rare event in America's transportation field, future tendering-procedures will increase the number of bidders (only two in the case of the Hudson-Bergen-line) and contribute to substantial financial gains for the public sector. In order to move forward with this, the relationship between the goal-setting public authority and the transport agency has to be redefined. As in the case of Portland/OR, in New Jersey as well as in merely every US state, the transport agency acts as an integral part of the authority and as transport provider at once. This role has actually led to a sub-contract nature of the relationship between NJ Transit and the Hudson-Bergen Light Rail consortium. This role excludes a far-reaching transfer of investment risks in the PPP deal.

A comparison of the American projects with British cases makes clear, how important the experience in dealing with the private sector is.

The "Private Finance Initiative (PFI)" of the British government, and its preparation phase, led to a series of projects in which the risk-reward ratio between the public and the private side has gradually improved. In many cases, it has achieved an optimal level for the public side. As a result, the already impressive financial performance of the Manchester Metrolink could even be surpassed through the more current Croydon Tramlink.

One of the major differences from the American projects is the transfer of the ridership-risk to the private side in Manchester and London-Croydon. This transfer is based on the British understanding of a maximization of private entrepreneurship in Public Private Partnerships.

The second major difference is the fact that due to the accumulated experience on the public and the private side, the number of bidders gradually increased. In the most current case of the substantial system extension in Manchester, almost the entire "who's who" in transportation, construction and consulting expressed interest to participate in the tendering procedure. This maximization of potential bidders could be achieved despite the sharp financial, technical and security requirements of the Greater Manchester Public Transport Executive, one of Europe's most experienced Public Transport Authorities.

The third difference is the fact that on the basis of the public acquisition of Rights of Ways, the bidder has the chance to influence every aspect of the project, from the early design phase on. This is reflected in the concession agreement. One example, the concession agreement of the first extension of the Manchester Metrolink, is therefore attached to this study (see 10.2).

The fourth difference is related to the urban structure of the Manchester and Croydon area. The cities themselves as well as their suburban areas are much more densely urbanized than typical metropolitan areas in the USA. As a consequence the number of transit riders per kilometer/mile is substantially higher than in the US.

The fifth difference is the diverging legal frame for tendering public tasks. The tendering procedure in the UK is easier to handle than in the US (and Germany). It allows negotiations with the "preferred bidder". As a general rule of public procurement in Germany (as well as in the US) these negotiations are forbidden. They are considered impure competition, potentially threatening the rights of the other bidders. As a result the upfront description of the tendered task has to be so detailed that the preparation takes a very long time and the procedure is extremely focused on legal aspects. As long as they are not obliged to tender, public authorities therefore tend to try to avoid entering into competition.

The result of these differences from the first turnkey experiences in the USA contributes to a much lower public investment rate per passenger. As shown in the table below, the investment per yearly rider is at least four times lower in the UK projects.

Despite these financial differences, the developments of relevant projects in both countries have common trends. Although not directly reflected in the figures below the following trends seem to exist: more private money is achievable where competent local authorities are acting as a professional agent, clearly distinguishable from the service provider, where experience in setting up partnerships exists, where high ridership expectations are justified, and where the regional or national government can ensure the stability of the political context of the project-related involvement. The possibility to include private investors under these conditions may be characterized as follows:

- The geographical pattern of the urban area with a future rail system plays a major role that is independent from organizational and institutional patterns. The denser the Light Rail corridor is, the easier it is to attract private investors to participate financially in the investment.
  On the other hand,
- It is more likely to attract private investors if the region where the investment is planned has a long-term transit-oriented policy and a longer record of successful transit development and,
- It is more likely to generate private money if the government has clear priorities for public-private partnerships, elaborate policies, tools and investment-incentives.
  Most of all,

- The conditions under which private investors are involved depend heavily on the ability of the public agent to grant the requirements of the principal while maximizing the private decision-making power.

The available data does not permit a clear conclusion in how far a regulated market (fares, protection from competing transit providers, etc.) restrains or promotes private investment. The Manchester and the Portland Airport extension examples support at least one supposition – the earlier the project planning and project management shifts from the public to the private side, the faster the project will be realized.

Table 5.2:

Comparison of public investment costs per rider of new Light Rail systems

United Kingdom

1992

Manchester, Phase 1	31 km/ 19 miles, 10% new construction, 90 % existing British Rail Track (lease), start in 1992
Total infrastructure cost	$232 million (1992), 4 % private, 96 % public ($8 million concession fee, $111 million GMPTA, $77 million Department of Transportation, $24 million European Investment Bank, $21 million European Regional Development Fund, $7million other bodies)
Costs per km/mile	$ 7.5 million per km, $ 12.2 million per mile
Ridership number	14 million passengers in 1999 (forecast: 12 million passengers)
Cost per rider	$16.57 total investment per annual passenger,
Public cost per rider	**$ 15.91 (96 % of total cost)**

1999

Manchester, Phase 2	6.4 km/ 4 miles, 100 % new construction (start between late 1999 and summer 2000)
Total infrastructure cost	$ 256 million total, 67 % private, 33 % public ($153 Altram, $69 GMPTA/DOT, $19 Developers (land donations), $16 European Regional Development Fund)
Costs per km/mile	40 million/km, 64 million/mile
Ridership number	6 million passengers (forecast)
Cost per rider	$42.67 total investment per annual rider
Public cost per rider	**$14.08 (33 % of total cost)**

2000

London Croydon	28 km/ 17.5 miles, more than 50 % new construction (15 km), less than 50% (13km) existing British Rail tracks, start between May and July 2000
Total infrastructure cost	$320 million, 45 % private, 55 % public ($96.5 Tramtrack-lease (Rolling stock and tracks), $ 45 **3i** risk capital (subordinate debt), $5 shareholders equity, $176 London Transport/DOT)
Costs per km/mile	11.4 million/km, 18.3 million/mile
Ridership number	20 million per year (forecast)
Cost per rider	$16 per annual passenger
Public cost per rider	**$ 8.80 (55 % of total cost)**

United States

1998

Portland/OR Westside	29 km/ 18 miles, 100 % new construction but approx. 50 % on existing ROW, start Sept. 1998
Total infrastructure cost	$963.5 million, 100% public (73 % federal grants, 27 % state and local funds, of which $113 from lottery funds, $21 million local grants, $125 million project related municipal bonds, based on property tax)
Costs per km/mile	$33.2 million/km, 53.5 million/mile
Ridership number	25,600 per month (March 2000), 7.7 million in 1999 (author's estimate)
Cost per rider	$125.10 per annual passenger
Public cost per rider	**$125.10**

2000

Hudson-Bergen IOS	15.3 km/ 9.5 miles, 60 % on existing (former) Conrail tracks and ROW , start between April and December 2000
Total infrastructure cost	$778 million, 100% public ($605 million federal (ISTEA and New Starts) grants – rest through State Transportation fund)
Costs per km/mile	$50.8 million/km, $81.9 million/mile
Ridership number	30.000 per month (forecast), 10.8 million per year (author's estimate)
Cost per rider	$72.00 per annual rider
Public cost per rider	**$72.00**

2001

Portland/OR AirMAX	8.8 km/ 5.5 miles, 100 % new construction but approx. 60 % on existing ROW (highway I 205)
Total infrastructure cost	$125 million, 22.5 % private, 78.5 % public ($28.2 million Cascade Station Dev. Corp., $ 28.3 million Port of Portland (Airport passenger fee), $ 45.5 million Tri-Met (project bonds), $23.0 million City of Portland (municipal bonds based on tax increment from the Urban Renewal District)
Costs per km/mile	$14.2 million/km, $22.72 million/mile
Ridership number	2.7 million per year after system operation in 2001 (forecast)
Cost per rider	$46.30 per annual passenger
Public cost per rider	**$35.90**

6. Transit Joint Development (TJD)

As already explained in chapter 1, the most important data collection and analysis about "Transit Joint Development in the United States" has been undertaken by Robert Cervero, Peter Hall and John Landis of the Institute of Urban and Regional Development at the University of California at Berkeley. The study was finished in August, 1992 (Cervero 1992) and later published as a Research Paper for the Federal Transit Administration. According to this study, 114 joint development projects in more than two dozen US cities have been completed up until October, 1990. The important decade between 1990 and 2000, when transit was a more important issue in many of these cities, has not yet been investigated in the same way. This remains to be done, because the examples of Washington D.C., Atlanta/GA, San Diego/CA and Portland/OR show, that since that time, more initiatives than in the decades before have been started, most of them were successful, while others failed or slowed down. (In August 2001 the FTA has in fact contracted a new Joint Development study. The study will be undertaken by a consortium that includes the University of Berkeley (Cerbero), the Urban Land Institute (Dunphy) and Parsons Brinckerhoff (Arrington).)

With increasing numbers of rail systems and permanent extension of these rail systems, the question of how to take advantage of the development impact of this infrastructure, in the context of an extremely car-oriented urban pattern gains importance. It is directly connected with the broader question of the next chapter of how, and with which potential results, urban development around stations can be promoted, no matter who owns the specific real estate.

6.1 Joint Development Forms

The Berkeley study presented a very detailed distinction between different Joint Development Forms. As the joint development policies and the resulting contract forms were not,and cannot be, that strongly differentiated, the following distinction seems detailed enough:

- Leasing of train stations and / or space within the stations:
  This is seldom the case in the USA for subway stations, and above-ground Heavy Rail stations or for Light Rail stations because these are limited to as

little space as possible. It is relevant though for commuter-rail stations which are generally several centuries old and in need of renovation.

The Southern Pennsylvania Transportation Authority's (SEPTA) "Lease and Maintenance" program offers many examples. 50 of the 223 stations have been partially or completely leased to interested clients: stores, offices, banks, public institutions, organizations and apartment renters.

SEPTA's interest is less a matter of earning money as it is in retaining and modernizing the buildings, strengthening their urban functions, renewing and maintaining the platforms and keeping operating costs at a minimum. The contracts with the clients are flexible and based on the level of building and maintenance required. Some contracts include the operation of the transportation functions depending on whether or not they are long-term and low-cost, there is a high level of modernization necessary, or the clients are willing.

Other commuter-rail regions are striving for similar measures and pilot studies have been undertaken with success, for example in the framework of the "Station Renewal Program" in New Jersey.

- Leasing property directly adjacent to stations:
  The land in this case was generally acquired during planning processes or through voluntary sales by property owners. As described above, the opportunities in the USA for acquiring land through "eminent domain" are limited especially for uses not directly in keeping with the proposed use. An example of this type of joint development policy, presented in the appendix, is from Washington.

- Leasing of "air-space" or underground development rights:
  Leasing or fee-charging of this sort can be done in inner-city areas and when property prices in the area are high. The legal basis for this type of activity is laid in the local zoning plan. The permitting department offers developers a bonus (usually a density bonus or the transfer of development rights from other sites to the project), if they are willing to pay for part or all of the transit infrastructure costs. This can be for pedestrian connections to office towers or other development projects. Examples can be found in New York, Washington, Montreal and Toronto.

- Station connection fees:
  These are a one-time fee or regularly-paid fee for a direct connection of a development project and a station, generally a tunnel passage or direct entrance to a shopping center. This type of link was especially sought after and achieved in Washington, New York and Montreal. In New York though there is usually no fee because of the interest of both parties in transforming narrow entrances on sidewalks into publicly accessible entrances on private property.

- Property sales:
  Similar to leasing, but less often used, because it guarantees no long-term income. Unfortunately, vast amounts of property were sold at New York commuter-rail stations in order to (unsuccessfully) renew certain privately run transportation systems, limiting later possibilities for transit-oriented development in areas surrounding the city.

6.2 Joint Development Policy in Washington, D.C.

According to Cervero, Hall, Landis (1992) Washington D.C. "has emerged as the national leader in joint development". The following section triwa to describe the policy context for the connection of rail investments and land-use impacts, and the planning and implemetation tools applied in the D.C. area, development examples and financial and economic impacts of this policy.

Rail-transit as an Element of Development Policy

The U.S. Congress enacted the National Capital Planning Act in 1952, thereby mandating preparation of regional plans for transportation systems, which was followed in 1954, by the establishment of an interjurisdictional commission. In 1960, the National Capital Transportation Act created an agency to plan a rapid rail system. Upon completion of a plan for a 25-mile system capable of being expanded into the region, the Washington Metropolitan Area Transit Authority (WMATA) was established by Congressional action, and an interstate compact was signed in 1966 by the states of Maryland and Virginia and the District of Columbia.

The rapid transit system envisioned by the compact was designed to serve radial corridors extending from downtown Washington into the suburbs, thus becoming a key component of planned metropolitan growth patterns laid down by the National Capital Planning Commission. In fact, joint development or transit-oriented development has taken place at many of the stations, especially those in the District's downtown area and in certain suburban centers.

When planning for the rail-transit system was initiated, the potential relationships between rail-transit and development were understood differently among the jurisdictions involved. The jurisdictions most immediately affected by the construction schedule for the transit system were the District, Montgomery and Prince George's counties in Maryland, Arlington County in Virginia, and the city of Alexandria. These jurisdictions were highly receptive to the potential advantages of rail-transit in promoting and directing development, particularly economic development.

By contrast, jurisdictions scheduled for Metrorail service at a later time (some of which are still waiting for completion of the system) have been considerably less enthusiastic about transit-supportive development. Fairfax County, to which service was extended in the mid1980s (with another extension still planned), was unable to reach consensus on station area development opportunities, in part because so much business development was taking place in areas not served by rail-transit, including the Tysons Corner megacenter. Prince George's County, whose expectations for development around its first transit extension proved overblown, has found communities along the line planned for the late 1990s, extremely reluctant to respond to growth opportunities. Also, although ideas for additional lines and extensions have been explored, the jurisdictions most affected by them have remained decidedly cool about their potential impacts. In addition, in this fiscally conscious age, all Washington-area jurisdictions are greatly troubled by potential costs of such extensions.

As a consequence of both, these weak regional planning conditions and the geographically disperse economical development, described above, "transportation continues to be the region's primary public issue" (REAL ESTATE 1999, p.305). In the outer parts of the region these problems are approached by road construction, in the inner parts through rail-transit. Outside the Beltway, "Virginia is studying the feasibility of a western bypass linking I-95 and Route 7, but a northern bypass proposal in Montgomery has been killed. The 14-mile Dulles Greenway (toll road) between Dulles

International Airport and Leesburg, Virginia, has continued to suffer from low use and is on the verge of bankruptcy. Construction has begun in Springfield on reconstructing the "mixing bowl", the interchange between the Beltway and I-395. This ten-year project is expected to cause significant gridlock unless 2,500 commuters switch to public transportation permanently." (As one reaction the Virginia Railway Express saw a 23 % passenger increase in only one year). Inside the Beltway the Metrorail system is seen as the predominant strategic transportation element. This view is underlined by the fact that from the beginning on, a newly opened WMATA station drew 10,000 riders a day.

Transit Supportive Policy and Tools

For many local jurisdictions, WMATA's Metro rail and bus system are considered a key component of metropolitan growth strategies.
As described in the next sections, the agency's and jurisdictions' policy and regulatory efforts at supporting development around transit stations, combined with a decades-long real estate boom, have transformed the region's development patterns, at least in the inner parts of the region, within the Metrorail corridors.

Regional Guidelines

The overall policy guidelines for relating regional development to rail-transit service, formulated in the 1960s by the National Capital Planning Commission (as mentioned before), set the stage for transit-focused planning. Transit corridors were defined and nodes of intensive development that would serve naturally as station locations were identified.

These guidelines had a strong influence although no powerful regional planning board was created. In fact, the National Capital Region Transportation Planning Board, the region's MPO staffed by the Washington Council of Governments (WashCOG), has no authority to encourage transit-focused development through its project prioritization. The most recent policies adopted by the Transportation Planning Board provide only general support for transit-focused development. This is one of the major reasons why despite the very attractive Metrorail system, a very important part of the development mentioned in the Times article, occurred in areas outside this system's reach.

Local Zoning

As construction of the rail lines proceeded, the most immediately affected jurisdictions (the District of Columbia, Montgomery and Prince George's Counties in Maryland, and Arlington County and the City of Alexandria in Virginia), responded with supportive planning, zoning, and joint development actions. The counties have continued to support station area development through redevelopment actions, parking and other infrastructure funding, and zoning revised to encourage station-area development. The robust real estate market in the Washington region during the 1970s and 1980s also responded positively, since locations of stations were considered prime real estate locations.

The jurisdictions interested in station-area development opportunities were assisted by WMATA's early support for joint development described below and other transit-related development.

Parking Policy

The variety of jurisdictional attitudes toward the rail system is reflected in parking policies. In the main group of federal buildings in the Federal Triangle, which includes buildings bordering the Mall, the General Services Administration provides free spaces mostly for official vehicles. Few other parking facilities except on-street parking are available within the area, which encourages most employees and visitors to use transit. In the District outside the Federal Triangle, federal and other employees pay rather steep parking rates (currently about $8 to $10 per day), although private firms often provide some free parking for employees. WMATA provides no park-and-ride facilities in the central area.

In suburban jurisdictions, parking generally is less costly and more plentiful. Federal facilities, depending on the facility, provide some free parking for employees, and some to pay modest rates. Thus, employees working in these areas have less pressure to use transit.

Transit Joint Policy

After a relatively long period of case to case decisions, WMATA set up Joint Development Policies and Guidelines in 1986. On the basis of the experiences, these guidelines were reviewed in 1995. They seek to achieve the following objectives:

- Attract new riders to the transit system by fostering commercial and residential development projects on WMATA owned or controlled land, and on private properties adjacent to Metrorail stations;
- Create sources of revenue for WMATA to operate and maintain the transit system by expediently negotiating Development Agreements between WMATA and public or private development entities; and
- Assist the viability of WMATA local jurisdictions to recapture a portion of their past financial contributions and to continue making subsidy payments by expanding the local property tax base and adding value to local revenue sources.

These guidelines describe procedures of publishing development opportunities, involving local jurisdictions, criteria of decision making and developer duties after submitting proposals. Due to the long experience with Transit Joint Development policy, these guidelines as well as their application are invaluable in understanding the procedures and possibilities of public-private partnerships to link transit and land-use development.

Other policy elements include the use of financing instruments such as tax increment financing, among others, and are not directly related to the Authority's joint development policy.

Station-Area Development Activities

As already mentioned, station-area development in Washington is strongly pushed by WMATA's real estate policy. The most successful projects and project corridors are in areas where early local support was provided.

There are two types of projects from which WMATA receives program revenue: 1) private development on property owned by the Authority and 2) private development on non-WMATA-owned sites with direct connections into Metrorail stations. On WMATA-owned land, the Authority generally executes a long-term, unsubordinated ground lease with private developers. In a few cases, it makes fee simple sales. The ground leases provide not only for a base rent, but also for a percentage rent which allows participation in the success of the project. In a number of cases, the Authority has participated in refinance or sale proceeds of the improvements. Connection agreements usually provide for a simple annual rental fee with periodic escalations.

WMATA's transit joint policy had significant and very encouraging successes. As WMATA was owner of large portions of land adjacent to its stations, and as the regional real estate market was generally dynamic, the development of this policy took place under very favorable conditions that are difficult to copy, but, generally applicable under very different market, real estate, and even transit system conditions.

Illustration 6.1: Cover of the Joint Development Solicitation

WMATA owns approximately 5,000 acres of land (2,000 ha), approximately 90% of which is used for transit facilities. The purchase of any other real estate is generally not allowed within WMATA. Only in certain instances where the Authority could not acquire a portion of the property without affecting the developability of the whole, was it permitted to buy the entire plat. About half of the 5,000 acres have been identified as having joint development potential and all of these properties have been offered for development.

According to WMATA's Real Estate Manager Alvin McNEAL and Rosa-lyn DOGGETT (1999, p.2) the first private develop-ment project was com-pleted in 1973 already, three years before the Metrorail system opened. To date, WMATA has negotiated agreements on 24 private develop-ment projects, providing the Authority revenue from 4 million square feet of office space, 0.5 million square feet of retail space, 1,000 hotel rooms and 300 residences. Since the inception of the program, WMATA has received over $60 million in real estate income. The yield has also included more than 1 million new rail trips per year, over $20 million in annual taxes to localities and 25,000 primary jobs.

These numbers will be far exceeded by the impact of three Joint Development Solicitations, issued in March, 1996, February, and July, 1999.

As a result of the solicitation issued in 1996, "the Authority has received 18 proposals for 12 sites and is in varying stages of evaluating and negotiating them. In all, they include: 7.4 million square feet of office space, 2.7 million square of retail space and 8,100 residences. Six projects alone for which preferred developers have already been approved by WMATA's Board of Directors, would yield the agency some $88 million in sale and rental revenue over the first ten years. In terms of rental revenue alone, the new projects combined with the old are expected to generate the equivalent of $12 to $15 million of income per year. They also anticipate adding 105,000 new daily trips with concomitant increases in annual fare box revenue" (McNEAL/ROGGETT 1999, p.5).

The two requests for development opportunities published in 1999 found even greater interest. The solicitation in February, 1999 received 20 proposals for 10 sites, the solicitation of July, 1999 received 29 proposals for 15 sites. As the majority of the locations offered in the solicitation are Park&Ride facilities, their increasing development can be a very important signal of the development possibilities of many comparably Park&Ride-dominated stations throughout the country.

On the other hand, many of the "difficult" sites had to be published several times before receiving development proposals. All of the 15 joint development sites presented in the latest development solicitation in July 2000 have already been offered at least two times without adequate proposals. But WMATA is convinced that the real estate market is so heated that it will be possible to actually develop these sites, for which stations like Brookland Catholic University of America is a typical example.

As the map and aerial photo in illustration 6.2 show, Brookland/CUA, well inside the city area, has 7.2 acres and contains a Metrorail station entrance (escalators and elevators), Metrobus parking (12 bus bays) and a Kiss and

Ride area with 32 spaces. The Brookland neighborhood is a middle income single family home community, economically stable, with more than 5,000 inhabitants within half a mile of the site. The station is adjacent to the Catholic University of America with more than 5,000 students. According to the solicitation, "potential development includes housing and retail to serve students and faculty". First time home buyers in the District of Columbia are entitled to a $ 5,000 Federal tax credit. But as the photo shows, development will have to create an environment of livability that will cost more than replacing surface car parking and transforming it into parking structures. Nevertheless, this has been done in many parts of the Washington area. This permitted a significant and almost unique switch between a very unurban setting at many stations with large park & ride facilities and other utilizations that won't fit into an urban mixed use setting.

Significant Examples:

Illustration 6.2:

Example of the 7-2000 soliciation – Brookland CUA

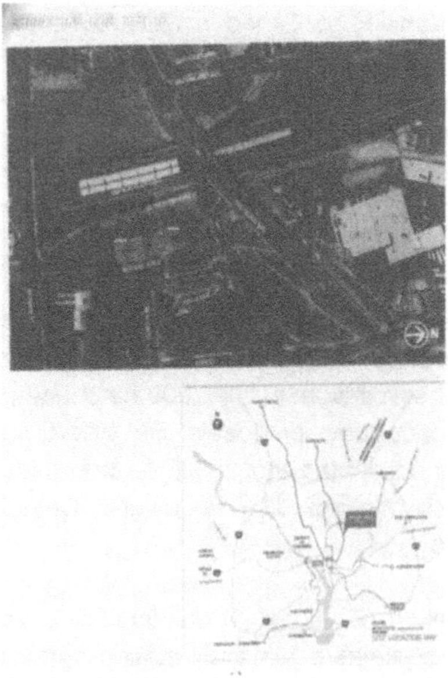

The description of the following examples is based on available WMATA data and very accurate Parsons Brinckerhoff analysis. The examples are analyzed under several aspects: planning procedures, cooperation bet-ween real estate developers, WMATA and the local com-munities, financial project contri-bution to WMATA, ridership results. The cases described stand for specific Joint Development forms, mentioned in the last chapter, sometimes they combine the different forms in one project. Three examples describe the developments before starting the Joint Development Solicitations, two of them are located immediately northwest of the D.C. area in Montgomery County, one just above the Potomac River in Arlington County.

Friendship Heights

The Friendship Heights Metrorail station straddles the line between the District of Columbia and Montgomery County about five miles north of downtown Washington. In the 1970s, Friendship Heights was a growing commercial, employment, and high-density residential center and the historic location of terminals for the former trolley lines and the bus network. Both District and county plans anticipated continued major development of the area as a regional center due to its accessibility by higher-income residents of Northwest D.C. and the Chevy Chase and Bethesda neighborhoods of Montgomery County.

When planning for the Friendship Heights Station began, a neighborhood shopping center adjoined the bus terminal and the quarter-mile area around the station encompassed two department stores and a number of small retail shops, some office and medical buildings, an insurance company's headquarters' offices, and several high-rise residential buildings. By 1995, Friendship Heights had become one of the premier regional shopping and office centers in the region, boasting five major department stores, two prominent retail arcades, top-of-the-line retailers, several major office buildings, and additional luxury high-rise residential buildings. At the center of this mixed-use regional complex, with direct access via a joint development project and three system interface projects, is the rail station and bus terminal.

The joint development project was constructed over the rebuilt bus terminal which, with an adjoining private tract, provided a 60,000 square-foot site at the corner of the two main streets, Wisconsin Avenue and Western Avenue. The owner of the shopping center adjoining the site had already indicated interest in developing a mixed-use project. After a zoning skirmish with area residents over initial development proposals, the Montgomery County Planning Board adopted a special zoning district for the site, that allowed an optional doubling of density under special hearing and design review procedures.

With this policy framework in place, and planning board staff cooperating, the developer entered into negotiations with WMATA. Each party had something to gain from joint development. The developer, Chevy Chase Land Company, needed to consolidate WMATAs and its own properties to create a buildable site. WMATA also required the larger site to enable reconstruction of the bus terminal, and provide convenient access to the underground transit station.

The planning board hoped for a well-designed project that would stimulate creation of an attractive regional center at a key down-county location.

Illustration 6.3:
Joint Development Project at Friendship Heights Metrorail Station

The resulting development is a 13-story, 240,000 square-foot building with 11 floors of office space and two floors of retail space, constructed over the ground-floor bus terminal and Metrorail escalators and three floors of underground parking with 381 spaces. This project is shown in illustration 6.3.

Although WMATA established basic guidelines for ensuring adequate bus and rail service, such as geometrics for bus bays, bus turning radii, specifications for park-and-ride lots, and so forth, it allowed the planning board to advise on major design aspects of the project.

A small design group created by the board worked with the developer and WMATA to ham-mer out a host of design issues, including the configuration of bus bays, pedes-trian access, and safety and secu-rity. Protracted re-views by local citizen groups concerned with proposed densities, and impacts on pedestrian movements and nearby uses required special analyses and redesigns.

Negotiations over details of the joint development agreement were extended and complex. The final agreement, signed in 1979, conveyed the Metro property to the developer in fee simple, with WMATA carrying back a permanent easement for bus operations and Metrorail access. The developer was to construct all facilities except the Metrorail entrance, including bus terminal facilities, and agreed to pay an annual fee of $26,600 as a license for the direct connection to Metrorail. Covering a period of 30 years, renewable, the license has generated $270,000 to date for WMATA.

Interface connections with other nearby developments included one with the existing Woodward and Lothrop department store (now Hechts), executed in 1972, as part of the downtown store connection agreement, a second in 1983 to the Mazza Gallerie shopping arcade, and the third in 1988 to the Chevy Chase Pavilion, a mixed-use development. Another potential connection to additional development is available. All garnered fees for WMATA, some paid over extended periods.

Only a few park-and-ride spaces are leased by WMATA to serve the station. No other public parking is provided; WMATA's original plan to build a major garage was successfully fought by local residents who feared ensuing traffic problems. However, a considerable amount of parking was provided by existing facilities and all the new private developments constructed underground garages. At the present time, two hours of free parking is provided in much of the new space and long-term parking is relatively cheap.

The Friendship Heights station occupies a particularly central position in this regional center, and ridership has remained strong. Daily passenger boardings averaged 8,343 in 1995 compared to 5,674 in 1985. (No studies have been carried out to define the portion of station-area development ridership as related to the total.) Pedestrian connections between the joint development project and adjoining shopping center remain a problem, but the overall functional and financial performance of the project has been exemplary.

With completion of additional development expected over the next decade, Friendship Heights will present an unusually effective mix of employment, retail, and residential uses closely associated with rail and bus transit.

Bethesda

The next station north of Friendship Heights in Montgomery County is in Bethesda, the site of a much larger joint development project as well as a system interface. A traditional commercial and business center for Montgomery County, Bethesda was decidedly low-key in character when Metrorail arrived in the late 1970s. A few high-rise office and residential buildings contrasted with the predominantly one- and two-story buildings located on or near Wisconsin Avenue. However, its proximity to one of the highest-income residential areas in the region plus the presence of National Institutes of Health and Bethesda Naval Hospital less than one mile north, had stimulated increasing interest by developers. In addition, the area was designated as a regional center on county plans and a sector plan supporting a considerable amount of new development had been approved by the county in 1976. Accordingly, WMATA found a private sector ready to act, and the county government interested in promoting opportunities for joint development.

The primary site was a tract of 115,000 square feet purchased by WMATA in 1975 to provide space for Station construction. Located at the 100-percent corner of Bethesda, the intersection of Wisconsin Avenue with East-West Highway and Old Georgetown Road, the tract was bordered by properties ripe for redevelopment. The county planning board, in fact, designated the entire block for unified design treatment; the area included the WMATA property, a county property originally acquired for parking, the corner tract for which an office building had been proposed, and another large parcel. Two smaller parcels and the Bethesda post office were included in the block but excluded from the development.

In 1977, as acquisition of the Bethesda station site was being completed, WMATA joint development staff solicited the interest of the county's planning staff in combining the WMATA and county properties to form a developable parcel. Some studies were done, but not until late 1978, when a proposal for developing the corner property was submitted to the county, did the planning board seize the initiative. With a "handshake agreement," planning staff agreed to the idea of consolidating the site and preparing county guidelines for WMATA's use in selecting a developer. A design concept and urban design principles were soon completed and by the end of 1979, the planning board recommended council approval to concentrate planned business development around the WMATA station and to use an optional zoning district procedure that permitted an increase in densities from three FAR to six FAR in exchange for contributions of public spaces and amenities. Major design features are shown in Illustration 6.5.

The design guidelines called for creating an exciting mixed-use project that would become the center of Bethesda activities, including a lively urban plaza over a bus terminal, bordered by high office buildings, a retail complex, and a hotel. Building masses and open space diagrams were included in the guidelines. WMATA's request for developer proposals, incorporating the design guidelines, were issued in June, 1980 and attracted three serious proposals. The winning proposal, and the subsequently built project, included 370,000 square feet of office and retail space in a 1 7-story building, a 1 2-story, 380-room Hyatt hotel, 38,000 square feet of retail space mostly located in a food court on the plaza, and 1,400 parking spaces. The 90,000 square-foot plaza stepped down to the corner and contained a clock tower, sculptures, fountains, and landscaping.

The project was linked directly with the 17-story office building constructed separately on the corner parcel, and was to also connect to another office building still to be developed. A pedestrian bridge connects the project with a county parking and residential structure further west. An underground pedestrian passage also connects the rail and bus stations to an office building on the eastern side of Wisconsin Avenue.

The developer offered an annual payment of $1 .6 million for a 99-year lease on the site, including easement lease-backs to WMATA for the bus terminal, rail station access, storage facilities, and kiss-and-ride facilities. The lease also promises WMATA 7.5 percent of the project's gross annual income above a base of $31 million, an income level which has not yet been reached. The developer constructed all WMATA facilities above the rail-station escalators and the public plaza, and executed a cooperative agreement with the owner of the corner building to maintain the plaza.

Other projects developed near the station, including eight major office complexes and a hotel constructed through the optional zoning procedure that became known as the "beauty contest." The 1976 sector plan had established a ceiling on development. County planners announced that projects offering a high quality of construction and significant public amenities would be first in line for approval. In the subsequent competition, developers supplied open space, public art, and other community-oriented facilities to satisfy the pedestrian-oriented design criteria of the sector plan.

Illustration 6.4: Metro Center Project at Bethesda

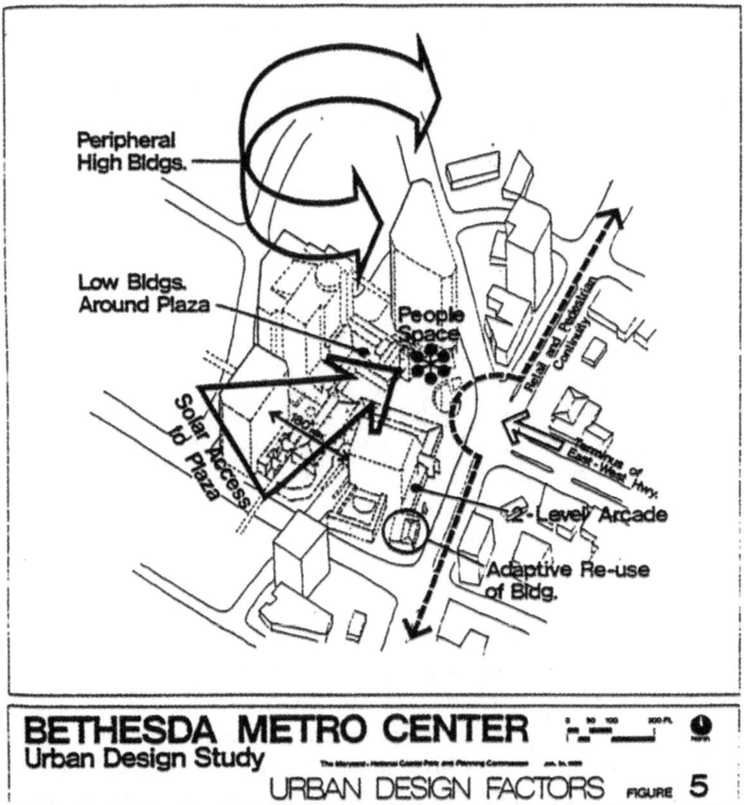

In addition, west and south of the commercial core hundreds of luxury condominium and rental apartments were built and the Bethesda Urban District raised funds to redesign and redevelop the downtown streetscape. The office boom in the 1980s coincided with a restaurant and arts boom that continues to this day. In 1995, Bethesda's downtown area, about two-thirds of a square mile, contains seven million square feet of office space, 2.3 million square feet of retail space (mostly small shops, services, and restaurants), and 5,000 housing units, with a total employment of 39,000.

Illustration 6.5: Arlington County Metro Corridors

This development has been supported by a county-initiated program to finance and build public parking structures. Bethesda has about 6,500 public spaces in garages and on the street. County garage spaces cost $75 per month or $.50 per hour for short term parking. These garages oper-ate virtually at capacity. Metro Center's garage, which char-ges more, is seldom full.

The Metro Center project has proven commercially success-ful, although the retail shops have never functioned as well as hoped, and the office tower, whose financing was highly leveraged, was taken over by the lenders during the recent real estate recession. Some of the problems are due to the postponement of the county's residential and parking project west of the site, on which construction is now underway, and the third office building south of the site; completion of these buildings over the next few years will generate increased activity on the plaza level as well as additional rail and bus ridership. Even without those components, daily passenger boardings have risen from

5,811 in 1985 to 7,501 in 1995. All in all, the Bethesda Metro Center joint development project – and station-area development in general – has transformed Bethesda's downtown area.

Ballston

Arlington County has been the most aggressive county in Northern Virginia in seeking to focus growth near transit stations to achieve tax and job benefits. It began planning as early as 1968, to evaluate the potential ways that transit might achieve its economic objectives, and a 1972 plan, RB '72: Rosslyn-Ballston Corridor Alternative Land-use Patterns, proposed to concentrate future intensive development around the five stations in that corridor. The plan reasoned that focusing intensive development around transit stations would help to preserve existing neighborhoods from commercial intrusions. However, the 1960s building boom in Rosslyn, just across the Potomac from Georgetown, proclaimed the potential downside of intensive development: massive buildings, a loss of pedestrian scale and street life, and wholesale change.

Illustration 6.6: Ballston (Parkington) in the 1960s

In response to that earlier experience, a citizen's advisory group bought the concept of intensively development station areas, but recommended that high-density development around transit stations be accompanied by attention to pedestrian access and mobility as well as architectural quality and amenities. Bailston represents the culmination of a series of county and citizen-supported planning endeavors to avoid repeating the Rosslyn experience.

Ballston is a 39-block, 270-acre redevelopment area, located just ten minutes from Capitol Hill and the White House. Metro service to Ballston began in 1979, when the area consisted of parking lots and aging commercial buildings along the main streets. The Ballston sector plan, completed in 1980, however, envisioned Ballston as a new mixed-use center, combining high-density commercial and residential development within a one-quarter mile radius of the transit station. The area was to include open space, neighborhood retail shops, and pedestrian walkways. Soon after the plan was issued, the area immediately around the station was zoned for coordinated mixed-use development that provided major density incentives for projects that are half-commercial and half-residential.

Illustration 6.7: Ballston (Parkington) in 2000

The permitted floor/area ratio of 3.5 for commercial uses could be increased to six; even higher ratios could be achieved with more residential space. Street-level retail uses were required in all commercial buildings.

In 1982, the county agreed to help finance a 3,200-car parking structure, to assist in development of the new Ballston Commons shopping center on the site of a 1950s center. The garage also provides Metrorail parking, just three blocks from the Ballston Station. In 1985, a group of developers, businesses, residents, and public officials formed the Ballston Partnership to promote high-quality urban design, and coordinate infrastructure improvements and marketing in the area. During the mid-to-late 1980s, bolstered by the robust real estate climate and Arlington County's prime location, nearly two dozen projects were undertaken within one-third of a mile of the station. About 3.7 million square feet of commercial space, 4,300 dwelling units, and three hotels have been built since 1984; 2.5 million square feet of office/retail space and 1,000 dwelling units have been approved for future construction. The joint development project in its current stadium is shown among a variety of new and older buildings in Illustration 6.7.

One of the major new projects was Ballston Metro Center directly above the WMATA station. It consists of a 12-story, 217,000 square-foot office and retail building, a 26-story building, housing 277 condominium units and 209 hotel rooms, both over a platform that contains 760 parking spaces plus rail and bus facilities. The $96 million development was completed in 1990.

WMATA had marketed the site in 1982 as a joint development project but could find no takers for the 72,000 square-foot parcel. Convinced that the parcel should be combined with an adjoining one of 31,000 square feet to produce a developable site, WMATA granted the owner of that parcel, exclusive negotiating rights to find a developer capable of undertaking a mixed-use project on the entire tract. In 1984, the owner entered into a partnership with a local developer and with several minority partners to develop the project.
Several issues were resolved during negotiations over the final agreement:

- The developer persuaded the transit authority and local government to accept seven,
  instead of 13 bus bays to simplify the site design;

Illustration 6.8: Joint Development at Ballston Metrorail Station

- The bus bays were provided on Stuart Street in front of the project and separated from normal traffic circulation by restricting movements of private vehicles on some parts of the street, thus effectively enlarging the site;

- The county refused to grant additional density bonuses in return for the develop-per's construc-tion of the public plaza, but did allow the buil-dings to rise 18 feet higher than nearby buildings;

- Recognizing that condominium sales would require a fee-simple land transaction, the site was divided into two parts, one conveyed to the Ballston Metro Partnership for the residential and hotel tower and the other leased by WMATA for the office/retail tower and public facilities; for the latter part of the project, WMATA receives its usual periodic payments based on eight percent of gross commercial income above a threshold level; for the housing/hotel part, WMATA participates in the gross proceeds from condominium sales in addition to three lump-sum progress payments.

Project construction began in 1987. The hotel and retail shops opened in 1989, and the condominiums were sold in 1990. The office tower, hit by the late-1980s real estate recession, was slower to lease, but is now fully occupied. Some small problems have arisen. Because there is only one access point to the rail station, the escalators and elevators often operate at capacity and experience frequent breakdowns. Constructing additional underground connections would be quite costly. In addition, bus operations create a complex mix of bus, auto, and pedestrian traffic that will grow worse with increasing traffic. Pedestrian movements also have been hampered by the state department of transportation's insensitivity to pedestrian needs at intersections on the several state highways traversing the Ballston area.

The Ballston project has been commercially successful, and, it has produced $ 600,000 yeary rent to the authority. But despite the commercial success, based on the high number of access to the area, in terms of transit ridership, for a long period the record didn't seem to be so clear. Daily passenger boardings for the rail station averaged 9,482 in 1991 (Brosnan 2000), only modestly up from 9,352 in 1980. In the interim, however, the line to Vienna opened so that stations farther out on the line captured a substantial part of the park-and-ride market.

Illustration 6.9: Arlington County at the end of 1960s, before Metrorail

The project at Ballston may have at that time forestalled an even sharper drop in boardings. In any case, a considerable amount of proposed development in the Ballston area was put on hold during the real estate downturn. During the course of the 90s and after completion of a number of private office developments though, the Ballston boarding numbers did in fact more than double and reached 21,892 in 2000 (Brosnan 2000). McNEAL and DOGGETT describe the Ballston development as "an outstanding example of how a community can use transit for economic development purposes".

The entire **Ballston-Rosslyn corridor**, "along an older commercial boulevard, contains five Metrorail stations. The county targeted the corridor and station areas for intensive, transit-oriented growth and provided planning incentives such as density/height bonuses to achieve that end. It is probably the most successful public-private development corridor in the United States.

The Ballston project has been commercially successful, and, it has produced $ 600,000 yeary rent to the authority. But despite the commercial success, based on the high number of access to the area, in terms of transit ridership, for a long period the record didn't seem to be so clear. Daily passenger boardings for the rail station averaged 9,482 in 1991 (Brosnan 2000), only modestly up from 9,352 in 1980.

Illustration 6.10: Ballston-Rosslyn corridor in 2000

In the interim, however, the line to Vienna opened so that stations farther out on the line captured a substantial part of the park-and-ride market.Since the stations opened in late 1978, it has achieved twelve million square feet of new office development, in addition to significant multi-family residential, university and hotel facilities". (McNEAL and DOGGETT,1999).

In a presentation at a ULI conference about "smart growth" in October 2000 in San Diego, the head of the Arlington county department of planning , Bob Brosnan, described what has been achieved since the Ballston-Rosslyn-corridor was opened: During the last 10 years from 1991 to 2000 ridership doubled or tripled at every station of the corridor, since 1969 office space within a quarter mile radius around the stations quadrupled from 4.4 Mio sq ft to almost 18.5 Mio sq ft, during the same period the numeber of residential units more than quintupled from 2,565 units to 14,346 units and between 1980and 2000 the employment numbers almost doubled from 73,790 to 128,553 (almost 200,000 expected in 2020) and the employment share in proximity of the Metro stations grew from 51 % of the total county employment to 67 % of the empoyment.

More recent examples include two different types: those based on the Joint Development Solicitations and those discussed independently from this policy:

One of the major examples related to the Transit Joint Development Policy are presented in McNeal's and Dogget's report:

Gallery Place - In the heart of downtown Washington, the proposed Gallery Place project will occupy 1.71 acres abutting H Street, the retail spine of Washington's Chinatown community, and the city's new 20,000 seat sports arena. The project will have a 22- screen movie theater, 300,000 square feet of retail space, 180 residences, and 900 parking spaces. Terms for the sale of the property at $25 million have recently been approved by WMATA's Board.
White Flint - This office/retail/residential project will occur on 32 open acres in one of Washington's most prosperous suburbs: Montgomery County, Maryland. The site is the last remaining large, developable parcel, along a well-established commercial corridor in the county. Though business terms are still under negotiation, it is likely that, as the White Flint site is developed in stages over the next 10 years, WMATA will receive substantial rental payments which will far exceed those from existing public/private development

projects. A Montgomery County conference center on an additional 13 acres of WMATA land is also slated for this location.

Greenbelt - Located within the City of Greenbelt, a Roosevelt-era new town in Prince George's County, Maryland, this project would reconfigure station facilities and a surface parking lot, which occupies 78 acres at the Greenbelt Metrorail Station. Required WMATA parking will be placed in a structure, pursuant to WMATA's policy that the developer must replace at its cost any WMATA facilities that need to be moved. However, the Authority will adjust rental/sale rates based on this requirement. The newly proposed suburban development will assemble the WMATA property with an adjacent privately owned parcel. Project plans include a major upscale shopping mall with 1.8 million square feet, two 200-room hotels, 1.5 million square feet of office space, over 2,000 apartments, and 300,000 square feet of entertainment retail space. This project is the largest WMATA has approved to date.

The following, last example is not directly connected with WMATA's joint development policy and it concerns a future concept. WMATA's real estate ownership is limited to the (future) station and necessary additional purchases are limited to the transportation purposes. Nevertheless – this project shows the enormous importance of Metrorail to stimulate economic developments and the possibility to take advantage of this impact to include investors into financing transportation infrastructure.

The **NoMa** area does not have the disadvantages of many of the surroundings of existing stations – it does not have a fixed urban setting and a given distribution of transportation facilities.

NoMa is one of the newest near-downtown development opportunities in the area „**No**rth of **Ma**ssachusetts Avenue". This area, directly north of the central business district, will be anchored by the new Washington Convention Center on the west, Union Station on the east, and New York Avenue on the north. According to the Washington D.C. strategic development plan (The Economic Resurgence of Washington, D.C., 1999) „the excitement generated by the MCI Center nearby has sparked interest in the potential of NoMa as a vibrant mixed-use community".

The area, now partly an inner-city brownfield with used and unused rail tracks and vacated or under-utilized warehouses and factories, is the major hope for a diversification and development of the District's economic future. The precise vocation had yet to be determined – the WMATA study of the possible new station predicts a transformation of the area „into a media and technology center that would rival the Dulles and I 270 corridors" (WMATA 2000, p.1-1) while the District's strategic development plan, mentioned above, believes that "it can become Washington, DC's answer to New York's SoHo and San Francisco's South of Market a multimedia and technology district that includes housing, arts and entertainment, and other attractions". Cable News Network, National Public Radio, Atlantic Video, and other media and technology companies already operate in the area,– which stretches along the New York Avenue corridor to the planned site of a new Metrorail station, serving the Red Line at New York and Florida Avenues, NE.

In any case – this well-located area provides very important development space. A report of Economics Research Associates (ERA) "estimates that the NoMa area could support about 2.3 to 4.4 million additional square feet of office space over the next 20 years" (ERA, 2000, p.2). There is also enough space for other functions such as housing ("essential for NoMa to thrive. From traditional townhomes to unconventional live-work spaces, both newly built and renovated housing will help attract the type of young and energetic, high-quality workforce that is particularly drawn to a vibrant urban lifestyle" Resurgence 1999, p. 43), culture ("a magnet for performing and visual artists, ...recreational and cultural activities ranging from restaurants and cafes, to art galleries and studios", Resurgence 1999, 43) and so on.

All of the many studies undertaken to evaluate the development potential of this area conclude that "a Metrorail station on the Red line near the intersection of New York and Florida Avenues, is an essential element in nearly all of the economic development initiatives that have been proposed for the area, and in so far has the wholehearted support of the local business community.

The station would significantly increase the attractiveness of the corridor by providing high quality and inexpensive access to the area from all parts of the region". (WMATA 2000, p.1-1) The ridership of the station is expected to be 8,652 in 2005, which means about 60 % of the current Metrorail passenger-numbers at Union Station.

The proposal for the new Metrorail station has been generated through a public-private partnership that includes not only community support but also significant private sector financial commitment

Illustration 6.11:

Development Projects in the Area „North of Massachussetts Avenue“

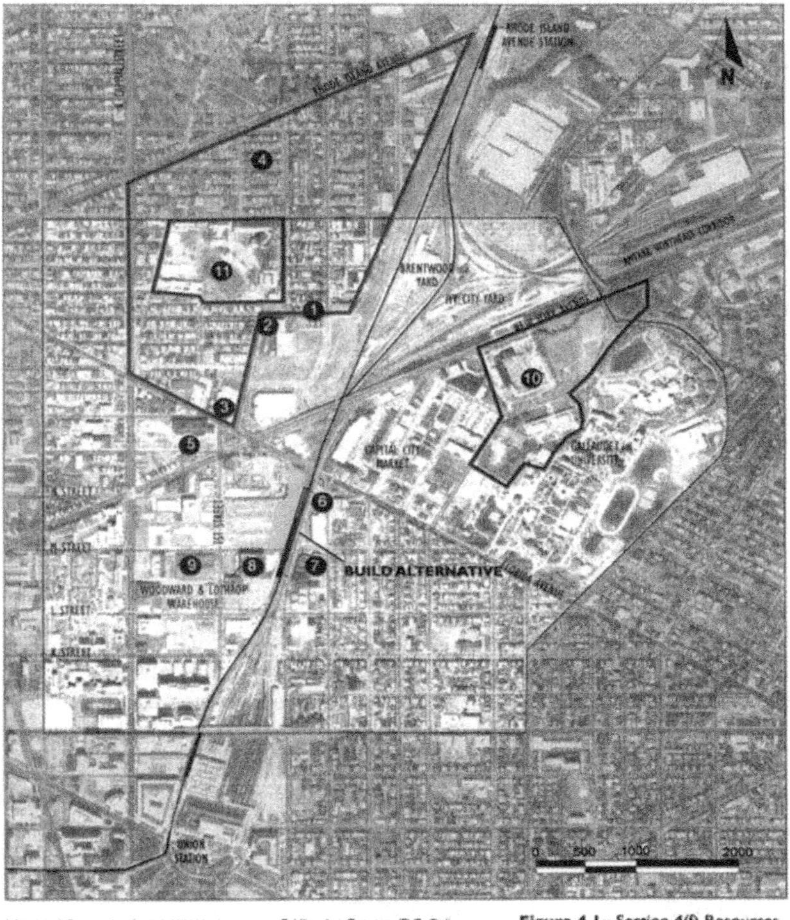

1. National Geographic Society Warehouse
2. Sanitary Grocery Company Warehouse
3. Judd & Detweiler Printing Company Warehouse
4. Eckington Historic District
5. L'Enfant Plan Streets
6. 301 N St. NE Warehouse
7. Uline Ice Company/D.C. Coliseum
8. Woodward & Lothrop Service Warehouse
9. Columbia Warehouse
10. Brentwood Park
11. Harry Thomas Recreation Center

Figure 4.1 – Section 4(f) Resources within the Study Area

According to WMATA sources, so far the area's real estate developers agreed to co-finance 50 % of the costs of the future rail station. In view of the expected impact on the real estate value of the area around (up to 100%, WMATA 2000, p. 3-23), this appears to be so low that WMATA is continuing to negotiate that.

Fiscal Impact of WMATA's Public/Private Land Development Program

The current contracts will provide a real estate rental income of more than $15 million per year. According to McNEAL/DOGETT (1999, p.5) "this amount is the equivalent of over four percent of all Authority earned gross revenue and, on a net basis, is even higher.... Real estate revenues, including parking, are the single largest source of non-farebox revenue for WMATA. Further, development earnings can be used at the Board's discretion, to provide incentives for additional real estate development on sites that are not as readily marketable as those already developed. WMATA has established a Transit Infrastructure Investment Fund for this purpose.
Public/private land development revenue will most certainly pay back the estimated $400 million invested since 1968, in WMATA rail system property acquisition by the national, state and local governments. Of that amount, state and local government provided 20%, or $80 million. By the year 2003, WMATA's receipts from the public/private land development program will be almost double that amount, a nearly 200% return on investment".

Regional Development Impact of WMATA's Metrorail System

Metrorail's role as a catalyst for transit-oriented development goes beyond Metro-owned station sites. The Urban Land Institute has estimated that $15 billion in additional development regionally has been generated by Metrorail, a number that will grow to $20 billion with completion of the 103-mile system. The international accounting firm of KPMG Peat Marwick has estimated that the state of Virginia is receiving a 19% annual rate of return on its investment in Metrorail, as a result of additional development attracted by the rail-transit system.

The basis for the success of WMATA's joint development policy is the management of the Metrorail system itself. It features frequent service (usually 5 to 10 minute headways) as well as clean cars and stations. As Washington-area residents see the system as user-friendly, developers can count on its use by employees and residents located near stations.

WMATA has used its large real estate property in a strategic, innovative and entrepreneurial way, so that WMATA's public/private land development program can be a model for other agencies.

The WMATA real estate management also demonstrates the importance of the real estate market in securing desired development. High-density development around the stations, especially the current transformation of Park&Ride facilities, is based on a strong real estate demand. The process slowed down in less favorable real estate periods, such as the late eighties and early nineties.

It also shows, that significant parking costs and parking availability constraints are strongly promoting the chances for Transit-oriented Development. The effect of the parking policy in suburban locations though is less evident. Until now, parking there is often free and more generally available; PARSONS BRINCKERHOFF (1996, p.67) point out, that "public programs have provided a great amount of parking in Bethesda, Silver Spring, and Ballston that supports ridership to downtown but probably diminishes potential ridership to those destinations.

One of the most difficult issues that project designers wrestled with at every station is reconciling car, bus, and pedestrian movements. Fitting new travel patterns into existing street and path networks and development patterns has proven a prickly problem, without ideal solutions, and the problem changes over time as development occurs".

According to PARSONS BRINCKERHOFF (1996, p.65), Washington's experience points also up "the immense importance of coordinating transit and land-use planning to achieve transit-focused development. In the Washington area, regional planning for both transit and regional development began with agencies established by federal action that took the long view and provided a strategic context for local planning. The regional plan formulated in 1960, shortly before planning began in earnest for the rail-transit system, emphasized concentrations of development along transportation corridors that would provide transit as well as highway service. This preplanning for matching transit construction with development, although advisory in nature, gave local jurisdictions a head start in planning as the transit system was being constructed". As they say, several local jurisdictions (starting with Arlington County) took the initiative to base their future plans on development of intensive centers around transit stations. Their primary objective was to steer expected major economic development to locations that could be served by transit, and act as community nodes. Their early interest in pursuing transit-focused develop-ment has succeeded in promoting a substantial amount of station-area development.

The fact that most suburban development is controlled by a few large and powerful counties seems both to have aided and hindered coordination of development planning with transit construction. They point out that on the one hand, the jurisdictions that chose to pursue transit-focused development were able, with strong citizen support, to direct development and redevelopment to that end. On the other hand, jurisdictions that were uninterested in supporting focused, higher-density development around rail-transit stations were free to ignore the 1960 regional plan. The federal agency that formulated that plan had no implementing powers except with regard to federal facilities. The voluntary council of governments that might have urged adherence to the plan deliberately foreswore any involvement in regional planning.

The recent development activity has resulted from new interest in suburban infill locations and previously unmarketable inner city sites. WMATA is moving expeditiously to capitalize on a healthy real estate development market and to sponsor creative approaches, which will likely include special financial incentives, to spur development on certain remaining sites.

Without a doubt, suburban traffic problems (Washington is second only to the Los Angeles area in traffic congestion) have helped spark the interest in concentrating development near Metrorail stations.

6.3 TJD-examples in Atlanta/GA

Transit Joint and Transit-oriented Development

While in the future a closer link between transit and urban development seems to be probable, the current situation is far more modest, although efforts to create such a link have been undertaken since Alan Kiepper's MARTA leadership, coinciding with Atlanta's planning and construction in the early seventies.

Early successes at joint development included construction of two state office buildings on air rights over the Georgia State Station in 1982, a land swap with Southern Bell that resulted in development of a $100 million project over the Worth Avenue station, leasing of air-rights over the Ashby Street station parking garage for a nonprofit community organization's retail venture, and interfacing of several stations with adjoining retail stores and office buildings.

Most of this activity ended in the late 1980s with the downturn in the real estate market. Construction of Resurgens Plaza in 1988, over the Lenox station, which was to be part of a large development complex, was the last major joint development venture before the mid-nineties.

Recently, in the context of the political and institutional changes described above, transit stations became a prime location for any type of real estate development. Since 1998, MARTA issued requests for proposals for a number of their real estate property.

Most of this property consists of Park & Ride facilities close to transit stations. Also transit-oriented developments on non-MARTA property were more closely surveyed and supported. In some cases agreements between MARTA and companies located at stations went beyond the location purpose.

The partnership between BellSouth and MARTA

The best case is BellSouth. In 1999, BellSouth and MARTA made a very complex and unusual agreement through which transit-oriented development contributes indirectly to increase farebox revenues and raise ridership numbers. Within three years from now (completion scheduled in 2003), 15,500 of the total 23,000 BellSouth employees in the Atlanta region will be located at three MARTA stations. At the moment, Bell South's office locations are quite decentralized and only the major facilities are located at MARTA stations.

The agreement has the following components: reduced fee for MARTA's monthly pass, increased parking fees at transit locations, construction of three large office complexes (a total of 3 million square feet) at the above-mentioned stations and 3000 more reserved Park&-Ride facilities at the terminal stations of each of the Heavy Rail branches.

Illustration 6.12: Future central BellSouth locations

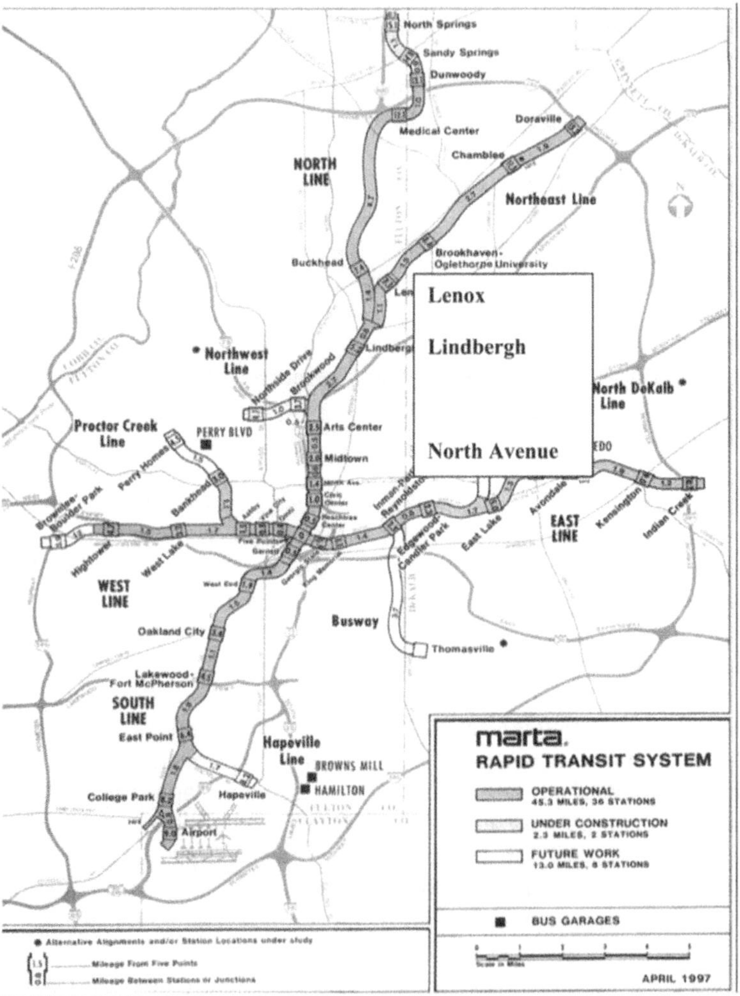

The price for the MARTA month pass will be $38.50 instead of $45. BellSouth sponsors the pass with an additional (tax-bill-reducing) $20 deduction. The employees have to pay $18.50 a month, which leads to a real cost of $8.5 after income-tax-deduction. The initial MARTA-price may be further stepped down if more then 2000, 3000, 4000 month-passes will be bought.

According to Richard Gilbert, BellSouth's Metro Plan Director, the current modal split of the 3,500 employees being already located at MARTA's Midtown-station is 30 %. According to an internal poll, 64 % of the MARTA riders are interested in parking their car at a P&R facility at a MARTA terminal. Adding 12,000 new employees at transit locations and assuming they will have similar MARTA ridership quotas and parking-requirements, necessitates 3000 reserved P&R facilities.

The costs will be entirely covered through the fact that parking requirements at the new BellSouth facilities will be lower than the original parking ratio provided by the zoning ordinance. Whereas the original requirements range from 2.5 (midtown) to 4.0 (Lenox) per 1000 sq feet, they now will be 0.5 to 0.7 lower, contributing thus to a saving of 1600 new inner-city parking spaces.

The centerpiece of BellSouth's transit activities is to build three huge "business centers,"shifting about 12,000 employees from 75 other offices in the next three years. "BellSouth's estimated $750 million will relocate most of its metro Atlanta employees to within walking distance of MARTA transit stations. At the same time, the project will deal a blow to the suburban office space market. The company will vacate 2 million square feet in the suburbs, while it builds 3 million square feet in the city." (Atlanta Journal Constitution, 01/27/1999). These buildings will be located in proximity to the Midtown, Lindbergh and Lenox stations

The BellSouth example will be repeated through other companies: According to the same article, "two weeks ago, Coca-Cola Co. said it is working on a consolidation plan to relocate 2,500 employees from the suburbs and Midtown, to sites near its 4,500-employee North Avenue headquarters in the western sector of downtown".

Station Area Development:

In the 1980s, station area development took place mostly in inner-city locations. At the **Five Points station** in downtown, the crossroads of the transit lines, a substantial amount of development occurred during the 1980s, together with construction of a pedestrian mall, connecting the Five Points and Garnett stations and underground connections between the station and adjacent development. The subsequent decline of the adjoining Underground Atlanta area dampened developer interest in this area. Now a multi-modal facility linking MARTA with Amtrak service is being designed in coordination with a planned federal building and the new Olympic Park. However, state funds required for the project appear uncertain.

Now, new strong developments occur at inner-city-stations, although not primarily on MARTA property. The most important one is currently the **Midtown** station. As already mentioned, in Midtown, BellSouth plans to build three buildings of 350,000 square feet each on the seven-acre site of the vacant First Baptist Church at Fourth and Peachtree. The telecommunications company has offered to give the sanctuary building to the Atlanta Symphony Orchestra for a concert hall. The new office would be near the North Avenue MARTA station and a block from the 1 million-square-foot BellSouth Center at 675 West Peachtree. It will have retail among other uses, and will have additional walking access from the highly frequented Peachtree-street east of it. The Midtown land was part of several blocks assembled by a Swedish investor in the 1980s for a massive high-density development. It is now owned by a Swedish lender of the developer who went bankrupt. A direct access between the MARTA station and the new buildings will be financed through BellSouth.

Major new developments on private property will occur at **Civic Center**. 1.2 million sq foot office-space, a 360 units residential tower, a 300-room hotel as well as retail and restaurants at the ground level will contribute to further densification and diversification of the downtown district.

A number of new developments are currently under way at suburban stations. Many of these developments will be built over Park&Ride facilities at or in proximity to these stations.

One of them is Abernathy Road (see design-draft), an 11,4 acre P&R facility at 1/3 mile near to **Sandy Springs.** The station was opened in 1999. The former Park & Ride offered drivers on I-85 the possibility to transfer to a shuttle bus leading to downtown Atlanta. The development will occur in two phases and contribute to the realization of a mixed-use residential, retail, restaurant, hotel environment, including 600,000 sq foot of office space. Due to the strong visual and functional separation through the Interstate-highway, pedestrian access to Sandy Springs will be very unattractive. The map shows the future shuttle service to the station. It will be important to investigate, in how far a frequent shuttle service may lead to a reasonable transit usership.

Illustration 6.13:
Construction works at Sandy Springs

Other developments on MARTA property will happen at **Medical Center**. The RFP, issued in February , 1999 received two proposals by June, 1999; in January, 2000 the MARTA board selected the developer who will build 200 multi-family residential units and a 400,000 sq foot medical office building within the next few years.

At **East Point** station, as well as at **Hamilton E. Holmes** station, developers will build multi-family units, each with 210 units plus, at Hamilton, 136 townhouses on non-MARTA property. At **Kensington** station the DeKalb County Workforce Center, with 100,000 sq ft will be built next to the heavy rail entrance.

A number of transit-oriented developments on private land property are concretely planned at **Decatur** station (105 condos), **Ashby** station (historic Westside village), **College Park** (Princeton Village) and **West End** station (large multi-family apartment complex with 112 apartments in phase 3, to start soon).

At the **Lenox** station about four miles northeast of downtown, an explosion of office and retail development has occurred driven completely by market forces.

Despite the connection with the MARTA system, these developments have been very strongly car-oriented and don't contribute much to increasing MARTA usership. Also – concerns were raised from those living in the surrounding communities, as to the amount of traffic these new developments would generate. They are concerned that the developments will bring the already unbearable traffic level to a gridlock.

New residential developments (PostProperties) in a distance of over half a mile away from the station could have been developed during the last year but access to the station requires shuttle bus service. Trammel Crow will add another 286 residential units.

North of the Lenox station, BellSouth has acquired 12 acres of land from a private owner. As already mentioned, the company will build three office buildings containing a total of 640,000 sq ft alongside three existing office buildings containing 360,000 square feet. The site is zoned for one additional building.

Lindbergh station as a national showcase of transit joint development:

A major TOD project is being developed at the **Lindbergh Center** station. The Lindbergh Center Station will be a multi-use development consisting of commercial office towers, retail stores, restaurants and residential buildings The station location between Buckhead and Downtown is considered ideal for high-density development.

All of the planned development will be built on property owned by MARTA. Based on FTA's new TOD policy of 1997, the company acquired 3 acres of land with federal subsidies. Apart from the potential revenue generated through the lease of this property, the land ownership allows MARTA to control the development, and contribute concretely to the intended mixed-used urbanization. Also, zoning was changed to allow for high-density development, and steps were taken to get community groups heavily involved in the process to generate local enthusiasm. Private investors, like Home Depot and an apartment complex in the area **(PostProperties)** have also donated $30,000 to finance a land-use, transportation, and economic development study at Lindbergh station in 1999. The surrounding residential community was not very receptive to the TOD project at Lindbergh Station. The increase in traffic congestion remains a major concern. Neighborhood Association groups have asked Atlanta City Hall to guarantee that impact fees collected from the project will be used to lessen the effect that the additional traffic will have on the area.

Illustration 6.14: Lindbergh station development plan

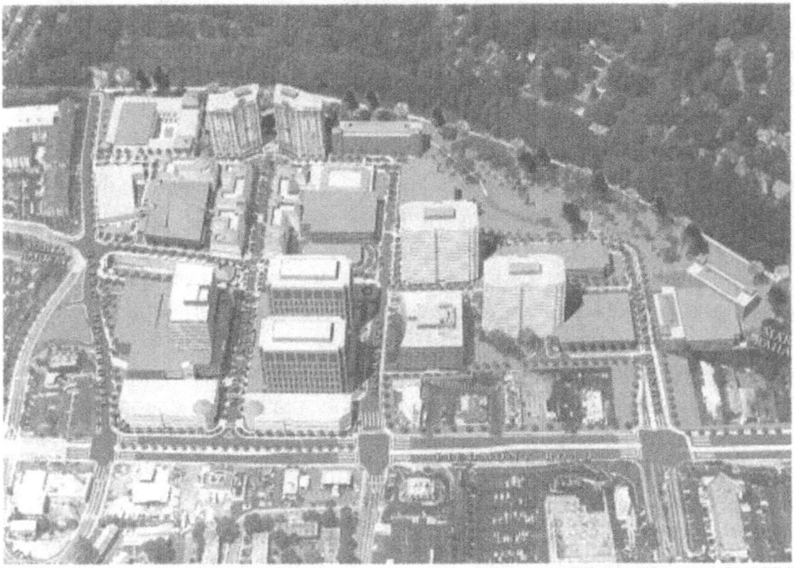

Despite this opposition, the project went ahead relatively quickly. After acquiring the additional land, MARTA issued an RFP in August, 1997). The RFP received two proposals in January, 1998. In March, 1998 the MARTA board selected Carter with a development concept as shown above. It has the following components: phase 1: 1.1 million sq ft BellSouth tower, 0.225 million sq ft multi-tenant office, 0.300 million sq foot retail and restaurants, 315 apartments units, 175 room hotel. In phase 2, an additional 1.1 million sq ft of office towers (owned, but not necessarily used by BellSouth) as well as 30,000 sq ft of retail and restaurant and 600 residential units will be built in the northern part of the area. More than half of this will be built by 2003.

In so far, by 2003, Lindbergh is supposed to be a heavily landscaped place where people can buy a condominium or rent an upscale apartment, purchase groceries, see a movie, shop in boutiques, and work in office buildings of about 17 stories. All these are elements for a completely different urban

setting, changing the usual monofunctional development type into a mixed use, carefully designed, pedestrian-friendly urban core.
The Lindbergh station is supposed to be the largest TOD in the United States: The live-work-play community to be anchored at MARTA's Lindbergh station in Buckhead is believed to be the most complex attempt by any authority in the country to develop land surrounding a transit station. "It's certainly one of the most visible projects," said Richard Steinmann, director of policy development for the Federal Transit Administration.

The development is based on the following conditions: MARTA is entering a 99-year agreement to lease 43 acres to Carter & Associates, the Atlanta-based winning real estate development bidder. Although MARTA had not intended to sell any land, 4.2 acres will be sold outright for condo construction. Planners presumed that bankers would not make loans on housing built on leased land. MARTA expects to unveil that project by mid-February.

At Lindbergh, the transit system is putting $40 million of its own into the deal. The money will be used to renovate the station to accommodate the development and help pay for a system of roads, parking and sewers.

"It's from the real estate fund, money which accumulated over the years as MARTA sold land that was excess," said Paul Vespermann, MARTA's director of property development. "With the recent change in federal transit policies allowing for these joint developments, they will allow that money to be spent for infrastructure, the purchase of property and whatever we need to further transit-oriented development."

MARTA agreed to increase its financial stake, from $20 million to $40 million, to fund a station renovation not envisioned before the board approved the concept site plan. The station's roof is to be knocked off, beams put over the platform, and the whole place covered over with concrete and earth to allow a so called Main Street to be built from Piedmont Road to housing planned on the back side of the station.

The development team has Carter handling office construction; Post Properties, the apartments; Federal Realty Investment Trust, the retail areas; and Harold Dawson Co., the condos, in conjunction with Southeast Capital Partners. According to Sam Massell, president of the Buckhead Coalition, a group of business leaders (Atlanta Journal, 02/01/1999), "Dawson is the first African-American company to do a major development in Buckhead.

According to the article mentioned above, "details of the Lindbergh development other than office construction remain sketchy". Conceptually, an unspecified number of condos and apartments will be built on the west side of the property, as a buffer for residents on the other side of the Southern Railway tracks.

"MARTA expects to take in more than $4 million a year", plus increased farebox revenue as ridership grows. "One question is whether BellSouth will take all 2.2 million square feet. It has contracted for 1 million square feet and took an option on another 1.2 million square feet, Vespermann said.

The project also still faces a re-zoning hurdle. Carter will ask the Atlanta City Council in March to downzone the 47-acre site from 10 million sq feet of office space to 5 million square feet of total construc-tion. The heavy density existed when MARTA bought the site for its headquarters, in the early 1980s.

In exchange for less density, Carter wants the council not to lock the company into a specific site plan. It wants to be able to place buildings where it appears they should go, as the market develops. The same type of zoning was approved for the site of the old Atlantic Steel site in Midtown, where developers envision a sweeping mixed-use development.

Carter expects to start demolition of old warehouses on the site by mid-1999. Construction of several buildings will occur simultaneously, with a garage for MARTA riders to be the first building to open, according to Chuck Konas, who heads the Carter team at Lindbergh. Opening dates have yet to be determined.

In relatively close proximity of up to one-third mile, east of the station, additional transit-oriented development opportunities may be possible in the future.. At the moment, Piedmont Road (see illustration 6.14) boldly separates the future new TOD, west of it, from the one-story big box retailers, and its very extended parking lots on its eastern side.

According to Paul Vespermann, the expectation of land value, accrued through TOD and higher zoning rights, has prevented land owners from offering long-term lease contracts. The largest mall, including a K-Mart has only another three years of guaranteed existence at these locations. The area east to Piedmont Road has a similar extension to the station area and is still located in a quarter mile radius around the station. Behind is another large slice of totally car-dependent retailers that could potentially also be relocated, or upzoned, if the future urban core at the station needs expansion.

Illustration 6.15: The station as the urban center

Outlook:

MARTA's initiation of operation coincided with a major development boom in many parts of the Atlanta region throughout the 1980s. Stations were located in many of the most desirable real estate market areas, and thus benefited from a considerable amount of air-rights joint development and nearby development. In recent years, however, neither MARTA, nor public agencies, have aggressively promoted close linkages between stations and adjoining development. That, coupled with the decline in the real estate market beginning in the late 1980s, has resulted in little station area activity, except that related to the 1996 Olympics.

This has been clearly changing in the last few years. With the business community leading the change in development patterns, chances are high, that not only the projects described above will be realized, but that they may serve as initiators for further market driven TOD in areas with development potentials. The office development at MARTA stations, will drastically increase during the next years. The available figures show that 6.3 million sq feet of office space are planned, much of that has already started or will start during this, or next year. The total amount corresponds to the average yearly office construction during 1997 and 1998; so the faster it'll get built, the more it affects the regional distribution of new office locations during the upcoming years. About 70% of that will occur on MARTA property.

Housing construction in proximity to stations is far less important. Even in the category of multi-family housing, the percentage of transit-oriented development of the total housing market will be relatively low. There is practically no single family housing in walking distance to heavy rail stations planned.

6.4 Upgrading Joint Development in New York

Most of the nation's established rail-transit systems have not had the same opportunities as MARTA or Metrorail to plan for joint development. Older rail-transit systems such as New York's MTA and Philadelphia's SEPTA, have little or no land available for direct development as their rights-of-way pass under, or through, sites that have long been built-out. Real estate markets in many older cities, even New York City, have tended to be less buoyant and predictable than in newer cities, thereby reducing the opportunities, or increasing the risks for joint development. Most older systems suffer from large and persistent operating deficits, and thus, lack the capital to seed joint-development opportunities. Finally, many established rail systems, being in older cities, are burdened with jurisdictional barriers that limit their ability to carry out a comprehensive, cross-jurisdictional program of joint development (CERVERO/HALL/LANDIS 1992).

For these cities and their transit operators, the task of promoting joint development has focused on renovating and re-developing existing transit stations, rather than on developing new stations or on promoting large new commercial projects adjacent to new stations. This section examines the process of joint development as undertaken by two older rail-transit systems: New York's Metropolitan Transportation Authority (MTA) and Philadelphia's Southeast Pennsylvania Transportation Authority (SEPTA). In the case of New York, joint development has gone forward, often on a grand scale, because of the proactive stance taken by the New York City Planning Commission. In Philadelphia, joint development has occurred on a much more modest scale, in part because of the lack of coordination between SEPTA and other local jurisdictions.

MTA and New York City's joint station development policy

MTA has been very active in pursuing joint development. CERVERO/HALL/LANDIS (1992) listed almost 40 projects up to1990. The present and future possibilities are limited through MTA's limited Real Estate Ownership around transit stations. During their last years, the MTA predecessors had to sell almost the entire Real Estate Property of the respective Companies. Also – within the City of New York, MTA faces a situation in which improvements of the subway and station infrastructure takes place in a built-up environment, with little additional construction. This neither allows the real estate marketing policy of Washington and Atlanta, nor the possibility of tax increment financing as a major local source to finance transit improvements in other cities.

The MTA-policy mainly strives to achieve cost-sharing agreements with owners or developers of adjacent properties. MTA has the jurisdiction over land-use at stations and at its right-of-way. But unless heavy legal procedures are applied, it depends in many cases on the readiness of the building owners on top of their stations, or of adjacent land owners, to agree with the necessary underground construction. It also relies on the legal authority of the City of New York to create a regulatory environment, favorable to cost-sharing.

In fact, it is only because the New York City Planning Commission and MTA have nurtured a good working relationship, that joint development has prospered in the city. Both agencies see joint development as serving their respective missions: MTA is interested in rebuilding and renovating old stations, and the Planning Commission wants to steer Manhattan's ever-worsening traffic congestion.

To promote joint development, the New York City Planning Commission has modified the city's zoning ordinance in two ways: first, by including specific "transit provisions" in the New York City Zoning Resolution (see the Transit Joint Guidelines[13]) and, second, through the dedication of Special Transit Districts.

Transit Provisions: The transit provisions of the New York City zoning ordinance stipulate subway station improvements that are to be completed by developers in exchange for zoning bonuses that allow up to 20 percent increases in floor area ratios (FAR). Station improvements are negotiated on a project-by-project basis, and focus primarily on facilitating pedestrian movements, providing free transfer points for subway riders, and improving station amenities. Between 1980 and 1988, NYCTA estimates that private developers constructed over $125 million in station improvements ($70 million in developer-sponsored capital improvements were budgeted for fiscal year 1987-88 alone). The transit provisions of the New York City Zoning Ordinance

---

[13] Guidelines for Developer-Proposed Transit Improvements,
New York City and The Metropolitan Transportation Authority

The following guidelines are used by the New York City Department of City Planning to direct developer-fmanced and developer-built subway station improvements.

1) Floor Area Ratio bonuses are, in general, granted for agreement to construct a specified transit improvement and not for a developer financial contribution. This policy is intended to allow the MTA to reduce the high costs of using in-house resources to build improvements by taking advantage of the cost savings from private-sector construction. In addition, the policy eliminates the appearance that developers are 'buying' zoning changes.

2) The developer's commitment to complete an improvement is secured with a letter of credit held by the NYCTA, to be claimed in the event a project is not finished as specified.

3) Developers that build new facilities or perform renovations required to maintain the mprovements.

4) Developer proposals that increase the operating expense for the station should be avoided (i.e. the addition of a token booth).

5) The MTA must verify the value to the agency or the station of developer-proposed improvements.

6) The NYCTA engineering staff must study the effects of each improvement on transit operations. –

7) The Board of Estimates of the City of New York and the public must give final approval to all plans.

Source: New York City Department of City Planning, 1989.

fall into three areas, each designed to improve pedestrian flow within, and access to, subway stations:

Mitigation to Alleviate Building-Induced Impacts: This element of the City's zoning resolution requires developers to mitigate the impacts that their projects have on the surrounding area, as identified in the project's Environmental Impact Statement (EIS). Required impact mitigation measures need not be transit-related.

Mandatory As-of-Right Zoning: Under this provision, developers are required to improve subway facilities that are adjacent to their projects, regardless of whether they are seeking an FAR bonus. Typically, developers are required to relocate a subway entrance from the sidewalk to within the lot line, taking due care to incorporate the entrance aesthetically with the new development. Stairs and elevator entrances to the subway, must be either located in the building lobby, or in an adjacent outdoor plaza area.

Floor Area Ratio Bonuses: For significant improvements in station circulation and access, the City Planning Commission is empowered to award a floor area bonus of between 5 - 20 %. Originally, these regulations only applied to the Midtown district. Since 1984, however, FAR bonuses have been available for any development in Manhattan, with a current FAR of 10 or more. Projects given higher priority are those offering construction of free transfer points, or other significant access improvements.

If developers are ready to pay a more substantial financial contribution for station- or other infrastructure-improvements, they may obtain a "floor area ratio" (FAR) bonus up to 20 %. These regulations have longtime only been applied in midtown Manhattan with FARs of 10 and more. They have contributed to the financing of station improvements at Times Square. Since the mid-eighties they have been extended to other areas where density could be increased without disturbing the neighborhood. But, due to a lack of real developers' interests, it has only been applied in Long Island City in Queens, where Citicorp has located a new high-rise office tower next to the LIRR station, and in Downtown.

Special Transit Districts: To further expand the scope and applicability of the transit provisions in the City's zoning resolution, the New York Department of City Planning established 33 special districts for needed transit improvements and likely development. Under the Special Transit District program, developers and regulators are allowed extra latitude in negotiating transit improvements.

According to CERVERO/HALL/LANDIS (1992), staff in the New York City Department of City Planning view the Greenwich Street District as a model. Whereas most special district programs provide for FAR bonuses on projects adjacent to a transit stations, within the Greenwich Street Transit District, developers have been allowed to transfer their FAR bonuses to other sites. Lot improvements that indirectly improve subway access are also eligible for bonuses within this district; the provision of arcades, covered pedestrian spaces, or pedestrian connections also entitles developers to a density bonus. Finally, developers in the Greenwich Street District have the Option of contributing to a fund, in lieu of undertaking actual construction. This feature allows development to proceed, while funds for future improvements are accruing in a reserve account.

The high level of coordination between MTA and the City Planning Commission notwithstanding, the potential of joint development in New York City is relatively limited. The high land values and rents required to spark developer interest in density bonuses are rarely present. According to MTA's Real Estate managers public-privatepartnerships didn't and don't occur often enough. In some cases they are facing heavy and irrational resistance through developers. This resistance seems to be related to the bad reputation of the public sector as such.

One example is the improvement of the LIRR – entrance at Penn Station. The LIRR ticket counters are located on the second underground level. The first level contains only retail stores and had some vacancies in the beginning of the nineties. The new entrance had to go through two vacant stores and could have created an additional street entrance for the retail owners at the first underground level. As the owners of the One Penn Plaza properties were fundamentally opposed to any change of the given situation, the necessary space for the new entrance had to be assured through the declaration of "eminent domain". This was confirmed through a court decision, and has led to an entrance that went directly down to the second underground level without creating any connection to the first level.

Under these circumstances, it is no surprise, that the chances for public-private partnerships are better where MTA is the main landowner. On the other side – the remaining large properties are facing the problem that their development preparation requires long procedures, which may very well be interrupted by downturns of the real estate market or management changes at MTA or the city administration. One such case is the Caemerer railroad yard in midtown Manhattan. According to CERVERO/HALL/LANDIS (1992) in the beginning of the nineties, prior to the real estate boom of this last decade, MTA had abandoned plans for an air-rights development over the this railroad yard. "Had the project gone forward, it would have been the largest joint development project yet undertaken in New York City". Another case is Atlantic Avenue, one of the major public transportation hubs of the city.

Atlantic Center – the slowdown of a promising joint development project

The station area plan involved two nationally-known design firms - Peter Calthorpe and Skidmore Owings & Merrill (SOM) – as well as a local government willing to write down the cost of land. But despite these favorable conditions, the ambitious plans did not go forward. They were finally abandoned and changed into a torso of the original concept.

The project had its roots in the mid-1980s, when New York City government decided that too much back-office space was relocating to outlying suburban areas. Hoping to stem the loss of jobs and tax revenue, Mayor Ed Koch launched a program of financial and development incentives aimed at retaining back-office activities within the city limits.

Downtown Brooklyn's Atlantic Center seemed a perfect site for back-office space, combined with a major new residential and retail development in a type of urban transit village. Atlantic Center included a largely vacant 24-acre site, owned by the City, over a Long Island Rail Road commuter rail terminal. Nine subway lines and fourteen bus routes converge at the site.

On the basis of a request for development proposals, the city hired Rose Associates, an established development company. Mr. Jonathan Rose, a member of the company and the lead developer, was attracted in good part by the transit connection that he thought would add value to the project. So it was he who hired the design firms of Peter Calthorpe and SOM to design not only back office, but also housing, and retail linked to the station.

Their design included 2.7 million square feet of office space – half in two large office towers directly over the terminal, and near the Williamsburg Bank Building. A skylit retail concourse with restaurants, shops and a 10-screen cinema is near the center of the complex. A 688-unit neighborhood to the east, Atlantic Commons, aims at medium-and-low income rent, along with several street-level retail businesses.

The housing design organizes four-story Brownstone courtyard apartment buildings around a crescent park, and along streets, which according to Calthorpe, "re-establish the lost fabric of a neighborhood decimated by 1960s redevelopment." An office building along Atlantic Avenue would shield the residential neighborhood from the adjacent train tracks. Daycare and community centers are situated at the base of the recent park, while neighborhood grocery stores and small retail stores line the neighborhood's edge.

The project won various planning approvals and was expected to move into pre-construction in 1987. At this point though, a lawsuit was filed by a neighborhood group claiming that the project was of too high density for the neighborhood, and also would lead to a gentrification and displacement of the low-income population. The nationwide environmental group, the Natural Resources Defense Counsel, joined the lawsuit.

Architects, developer and transit agency are convinced that that this lawsuit doomed the project. It wound its way through the courts for three years before being dismissed. By 1990, the market for office, including back-office, had weakened, and the likely main tenant, the City Department of Community Development, went elsewhere.

BERNICK, evaluating this project several years later, sees the absence of a powerful public promoter as another reason for the project failure. "Certainly, the lawsuit undermined the project's momentum, and made development more difficult. But the absence of continued support from the city government and transit agency was also significant in ending the project. By 1990, no one in the city government or transit agency functioned on a day-to-day basis as the project champion. Without a public champion, without someone committed to pushing the project forward on a daily basis, it did not survive." (BERNICK 1995, p. 17)

In the mid-nineties, new development has come to the site, though it is anything but transit-oriented. Forest City took over for Rose Associates as the developer, and set out to use the site for a big-box retail project, complete with a large parking lot. It moved forward on housing, but in low-density two-story townhouses, amounting to less than 100 units.

Now, 15 years after the project start, construction work is going on for a new three-story building on top of the underground station and the LIRR-tracks. The building has foundations for a later high-rise extension, if the respective real estate demand occurs.

Although it very far from the original concept, it will finally improve the visual appearance of this important transfer-point between subways and the LIRR, while contributing to the complex reorganization of the transfer connections below ground. The investor contributes 100 Mio $ to the entire construction work; MTA, $180 million. The investor has therefore a low rate long-term lease.

Very little attention to MTA's suburban rail network

Up until now, **only few station-related partnerships** took place in the suburban area. One is **Ronkonkoma** in Long Island. Once again, MTA (LIRR) owned a piece of land at the train station. A development "request for proposals" (RFP) was published.

The RFP had only one response. The developers suggested retail, instead of office space. The lease contract was concluded under these development conditions, but with a serious frame of architectural requirements, which were supposed to lead to the creation of a town center of this very sprawled-out community.

Although the local jurisdiction wanted changes to the original plan that contradicted this idea (such as an elevated protected connection between the parking garage, and the station platforms that run over the retail building and has no connection with it), the development still has the potential to become such a center. Due to its architectural success, the Ronkonkoma station serves as an example for similar suburban stations in Long Island, e.g. at Hempstead.

Outlook:

On the whole, the financial impact of transit joint development seems be relatively low. The MTA Real Estate Managers estimate that the revenue generated through transit-oriented partnerships in the last twenty years is not higher then $100 million, and the total revenue generated through Real Estate Policy (including the sale of a 4 acres piece of land at Columbus Circle) as not more than $ 500 million.

In addition, transit-oriented development, where it's not market driven, seems to be very difficult to generate, both within the city of New York and at stations of the suburban railway networks.

One key reason therefore is the public funding disequilibrium between capital and operation funding: For instance, it seems to be relatively easy for MTA to receive capital funding for parking structures (highway funds) and relatively difficult to fund the operation of a bus service, convenient enough to pick up commuters at home. This could reduce the need for parking space at the station and open new development possibilities at suburban stations.

6.5 SEPTA 's Lease and Maintain Program in Philadelphia[14]

Philadelphia's Southeast Pennsylvania Transportation Authority (SEPTA) is the third-largest public transit agency in the country. SEPTA's jurisdiction includes the city and county of Philadelphia, Bucks County, Montgomery County, Delaware County, Chester County, and the scores of townships throughout the Philadelphia metropolitan region. SEPTA operates more than 1,500 diesel buses and 110 electric trolley buses. SEPTA rail operations include over 300 Light Rail and 600 Heavy Rail subway and commuter trains.

Throughout the 1980s, SEPTA has been able to maintain an overall farebox recovery ratio across all the modes it operates at almost 50 percent. In addition to covering these operating deficits, SEPTA must also provide capital funding, to maintain and renovate its aging infrastructure including vehicles, rights-of-way, and stations. These capital needs have prompted SEPTA management to explore options for generating non-farebox revenues,

[14] This chapter is based on CERVERO/HALL/LANDIS' 1992 publication. Adjustments and updates were made where this was necessary and possible.

including private-sector funding for capital projects through public-private ventures.

In 1982, SEPTA's Real Estate Department began to explore techniques, for using the system's property holdings, to generate revenue, fund capital improvements, and reduce operating costs. Since then, SEPTA has successfully attracted private investment in needed capital improvements on its suburban Heavy Rail lines, through its Lease and Maintain Program.

The Lease and Maintain Program involves public-private cost sharing in the purest sense. Under the program, private developers - through a competitive bidding process – lease commercial space within existing suburban rail stations, under the condition that they maintain or upgrade some stipulated part of the station proper. The primary distinction between the Lease and Maintain Program, and a conventional commercial lease arrangement, is that SEPTA grants a rent-credit to the developer for completion of specified capital improvements. These improvements can include station renovations, the rehabilitation of commercial space, and developer-funded maintenance and property-management programs.

As of late-1990, SEPTA had 19 transit stations operating under the Lease and Maintain Program. All of these stations were part of the suburban Heavy Rail system and all projects except one were outside the city of Philadelphia. According to SEPTA, these 19 stations have attracted $2.4 million in private investment for station rehabilitation and have saved SEPTA approximately $7,000 per station in annual maintenance, cleaning, and utility costs.

The station areas typically consist of an older free-standing station building, a passenger platform, and adjacent commuter parking lots. Most existing Lease and Maintain projects are located in neighborhood retail districts or in areas zoned for residential use. Given the small scale of the SEPTA properties and the modest prospects for economic growth in these areas, SEPTA has tailored the program to fit the general economic conditions found along its suburban lines. Most development proposals received by SEPTA have been for small-scale commercial projects, located entirely within the existing rail station complex. None of the completed projects involve owners or developers of adjacent land.

The Lease and Maintain Program faces a number of institutional constraints which have limited its use. SEPTA is allowed to condemn land with board approval for non-transportation projects. The agency is required, however, to conform to local zoning laws at all of its stations. Due to local opposition, several proposed commercial projects and station renovations in residentially-zoned neighborhoods have been denied local approval. SEPTA is seeking to bypass local zoning ordinances by requesting a broader definition of allowable uses at a transit facilities to include commercial uses.

One dilemma is that SEPTA actually has very little control over how stations are to be improved. Current SEPTA budget constraints preclude the use of agency funds to renovate stations in the absence of private sector contributions. Additionally, Pennsylvania state law requires state agencies like SEPTA to put capital projects out for competitive bid; and, contracts may only be awarded to the bidder with the highest total value of capital improvements.

The practice of choosing projects and developers by competitive bid has substantially constrained SEPTA's ability to negotiate project-specifics (e.g. design standards, preferred uses, and maintenance duties). The types of proposals received by SEPTA are entirely the prerogative of the individual developers who submit bids. To remedy this problem, SEPTA is seeking to revise state-enabling legislation, that would allow the agency to use Requests for Proposals (RFPs), as a method of choosing developers and projects under the Lease and Maintain Program. RFPs would enable SEPTA to select projects which offer capital improvements that meet particular design standards and development objectives.

AMTRAK policies have also been an impediment to the Lease and Maintain program. SEPTA currently leases 47 of its 174 suburban rail stations from AMTRAK, and had negotiated Lease and Maintain agreements at four of the stations: Berwyn, Haverford, Rosemont, and Wynnewood. Subsequent to the conclusion of these contracts, AMTRAK invoked a specific clause in its lease contract with SEPTA allowing it to reclaim authority over the operation of these stations.

Thus it is AMTRAK, not SEPTA, that now receives the tenant income at these 47 stations. This type of conflict has prompted SEPTA to limit bids to those stations over which it retains clear title - a constraint which has precluded the joint development of stations on the Northeast Corridor (NEC) and on the main line from Philadelphia to Harrisburg.

6.6 Federal Support of Joint Development

The FTA has recognized the positive impact of joint development on the value of transit systems . Paul Marx (FTA 1998) describes how joint development issues were pursued on the federal transit funding level: "Urban Mass Transit Program Authority was expanded significantly in 1974, by passage of the "Young Amendment," Section 3(a)(1)(D) of the Urban Mass Transportation Act, This section made joint development projects eligible for grant support. It took some time for the agency to incorporate this potential into its overall mission, through what was called the Urban Initiatives Program; and, it took even longer for transit systems to begin proposing joint development in conjunction with their planned rail-transit projects. Nevertheless, by March of 1978, UMTA was reviewing joint development proposals from over 20 cities. The focus of this effort was a region's central business district and, with few exceptions, development around rapid rail stations. Some of the major projects included: Miami's Civic Center rail station, Portland/Oregon's Banfield line as well as property development and air rights next to existing, or new stations, in Cleveland/Ohio, Baltimore/MD and Washington/D.C.

During the 1980s, to prevent transit systems from "double-dipping" on their federal subsidies, it was decided that federal transit dollars could be used to defray the "net" costs of a joint development project on the same ratio as an otherwise eligible transit project. The term "net" referred to costs remaining after any economic or other return from the project's private partner. The effect of this interpretation on joint developments was to halt many of them in their tracks. There was very little incentive for transit systems to undertake joint development projects, if the federal interpretation of "value capture" was going to create a direct substitution effect between private and federal dollars.

In very short order, the concept of joint development switched from incorporating development plans at the design or preliminary engineering stages, to taking advantage of "discovered" uses of existing property – particularly air rights that had no direct Federal cost component. UMTA viewed leases of air rights for 50 years or less as not being under the Common Grant

Rule and its predecessors, and thus not restricted by the new interpretation of the Young Amendment.

Another change in administration was marked by a steady, long-term economic growth cycle that increased commercial real estate values. At the same time, the Federal Transit Administration revisited its joint development policy in the context of the “Livable Communities” Initiative. This new effort was targeted specifically at demonstrating and reinforcing, the link between transit and the community that it serves. The concept of joint development, therefore, was reexamined in the context of land-use planning and community-building.

On March 14th, 1997, FTA issued a revised ‘Policy on Transit Joint Development’. The purpose of this policy was to "clarify the relationship between transit regulations and FTA policy regarding property disposition, leases of property, and sale of property for joint development. This FTA policy statement affects primarily the treatment of program income with regard to joint development and the definition of "highest and best transit use" in joint development." The policy statement announced to all transit grantees that real property acquired with Federal grant funds could be used to support a transit-oriented joint development. Further, if the joint development project produced income for the transit system, this was considered to be "program income" as defined in the Common Grant Rule, and freely usable by the transit system for eligible transit purposes. The only restriction placed on such transactions was that the transit system must retain effective continuing control of the joint development for transit purposes. Simply put, the property being used for joint development could be sold for this purpose to the developer, but the transit grantee must retain some assurance that the joint development will remain accessible to the transit system during the life of the project.

The new FTA policy is intended to make it easier for transit systems to "capitalize" on the increased value of property acquired for their transit service. The increased value comes from two factors--the basic function of transit as a collector and mover of people, and the ongoing economic growth of communities served by transit. FTA is encouraging transit systems to undertake transit-oriented Joint Development projects either under new grants or with property acquired under previous grants, whether the property is associated with a rail, bus or other transit facility.

The purpose of this Joint Development should be both to secure a revenue stream for the transit system and to help shape the community that is being served by the transit system. Where the grantee retains effective continuing control over the joint development for mass transportation purposes (such as an easement, or a contractual arrangement), all proceeds of sale, lease or other encumbrance of the property will be treated as program income for use by the transit system to meet capital and operating needs, for as long as the joint development lasts.

This is a departure from previous policy in two areas. First, FTA will now define all revenue derived from such joint development to be program income as defined in the “Common Grant Rule”. Second, grantees may use the new concept of "highest and best transit use," as an alternate to "highest and best use," in valuing real property for transit-oriented joint development.

To accomplish this change, the FTA Master Agreement has been expressly modified to include joint development as an eligible activity in all capital grants to which it applies. Further, grantees may request amendment of grants issued prior to FY 1997, as desired, to expressly include joint development within the scope of such grants.

6.7 Real Estate Policy of the Deutsche Bahn AG, private development examples

The Deutsche Bahn AG is fundamentally different from US regional local transit companies in regards to its size, tasks, internal structure and property ownership.

However, on closer inspection, there are similarities within regional transit tasks. Under the current situation, the tasks, which local American transit companies perform for regional transit, are essentially carried out by the Deutsche Bahn AG in Germany (although due to the European regulatory framework, important changes of this situation may occur over the next decade – see introduction in chapter one). There are also basic similarities in the cooperation with private investors, where the DB AG looks to connect its own properties with the private development and marketing process.

Beckmann/Perlan/Wulfhorst (1999) offer a comprehensive overview structure of the structural background of the DB AG real estate policy, on which the following summary is based. Additional footnotes supplement the summary. Examples of small scale cooperative projects will complete the picture.

The Structural Railway Reform

In early 1994, the Railway Reform introduced a meaningful step towards the new organizational, economic, and legal orientation of the Federal Railway Company (Deutsche Bahn AG, DB AG).
Upon the foundation of the Reform Laws of December 20, 1993 (Change of relevant "articles" of the German Constitution – Grundgesetz, GG) and December 27, 1993 (Railway Reorganization Law), the merger of the West German Federal Railway (Deutsche Bundesbahn, DB), and the East German State Railway (Detusche Reichsbahn, DR) took place.

This was formed to transform the state-owned Bundesbahn of the West & Reichsbahn of the East into a new market-conforming company. A business section and an administration section were created in addition to the following organizational entities:

- The DB AG, which was given the business task of infrastructure supply and transport.
- The „Federal Railway Authority „ (Eisenbahn-Bundesamt, EBA), which serves as upper federal authority for planning approval and supervision.
- The „Federal Rail Property Fund" (Bundeseisenbahnvermoegen, BEV) as the overriding power to merge former special assets of the Federal Government , manage debt and handle personnel affairs.

The federal government is responsible for the extension and maintenance of the rail network (a legal obligation to supply infrastructure) and for meeting the public's transportation needs (a legal obligation to supply what the citizens need)

The Railway Reorganization Law led to the amendment and creation of a number of implementation laws. Specific examples include: the law governing the merging and subsequent new arrangement of the two federal railway systems, the law which founded the new Deutsche Bahn AG (Deutsche Bahn Gründungsgesetz), the law concerning the federal government's management of the railway system (Gesetz über die Eisenbahnverkehrsverwaltung des Bundes), the "Regionalization" law (Regionalisierungsgesetz), as well as the General Railway Law (Allgemeines Eisenbahngesetz).

The main elements of the reform are:

- The structural reform of the Federal Railway through the fusion of the West German Deutsche Bundesbahn and the East German Deutsche Reichsbahn. The transformation into a public limited company and therefore, into a commercially-led rail business (as mentioned before).
- The separation of technical infrastructure from transport service by creating independent business branches for passenger traffic (local and long distance travel), freight traffic, and railway infrastructure, which in the third stage of the Rail Reform would be converted into independent corporations.
- The abolition of the railway monopoly and the opening of the railway to third parties (non-discriminating access).
- Extending rail-transit to meet regional needs. And since 1.1.1996 the shifting of the responsibility for rail-transit to the state level.

After the implementation of the first steps of the Rail Reform was concluded, the legally required breakdown into independent corporations followed on June 1st, 1999.

In addition to the four independent divisions required by law – railway infrastructure, local passenger traffic, long distance passenger traffic, and freight traffic – a fifth division was created to address passenger stations. These divisions would be formed into independent public limited companies within three years at the earliest, and five years at the latest, under the umbrella of a holding company called Deutsche Bahn AG. They consisted of:

- DB Reise und Touristik AG (Travel and Tourism - long distance passenger traffic)
- DB Regio AG (local passenger traffic)
- DB Cargo AG (freight traffic)
- DB Netz AG (railway infrastructure)
- DB Station & Service AG (passenger train stations)

The company's management was assigned service and thematic centers for higher priority tasks (i.e. Service Center for Training, Research and Technology Center, Train-Environment-Center). Further company divisions, which belong to the „Deutsche Bahn Group“ and are part of the DB AG Holding Co., complete other aspects of the group's business (i.e. DE Consult GmbH, MITROPA AG, Deutsche Bahn Real Estate Company (Deutsche Bahn Immobilienmanagement, DBImm), Railway Property Management (Eisenbahn-immobilienmanagement, EIM).

Consequences for the Railway estate policy and the development of "dispensable" railway land

After the 1960s, the management of the Real Estate and premises of the German Federal Railway had been subjected to a trend of „ Maintaining the Status Quo“; in the 1970s there was an effort that excess Real Estate Property be utilized for commercial purposes.

According to available information, the "Bundesbahn" (former West German National Railway Company) property ownership in 1986 (former West Germany) included a total area of 104,250 hectares (BECKMANN et al. quote Fischer, 1986) of which about 89,000 hectares were allotted to the rail tracks and other third party business properties, 12,000 hectares were used as campsites and railroad employees homes. About 3,000 hectares served unrelated business purposed, and are regarded as freely available. (BECKMANN et al. quote Groben, 1983 & 1986).

According to its own records, in the period between 1970 and 1983, the Deutsche Bundesbahn sold over 18,000 hectares of land, for which it received a profit of 1.7 billion DM (Deutschmarks) (Groben, 1983), representing an average profit of 9.44 DM per square meter. In the same period, the regular (steady) proceeds from property use through rentals and leases of the DB Service Operation and Advertising revenues had doubled from around 200 Million DM/a (in 1970) to over 400 Million DM/a (Groben 1983.).

Reorganization of Real Estate Holdings through the Rail Reform

The prevailing business conditions and economic goals of the Railway Reform considerably intensified the dynamic of rail property development. Through new operational and organizational techniques, as well as the diminishing traffic revenues – especially in regards to freight – the low demand for necessary business structures was further reduced. But, the increasing pressure related to economic results, led to a progressive concentration of business sites, and also to a more efficient use of existing properties. In particular, the Railway Reform's framework compensated for certain settled events such as the federal government taking over old debts, and this circumstance led to a very strong commercialization pressure for rail properties.

In the course of the Rail reform, the federal railway's land was transferred to different property owners and responsible parties.

At first, the entire real estate concern of the Deutsche Bundesbahn and the Deutsche Reichsbahn was turned over to the Federal Railway Property Fund. The exclusion of business areas of DB AG and the Administration Authority (EBA and BEV) had divided the properties out of DB AG and BEV as a result. However, the concrete agreement over the single surface could first and only partly be completed in 1998.

In the Federal Railway Property Fund (Bundeseisenbahnvermögen, BEV), most of the home purposes serving real estate – social public housing facilities, leisure and sports grounds, as well as cooperative (community) areas – have remained standing. From here on they would be managed (maintained) by the BEV.

Within the Federal Railway Property Fund sprang a real estate parcel (so-called "Targeted projects", from which some 3,000 objects (parcels) (about 8,000 hectares with an estimated total value of about 13 billion DM would be formed) – averaging about 162,50 DM /square meter.

The commercialization of this so-called "real estate package" was supposed to compensate the remaining liabilities of the Deutsche Bahn AG. The Railway Real Estate Management (EIM), a 100% subsidiary of the Federal Railway Property Fund, was founded in September, 1996 to fulfill this commercialization mission within a time period of 15 years. The proceeds from this utilization would be directly transferred to the German Federal Republic.

All of the remaining real estate (about 1.4 million square meters, meaning 140,000 hectares or 350,000 acres), in the "old" and "new" federal states (i.e. West- and East-German states), were connected to the DB AG, some to have their property uses be economically optimized (sales, leases, rentals, etc.). This was done in the beginning of 1996, through the founding of the Deutsche

Bahn Real Estate Company (Deutsche Bahn Immobiliengesellschaft, DBImm) which was put in charge as business product manager. The use of the mission covered the "dispensable" real estate, i.e. real estate which no longer had transit-function significance.

Expected Profits, Conceptual Problems, and Legal Peculiarities with regard to the EIM Areas

The entrusted EIM land areas were subject to a very high commercialization pressure to fulfill the expectations of the federal government (realization of 13 billion Deutschmarks through land sales within a 15 year period). As a consequence, the EIM in most cases, is less interested in promoting a long-standing high quality urban development than in achieving short-term sales profits (capital gains). As EIM sells high portions of land that is still under the special right of railway-dedicated land (similar to the legal frame of "right-of-way"), the sale-activities may in many cases not be coordinated with the local urban planning policy.

In addition, the real estate properties of the EIM often were enclosed by more rail land, and thus found in isolated locations.

Development of the DB AG real estate through DBImm

The DBImm, as the business manager for DB AG Holdings (probably in the future also for DB Netz, DB Station & Service) pursues similar objectives as the EIM for the Federal Railway Areas (first priority: commercialization of the real estate holdings for a maximum price). However, in the fulfillment of its duties, it is subject to other marginal requirements.

The excess property of the DB is not subject to any direct outside sales or profit pressure. However, the DBImm has instructions, through its activities, to contribute to the business outcome of the Deutsche Bahn AG as a whole. Therefore, its aim is oriented towards producing balance sheet profits. This orientation becomes reinforced through the private business interest commitments to the DBImm (for example, the Allianz Insurance Company has a share as partner of DBImm).

Fundamental options of the business utilization of the excess rail sites are the result of different types of market activities, including residual sales to a third party (one-time capital formation), steady development, leasing and rentals.

It is difficult to determine what the amount of land areas to be marketed is. In an interview in June 2000, the head of the train station development department of the DBImm, Mr. Gerlein, had estimated the entire amount of the land marketing (commercialization) at about 90 square meters (9,000 hectares or 22,500 acres). According to this information, one third of this amount is related to“ sell-offs“ (sales), one third to “leases“, and one third to “development.“

The sell-off does not generally relate to the transit goals of the DB AG, (in certain ways analogue to the EIM land sales), the lease share generally calls for value-maintaining or market-improving investments through DBImm in regards to respective business areas. The biggest piece of the „development“-related land are rail station areas or rail stations themselves. The development of this latter real estate does contribute to the transit goal although the main objective of this development is generally not the maximization of the transit impact but the maximization of real estate revenues.

Recently (spring 2001), DBImm radically changed its mangament strategy regarding excess land, considered not directly developable. It was offered as enormous land “packages”, each containing thousands of acres, to the state governments. The state of Brandenburg (2.5 Mio inhabitants) for example was offered, land worth 700 Mio DM. Now is the time for many states, to seriously estimate the real market value of this land. At the moment, it is in most cases considered to be highly overpriced. If, after negotiations with DBImm and the federal government, the land evaluation becomes more realistic, this new policy might contribute to new dynamic and flexibility in dealing with the railway real estate, and also to a more transit-oriented use of this land.

The necessity for investment in train stations

Various examples of DB-initiated railway station developments, before and after the aforementioned structural reform, exist. These developments were generally realized in partnership with private retail owners. After the creation of DB Station and Service, the official and broadly publicized goal (e.g. Architecture Bienale in Venice 1996) was to achieve the “renaissance of railway stations". The first priority of this concept was to modernize and show the existing railway station (a high portion of which is protected) in its' original function and to add new utilizations, particularily retail.

Some of the recent examples already completed or under construction have been realized in conjunction with private investors, and are impressive signals of the new role of rail and rail station buildings in the urban context. But as almost only large main stations have been renovated so far (with a real estate value stemming from long distance, generally high speed rail), these examples are not significant, in the context of this study, about how private investment can improve regional and urban rail systems.

In a thesis written at the Technical University of Berlin in 2000, Ludger STRATHMANN (Strathmann, 2000) examined the investment needs for train stations and the prospect of public-private partnerships in developing regional train stations.

According to his study, the compounded investment and maintenance deficits of the Deutsche Bahn AG, amount to a total of nearly 18 billion €. Of this sum about 14.5 billion € are necessary for maintenance deficits, and approximately 3 billion € are needed for train station development.[15] The budget set aside by the Deutsche Bahn AG (DB) for investment in this area amounts to 230 million €, which, according to his calculations, is far less than is necessary to meet these needs. An additional 300 million € is expected from public entities.

As a consequence, the large number of regional railway stations, in many cases 100 years and older, cannot be renovated without additional private or public money. Numerous cases have been realized so far, in which development programs were initiated and financed by the states. A number of success stories of regional rail stations being improved for transportation and for urban design purposes are documented in state owned or private publications, including Schriftenreihe ISW, Schriftenreihe DSSW, Schriftenreihe ILS, Schriftenreihe TH Aachen, BahnStadt-Report etc.

Examples in which private investors financed, or partially financed, the new construction or renewal of regional train stations are very rare so far. STRATHMANN (2000) describes six significant cases in Berlin/Brandenburg

[15] Strathmann quotes from German Railways, Passenger Train Station Department (Ed.): Strategy Conference, Frankfurt am Main (Strategy Conference), 87.

and the Rhine/Ruhr area:

Bernau-Friedenstal: Housing park developer finances transit station

In 1997 the train stop Bernau-Friedenstal on the Berlin-Bernau route was financed and built by Wohnpark Bernau-Friedenstal Immobilien GmbH, a real estate development firm. The site was first considered as a train stop in plans by the national railway (Reichsbahn) and the city of Bernau in 1910. After German reunification the regional transit authority, S-Bahn Berlin GmbH, estimated costs for a stop at a slightly more advantageous location at approximately 25.6 million €. In fact, the actual cost of planning and building this almost completely privately-financed project, proved to be 2.8 million €. Not only this, but planning and construction went much faster than was customary for comparable projects.

Plans for this project disappeared into transit authority archives for 87 years. The stop was finally built on private initiative and took only five months to complete.

Bernau is located on the northeastern edge of Berlin, and has a population of 24,000. As is true of other towns on the outskirts of the German capital Berlin, Bernau profits from an influx of new inhabitants, and is witnessing an increase in housing construction activity. Bernau expects to be home to nearly 30,000 people in the next few years. It has excellent access to transportation systems reaching beyond the region. It is connected to the Autobahn, regional transit and the regional railway.

Bernau lies on one of the train lines that runs radially from Berlin. The areas along these lines are at an advantage for development because of their proximity to the capital, and also their location on the line.

The neighborhood Friedenstal lies at the south end of the old part of town. It was reconstructed in the 1970s. New housing blocks were built and additional land was developed for housing. In 1995 the developer Wohnpark Bernau-Friedenstal Immobilien GmbH initiated the second largest privately-financed housing development project in the state of Brandenburg. On a 30 ha site, 2000 units were planned, almost 500 of them have been realized until 1999. They were to offer high-quality housing in an all-new, self-sufficient quarter with its own center and transit station. Investment was to amount to a total of approximately 385 million €.

The initiative to build a transit station came from the investor in 1995. His interest in improving access to transit for his housing park was based on examples of other housing development projects that had been started or already completed by other investors, in the areas surrounding Berlin. He chose not to apply for state funds because of the expected delays it would pose for beginning construction of the station. The transit stop was to be completed soon after the first sections of the housing park were finished, in hopes of attracting potential buyers and renters. Neither the shop owners nor other developers of housing projects agreed to participate in the costs.

The project included the construction of station platforms, service building, access routes and car- and bike-parking facilities. A contract in which the Deutsche Bahn allowed the investor to build the station was signed in June, 1996 and the federal agency in charge of the railways gave its official go-ahead in February, 1997. Construction began in April, 1997, and the station was completed within five months. In late September, 1997, the station was put into service.

Illustration 6.16: S-Bahn-Station Bernau-Friedensthal

The fact that in August, 1998 the investor was forced to declare bankrupcy, had nothing to do with this particular investment. It underlines, though, the risks of an "urban" rental housing project in a suburban setting.

Without this "urban" approach, the station may not have been built. To this day, 454 housing units and some commercial units have been completed, and the transit station is in service. The areas where access has already been developed are to be sold as part of the bankruptcy contract.

Hennigsdorf: Construction of a new entrance building by a private investor

Hennigsdorf has a population of around 25,000 inhabitants, and is located right on the northern Berlin city limits. The major economic sectors include rail vehicle manufacturing and steel processing, i.e. economic sectors that after the unification were supposed to be strongly endangered. The fact that they could survive in Hennigsdorf did not only contribute to a relatively healthy local economic situation, but also to a relative attractiveness for small engineering and computer companies. The city also lies directly on the edge of Berlin and benefits from this vicinity, but it does not have good car-access to the capital.

The new entrance building of the Hennigsdorf train station: Between the two wings is a pedestrian passage through the railway embankment that also leads to the platforms.

Since the German reunification, in 1990, the city has made considerable efforts to develop its new urban core, an undertaking that represents the completion of a project begun during German Democratic Republic times. The train station plays a key role in this scheme. The square at the train station's entrance and the pedestrian tunnel that crosses under the north-south running railway embankment are some of the reasons the train station is central to the urban design concept of the city. The station represents the easternmost point of the new central axis and connects the new core to the old town center located on the other side of the train lines. The background of this strongly transit-oriented urban development was the plan to re-install of the former Metrorail (S-Bahn) connection to the center of Berlin, and the city's eagerness to acclerate the realization of this connection. The S-Bahn-line was finally reopened in December 1998.

As the existing station building was incurring unreasonably high maintenance costs and was unattractive, it needed to be replaced. The city, in deliberation with the investor, was able to realize its ideas on the design of the new train station. The initiator of the project was the investor BC Berlin Consult, who was looking for an investment object and came upon the Hennigsdorf train station in 1994. The impetus for the Deutsche Bahn AG to agree to the project was the exceptionally poor structure and design condition of the old train station.

The investor paid for a design-study of a new station building. The resulting urban and architectural design concept was presented to representatives of the city, the Deutsche Bahn AG and the federal parliament in November, 1996 at a "train station conference."

Illustration 6.17:
Hennigsdorf: S-Bahn and Commuter Rail Station

The participant's ideas on the content of the project were in part very divergent leading to an intense discussion after the conference. Once they were brought more into line, a consensus was found in February, 1997, and was documented in the development con-tract. In April of the same year, a building permit was issued. Construction began immediately, and the buildings were finished in April, 1998.

Similar to several US-projects presented above, and in contrast to other German projects examined in this study, the private investor financed the entrance building and not the railway-related infrastructure. The costs of the building that was completed in 1998, were around 5 million €. Approximately 0.75 million € of this sum was contributed by the S-Bahn Berlin GmbH and the Deutsche Bahn AG.

An interesting aspect of this project was that the deliberations held between the investor, the city, and the Deutsche Bahn, resulted in a "new" form of entrance building. The unprofitable space, such as the entrance hall, waiting areas and ticket center was reduced to a minimum and the biggest portion of the building was commercially used. It is no longer a train station in the classic sense, but instead, more of an office and commercial building near the tracks.

Since the completion of the station building, other projects in the immediate vicinity of the train station have followed (compare MSWV aktuell 3/2000). As a result, Hennigsdorf, along with Fuerstenwalde perhaps (compare MSWV aktuell 3/2000), can be considered the city in the Berlin region with the most thoroughly transit-oriented urban settlement development. In this way, the common problem of commercial developments on the edge of town could also be avoided, and buying power could be encouraged to remain in the city center.

IKEA Kaarst: "Big box retailer" co-sponsors a stop of a new regional railway line

Similar to the pre-development situation in most suburban areas of the US, the area where the city Kaarst is located, was rural in character until late in the post-war era. The migration of new inhabitants in the last few decades, has led to new single-family and multi-family housing projects, and commercial park developments, changing the face of the area almost completely.

The two areas: Kaarst (population approximately 22,000) and Holzbüttgen (population 6,500), that are separated by the railway line, were once independent entities, but exist today as one town center. Three surrounding settlements are separated from this center by farm land. The total population of Kaarst is now 41,000. The town is located in the urban area surrounding

Düsseldorf.

As a reaction to plans by the national railway company to shut down the railway line into the major regional economic center (Düsseldorf) and encouraged through a study that attested great user potential, the cities along the Mettmann-Düsseldorf-Kaarst line founded the regional railway company Kaarst-Neuss-Düsseldorf-Erkrath-Mettmann mbH (Regiobahn GmbH).

Their first goal was to retain service along the line, but also to renew it while expanding service. In November, 1998 the state government approved the financing of 90 % of the 50 Mio € construction costs for the renovation of the rail line. Service began in September of 1999. Because of the many agreements that had to be made during construction of the whole line, the opening date was delayed several times. As part of their aim to improve rider potential, the Regiobahn approached Ikea in 1994, with an idea to move one of the train stops that was due to be renewed, to a site closer to the store. Ikea reacted positively, and after deliberations about their financial contribution, a contract was made for co-operation in December, 1998, and signed by both parties.

The company IKEA, which sells furniture and home supplies in 25 stores in Germany, contributed 150,000 € to the construction of the new train stop Ikea Kaarst. The stop lies on the Mettmann-Kaarst line of the municipal "Bahngesellschaft Regionalbahn". The line was reopened in September, 1999 after extensive renewal work. The construction of the new train stop costs approximately 500, 000 €. Besides its contribution to construction, Ikea pays 40,000 € a year for the cleaning and maintenance of the station. In July 1999, the train stop Ikea Kaarst was still under construction; the company Ikea had been waiting three years for its completion.

Leverkusen – Bayerwerk: Additional provisions at a new transit station are funded by Bayer AG

The city of Leverkusen is located on the right side of the Rhine, between the larger cities of Cologne and Düsseldorf. In 1930, it was combined with three small settlements in the surrounding rural areas, as part of a scheme to offer the many employees of the expanding Bayer company, adequate urban infrastructure. Its origin can still be seen in the polycentric structure of the city and the sprawling facilities of Bayer (on approximately 3.4 km^2). Leverkusen is located near the city of Cologne.

The economy of the city is dominated by the chemical company, sited in Leverkusen's southwest, and by its suppliers. About half of the transit stop Bayerwerk is located in the city of Leverkusen, and half in the neighboring city of Cologne. To the west of the station is the Bayer facility, and to the east is undeveloped land, belonging in part to the company. The station, thus, almost exclusively serves the company Bayer.

The transit station (Leverkusen) Bayerwerk was built partially over a street connecting two parts of Bayer's plant.

In 1985, an agreement was made between the state and the national railway on the financing of a project to improve the line, and bring it up to transit standards. In the framework of this project, the new station Bayerwerk was planned. Bayer AG had additional wishes that they brought into the project: The connection between the two areas opposite the station was to be improved, and the platforms were to receive a more costly roof. In an agreement, the Bayer company agreed to pay for the additional measures.

The transit-stop Bayerwerk was built at a cost of approximately 56 million € and went into service in 1991. It was financed primarily by public entities. The federal government provided much of the funding for the project according to the Municipality Transportation Financing Law. The state of North Rhine – Westphalia contributed 10% of the construction costs in the form of a flat rate for planning measures. Bayer AG financed the aspects of the project that went beyond what was foreseen in the standard version of the plan. This included a roof over the platforms and widening of the street that crosses under the station. This amounted to a 4.5 million € contribution from Bayer AG.

Common aspects of the projects

The most common driving force for private investors to finance stations or to contribute funding was the necessity to improve access to existing stations. In the case of Friedensthal, the project accelerating though private financing was an additional motivation.

For the Deutsche Bahn AG, the interest to participate in public-private partnerships is only partially a matter of financial savings. It is also a matter of improving rider potential (Friedensthal and Ikea), of improving their own image (Hennigsdorf and Ikea), and, sometimes, exclusively a question of political pressure. This attests to the relatively passive role the Deutsche Bahn AG plays in such projects. Although according to various statements by the company's upper management and the leaders of their subsidiaries "DB-Imm" and "Station&Service", it must be assumed that at least the willingness to work together is increasing.

The examples are on the one hand important and instructive, not only for the station-renewal policy of the Deutsche Bahn AG, but also with regard to the situation in the USA and other countries. But each case is very specific to the local situation and hardly allows conclusions for potential strategies and results of Transit Joint Development policy in Germany.

6.8 The transfer of restrained property rights as a means to spur transit oriented urban development and generate ridership-revenue

Despite strongly diverging project scopes, local political situations, socio-economic conditions and legal frames, a comparative summary of the examples quoted above helps to better understand under which conditions real estate related cooperation may lead to transit-oriented partnerships.

The American transit agencies presented in this chapter have a relatively clear transit-oriented goal when they offer available real estate property to the real estate market. The goal is not to maximize profits through the real estate deal as such, but to use their property to increase ridership or to improve system access and thus rider comfort.

This is the case for both: excess property, no longer needed for transit purposes, and transit- relevant real estate which, adjacent to stations, generally serves as park & ride facilities. As opposed to the situation in Germany and other European countries, park & ride and other transit access facilities generally belong to transit agencies and not to local communities.

The decade-long economic boom of the nineties contributed to a heated real estate market in almost every urban area of the United States, which led to a good opportunity for transit agencies to increase revenue with both types of real estate.

Especially in Atlanta and Washington, Park & Ride as well as service and storage buildings were accepted on the market, if the pieces of property offered substantial development potential. This was often the case despite the burden of integrating these infrastructures into the development project.

The repeated presentation of property dominated by such type of technical transit equipment in WMATA's requests for proposals show both: the optimism to find a serious developer despite the difficult technical requirements he will have to face, and the difficulty to develop a site with too many constraints.

This is the reason for FTA's joint development guidelines. These regulations encourage the purchase of additional real estate (with transportation funds) to improve the developability of property adjacent to urban rail stations. Atlanta's MARTA used this possiblity to add parcels to its' park & ride and technical infrastructure sites close to their headquarters at Lindbergh station. This was necessary to substantially improve the development potential of this site.

Although the Lindbergh station project is still in the planning phase, the probability is very high that the costs of the real estate purchase will be far exceeded by the potential gain through lease revenue.

The best example is Washington D.C. In 1995, since the inception of the Transit Joint development program, WMATA has received over $60 million in real estate income and realized more than 1 million new rail trips per year.

Another $88 million in sale and rental revenue over the first ten years are expected from new projects through new development solicitations that the WMATA Board of Directors has approved since 1996. In terms of rental revenue alone, the new projects, combined with the old, are expected to generate the equivalent of $12 to $15 million of income per year. They are also anticipated to add 105,000 new daily riders.

Public/private land development revenue will most certainly pay back the estimated $400 million invested since 1968 in WMATA rail system property acquisition by the national, state and local governments. Of that amount, state and local government provided 20%, or $80 million. By the year 2003,

WMATA's receipts from the public/private land development program will be almost double that amount, a nearly 200% return on investment[16].

The cases of San Diego/CA and Portland/OR (presented in the following chapter) show that these impacts are not limited to heavy rail systems. The relative importance of development (compared with the regional real estate market) at future or current Light Rail stations may even go beyond the development potential of existing heavy rail stations.

So far, the case of commuter rail in the US seems to be a little different. SEPTA in Philadelphia,PA has achieved the best results in gaining private investment for transit purposes. Nevertheless, the impacts seem to be limited to the passenger building, i.e. mostly the commercial parts of these buildings. One reason for this is the very limited real estate property outside of the station building; the other is the fact that in the US, commuter rail serves as a transit collector in a relatively low-density suburban area. Public-private Partnerships at regional rail stations in Germany go beyond the American possiblities. But as already mentioned - the location of the stations and the frequency of the rail service is more comparable with the suburban portions of American heavy and Light Rail systems, and needs thus to be compared with those.

New York's old heavy rail system has very important development potential. Although quantitatively, compared to other Metropolitan Areas, alot of joint development took place during the last decades, relatively few projects have been started lately. Several reasons have led to this situation: the close proximity to existing urban structure creates conflicts for almost any type of project, important development projects require a long preparation period, and very often, public pre-investments are necessary to generate private development.

In the case of either light or heavy rail, transit agencies try to optimize the financial impact and the transit value of partnerships through land-leases. Land sales are rare for US transit agencies. The agency-statutes generally prohibit the sale of excess land. Exceptions are permitted only if the project or parts of the project cannot be financed or developed on a leasing basis. This may be the case for residential projects, in particular, condominiums. The

[16] In the light of these results, it must surprise, that WMATA does not intend any additional real estate purchase.

question as to whether this policy may contribute to a relative limitation of transit joint development in favor of the construction of office, commercial and hotel space and in disfavor of more mixed use developments should be investigated more in depth.

From a neo-institutional perspective, transit joint developments generate contradicting property rights transformations. On the one hand, real estate assets that would stay disclosed under "normal" conditions, are being released and transferred to the private side. On the other hand, this transfer is only happening under fairly restrictive legal conditions, which are supposed to guarantee economic goals of the transit agency, and political goals of the local community (as the prinicipal of the transit agency).

The table below contains a brief comparative summary of property rights attributes, as well as agency, municipal and regional transit policies, project focuses, and their respective financial and transit results. The table shows that while US transit agencies are generally supportive of joint developments[17], the regional policy context is almost hostile to it[18]. In Germany the opposite is the case.

It is surprising to see, that despite the provision of an almost unlimited real estate investment allocation frame on the regional level, investors accept the property rights limitations of transit joint development projects in the US. This acceptance is once again a sign of two tendencies that have been described further in chapter 4: The heated real estate market of the nineties, and the reorientation towards inner-city areas with transit access.

[17] Some seems to have slowed down their activities (e.g. SEPTA)

[18] The „home rule" and the generation of uncoordinated urban development offers throughout the entire region being the most important reason therefor.

Table 6.1: Specific property rights attributions versus financial and transit impact

	Station infrastructure	Commercial space in station	Station-connection	local transport connection	Air rights	Adjacent real estate	Agency's real estate policy	Regional policy	Local zoning policy	Local parking policy	**Financial Impact of private contributions**	**Transit Impact**
Washington D.C - WMATA.							++	--	++	o	+	++
Friendship Heights			x	x	x	x					+	++
Bethesda	x		x	x		x					+	++
Ballston			x	x	x	o					+	o
NoMa	x			x							+	++
Atlanta/GA - MARTA					x		+	-- ++	+	o	+	+
Lindbergh				x		x					o	+
New York City - MTA			x		x		+	-	++	++	o	o
Atlantic Center	x	x	x	x	x	x					+	o
Philadelphia/PA – SEPTA	x	x				x	+-	o	o	o	+	o
L&M Program	x	x				x	+-	o	o	o	+	o
Berlin/Brandenburg - DBAG							-	++	+-	o	o	-
Bernau-Friedensthal	x			x							++	+
Hennigsdorf		x				x					+	+
Rhein/Ruhr - DBAG							o	++	+	+	o	-
IKEA Kaarst	x										+	o
Bayer Leverkusen	x										+	o

7. Transit-oriented Development

Although urban development around transit stations doesn't lead to a direct financial contribution for the Transit Agency (or other infrastructure or planning body) it is "absolutely essential" to the long term viability of the transit investment (SKMG 1996, p. 4). The transit accessible area around the stations is generally far larger than the Transit Company's real estate can reach. Many studies have been undertaken to define the influence zone of transit stations, i.e. the probability that at a certain distance from the station an employee or resident is ready to use transit as a transportation alternative for commuting or other travel purposes. "Walking distance" is the general qualification, that means five to fifteen minutes walking time, depending on the travel purpose, the travel alternatives and the system performance. It is obvious that the attraction is more important at stations of highly performing transit systems. Frequent Rapid Transit service has potentially more impact then Light Rail Service, especially when the Light Rail line is short and/or when the station is less frequented.

A large number of studies have been made to estimate the land value effects of transit access. ANAS and ARMSTRONG (1993) didn't doubt the positive influence of transit, and developed two different mathematical models to estimate the accrued value in the New York Area. The idea was to capture these land value gains to have adjacent landowners co-finance necessary improvement of the city's transit system.

In a "review of the academic and professional literature" WEINSTEIN/CLOVER (1999, pp. 3-10) came to the conclusion that no unanimous opinion about these effects existed. They cite early studies about the BART system (Bay Area Rapid Transit) that concluded that the system contributed to a decrease of inner city land value and an increase in suburban land values. 20 years later however, studies showed, that homes with access to *any* BART-station had a "premium" (Landis et al 1994), which leads to the conclusion, that "there probably is a significant time lag involved in the capitalization of transportation improvements" (Guiliano 1986) (WEINSTEIN/CLOVER 1999, p.5).

According to their finding only in Toronto every study showed a **positive** impact of the Metro-system on the transit corridor's land values. Interestingly Weinstein/Clover's own study about Dallas came to the conclusion that immediately after the opening of the DART-system (Dallas Area Rapid Transit) land values around transit stations increased an average comparative rate of 10%.

This seems also to have been the case for the WMATA-system. In 1981, a U.S. House of Representatives Staff Study, "Metrorail Impacts on Washington Area Land Values," determined that homes within 1,000 feet of a transit station ha[d] a property value premium of $12,300". (LANDIS et al. 1995)

HOEVELER (1997, pp. 4,5) cites a number of studies where land value increases are quantitatively estimated: Robert A Fejarang's 1994 report to the Transportation Research Board found that properties near rail lines have mean sale prices of $102.13 per square foot compared to $71.13 for non-rail properties (a difference of 30.35%). (FEJARANG 1994).

In a 1996 Federal Transit Administration (HLB 1996) study, researchers examined the value that public transit imparts to real estate in a variety of urban settings including San Francisco Bay area communities in proximity to the BART System and neighborhoods in Portland, Oregon in proximity to the MAX System. Hickling Lewis Brod, (HLB 1996, p.15), the consultants who authored the report, found that "BART access is worth $15.78 more every foot closer to the station. This means that an average home in our study area would be worth over $15,000 more if it were 1,000 feet closer to BART than its original location."

They also quote a 1995 study showing that three BART-accessible counties demonstrate a price appreciation for East Bay residential neighborhoods of $1.96 to $2.26 per meter closer to the BART station, or approximately a $70,000 depreciation in property values at 35 km from the station.

HLB researchers for the 1996 FTA study also found that access to highways has an entirely opposite effect: ". . . closeness to highways has a negative effect on housing values within the study area. The regression analysis shows that homes further from a highway interchange are worth $7.94 more on average for every foot further from the freeway interchange [than from their original location]." (HLB 1996, p.15)

The basic assumption here is that urban rail-transit generally can influence urban development (much more than bus service). As a consequence, it is essential for the long-term perspectives of any rail-transit mode that urban development and the densification of transit perceptive uses, occur at transit nodes. Due to different conditions of the transportation market and important differences of the urban form, with a much wider "Urban Field" (GRAVA 1999), the usership rates after a maximization of Urban Development in these areas will probably be higher in Europe then in the US. Genevieve Giuliano quotes a study citing the San Francisco area in which, even under optimal conditions, only 7 to 10 percent can be expected (GUILIANO 1995).

Despite these differences, research findings in America on how to maximize the impact of a transit station on travel behavior may be also applied in Europe. Sam Seskin (together with Robert Cervero, Jeffrey Zupan and others, PARSONS BRINCKERHOFF 1996) summarizes, that "density or compactness of employment and population is the most important factor associated with transit use" (p. 32). As a second priority "within areas served by transit, land-use mix and urban design can encourage transit use, balance directional flows along transit lines, and reduce automobile use". And it is probably true in Europe, as in America, that "above all, those communities with a vision that includes good transit access should adopt regional and local transportation policies that put transit first in order to sustain the positive effects of transit on land-use" (p.32).

In order to set up a policy to promote real estate investment at transit stations a bundle of measures through the transit agency as well as the local jurisdiction, the state and the federal government can be set up.

Due to the lack of data it is difficult to evaluate the impact of the measures taken on the actual development. It is not possible to systematically compare the different cases and to draw empirical conclusions about the relevance of specific factors to attract transit friendly developments. It is also difficult to evaluate quantitatively the development risk of transit projects (also because many of these projects have only recently been completed or are still in the planning phase).

Therefore, the presentation will focus on a relatively broad description of the following aspects: the political context of these developments, the planning and financing tools applied on the local level, the financial dimension of the project, its financial impact for the transit agency or the community, the development type, the regional development impact, and the number of additional passengers through the project.

Five of the seven researched metropolitan areas will be presented in this chapter. The case study of the Orenco Station development will describe more in detail the aspects mentioned above.

7.1 Administrative and Regulatory Framework of Transit-oriented Development

Statutory Legislation of Transit Agencies and TOD – Organization

Many transit and other single-purpose agencies face a question of "institutional legitimacy" when they attempt to conduct activities that are not explicitly a part of their mission. Some agencies have been resolving this problem, e.g. the Los Angeles Metropolitan Transit Authority (LA-MTA) and the Washington Metropolitan Area Transportation Agency (WMATA). They both have a development mission within their respective agencies. According to the above mentioned SKMG-study for BART, the Californian "Transit Village Planning Act" of 1994 is a law that explicitly permits and promotes "joint powers agreements between transit agencies and local governments or redevelopment agencies to pursue more transit supportive development within Transit Area Development Zones (TADZ), defined as within one-third of a mile of any existing or planned transit station" (p.7).

In other cases, the agency or the community can create an attached or independent public/private development entity. This may be the case at specific stations or transit-oriented inner-city-corridors such as the Union Station Redevelopment Corporation in Washington D.C. or the Pennsylvania Station Redevelopment Corporation in New York City or the Pennsylvania Avenue Development Corporation (PADC) in Washington D.C. It can also cover inner city districts as in San Diego (City Centre Development Corporation) or larger areas, with the general target to promote transit friendly urban development, such as the Philadelphia Industrial Development Corporation (PIDC) or the New York State Urban Development Corporation.

Regional and Local Planning Incentives

Transit-friendly incentives can be dispensed on the federal-, state-, metropolitan- as well as the municipal level. More and more US-State-governments, aware of the sprawl-related environmental and congestion-problems, set up policies to get control of further urban and regional development.

State-policies to enhance the conditions for transit-oriented developments have been described in the case studies of Atlanta/GA and Portland/OR.

The geographical pattern of local transportation and land-use policy is very fragmented. In order to enhance its coherence on the regional level, **Metropolitan Planning Organizations** were created all over the US. Their role, geographical context and names differ between regions. Their tasks include gathering information about the regional transportation situation, drafting regional transportation plans, and contributing to a better coordination of publicly funded transport investments on the regional level. Federally funded projects must have the approval of the MPO of the specific area. Therefore, the MPO board of directors generally consists of authorized members of the central city - government and the government of the surrounding counties. As general political agreements are made, the MPO, and its plans and project-statements, has a consulting role. In some cases its role may be more active through a budget that permits the funding of (smaller) projects on the local level.

The following description of the San Francisco Bay Area's Metropolitan Transportation Commission (MTC), a very active institution, may highlight the variety of actions that an MPO can undertake:

San Francisco Bay Area's Metropolitan Transportation Commission (MTC) comprises the entire regional area, including the city of San Francisco and nine surrounding counties. The following description underlines the commission's active role as a promoter of a transportation change in the Bay area. MTC was created by the state Legislature in 1970 (California Government Code § 66500 et seq.), MTC functions as both the regional transportation-planning agency – a state designation – and for federal purposes, as the region's metropolitan planning organization (MPO). As such, it is responsible for the Regional Transportation Plan, a comprehensive blueprint for the development of mass transit, highway, airport, seaport, railroad, bicycle and pedestrian facilities. The Commission also screens requests from local agencies for state and federal grants for transportation projects to determine their compatibility with the plan.

A 19-member panel gives MTC policy direction. Fourteen members are appointed directly by local elected officials. Two members represent regional agencies – the Association of Bay Area Governments and the Bay Conservation and Development Commission. In addition, three non-voting members have been appointed to represent federal and state transportation agencies, and the federal housing department.

The region MTC serves has eight primary public transit systems as well as numerous other local transit operators, which together carry an average weekday ridership of about 1.5 million. The combined annual operating budget of the transit agencies is over $1 billion, placing this region among the top transit operating budgets in the nation. In addition, there are numerous specialized services for elderly and disabled travelers, some 18,000 miles of local streets and roads, 1,400 miles of highways, six public ports and five commercial airports. The Bay Region embraces nine counties and 100 cities. Over 6 million people reside within its 7,000 square miles.

Over the years, state and federal laws have given MTC an increasingly important role in financing Bay Area transportation improvements. Most significant at the federal level was the 1991 Intermodal Surface Transportation Equity Act (ISTEA), which increased the powers of MPOs like MTC to determine the mix of transportation projects best suited to meet their region's needs. To foster consensus in the implementation of ISTEA and develop agreed-upon spending priorities, MTC created The Bay Area Partnership - a consortium of local, state and federal agencies. With the cooperation of these partners, MTC administers federal funds - such as those from the Surface Transportation Program and Congestion Mitigation and Air Quality Improvement program laid out in ISTEA – to combat congestion and air pollution in the Bay Area. MTC administers state monies, too, including those provided by the Transportation Development Act. Legislation passed in 1997 gives MTC and other regional transportation planning agencies increased decision-making authority over the selection of projects and allocation of funds for the State Transportation Improvement Program (STIP). Also in 1997, the state Legislature transferred the responsibility for administering the base $1 toll from the Bay Area's seven state-owned toll bridges to MTC (from the California Department of Transportation). A new entity, the Bay Area Toll Authority (BATA) was created for this purpose.

- MTC oversees the efficiency and effectiveness of the region's transportation system. It monitors transit operators' budgets, conducts performance audits, and adopts a yearly productivity/transit coordination improvement program.
- To win state and federal support for regional priorities, whether in terms of funding or policy changes that may affect the Bay Area, MTC devotes considerable energy to advocacy efforts on both the state and federal level.
- In recent years, MTC also has added to its activities some "hands-on" projects to promote the efficient monitoring and operation of the regional road transportation network. MTC set up projects to help Bay Area cities and counties to better maintain their local streets and roads, to install and operate call boxes along Bay Area freeways and to set up and apply ITS deployment plans to provide the public with real-time transit, traffic and ridesharing data.
- A historic agreement forged by MTC with local officials, as well as state and federal legislators in the late 1980s set forth a $3.5 billion program to extend a total of six rail lines in the Bay Area. This added 40 miles to the region's rail-transit network. The extensions include four Bay Area Rapid Transit projects, a Santa Clara Valley Transportation Authority Light Rail line, and an extension of the Caltrain commuter rail system into downtown San Francisco.
- MTC has created a regional program to enhance "livability" on the local level, so called "Transportation for Livable Communities (TLC)". On the basis of federal money, it covers the funding of small-scale transportation investments, such as streetscape improvements, and transit-, pedestrian- and bicycle-oriented developments. During the two years of 1998 and 1999, almost 10 million dollars for 35 projects, covering every county of the region have been approved. MTC expects a growing number of grant requests as a consequence of previously successful examples. The important role of this program is to nurture a desire for a transit friendly, more community-oriented lifestyle.

The Bay Area Transportation Commission is one of the most active and innovative Metropolitan Planning Organizations of the country. It is one of the leading MPO's to promote the concept of livable communities. It has started and coordinated many projects to enhance the regional coherence of mobility networks.

And yet it has remained an institution with a consulting role, but with no executive powers and very little power to prevent local transportation or development projects that are not coherent with its envisioned development strategy. As no zoning regulation needs to be approved by an MPO, its specific influence on decisions of real estate investors is very low. (The only exception is Oregon, where regional councils of government (incorporating also the competence of MPOs) have a decisive role on land-use planning. This example is described below for Portland, OR).

Although MPO's generally have an important knowledge and expertise on the regional level, these assets can only be useful if they succeed to convince local and state decision-makers. As long as developers and local politicians do not look for new forms of developments with a broader choice of accessibility modes, this is a very unfavorable framework for transit-oriented development. If in the chain of decision-makers including investors, local and state administrations and politicians one is reluctant to innovative approaches, the chances of pushing and realizing a transit-oriented development project is very low.

And yet – the rapidly growing number of transit-oriented development-examples shows that the efforts of transit promoters have rendered some results. The rationale behind the cases differs from case to case. A summary and evaluation what the decisive factors are will be given in the summary after the following case descriptions.

7.2 Transit-oriented development in New Jersey

During the last few years, strongly pushed by Shirley De Libero's leadership, NJ Transit undertook many efforts to improve their stations and to create a better link with the surrounding neighborhoods.

The agency started this work with station problems very similar to the problems found at stations of regional railway networks in Europe: vandalism, poor maintenance, deterioration, lack of site management, lack of passenger-oriented amenities, safety problems and insufficient investment and operation funds. Three different types of strategies were selected: community -oriented station renewal, transit-oriented real estate policy and (as a new approach) "transit villages".

In 1991, the goals of a station renewal program were developed through discussions between NJ Transit and Project for Public Spaces(PPS), a New York based non-profit organization, specialized in community-oriented design of public facilities. "The goals of the program were to improve the condition, appearance, uses, and, most important, the management of its commuter rail stations to serve passengers more effectively, promote public transit, and act as a catalyst for economic development in the communities in which they are located" (PPS 1997, p. 79).

Five stations were selected, representing the range of suburban and rural stations and station area situations: Bradley Beach, Maplewood, Netherwood (in Plainfield), Rahway and Woodbridge.

Rick Mariani, the responsible manager at NJ Transit, says the program is an initiative in which individual communities share responsibility for designing and implementing station improvements as well as for ongoing maintenance and management of stations and adjacent public spaces. Moreover, activities such as supplementing existing security services, retail leasing, and coordination of customer and community information is provided by communities in partnership with NJ Transit... In this approach, communities have a major impact on the quality of the station environment. The measures undertaken are not necessarily heavy investments but rather activities that could increase local identification and thus, on the long term, private capital investment. Examples are: Working with the community to define issues and potential solutions and implement changes at the Woodbridge and Netherwood commuter rail stations, providing maintenance for the station building (excluding major capital improvements), painted murals in passenger tunnels and buildings by local artists or students, just to name a few.

At the end, the stations were completely reshaped with many new services offered, the most inspiring being the so called "concierge" service at the Maplewood station, offering any kind of errands realized during the absence of the commuter.

The program has now been extended to 50 additional stations in New Jersey. Funding for the necessary improvements comes from various sources, most of them public: For example, the 2.1 million dollar Netherwood Station Renewal Project is a combination of grants to NJ Transit from the FTA, the State Transportation Trust Fund, grants of the city of Plainfield from the federal

Highway Administration, the State of New Jersey, the Urban Enterprise Zone Authority and private developers (for the station tenant).

In many other cases, NJ Transit property is used to promote Transit-oriented Development, e.g. the "Transit Village" – program, called FIRST (Future Investments and Reinvestment in State Transportation), set up by the State of New Jersey together with NJ Transit.

Five stations have been selected, in which NJ Transit owns key properties adjacent to the train stations and where the communities are interested promoting urban developments on these properties and additional developable land at the stations. The idea is to show how the Park & Ride orientation that commuter rail stations generally have can be turned into a community center function, comparable to developments that are thought to happen only at urban heavy or Light Rail stations. The station area of South Amboy will become a new town on the New Jersey Coastline, Morristown will permit the "urbanization" of a Park & Ride facility and South Orange could become a residential area, closely linked with the train with the city of Newark. The station of Rutherford will be the extension of the main street business area, very likely to attract private money and in Pleasantville the community wants to promote residential development at the local bus terminal.

A major TOD project will be the Secaucus Transfer. This new station is now under construction and will serve as an interchange for passengers from northern counties into Manhattan, a hub for 11 of NJ Transit's 12 northern New Jersey lines. The construction costs of the station itself will be 150 million dollars, the entire project (including the track work portion) is worth about 450 million dollars. 12,000 passengers are expected to transfer at this station. 4,000 more are expected if the station becomes a "destination". This will be the case when the office development, planned by the owners of the adjacent properties, will be realized. The project includes 5 million square feet of office space in its final state. As a first step an office tower on top of the new station is planned-- an example of the "overbuilt" possibilities of the station. The 10% surplus costs will have to be paid by the future developers (Allied Junction Corporation).

In some relatively rare cases, transit-oriented development is just market driven. The most prominent example is the development around Newark Penn Station, the largest station of the NJ Transit system. Over a period of 15 years, the adjacent private property was developed as a huge office and shopping mall with 4 million square feet of office space. The various Plaza buildings are linked with skywalks and thus isolated from a less prestigious urban environment. Despite this isolation the office complex turned out to be the starter investment for a major change of Newark's Downtown district, where an image of an unsafe area has been replaced with an image of development opportunities.

Outlook

The state of New Jersey and NJ Transit are trying very strongly to use stations and station areas as assets to attract developers. Station upgrading and major new rail-line-investments are supposed to contribute to a policy of creating an image of progress and modern management.

However until now, only few innovative planning and financing tools have been applied to maximize the effect of new railway investments on the urban development patterns of the benefiting communities.

7.3 Private initiative and Transit-oriented Projects in Dallas, TX

Transit-oriented Development Tools

Planning tools to attract developers to transit stations exist also in Dallas, although they have not been applied very aggressively. They concentrate on those tax-abatement instruments that are applied in the general context of urban renewal. Susan MEAD (1999) describes the instruments to be applied in Texas, although she does not give examples where they have been applied. But independently of how often, and under which conditions they were applied, the toolbox is very inspiring and merits thus to be described more in detail:

Texas Urban Renewal Statute

In 1957, the Texas Legislature enacted the Texas Urban Renewal Law. In order to utilize the authority granted, a municipality must hold an election authorizing the establishment of an urban renewal authority. Since establishment of the urban renewal authority is difficult to achieve, most Texas cities have used other statutes to improve blighted areas.

The original Texas Urban Renewal Statute (V.A.C.S. art. 12691-3), was adopted in 1957, and was used sparingly, if at all. The author is aware of only one Texas city, San Antonio, which used the statute to call an election and set up an urban renewal authority. In 1987, the Texas Legislature repealed the previous legislation and replaced it with the Texas Urban Renewal Law, Chapter 374 of the Texas Local Government Code. However, the more recent statute continues to have the burdensome requirement of calling a local election before an urban renewal authority can be instituted.

Texas Enterprise Zone Act

The Texas Legislature enacted the Texas Enterprise Zone Act (the "Enterprise Zone Act") in 1983' as a means of assisting communities to create the proper economic and social environment to induce the investment of private resources for productive business enterprises located in severely distressed areas.

The Enterprise Zone Act is specifically aimed at severely depressed or impoverished areas, whether urban or rural in character. The criteria described under the Enterprise Zone Act are similar to the criteria provided in the Texas Tax Abatement Act.

However, the criteria for creation of an Enterprise Zone are more specific, and it must be proven upon written application to the Texas Department of Commerce, that the particular area meets the criteria set forth in the statute. One of the stated purposes for the Enterprise Zone Act is removal of unnecessary governmental regulatory barriers to economic growth, while the required criteria, and the procedure involved in petitioning the Texas Department of Commerce, seem to inject a new level of state governmental involvement in these areas. However, supporting this contradiction are some far-reaching incentives made available by the designation.

Upon determining that the area meets the criteria of the statute, the Texas Department of Commerce "shall negotiate with the nominating body for a designation agreement." Specific time limits apply to the negotiation of such an agreement, and if the time limits are not met, the application is considered to be denied.

Tax Increment Financing Zones, as described in chapter 3.

Public Improvement District Assessment Act

Public Improvement Districts in Texas have been utilized since the passage of the state enabling legislation, known as the Public Improvement District Assessment Act (as amended, the "PID Act"), (V.A.C.S. Article 1269j-4.12 in 1977), as amended in 1983, 1987 and 1989. Similar to the special assessment district, which is widely employed in many states, the Texas equivalent was named a Public Improvement District (PID).

Illustration 7.1: Cover of a DART magazine

As the name reflects, the original statute restricted the use of funds to capital improvements. A 1983 amendment, however, permitted among other items, the funding of special supplemental services for improvement and promotion of an area (such as advertising, health, safety, and cultural enhancement) through a PID.

The PID performs the same functions as a special assessment district, and for purpose of this analysis, the two terms are synonymous. The PID is a funding mechanism created for the sole purpose of financing improvements and/or services that will benefit a defined, but limited, geographic area of a municipality and/or a municipality's extraterritorial jurisdiction (ETJ). A special assessment is levied against a piece of property because that property has theoretically reaped a benefit from some public improvement initiated by the local government. Typically, the improvements are financed by the sale of bonds, which are secured by the assessments.

The supporting theory behind assessments is that parcels that are similarly benefited should be similarly burdened. The dollar amount of an assessment is therefore apportioned according to the degree of benefit received, which may result in the assessment varying in proportion to the proximity of the assessed parcels to the improvements. An assessment formula may be based on a variety of measures, including square footage of land and/or building, front footage and assessed value of property, so long as the formula imposes equal shares of the cost on property similarly benefited.

A PID serves two very important functions. First, the assessment levied on property within a PID is designed to reimburse a municipality for a public improvement by placing the cost of improvements upon the benefiting property owners, thereby establishing one -basic form of public/private partnership in which both sectors pair their resources for the benefit of all within the PID. Second, a PID allows a municipality to fund much of the cost of public improvements without increasing the burden on its general revenue funding. As fiscal constraints become tighter, this is an increasingly important aspect of special assessment, as it allows the provision of public improvements that otherwise may not be economically feasible.

The Texas PID Act itself enables the innovative use of special assessment funds. The improvements or services, which may be funded through a PID, include a specific list, set forth in the PID Act, as well as authorization for other improvements similar to the listed projects. The improvements and services listed are not typically available through the normal range of city services funded by the general revenue sources. For example, the statute specifically authorizes the use of funds for such projects as landscaping, "distinctive" street lighting, pedestrian malls, fountains and parks, and off-street parking facilities.

It should be remembered, however, that the PID assessment is an additional tax, so the tool is not viable as an incentive for encouraging development that otherwise would not occur. For example, an additional tax on the land-used for housing in or around a downtown would only serve as a disincentive when urban land prices already make housing economically difficult to achieve. There is disagreement as to whether a PID ordinance can exempt a certain type of property or use, housing for example, from the special assessment.

Texas Tax Abatement Act

Tax abatement is yet another public incentive for development. Like TIF, it is based on the premise that a development or redevelopment project in a particular area will result in both increased real or personal business property values and hence, an increased tax base. However, unlike TIF, the Municipal and County Tax Abatement statutes do not authorize a recapture of the tax increase, but rather, a partial or total exemption from increased taxation for a period not to exceed 10 years. This is provided that the owner agrees to make specific improvements or repairs to the property. Regardless, only the incremental tax is available for abatement. It should be noted that tax abatement, by its very nature, is not used to build public improvements, such as streets and sidewalks, but is intended to encourage specific private improvements such as downtown housing.

An equivalency between the relationship of the dollar value of the abated taxes versus the dollar value of the improvements is not a statutory requirement, although it is a point of negotiation during the agreement deliberations. Unfortunately, this tool may have been overused as adjacent municipalities use incentive packages as they bid against one another for corporations relocating.

Perhaps tax abatement is best used as a method of implementing public policy, i.e., filling part of the "gap financing" needed to entice an owner to risk using this property for the development of a needed and desired use, for example, downtown housing or factories in a high unemployment area. In contrast to the TIF, the payment for the specific improvements by the property owner would occur initially, but the property taxes may be abated for a number of years after the improvement is installed. In an abatement program, specific improvements by the property owner are likely to be constructed on private rather than public property. The municipality may, however, find the need to agree to the upgrading of certain public infrastructure as part of the abatement agreement.

Texas Local Government Code

A more recent, yet related, law is designed to provide flexibility to municipalities in funding economic development programs. Chapter 380 of the Local Government Code; "Miscellaneous Provisions Relating to Municipal Planning and Development", provides that a municipality may administer programs and loan or grant public money to "promote state or local economic development and to stimulate business and commercial activity in the municipality. Chapter 380 thus implicitly asserts that an overall public purpose exists in promoting private commercial enterprise spur the economy. Although Chapter 380 does not refer to condemnation powers, it does accord tremendous discretion to a municipality to fund any type of private project that promotes economic development.

Station-Area Development Activities

Until the system was in operation, DART officials have found little interest among developers in considering joint development or station interfaces. An early experience with joint development has yet to succeed. The City Place project, including twin office towers adjacent to a proposed DART station halted with one tower built when the market soured, and the second tower was never undertaken. Neither was the developer's contribution to station construction, which was nullified by a negotiated agreement. As a result, the opening of the partially completed station will be delayed pending further negotiations with the developer. However, since the opening of the initial segment, restaurant business in the West End entertainment district has improved by 10 to 20 percent.

The West End, downtown Dallas' first entertainment district, was one of the first downtown locations to experience residential development. In 1996, developers converted a 6-story former saddle factory, built in 1901, at Elm and Houston into 29 loft condominiums, from 700 to nearly 2,600 square feet. "Our location is great, with the West End and DART just outside the front door," says listing agent Paige Compton of Coldwell Banker. "What more could you want?"

DART recently published on its home page (www.dart.org) the following Light Rail related developments:

"Union Station/West End/Akard/Pearl: Two weeks after the trains began running in 1996, most West End restaurants reported a boost in their lunchtime business - some by as much as 40 percent. At Sonny Bryan's Smokehouse, meat consumption doubled because of the crowds. Lunch sales at Hofbräu Steaks increased about $1,000 a day, said Greg Schooley, the restaurant's general manager. "The rail line has made it possible for people to get away without parking or walking in the hot sun," said Mr. Schooley. "It's been exceptionally wonderful."

Adam's Mark Hotel: The HBE Corp. invested more than $150 million converting the former Southland Center into a new Adam's Mark Hotel, one of the most costly real estate projects in the central business district. The hotel opened in fall 1998. But the St. Louis hotel company would not have invested a dime on the deal if the DART rail line didn't run by the new hotel's front door, officials say. "DART is the reason we did the project," said Stan Soroka, general manager of the 1,900-room hotel, the largest in Texas. "That Light Rail line is our life blood – our connection to the Convention Center. It also gives our guests direct access to the West End and North Park."

Bryan Tower: The Spire Realty Group is nearly finished with a $30 million renovation of the 40-story Bryan Tower, located on the DART rail line near the Pearl Station. A key architectural feature was opening the ground floor to the street by replacing brick and concrete walls with glass.

Office Leasing: In mid-1999, advertising giant Omnicom Group decided to leave the Crescent complex on Cedar Springs and move downtown, taking its 1,000 employees to 200,000 square feet of space in Harwood Center. The company had planned to move to a large suburban campus, but changed its mind due to the attractiveness of downtown, especially the urban environment with good public transit. Blockbuster Entertainment, one of the area's largest relocations, cites DART as major factor in establishing its headquarters in the central business district, across from DART's Akard Rail Station for its 1,000 employees.

Other Downtown Development: Within two blocks of the rail line, developers have renovated the historic Magnolia, Wilson, Santa Fe II and Kirby buildings for hotel, restaurant and residential uses. Also: Four historic buildings will be transformed into a complex of 120.000 square feet offices and 40 condominiums. On seven acres of open space a new mix-used development called "West-village" is planned as a $ 50 million project with 160 apartments, 45 retail shops and restaurants and an art movie theater.

Outside the Downtown area, DART publishes the following developments:

"South of Downtown:

Cedars Station: Matthews Southwest is converting a former Sears warehouse, built in 1913, on South Lamar into 450 loft apartments, scheduled to open in summer, 2000. Southside on Lamar, a 30-acre project located one block from the Cedars Station, will also include retail, commercial and restaurant space.

Illustration 7.2: Transit accessible area at Cedars Station

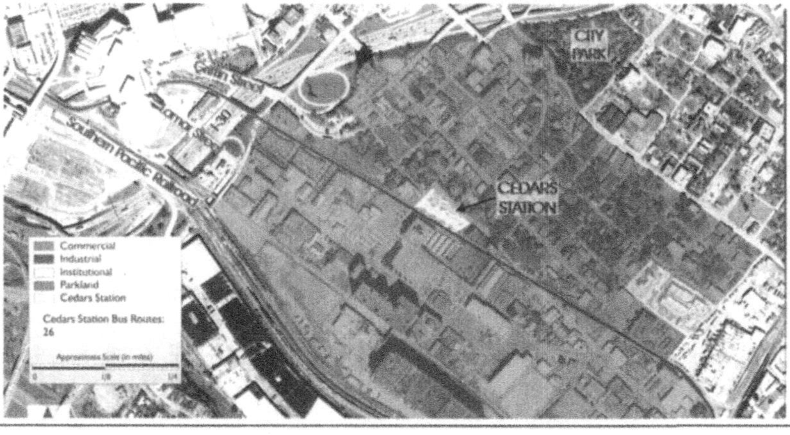

The developer is investing $65 million in the 10-story warehouse, and plans to put $35 million more into adjacent buildings to create an arts and entertainment district. Gilley's Dallas will be opening a new country western bar nearby. From that transit station across the street, we have access to downtown, to the medical center and all the way up to North Dallas," said Pete Coughlin of Matthews Southwest. "The critical factors in the decision to purchase that property were DART's Cedars Station and the proximity to the Central Business District and Convention Center."

A 165,000-square-foot Gilley's nightclub in the neighborhood is under construction as part of the project, and Matthews Southwest donated land across the street from the Sears building for a new police headquarters.

Illustration 7.3: Old Sears Warehouse at Cedars Stastion

Illinois station: DART received a $26 million federal grant to renovate a historic trolley car storage building to be used as a station and community retail center. The 30,000-sq-ft station will include a transit museum and police office and over 20,000 sq ft of retail space. DART selected the developer and renovations were scheduled to begin in 1996.

Kiest Boulevard station: DART used part of its federal grant to pay 70 percent of the cost of a 275-space parking facility that will he shared with an adjacent shopping center. The facility and station were scheduled to open in late 1996.

New banking and retail establishments are cropping up around DART rail construction along Lancaster Avenue. New businesses include Chemical Bank, Bank of America, Fiesta Mart, Minyard Food Stores, Walgreen drug store and Weiner's department store.

AHC: Affordable Housing Corporation is proposing a 160-acre senior housing and single-family development close to Dallas Southwest Medical Center, near DART's Kiest Station. "There's a great demand for this type of housing that's near the hospital, shopping and has DART access," says AHC's Brian Potashnik.

North of Downtown and "Telecom Corridor"

Illustration 7.4: DART system extension, North Central Corridor

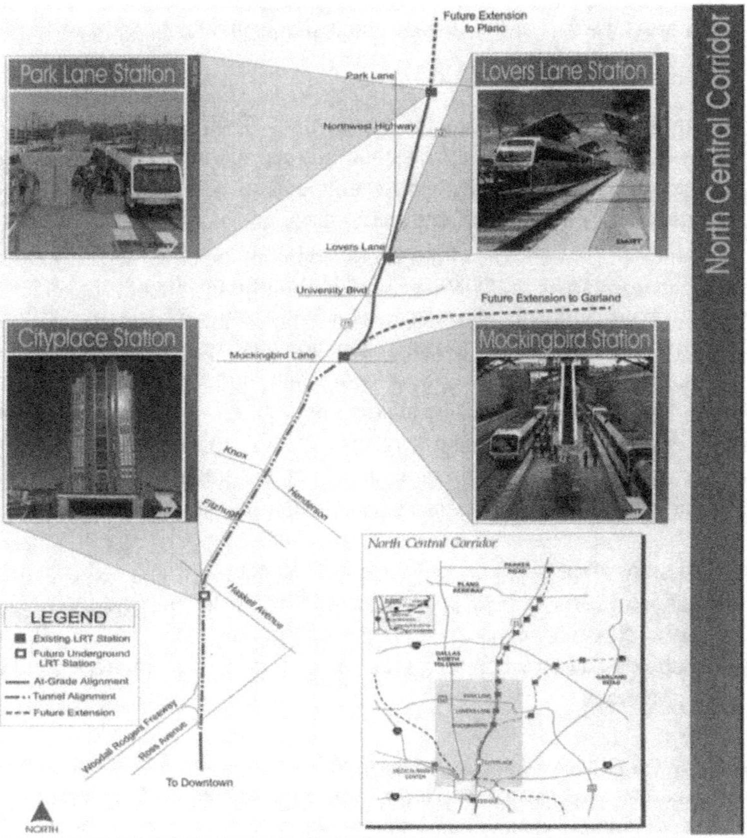

Cityplace Station: DART will complete an underground station below the Cityplace office tower at North Central and Haskell in late 2000. Cityplace

Company developers are planning 230 adjoining apartments, a 300-room hotel and a 43-story office tower in the area, and Cityplace Company's Neal Sleeper says "DART is a very key factor in all that development. We think DART is going to be a tremendous catalyst." Across the expressway from Cityplace, Urban Partners and Phoenix Property Co. are developing the $50-million West Village, 7.5 acres with six buildings to house townhouse lofts, retail, and a theater. The project will benefit from an entrance to DART's Cityplace Station on the west side of the expressway, which will also be served by the McKinney Avenue Trolley. Nearby, McCaslin Development is building the $23-million Quarters at Cityplace, a 244-unit luxury apartment complex. Developers say they'll market the fact that the DART station is within walking distance of their project.

Mockingbird Station: Across the tracks from DART's Mockingbird Station, developer Ken Hughes' UC URBAN and a group of investors are renovating a former Southwestern Bell telephone warehouse and office tower that fronts on Mockingbird Lane and North Central Expressway. On the 10-acre site adjacent to Mockingbird Station, UC Urban's development includes adding four stories to the old warehouse to make a 200-unit apartment project, building a new 250-room hotel, creating new office, retail and restaurant space, and building an eight-screen art movie theater. The complex will be connected to the below-grade DART station with a pedestrian bridge. East of the station, Phoenix Property Company is building a 449-unit apartment community on the old Dr Pepper plant site. "The proximity of the DART station and growing ridership made the Mockingbird Station project attractive and doable – and we're not doing it half-way," says Ken Hughes, president of UC Urban.

An eight-story office complex, 6060 Central, is located within walking distance of Mockingbird Station. The property is connected to the Radisson Hotel. A multi-million-dollar renovation features an updated exterior and improved interior lobbies and common areas providing more convenient access between the two properties.

Park Lane: On Park Lane just west of the DART stop, a Canadian investment group has acquired two of the North Park East building and is studying plans for more. "They've made a major play at two stops, and the rail head was the impetus for that," said real estate broker Jerry Fults. "These people are from an area where mass transit is a way of life and it is a real important issue for them."

Illustration 7.5: Development at Mockingbird Station – rehabilitation and new buildings

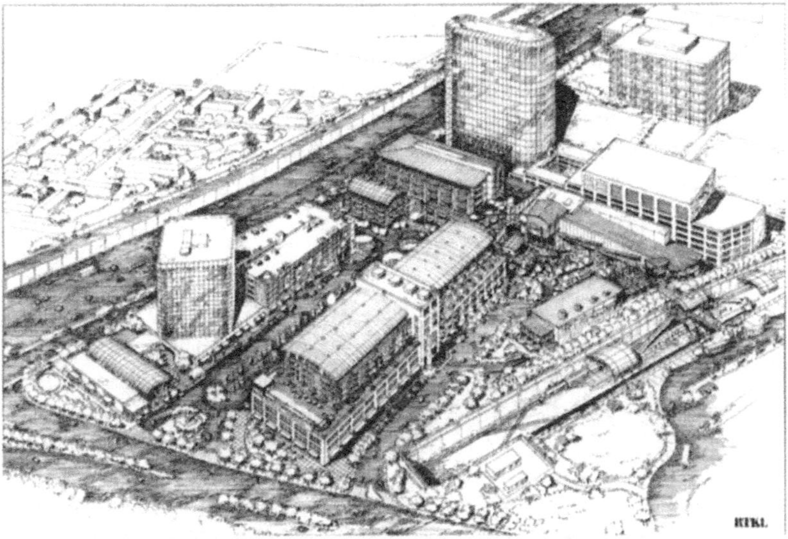

Garland: At the future extension to Rowlett, plans are being developed by the City of Garland to lay the groundwork for new transit-oriented development in downtown Garland around the downtown Garland rail station and at the Forest/Jupiter Station opening in 2002.

Telecom Corridor: DART, private developers and the City of Richardson are participating in the Galatyn Park project – an expansion of the Telecom Corridor that could rival downtown Dallas in employment, and add another transit mall to the region. Jobs in the Telecom Corridor will grow from 70,000 to nearly 127,000 by 2010, according to the North Central Texas Council of Governments.

Two examples of station area plans on this corridor are:

Galatyn Park Station: When this Richardson Light Rail station opens near North Central Expressway and the new George Bush Turnpike in 2002, riders can step off the train and into the 25-acre Urban Center of Galatyn Park, a project developed in conjunction with Hunt Petroleum Corporation, the City of Richardson and DART, featuring a central plaza, a 330-room hotel and an auditorium/meeting facility all clustered around the station. The station and plaza form the center of the larger Galatyn Park, a 500-acre mixed-use development in Richardson's Telecom Corridor. Nortel Networks is building new offices on a 50-acre tract, and walking trails and roads will allow easy foot and car access from retail, restaurants and upscale housing to be built at the edge of the business development. (Station has been opened on schedule in 2002, see URL: www.dart.org: InMotion, Summer 2002: "7 Brand New Light Rail Stations", including New Park Lane Station, Walnut Hill Station, Forest Lane Station, LBJ Central Station, Spring Valley Station, Arapho Center Station and Galatyn Park)

Illustration 7.6:
Amicus Partners at Plano's future development site

Plano's 15th Street Station: Plano Transit Village, a $16 million development of Amicus Partners in collaboration with the City of Plano and DART, is a 3.5-acre development of new buildings adjacent to Plano's Historic downtown, facing the planned DART Station. It opens on 15th Street near North Central Expressway in 2003. New buildings designed to match the historic character of the surrounding 19th century architecture will include 246 upscale apartments, with a city conference center and small retail shops on the ground floor. Construction begins in spring 2000.

"The future DART station gave us the impetus to launch the Plano Transit Village project. We have seen great interest in the rebirth and rediscovery of older neighborhoods in our inner cities and suburban cities, and the need to create more livable, compact communities. DART and the City of Plano have given us an extraordinary opportunity to add to and enhance an existing small Texas downtown — and working together has definitely enhanced the whole development," says Amicus Partners President Robert Shaw.

7.4 Light Rail generates privately co-financed development projects in San Diego/CA

San Diego's transit-oriented development has been relatively well investigated. The following presentation is based on reports, mainly by Bob Dunphy (ULI), Robert Cervero (Berkeley) and Nancy Bragado (MTDB) (see bibliography in chapter 9.2).

MTDB has developed a very active joint development strategy. According to Cervero (1992) this policy saved "an estimated $8 million in construction costs" up until 1990. The policy to locate stations at sites where private investment is already scheduled has also been applied to areas where MTDB did not own land. The agency and many other regional players work together to increase the land development impact of the trolley lines.

Policy Framework

The city and regional planning agencies and the transit agencies in San Diego County have taken impressive steps to establish a policy framework for transit-focused development. The San Diego Association of Governments (SANDAG), consisting of all local governments in San Diego County, is both the regional planning agency and the metropolitan planning organization for the region. Its regional growth strategy, found in its 1993 Blueprint for the San Diego Region espouses changes in land-use patterns to result in better use of transit and increasing development intensities within walking distance of transit stations and major bus routes.

SANDAG's 1995 Land-use Distribution Element of the Regional Growth Management Strategy incorporates land-use policies calling for higher-density, mixed-use development in transit access areas and for local governments' adoption of design guidelines and consideration of local zoning and subdivision revisions that would encourage such development. SANDAG also commissioned plans for five station areas to demonstrate the physical feasibility of implementing the station-area development policies. A major outreach program is now underway.

BRAGADO (1999) summarizes the major Station Area Development policy-elements and tools as follows:

MTDB Policies

There are several policies, publications, and programs that together form the foundation of MTDB's TOD program. These include:

TOD-Guidelines which were published in 1993 under the title: Designing For Transit – A Manual for Integrating Public Transportation and Land Development in the San Diego Metropolitan Area.' This document contains technical design standards for bus and Light Rail-transit, and summarizes basic transit-oriented land development policies.

A video, called *"Cities in the Balance",* produced by MTDB for the Federal Transit Administration (FTA), illustrates the relationship between transit and land-use, and ways to make transit an attractive alternative to the automobile. The *MTDB Board Policy (No. 19)* defines joint development, states goals that joint development projects are to achieve, and establishes guidelines and procedures for bringing a project to fruition.

An *agreement of MTDB with the City of San Diego* that a City of San Diego senior planner works full time at MTDB as an agency liaison.

Another way MTDB works to encourage and support good projects is to offer the political support of the agency early in the planning stages. This is possible as the MTDB Board of Directors consists of 15 elected officials from throughout the region. An early show of support from this Board can be a powerful tool for smoothing the path to entitlements.

City of San Diego Policies

The City of San Diego has been a willing partner in supporting transit and transit-oriented development. Over the years, the City has initiated programs and adopted several policies and ordinances that have enabled MTDB to benefit from agreements with private developers. City of San Diego documents include:

The *Council Policy 600-34* about transit planning and development: This policy is intended to support expansion of the transit system. It identifies implement-tation measures to achieve this, including direction to City staff that transit is to be regarded as an integral component of all major planning studies and programs, and reservations and/or dedications of right-of-way (ROW) are to be sought in conjunction with development permit application review.

The *Council Policy 600-39* concerning "Transit-Oriented Development (TOD) Design Guidelines": The TOD Guidelines and associated Council Policy adopted in 1992 provide guidance on how to achieve transit-supportive planning and design at both a policy and project level.

Discretionary Project Review: A copy of all site plans that require a discretionary permit from the City of San Diego is forwarded to MTDB for review. This enables MTDB to request right-of-way dedications for transit facilities and to influence the design of projects.

Zoning Code Amendments: Transit and pedestrian-friendly zoning standards have been adopted that will strengthen the ability to implement transit-oriented developments and create more pedestrian-friendly neighborhoods code. These amendments were part of a comprehensive zoning code update.

Design Manual: A 1997 update to the City of San Diego's Street Design Manual has had mixed results. The City Council is currently considering amendments to the manual to narrow street widths among other changes.

In addition, various transit-supportive community plans have been adopted for specific communities within the City. A key barrier to implementing TODs is the lack of infrastructure in urban and some older suburban neighborhoods. While these neighborhoods are well served by transit, they lack the schools, parks, and libraries needed to support increases in population. Traffic congestion is another major concern of existing residents. Despite the regional benefits of building TODS, environmental impact reports and neighborhood concerns are typically focused on direct, local intersection impacts.

Regional Initiatives

At a regional level, a Regional Growth Management Strategy developed by the region's cities and county has been approved by SANDAG. This strategy calls for increased development in 'Transit Focus Areas' and decreased intensities in areas not served by transit. The distribution of density is a key factor in increasing the efficiency of the transit system. While multiple family units have long constituted a high proportion (about 37 percent) of the region's housing stock, land-use patterns have typically not created walkable activity centers.

SANDAG has undertaken several important tasks toward implementation of the growth strategy including: producing a 2020 region wide growth forecast, continuing public outreach efforts, providing limited funding for TOD planning, and promoting local government fiscal reform. The growth forecast will be used to evaluate the long-range impact of alternative growth management strategies. A key limitation facing the region is that it has been forecast that the region will run out of urban density residential land (densities of one unit per acre or higher) by the year 2010.

The draft fiscal reform initiative would require state legislation to guarantee a stable funding source for local government and reduce fiscal incentives in land-use planning. It would be accomplished by providing local government with a stable share of local property tax revenue, in exchange for other revenues and allocating revenues from a countywide tax base on the basis of population. This reform would help cities like San Diego tackle some of their unmet facilities needs, and address fiscal "localism," a major obstacle to transit village development.

Zoning

Zoning regulations offer an effective way to achieve transit-supportive development over time. Once regulations are written that support elements such as pedestrian orientation and mixed uses, the principles of TOD can be implemented slowly and consistently as a part of the way the City does business. Incremental implementation through zoning is especially important in cities that are primarily built out and experiencing infill development. In San Diego, tailored zoning has been used extensively in urban neighborhoods along bus corridors where a traditional "main street' type business district is sought to be preserved. Through the code amendments recently adopted in the City of San Diego, zoning is poised to become an even more important tool.

Key components of the new code include:

Urban Village Overlay Zone: This zone provides regulations that will allow for greater variety of uses, flexibility in site planning and development regulations, and intensity of land-use than is generally permitted in other citywide zones. Urban villages are characterized by interconnected streets, street-facing entrances, and architectural features and outdoor activities that encourage pedestrian activity and transit accessibility.

Transit Area Overlay Zone: This zone provides supplemental parking regulations for areas receiving a high level of transit service. The intent of the overlay zone is to identify areas with reduced parking demand and to lower off-street parking requirements accordingly.

Parking: Revised parking standards allow parking reductions of 10 to 20 percent for multi-family dwelling units and approximately 15 percent for most commercial uses located in transit areas. Additional reductions are allowed for mixed used projects based on shared parking ratios. There is also a requirement for bicycle parking spaces for commercial and residential development.

Small Lot Single Dwellings: The code provides for both attached and detached single-dwelling units on smaller lots than are required in the standard single-family zones. It is intended that these zones provide an alternative to multiple-family developments where single-family homes could be developed at multiple-unit densities. Minimum lot sizes for the small lot zones are 279 and 372 meters squared (3,000 and 4,000 square feet).

Townhouse Zones: These zones provide for attached, single-dwelling unit residential development on small lots with alley access. It is intended that these zones provide for more urbanized, single-family living at densities that are historically more typical of multiple-unit zones. These zones provide transition opportunities between single-family and higher density.

Commercial Mixed Use Zones: Zones permitting mixed use and requiring pedestrian orientation have been added to the City's base commercial zones. These zones require that buildings address the sidewalk with entrances, windows, and articulation among other things.

Concession Program

MTDB has contracted with a local firm to serve as a Master Concessionaire and to manage a concession program. This contract has been in effect since

1991 and has been extended until the year 2000. The contract requires the firm to develop and implement a full range of concession services and facilities at the largest possible number of Light Rail stations within the San Diego Trolley system. In addition to selling products and services, the concessionaire provides transit assistance and information to patrons at some of the sites. San Diego Trolley receives 25 percent of the gross revenues derived from this contract.

Cooperation between communities and public agencies

The relationship between transportation and land-use in the San Diego region has many key players – 18 cities, the county, two regional agencies, a variety of transit operators, the state transportation agency (Caltrans), and two local development agencies (the San Diego Unified Port District and the Centre City development Corporation). For over a decade, a variety of formal and informal arrangements have helped foster cooperation and communications (see Lerner-Lam 1989), among them:

Cross-membership on policy-making boards. The mayors and council members who decide on local planning and growth management issues sit on the boards of SANDAG, the Regional Transportation Commission, and the two regional transit operators. Key issues often arise at the meetings of these regional agencies. Jack Limber of the MTDB points out proposals for transit-related development projects are often floated at MTDB meetings. By the time they are presented to the City council, they are not a surprise and often some of the concerns have started to be addressed.

Management groups: Senior-level staff managers participate in a number of working groups that are sanctioned by policy boards. For example, a City of San Diego management group involving the departments of planning, traffic engineering, and development services meets regularly, as does a group of general managers of transit agencies.

Shared staffing: The MTDB has regularly used staff from the city of San Diego, providing valuable experience to the transit agency and facilitating coordination with the city. Several Caltrans staff members work at SANDAG.

Task forces: Land-use and transportation agencies in San Diego often resort to task forces to deal with tough problems. An example is the Transportation

Financing Advisory Task Force, which reported to SANDAG on recommendations for the sales tax.

Contracting out to other agencies: The level of trust among technical agencies in the region is such that they often are willing to accept the assistance of another organization with special expertise. SANDAG provides design services to Caltrans and travel forecasts to MTDB. MTDB has contracted with the City of San Diego for assistance with land-use planning and traffic engineering along rail corridors. Local jurisdictions negotiate with developers to contribute to transit facilities, including rights-of-way for MTDB routes and, occasionally, stations.

Station-Area Development Activities

The MTDB and the NCTB both have publicized development opportunities for station-area sites. The NCTB has been pursuing an aggressive marketing program for its station sites and railroad rights-of-way. The MTDB has participated in joint developments in downtown San Diego and in other locations.

Downtown San Diego:

Imperial and 12th Transfer Station: The MTS/James R. Mills Building, a 10-story, 180,000 square foot office tower with a 1,000-car parking garage and a 15-story clock tower, was developed as MTDB's headquarters at the junction of three Light Rail lines in downtown San Diego. The 2.7-acre site was acquired in 1983 for use as a transfer station. The county became involved as a financial partner of MTDB and major occupant of the building. The Light Rail lines pass through a station under the building: the tracks are bordered on the ground floor by retail space. The 35 million dollar project was completed ahead of schedule on January 1, 1989. The MTDB receives an income stream from the ground lease and retail rents. The MTDB sees three major benefits in this project. The first is the savings in construction and financing costs that they were able to achieve through the joint venture deal with a private partner. They also hoped that this project would accelerate the redevelopment of this area from what has previously been a transition zone. Also due to the expected increase in passengers from its current level, and parking revenues, they expect to receive enough revenues to offset significant portions of finance costs of the station and adjoining tower over its service lifetime. (CERVERO/HALL/LANDIS 1992)

America Plaza: The 34-story America Plaza was constructed on a site just across the street from the AMTRAK and commuter rail station. As with the MTDB building, America Plaza straddles a Light Rail station and incorporates retail space. Adjoining the station is the Museum of Contemporary Art/San Diego. It was completed in late 1991. MTDB is responsible only for maintaining the station platforms, trackway, and equipment. The project's private developer financed about 80% of the 5.2 million capital cost of the station.

La Mesa:

The City of La Mesa has several TOD projects. These projects included the La Mesa Village Plaza at the La Mesa Blvd. Trolley Station, Villages of La Mesa at the **Amaya Station**, and Navy Housing at the **Spring St. Station**. Part of the reason La Mesa has so many TOD projects is because these projects satisfied many local goals that could not be achieved before. For example, the development of the vacant lot situated downtown at La Mesa Blvd, and the flood plain near the Grossmont station, along with the removals of the vacant dump near the Amaya station. Also the many successful projects could be attributed to proactive, cooperative planning for station-area development by the city of La Mesa and MTDB.

The **Grossmont Center Station** on the Orange Line is located below a regional shopping mall and adjacent to the "Grossmont Trolley Center' theater and shopping center in the City of La Mesa. MTDB owns a 3.3-hectare (8.1-acre) site, on what is currently a 600-car parking lot on the edge of the center. MTDB has an agreement with the theater for shared use of the parking spaces. The center is auto oriented in design, but a survey found that nearly one-third of Grossmont Trolley Theater employees surveyed used transit to get to work. Regionwide, only 3 percent of work trips are by transit. In addition, 8.1 percent of the people surveyed using the center took transit to get there.

The ultimate use of the site is expected to be a high-density, transit-oriented development that will create an upper level pedestrian link to the shopping mall. The City of La Mesa is currently initiating a master planning effort for the site. As MTDB wants this vision to be realized, there is an ongoing benefit from the revenue generated from the shared parking agreement. However, this agreement is also a hindrance to development in that the future project must accommodate parking for the theater.

Mission Valley:

One of San Diego's most successful examples of proactive long-range planning can be seen in the Mission Valley community (BRAGADO 1999, p.15). Mission Valley is located close to the geographic center of the City, and is the location of the latest extension of the San Diego Trolley. Light Rail-transit was a central part of the 1985 Mission Valley Community Plan, which sought to shape new development into a series of multiple-use, pedestrian-friendly centers, physically linked by the Trolley and a pedestrian path system.

Slowly, this plan is becoming a reality. The Trolley line is now operating, multiple-use developments are being built, and the pedestrian environment is improving. In addition to the new Trolley stations, notable pedestrian improvements include a bicycle/pedestrian path that flanks both sides of the San Diego River, the installation of noncontiguous sidewalks and street trees, new restaurants with outdoor dining, and enhanced street-facing facades. In addition, developers have provided various degrees of financial contributions toward the Light Rail line.

Rio Vista West is a privately initiated TOD in Mission Valley. The entire project is within walking distance of a Trolley station. It will include up to 1,754 dwelling units, 28,830 square meters (310,000 square feet) of commercial uses, a public "commons' area, and a trolley plaza at the Rio Vista Trolley Station. The developer dedicated the right-of-way for the LRT alignment and station.

The project was submitted as a TOD in 1992 in part because the developer was exposed to, and impressed by, the work of Peter Calthorpe. The developer also felt that if he followed the TOD Guidelines, the City of San Diego would readily approve his project. However, staff planners were not immediately supportive of the plan because it reduced office entitlements in favor of a large retail commercial center. The office use would have been favorable from a transit ridership perspective. In December of 1993 the developer gained the necessary approvals, as he was convincing in his argument that there was no market for the office use and that the retail component was the economic engine of the project.

As expected, the first portion of the project to be built was a retail center. The center includes an attractive and functional pedestrian walkway through the parking lot, outdoor eating areas, and abundant street trees. It is well done, but still primarily an auto-oriented commercial center. The next planning area to be built was the courtyard residential component.

The most exciting part of the project will be the mixed-use core around the Trolley station. This core area incorporates key components of a transit-oriented development such as: high-density uses near transit; interconnected streets, underground parking, public spaces and amenities, and ground floor “main-street"-type retail uses with upper-level residences. It is anticipated that construction of the mixed-use core will begin in 1999.

A joint development project currently under way is located at the **Morena/Linda Vista Trolley Station**, the first station of the Mission Valley West Line (BRAGADO 1999, p.14). MTDB owns a 2.1-hectare (5.27-acre) parcel at the station, with less than half of the site in use for the LRT station and park-and-ride lot.

A revived economy and the opening of the new Trolley line were the driving factors in seeking developer interest in the Morena site. The Board of Directors directed staff to issue a Request for Proposals (RFP) on the site that did not dictate specific uses or size and allowed for private sector creativity. Within a broad window of possibilities, developer candidates were told that:

- The entire site could be utilized using air rights and structured parking.
- The project should have a mix of uses that generate transit ridership and a revenue stream to MTDB.

The design should be pedestrian and transit-oriented. He project should become a landmark for the community and spark revitalization of the adjacent business district. evelopers were asked to submit site plans and pro formas among other materials that would be used to evaluate their proposals.

These broad parameters led to a wide range in the proposals received. Staff, together with economic consultants and an advisory committee, reviewed the submittals. After a lengthy and contentious selection process, a local developer won the support of the Board of Directors in April of 1998.

This decision was based on the developer's acceptance of tough business terms and strong support from local community groups. Development of the site continues to be challenging due to site constraints and community opposition to multi-family housing. Still, prospects for implementation of the project look good, as the developer has established an excellent relationship with the community and the local council member is a champion of the project.

In retrospect, it would have made more sense to proceed with a Request for Qualifications (RFQ) process that did not require the submittal of detailed projects, or to more clearly define project parameters as a part of the original developer solicitation.

Otay Ranch, the potentially largest transit-oriented development:

A major 'new town' planning initiative, and by far the largest regional development project, is the planned community of Otay Ranch, which covers approximately 9,315 hectares (23,000 acres) of land in southwestern San Diego County, just across the Mexican border. The development proposal is distinctive in that it would cluster much of the available development intensity into urban villages that are transit-oriented.

The plan envisions the extension of the regional LRT system to serve the now community. MTDB staff has been involved in the planning process to ensure that adequate transit right-of-way is dedicated and to work toward achieving an integrated land-use, transit, and urban design plan. Construction is now under way in two of the planned villages.

NCTD's first experience with the cities along the commuter route was in siting. This was controversial and sometimes resulted in poor station locations. Now it is working with several cities to encourage joint development projects in station areas.

Public Facilities

At many stations, MTDB and the local communities agreed to locate public facilities. Some examples:

Childcare facilities have been developed at two Light Rail stations. The **47th Street station** facility was a joint development project. A developer was persuaded to modify a residential project to also include a childcare facility on leased MTDB land next to the station. At the **Imperial and 12th transfer station** site on the Orange Line, MTDB encouraged development of a childcare center just a block east of its headquarters. (This center has since closed as a casualty of the economic recession).

The Sweetwater Union High School District, working with the Community Development Commission in National City, has built an adult education center on a 1.5-acre parcel at the **24th Street Station** on the South Line.

Other examples are the 73,000-visitor **Qualcomm Stadium** in Mission Valley, the Chamber of Commerce on top of the **Lemon Grove Depot,** and the visitor centers at the same station and at **Bayfront/E-Street**.

Outlook

San Diego's initial Light Rail lines were built along existing railroad rights-of-way, much of their length through older neighborhoods or industrial areas – not prime area for real estate activity. Also, since these are pre-existing development, the scope of any new TOD will depend on the city's willingness to redevelop the area. Cities like Chula Vista, El Cajon, Lemon Grove, and National City already have major developments near existing stations and they continue these developments. Finally, in some cases land-use along pre-existing rights-of-way are not considered conductive to residential use because of pre-existing freight rail. Market conditions and fiscal and economic incentives are also important factors in implementing successful TOD. Voter approved sales tax revenues are available for another 10 years but securing funding for planned rail extensions remains difficult.

As the map of ongoing development projects shows, a very large percentage of developments still seem to have no relation at all with the existing and future railway network.

This might change in the future, as San Diego has an elaborate public policy framework in place to encourage transit-focused development and the transit agencies have positive experiences on which to build future projects. The one future development to watch for is the Mission Valley Line. Together with the Santle extension this line is the only line that does not use a pre-existing freight right-of-way, but instead is placed on a high growth corridor to the north of downtown. Along with pre-existing developments like shopping malls, hotels, commercial and residential complexes, the corridor is still growing and has developable land. Therefore, the Mission Valley Line must be considered as particularly suitable for future TOD outside the City center of San Diego. DUNPHY (1998) believes that most near future TOD plans are going to be situated along the Mission Valley Line and as a result the MTDB may have created a situation in which TOD will be consistent with other local development plans, much like the La Mesa development.

Otay Ranch in Chula Vista, the largest potential regional development area, is also the most promising area for future TOD. But the feasibility of this project will depend on the realization of a potential Light Rail line that is now under consideration, the South Bay extension. Despite the readiness of the major investor in this area to participate substantially to the financing of the line, the majority of construction costs will be still have to come from the public side. It remains unclear, whether after the end of the 20-year contract sales tax period, described in chapter 4, a prolongation of this tax, will have a chance to be approved by the local voters.

Similar to Portland, Oregon, although under less favorable regional planning conditions, the development of these lines are important indicators of TOD-possibilities in other parts of the country, especially in other growth areas.

7.5 Transit-oriented Development tools and results in Portland/OR

The Portland region has used **a variety of tools to influence development in station areas**. With each Light Rail project, new lessons have been learned about what it takes for Light Rail to shape development patterns. Planning for the eastside Light Rail line focused on station area planning to allow transit supportive development to occur. According to Rajiv Batra, head of one of the planning offices involved in station area planning in Portland and throughout the country, the Eastside-planning tried to establish development (zoning) standards that could not be supported by the market. Planning for the Westside route has included greater involvement by landowners and developers especially in the development of master plans for four station areas with between 112 and 400 acres of developable land each.

These large tracts of land offer the possibility of creating transit-oriented communities, whereas on the eastside most development potential was infill and redevelopment. The Hillsboro extension of the Westside line brought urban design issues onto the table earlier, and explicitly included them in the process of determining the alignment and station locations. This inclusion of land-use impacts as a decisive element of the corridor planning was the first attempt in America to plan and build a new Light Rail Line in area that offered the best possibilities to maximize future urban densities and to attract a maximum of future riders.

Other tools used to influence development in station areas include local improvement districts to help finance streetscape improvements in business districts, locating public facilities or subsidized housing near stations, and using the powers and financing tools of economic development agencies to facilitate private development.

Station Area Planning

Eastside

In order to improve the land-use impacts of the so-called Banfield line, a "Transit Station Area Program" (TSAP), as a cooperative venture of Tri-Met, Metro, Portland, Gresham, and Multnomah County was established. The program prepared development plans for each station area by analyzing the demand for office, retail, and residential development at each station, evaluating park-and-ride, and other means of accessing Light Rail stations, studying urban designs, and changing zoning ordinances.

One result of TSAP was the decision to build only five park-and-ride lots with a total of 1,917 spaces. Most people would arrive at stations by walking or using a rerouted feeder bus system. Another product was the decision to move a station in the Lloyd District to better connect with planned office development. The major result was the development of special transit station area zoning that allowed higher density development near stations. The new zoning also regulated building setbacks, parking lot locations, and the pedestrian environment.

A recent evaluation of TSAP (Barney and Worth, 1993a, 1993b) identified the preparation of station area plans as the major outcome of TSAP, but noted the lack of implementation strategies, such as incentives to build transit-supportive development. In part, the lack of implementation was the result of dropping a planned implementation phase of TSAP due to a lack of funds. The evaluation also attributed the lack of implementation to the recession in the late 1980s / early nineties, confusions about responsibilities at a time when political boundaries were changing, and uncertainty about what Light Rail could do.

Due to the difficult market situation, to scattered and limited development opportunities, and to a less dynamic and less wealthy social context, the land-use impacts of the LRT on the eastside are still relatively small. Some of this is also due to political indecisiveness, especially in the city of Gresham.

In the case of Gateway, a suburban station that serves as a major transfer point between bus and Light Rail, representing one of the most promising development areas along the Eastside line, early successes would have been possible. According to PARSONS BRINCKERHOFF (1996), they were missed because of changing political boundaries. This area had vacant land and a shopping center that was ready for redevelopment. When Light Rail was built, Gateway was in unincorporated Multnomah County. Shortly thereafter the cities of Gresham and Portland began annexing all the unincorporated area between them, and Gateway became part of Portland. When Portland annexed the area, it did not keep the county's transit overlay as part of its zoning. The city, therefore, had no leverage to require the new shopping center to orient towards the transit station. The result was a standard auto-oriented shopping center.

As shown later under "station development activities", neither in the case of Gateway nor at other stations of the Eastside LRT will these initial failures prevent future developments or have prevented current developments that may lead in many cases to real urban transformations in the station surroundings.

Westside

A cooperative planning effort involving Tri-Met, Metro, the Oregon Department of Transportation, Portland, Beaverton, Hillsboro, and Washington County similar to TSAP has been set up relatively early for the Westside Light Rail. New land-use plans, capital improvement plans, and implementation strategies were developed for all stations by the spring of 1996.

A coordinated set of interim development regulations have been put in place in three of the four jurisdictions (cities of Portland, Beaverton, Hillsboro and the Washington county) to keep transit-supportive options open while final community plans were developed. As more precisely described for the Orenco station case, the interim zoning prohibited certain auto-oriented uses within one-half mile of stations, sets minimum densities, limited parking supplies, and required that buildings be oriented to the Light Rail stations (ARRINGTON, 1995).

Another innovation is public-private master planning. The Westside has four large tracts of vacant land where transit-supportive communities could be built. Tri-Met knew they needed a demonstration project for a transit-oriented community. They hired a new person to coordinate station area planning, which contributed, in conjunction with the local communities public-private partnerships involving Tri-Met, Beaverton, Metro and other institutions. These groups developed master plans that went beyond the development of comprehensive plans and zoning ordinances to site designs and market analysis for actual projects.

The landowners/developers paid over half of the costs for these master planning efforts. These partnerships were initially installed for all of the four major development sites along the Westside-line. They did not succeed in all of these areas. As will be described later the most important failure so far is the development of the large area in proximity of the Nike-production plant at Murray West/ Beaverton Creek. The most important success story so far is the development of the Orenco station area in Hillsboro.

The Hillsboro extension, the six miles of the line west of 185th, includes two further planning innovations. First, the Federal Transit Administration (FTA) made regional and transit area planning a condition for full funding. The region has five years to adopt transit-supportive plans based on Metro's 2040 plan and the state Transportation Planning Rule as well as develop station area plans that support ridership or Tri-Met will need to refund the $75 million from the FTA (ARRINGTON 1995). Second, prior to preliminary engineering, architects and urban planners sat at the table with engineers and environmental planners to determine the route and station locations. During the five-week process, the group moved four stations and eliminated two others. A committed and knowledgeable group of people, they were able to do this work in a relatively short period of time without any phase of the planning proceeding too far. The result is an alignment that costs less, and a design that maximizes the opportunity for transit supportive development.

Joint Development

Tri-Met has been pursuing the concept of joint development since the eastside Light Rail decision was made. The agency hired a joint development specialist (Phil Whitmore) to develop and negotiate these public-private agreements. Although large projects have been planned, only modest projects have come to fruition.

The first joint development proposal was for a YMCA over the parking lot at the Gateway station. The YMCA would provide off-peak riders and set the stage for further transit-oriented development at this major bus and Light Rail transfer station. The proposal made it through a complex Urban Mass Transit Agency (UMTA) approval process, but the YMCA withdrew from the project after it lost its tax-exempt status (HOWARD 1985; BARNEY/WORTH 1993b).

Failures and successes of transit joint as well as transit-oriented development can be seen ainthe example of large as well as of small projects. During the late eighties and early nineties, large projects (such as a commercial center in Gresham, described under "station area development activities") were more difficult to implement than smaller projects, i.e. affordable housing projects. This lead some authors to the (premature) conclusion that Light Rail doesn't have the possibility to generate large development. Longer experience shows that site control through Tri-Met or other TOD supportive public agencies is a key instrument to promote TOD.

Transit-oriented Development Implementation Program

A special form of transit joint development is pursued by the regional government. After 7 years of political, conceptual and financial preparation, the Metro council approved in April 1998 a Transit-oriented Development Implementation Program. This program is based on FTA's new Joint Development Policy, mentioned in chapter 6.3 and receives funding from FTA. It aims at non-conventional ways of realizing transit-oriented developments, necessary to achieve the goals of Metro's 2040 development plan. The program has a financial size of $7 million, assembling funds from different grant programs and for different specific purposes. The program activities so far include an RFP (request for proposals) from the development community for infill sites within a ¼ mile radius around any of the 24 LRT stations. On the basis of the incoming proposals 6 program sites were selected (see graph) (added later by other promising development sites). Metro has different activity options, including the purchase of an easement or the "outright"-purchase of underdeveloped land near transit stations and the resale of these acquired parcels to developers who agree with Metro's infill development goals for these areas. Another option is to fund transit friendly site improvements, such as adequate construction materials or additional equipment for pedestrian or public areas. Finally one of the options is also helping to achieve the completion of "old" projects (e.g. the Beaverton Round, see below).

In a recent publication GUICHARD (1998) describes the program goals: "The TOD Implementation Program will use joint development to address the risk and feasibility issues currently dissuading developers from constructing TODs. Joint Development refers to a collection of public and private sector partnership techniques, strategies, and development "tools" that can be used to link development to the transit stations to increase the efficiency of a mass transit system. The increase can take the form of new ridership (caused by the construction of TODs), new revenue to a transit agency, or a combination of both. Specific joint development tools that may be used include:

- Site Control (land acquisition and sale) to ensure design and density of a TOD can be determined before the land is developed.

- Pre-development Activities to assist in making environmental and programmatic determinations including financial analysis, conceptual design and permit acquisition. These activities do not include the preparation of architectural construction documents.

- Request for Proposals (RFP) to ensure the competitive offering of development opportunities.

- Development Agreements to establish a set of performances by both parties and to protect public interests in the sale or lease of TOD sites.

- Public and Private Co-use of transit station structures or land to reinforce the connection of a TOD to the transit system.

- Air or Subterranean Rights to increase the density, urban character and/or feasibility of a TOD.

Land sales to the private sector may include a "write-down" of land value, if needed, to assist in offsetting cost penalties associated with higher density, mixed-use, and/or strong pedestrian amenities. The write-downs will be determined by an independent appraisal or economic analysis utilizing the "highest and best transit use" approach. ...The proceeds from land sales will return to the Program for use on another TOD project".

Guichard describes one of the projects, the purchase of 4.88 acres piece of land next to the Eastside 60th street station ("Center Commons') from the Portland Redevelopment Corporation (PDC). PDC acted as a private owner but donated the part of the land, which was supposed to be a pedestrian only area. Then they sold it to a developer at a reduced price in order to offset TOD cost-penalties and design-requirements. The difference can be justified through the possible ridership- gains.

Local Improvement Districts

Local Improvement Districts (LIDS) have been created to finance the local share of public amenities that support transit use and transit area development. Property owners vote to form a LID with authority to levy a benefits-based tax. LIDs have raised the local share of funds for amenities that make station areas more attractive, but they have not been used to finance transit service itself.

Businesses along the Morrison-Yamhill Light Rail streets downtown formed an LID to upgrade the street pavement and add artwork and other amenities as shown in Figure 28. Property owners pay 20-year benefit assessments to pay off the $1.5 million in bonds that provided the local contribution to a $5.5 million project. UMTA provided the remaining funds. Merchants therefore received almost $4 in improvements for every $1 they contributed, which made selling the idea easy (HOWARD 1985).

Another LID was formed in the Lloyd District in the 1980s to turn Holladay Street into a pedestrian mall between the Arena, Coliseum, and Convention Center at the west end and Lloyd Center regional mall at the east end.

Businesses in downtown Hillsboro have formed another LID to improve the appearance of their station areas.

Locating Public Facilities

Another way to generate ridership is to locate public facilities at transit stations. Federal, state, and regional office buildings have been built or renovated near the line in the Lloyd District and downtown. These include a federal office building and the Oregon State Department of Transportation (ODOT) Region One headquarters in downtown and federal, state, and Port buildings in the Lloyd District.

Two generators of off-peak riders are situated at transit stations at the west end of the Lloyd Center area. Both have been built with limited parking. The $85 million Oregon Convention Center was built in 1990 fronting on a new station. Although the Convention Center is located near the intersection of 1-84 and 1-5, it has only 800 parking spaces that are in back of the building. Light Rail provides an easily understood connection between the convention center and hotels, restaurants, and shops both in downtown and in the eastern end of the Lloyd District. $34 million in public funds were invested in the $262 million Trailblazers Arena at the Coliseum (or Rose Court) Transit Station. The arena seats 20,340 people, but has only 3,446 nearby off-street parking spaces. Instead, most fans arrive on Light Rail or are shuttled on Tri-Met buses from parking garages farther east in the Lloyd District (ARRINGTON 1995).

Urban Renewal Districts

Under Oregon's state law Urban Renewal Districts can be designated for relatively large urban areas. Their renewal or development purpose must be of public interest and require the Urban Renewal District toolbox. Three major tools exist: land purchases at (predevelopment = low) market prices are eased through the possible menace of expropriation, incremental taxes are used to finance the public investments to improve the area (tax increment financing) and day to day decisions are made through the District management organization and don't require long administrative procedures.

Urban Renewal Districts played an important role to develop the most important station areas in the cities of Portland, Gresham and Hillsboro.

Among many other Renewal Districts, the Portland Development Commission is the responsible managing agency for the northern district, built to improve development opportunities along the future Interstate MAX.
PDC's project manager, John Southgate, expects a total tax increment of $180 million in this area. $30 million of that will be invested as local matching funds for the financing of the line itself. To leverage the money prior to the expected tax-revenue bonds, backed on the expected minimal increment, will be issued for this purpose.

Economic Development Agencies and Powers

Many of those who evaluated the TSAP process suggested that an experienced development agency provide a pro-active development program for the entire corridor. TriMet has been the only agency taking a corridor-wide perspective. Prior to Light Rail, they had no experience with economic development, and they do not have the powers of a redevelopment agency.

Although it does not have a corridor-wide perspective, the city of Portland's economic development agency, the Portland Development Commission (PDC), has been involved in a number of station area projects. PDC was the primary mover behind the development of Pioneer Place, a festive marketplace and office complex, at the intersection of the downtown Light Rail and bus malls.

PDC assembled the land, selected the developer and financed parts of the project with tax increment financing. The project opened in 1990 and includes two Light Rail stations. Figure 29 shows a Light Rail station at Pioneer Place. PDC has also helped finance the rehabilitation of historic buildings in the Skidmore/Old Town and Yamhill Historic Districts along the Light Rail line.

In addition, PDC created an urban renewal district around the Oregon Convention Center to facilitate the development process. Voters however, approved a statewide property tax limitation measure in 1992 that has eliminated PDC's ability to use tax increment financing. No urban renewal activities are, therefore, taking place in the Convention Center area.

PDC has also identified transit station areas in Portland as one of their ten target areas in their 1994-1999 business plan. PDC's goal for station areas is to provide technical assistance and facilitate private development using private funds and federal transportation funds such as Congestion Mitigation Air Quality (CMAQ) dollars (PDC, 1994).

For this purpose it works closely with other public agencies,such as the Metro government, to whom, in the meantime, the administration of CMAQ-funds was transferred.

Tax Exemption Program

The 1995 Oregon State Legislature amended legislation on Transit-oriented Development Property Tax Exemption. The TOD tax exemption is supposed to support high-density housing and Mixed Use developments, affordable to a broad range of the general public on vacant or underutilized sites along transit corridors whose design and features encourage building occupants to use public transit. This instrument is very important in so far as property taxes in Portland are the highest in the country. The reason is that they are the only major local income source. Through tax exemption thousands of housing projects with affordable prices have been attracted to transit-oriented locations. One of the major tax exempted housing developments is in the so-called Water District, the area of the future streetcar.

Subsidized Housing

PDC also coordinates a number of housing programs. Prior to the Westside line, none of them had specifically targeted transit station areas. Now, PDC has coordinated several important station area developments, one of which is a multi-family housing project on surplus land between the tracks at a station in Goose Hollow, a mixed residential and commercial area, immediately west of downtown Portland. Like other downtown housing projects, this project will require some subsidy (from FTA) to be feasible.

Station-Area Development Activities

A large number of studies have been undertaken to investigate the attraction of private capital to the MAX Light Rail stations.

The development opportunities offered by the Eastside line were quite different from the west side. This is due to different real estate market situations and different land-use possibilities. DUEKER and BIANCO 1999 point out that “the motivation for Portland's eastside LRT line in the 1980s stemmed from an earlier freeway revolt and federal legislation allowing for the substitute of transit for highways. However, transit-oriented development was not a central part of the project, although there was some station-area planning in the LRT corridor. This took the form of densification via redevelopment of low-density areas" (p.4). According to CERVERO 1998 "the east-side line has failed to spawn the amount of development that was hoped for: This is mainly because it passes near established single-family neighborhoods and lies partly in a freeway median. A recent study (K.Dueker and M.Bianco: Effects of Light Rail-transit in Portland: Implications for Transit-oriented Development Design Concepts, Portland 1998) found multi-family housing development is actually occurring at a faster rate near bus stops and arterials along the Eastside corridor than around Light Rail stops. Still, more than 1000 multi-family housing units have been built on in-fill sites near the rail corridor, in no small part due to aggressive efforts to leverage these projects through such steps as fast tracking the review of building permits for transit-supportive development. It has been downtown Portland and the Lloyd District where transit's presence has been most felt" (p.417).

The estimations of the amount of development spurred by Portland's LRT are varied and sometimes contradictory.

A 1995 summary of development in rail station areas, quoted by PORTER 1999, determined that "$396 million in development had occurred in downtown since the decision to construct the east-side line. A similar coincidence of public and private forces occurred in the Lloyd district near downtown. The robust real estate market in that activity center produced $715 million in development after the Eastside-line was announced, over half of all investments along the length of the transit line. Most of this development took place with no direct input from Tri-Met other than station-area planning". According to Tri-Met's figures, transit related developments in these two districts alone generated more than $1.5 billion worth of private development; Another $400 million investments are under construction in the suburban parts of the east-side line. Altogether, both lines generated real estate developments worth more than $2.4 billion (TRI-MET 1998, p. 2, 21).

More is to come although "station-area development outside central Portland has lagged somewhat, due in part to the market decline that began soon after the Eastside line began operation, and in part to difficulties in obtaining coordinated agency and local governmental action to promote TOD. Some jurisdictions have enthusiastically planned for station-area development, but found implementation fraught with problems" (PORTER 1999).

Some of the **typical projects** and problems are described on the following pages:

Gresham, the terminus of the east-side line, can be mentioned as a significant example of development opportunities and difficulties. Gresham is a suburb 17 miles east of Portland's city center. With a population of over 81.000 in 1997 Gresham is Oregon's fourth largest city and is growing steadily (20% population increase between 1990 and 1997). Near the terminus, a shopping center developer (Winmar) had proposed development of a $100 million, 900,000 square foot regional mall as a mixed-use center on a platform over the tracks, with the station bridging the two halves of the development. Congress had earmarked $14.5 million in Section 3 funds for TriMet's share of the project. To aid the project, Tri-Met was to acquire and lease back to the developer about 65 acres of land around the station. (The difficulties encountered in Gresham later became one of the reasons to change the transit-funding regulations on the national level and led to the introduction of the "Transit Joint Guidelines", mentioned before.) Interagency discord and developer delay in signing anchor tenants stymied closure on the project until the market decline killed the development. Under pressure to develop, however, the landowner worked with Gresham and transit officials to prepare a new plan for the "Gresham Civic Neighborhood," a transit-oriented development with a mix of uses and a substantial expansion of city hall. Site infrastructure is being constructed and final designs prepared for the first phase to be initiated in early 1997. Tri-Met had to clear a number of easements on its properties and secure several grants to make the project financially feasible. The project was completed in early 1999. TriMet also worked with another developer to merge Tri-Met properties with adjoining properties in Gresham Central. As one of the first completed developments, the "Gresham Central Apartments" were built on a small 2.5 acre site, well linked to the nearby transit station by a promenade. Despite this small size, it is, according to Eryn DEEMING's 1999 MIT-thesis "affecting a change in the way development is happening in the entire area, just by example"(p.73).

The market situation for the Westside line was far better. Also, the west-side corridor offered a large amount of developable land around the stations. As a result of the relative Eastside success, developments around their future stations started relatively early, sometimes so early that they also had to face some of the real estate market problems of the Eastside.

The west-side MAX is described as "the region's most aggressive venture in marrying transportation and land-use...Even before the grand experiment opened for service in September 1998, new transit-oriented communities with nearly 7000 new residences were underway next to the Westside. The success or failure of the public's nearly $1 billion investment in the Westside will be determined in large part by what happens around the 20 stations (see graph). There is more vacant land around one station in the Hillsboro section than around all the Eastside stations combined" (TRI-MET 1998, p.20)

Illustration 7.7: Development potential at West MAX station areas

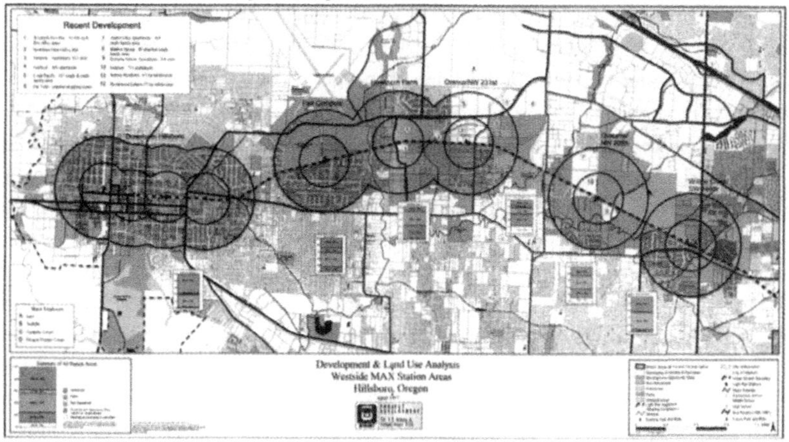

The **Orenco Station** project has emerged as one of the most important developments on the Westside MAX route and maybe one of the most significant examples of TOD in the US. On the one hand, Intel is planning a major new factory, a 4 billion dollar investment "in the nation's largest and most expensive silicon chip fab(rication) plant and research center" in proximity to the station. On the other hand more than 2000 new homes will be built close to station. "All the land between the Orenco Max station and the Intel plant – some 190 acres – is owned by PacTrust. The Land was originally acquired by PacTrust for industrial uses in Portland's burgeoning Silicon

Forest" (TRI-MET 1998, p. 21). The common vision of PacTrust, Tri-Met and the City of Hillsboro "was to create a community with a pedestrian oriented spine between Intel and The MAX station lined by parks, high density residential and neighborhood commercial and residential above" (ibid). Due to its importance as one of the nation's largest and most ambitious transit-oriented residential development the Orenco station development and its planning context will be described and analyzed more in detail in the attached documentation.

Beaverton Creek, a residential and retail shopping project on the Westside MAX line shows the problems that were also encountered on the Westside. Beaverton Creek was to be the first project developed under Portland's TOD guidelines and a showcase project for a growing upscale suburb. Involving four landowners but no Tri-Met properties, the project aimed at demonstrating the marketability of transit-oriented design. The Murray West station area has 112 acres of vacant land in large parcels near Nike's World Headquarters and a Tektronix campus. The initial joint planning process resulted in moving the station to the center of the parcel, changing the location of the park-and-ride lot, and developing detailed plans for apartments, small lot single-family, and commercial, light industrial, and community facilities. Private investors initially appeared to be quite interested in the project and individuals were already trying to obtain home sites. But then dissension among landowners, planners, and neighborhood residents over proposed densities and parking requirements apparently proved too vexing for the major developer involved, who sold his property to the Nike Corporation in 1995. Nike has revealed no plans for the property. On the southern half of the site, however, development has proceeded on two residential projects with about 840 townhouses and apartments designed to be "transit-friendly" and were opened in late 1996 and late 1997.

A critical analysis of another TOD example, the **Beaverton Round** at Beaverton Central, shows that the ambitious design and user-mix concept can encounter specific market problems, especially if the lenders' attitude remains conservative. The "Round" is a high density mixed used development on an eight-acre former waste disposal plant. The development is supposed to re-create the lost historical city center of Beaverton. As a consequence of the many goals, costs and problems of the project, "a high level of coordination between a variety of different agencies was required to make this project possible. 12 agencies were involved in planning for the site including: US

Housing and Urban Development Department, US Environmental Protection Agency, TriMet, Metro, Washington County and the City of Beaverton" (DEEMING 1998, p.82).

Illustration 7.8:

Plans for Beaverton Round at the WestsideMAX station Beaverton Central

But despite the involvement of so many different people and public agencies, the developer was unable to obtain financing and the project had to be sized down to almost half of the originally planned density. It includes now 100,000 square feet of office space, 59.000 square feet of retail, 53 townhomes and 54 apartments as well as a 200-seat theater. But still the parking ratio is much lower than average suburban developments. Based on their Transit-Oriented Development Implementation Program, described above (GUICHARD 1998), the Metropolitan government tried to encourage the completion of the rusting structure of the Round-Buildings through a grant, supposed to ensure a reasonable return-on-investment-rate. The failure of the Beaverton Round is in the eyes of many involved players not only related to the lack of experience of the development-group. It was at least partly caused by the structural inability of the financial sector to ensure financing of a true mixed use project, typical for the necessities of station oriented smart growth concepts but very atypical for the reality of the American real estate finance sector.

The smaller projects that Tri-Met has been more successful with (according to PORTER (1999)) include one example that "exemplifies the modestly scaled project that may be most suitable for Light Rail lines. A developer requested an easement through Tri-Met properties to allow development of adjoining properties a half-block from the **162nd Street station**. Tri-Met staff persuaded the developer to acquire and join the properties to develop a multi-family residential project. On the 1.7-acre parcel thus assembled, the developer built four two-story buildings incorporating 42 moderately priced units. Most residents are entry-level office workers who value their accessibility to downtown offices. Since completing that project, the developer has built or is planning eight projects with 300 units along the transit line, including another joint development project."

7.6 Toronto, ON: New need for development examples in North America's most transit-oriented city

Although the development of Canada's largest city before and after World War II is very strongly related to the development of the transit system, there are very few hints that in the past 10 or 20 years a formal transit-oriented development has been developed. Due to this fact, tools or institutions to promote transit-oriented development over the last 20 years have been hardly reported. The description has thus to be based on a selection of specific **station area development examples**:

High Park Station - High Park station is located west of Toronto's downtown in the suburbs. At least six high-rise (15- to 20-story) rental apartment buildings were constructed near the transit station during the 1960s in an otherwise single-family detached-home residential neighborhood - a "tower in a park" concept. Developers and the city put forth a cooperative effort, and the transit ridership impacts are considered very favorable.

During the planning stages, however, the high-rise apartment projects were not received well by the community as a whole. Local residents disliked the thought of high-rise projects and the injection of renters overloading schools and streets that would follow. In the early 1970s, for example, a westward extension of the Quebec-Gothic high-rise apartment complex became an item of contention. Concerns focused on land assemblage, demolition of existing houses, and the intrusion of further high-rise development in an existing residential community.

In 1974, the Quebec-Gothic Working Committee was formed by a group of representatives from local residents' associations, Gothic Developments

Limited, City Planning Staff, and a local Alderman to resolve the various issues. Supported with funds from the city, an architectural consulting firm was also brought on board. After a year of negotiations, a compromise plan was reached in 1975, allowing the construction of three apartment towers, but significantly altering the original site plan. The new plan replaced the two proposed 25-story towers with 533 two- and three-bedroom units, while preserving an existing string of houses.

North York Stations - Sheppard, North York Centre, and Finch: The local municipality of North York, located north of Toronto's downtown along the Yonge subway line, proposed a city center plan in the 1970s, and constructed the North York Centre Station between two existing subway stations, Sheppard and Finch, already located along the line. North York Centre Station was positioned adjacent to the North York City Hall and facilitated a $250 million mixed development consisting of a 250-room hotel, office towers, a shopping galleria, and a $20 million library, all flanking a central open civic space. Most of the new developments are connected via underground pedestrian passages. According to SCHNEIDER 1999 "over the last 10 years, development in suburban North York's downtown has been occurring at a slower pace than anticipated. Parking restrictions in downtown helped orient development to downtown stations".

Scarborough Centre Station - At the Scarborough Centre Station northeast of Toronto's downtown suburbs, direct connections to a regional shopping mall and City Hall are in place. Offices and residential high-rises are located next to the station in an emerging commercial, retail, and municipal center. The plan was met with some local opposition, but residents in the area are further removed from the station site. Unlike the traditional grid pattern in North York, for example, Scarborough maintains a cul-de-sac street plan. A possible line extension from Scarborough, complete with high-density mixed-use development, has been stalled due to lack of funding. According to TTC officials, the market seems to have shifted from housing to three- and four-story townhouses.

King Station - At King Station in downtown Toronto, a market square atmosphere has evolved. The station is lined with upscale five- to six-story condominiums. The market for this style of housing downtown seems to be prospering.

Queen, College, and St. Clair Stations - Queen, College, and St. Clair stations on the Yonge subway line are located along main streets with high commercial activity. Development is being encouraged along main commercial streets, where good street-level transit service is in place to feed the transit station. By revitalizing the traditional linear streets with mixed use, planners aim to make the best use of transit stations. However, eased parking requirements have been met with some local opposition, since parking along these commercial corridors is already scarce.

A pilot project at the **Warden Station** on the Bloor-Danforth line was planned by Metro to revitalize an existing commercial center and retain substantial amounts of commuter parking. The project, based on Policy 30, which calls for preparation of station area development plans, is now on hold pending an agreement between public and private participants. Planning studies, undertaken in connection with the Main Streets initiative have focused on increasing intensities of development and making streetscape improvements along streetcar lines, most notably on Spadina Street along a new Light Rail line. These planning efforts have encountered considerable neighborhood opposition to increased densities and reduced parking requirements.

Two "Gateway" projects promoted by the provincial government have planned intermodal centers and adjoining mixed-use development at the Malvern and Mimico commuter rail stations.

7.7 The Orenco Station Development as a national showcase of transit-oriented development

The Orenco station development became a model case of transit-oriented development in the USA. The reasons therefore are the large project-size, the typical suburban residential setting of the development and its innovative approach to this task. The Light Rail station serves as the focal point of the project and highlights very clearly the alternative to car usership.

The development breaks the monofunctional pattern of normal suburban areas. It tries to offer opportunities for community-building through parks, restaurants, business locations, shops and a mixed social context through a diverse housing offering, meeting points and others.

Regional Planning Context

The regional planning context has been described extensively in the presentation of the transit-oriented development context in Portland in general. To that end, some brief notes may describe the framework:

- Oregon Transportation Rule: This Rule, effective May 1994, requires vehicle miles traveled (VMT) reductions by increasing development densities and improving opportunities for pedestrian access.

- EPA Airshed Requirements / Clean Air Act CAA (1990): The Environmental Protection Agency, EPA, has stepped up enforcement of air quality requirements in the Portland Region due to rapid growth and simultaneous increases in VMT and resulting air pollution levels.

- Metro's Housing Rule / Periodic Review: requires that a minimum of 50% of all residential land be zoned for multi-family units. Often this has led to multi-family locations not easily accessible to transit.

- Metro's RUGGOS: Regional and Growth Goals and Objectives require greater integration of land-use and transportation planning. This will lead to new regional strategies to achieve compliance with Federal Clean Air Act requirements.

- Metro's 2040 Plan: This long range planning process is underway, and will test the ability of current transportation and land-use plans to accommodate growth within the region. [19]

---

[19] Extracts of Metro 2040 Growth Concept

As adopted by the Metro Council on December 8, 1994

11.4 Growth Concept

Fundamental to the Growth Concept is a multi-modal transportation system which assures mobility of people and goods throughout the region. By coordinating land-uses and this transportation system, the region embraces its existing locational advantage as a relatively uncongested hub for trade.

The basic principles of the Growth Concept apply Growth Management Goals and Objectives in RUGGO. An urban to rural transition to reduce sprawl, keep a clear distinction between urban and rural lands and balance re-development is needed. For its long term urban land supply, the Growth Concept estimates that about 14,500 acres will be needed to accommodate projected growth. These lands will be selected from about 22,000 acres of Urban Reserve Study Area shown on the Concept

Map. This assumes cooperative agreements with neighboring cities to coordinate planning for the proportion of projected growth in the Metro region expected to locate within their urban growth boundaries and urban reserve areas.

The Metro UGB would only expand into urban reserves when need for additional urban land is demonstrated. Rural reserves are intended to assure that Metro and neighboring cities remain separate. The result is intended to be a compact urban form for the- region coordinated with nearby cities to retain the region's sense of place.

Mixed use urban centers inside the urban growth boundary are one key to the Growth Concept. Creating higher density centers of employment and housing and transit service with compact development in a walkable environment is intended to provide efficient access to goods and services and enhances multi modal transportation. The Growth Concept uses interrelated types of centers. The Central City is the largest market area, the region's employment and cultural hub. Regional Centers serve large market areas outside the central city, connected to it by high capacity transit and. highways. Connected to each Regional Center, by road and transit, are smaller Town Centers with local shopping and employment opportunities within a local market area. Planning for all of these centers will seek a balance between jobs and housing so that more transportation trips are likely to remain local and become more multi modal.

In keeping with the jobs housing balance in centers, a jobs housing balance by regional sub-areas can and should also be a goal. This would account for the housing and employment outside centers, and direct policy to adjust for better jobs housing ratios around the region....

Centers

...

There are three types of centers, distinguished by size and accessibility. The "central city" is downtown Portland and is accessible to millions of people. "Regional centers" are accessible to hundreds of thousands of people, and "town centers" are accessible to tens of thousands.

The Central City

Downtown Portland serves as our major regional center and functions quite well as an employment and cultural hub for the metropolitan area. ....
Today, about 20 percent of all employment in the region is in downtown Portland. Under the Growth Concept, downtown Portland would grow at the same rate as the rest of the region, and would remain the location of 20 percent of regional employment. To do this, downtown Portland's 1990 density of 150 people per acre would increase to 250 people per acre. Improvements to the transit system network, development of a multi-modal street system and maintenance of regional through routes (the highway system) would provide additional mobility to and from the city center.

Regional centers

There are nine regional centers, serving four market areas (outside of the Central City market area). Hillsboro serves that western portion of the region, and Gresham the eastern. The Central city and Gateway serve most of the Portland area as a regional center. Downtown Beaverton and Washington Square serve the Washington- County area, and downtown Oregon City, Clackamas Town Center and Milwaukie together serve Clackamas County and portions of outer south east Portland.

The relatively small number of centers reflects not only the limited market for new development at this density but also the limited transportation funding for the high-quality transit and roadway improvements envisioned in these areas. As such the nine regional centers should be considered candidates and ultimately the number should be reduced or policies established to phase-in certain regional centers earlier than others.

- Tri-Met's Strategic Plan (1993 - 1998): (This plan recommends land-use intensification along bus and Light Rail corridors as one of several strategies to increase ridership and mobility. Further, the Strategic Plan recommends that 85% of new growth should occur within the Urban Growth Boundary UGB, and within a five minute walking distance from transit stations.

Hillsboro development indicators

As opposed to Gresham on the end of the Eastside line, Hillsboro is a wealthy, strongly growing community within the strongly growing Washington County (population increase of 88,000 or 28% between 1990 and 1998). On an area of 19.1 square miles it had 42,000 inhabitants and over 16,000 households in 1993.

Metro's 2040 growth concept characterizes it as a "Regional Center", which should "become the focus of compact development, redevelopment, and high-quality transit service, multi-modal street networks, and act as major nodes along regional through-routes".

One of the main objectives in these Regional Centers is to increase urban densities. "From the current 24 people per acre, the Growth Concept would allow up to 60 people per acre".

The city has a total employment of 25,000 people and a strongly computer-hardware oriented economy. The main companies include: Intel Corporation, West One Bank Oregon S.B., Lattice Semiconductor Corporation, Toshiba America, Microtek International Inc., Soloflex Inc., NEC, Oregon Garden Products, White Consolidated Industries, Inc., and Wilbanks International, Inc.

It has a vital housing market with almost 600 housing unit starts and a total major building permit value of 71 million dollars in 1993.

Station Area development planning process

Based on the experience with the lack of coordinated urban development at the Banfield line, TriMet initiated meetings of the institutions along the Westside extensions, responsible of urban development: the Westside MAX task force of the local jurisdictions, Metro, O-DOT and TriMet. The goal of these meetings was to coordinate land-use regulation and development in the future rail station areas. The meetings started early 1993 and ended after the approval of the design standards in 1997. Many of the planning tools developed in the context of this line were prepared through the task force.

Parallel to this taskforce, the City of Hillsboro and affected property owners prepared plans for transit-oriented and pedestrian-sensitive developments within an eight square mile study area surrounding the proposed 6.2 mile extension of the Westside Light Rail-transit (LRT) system in Hillsboro.

The emphasis on advanced land-use and development planning around LRT stations reflected both the regional objective of increased transit ridership, as part of the 1 billion dollar investment in Westside LRT, and Hillsboro's commitment to fostering transit-supportive and pedestrian sensitive development around LRT stations.

The concept of transit-supportive and pedestrian-sensitive development, which typically includes a mixture of housing, commercial and employment uses in an environment designed to accommodate pedestrians, implies densities that often will be higher than adjacent developable densities. Because development densities in Hillsboro have been traditionally low, though comparable to other suburban communities, the city recognized the need to evaluate its Comprehensive Plan and Zoning Ordinance to determine justification for modifying those plans to accommodate higher development densities at selected locations. It was assumed that for the market to induce land development at transit supportive-densities, station areas must also have good auto access, other infrastructure improvements and supportive community services.

The City was implementing a three-part station area development planning process:

Station Area Interim Protection Ordinance (SAIPO)

The first phase of station area development planning concluded with City Council's adoption of SAIPO on April 5, 1994. This zoning overlay district essentially prohibits uses that are not transit-supportive, establishes a minimum residential density of 9-12 units per acre, a minimum floor-area-ratio (FAR) of 0.5 for non-residential properties, and establishes design standards for pedestrian-sensitive features to be incorporated within new developments.

SAIPO was supposed to be in effect until at the latest, May 1996. It was anticipated that long range station area master plans and station community plans described below would be adopted by May 1996.[20] As the result of

---

[20] **(HILLSBORO LIGHT RAIL STATION AREA INTERIM PROTECTION ORDINANCE (SAIPO) (Effective May 1993)**

The City of Hillsboro has recently adopted a new ordinance affecting land-use in the neighborhoods surrounding the stations on the Hillsboro Light Rail Extension. This ordinance, called the Station Area interim Protection Ordinance (SAIPO). is intended to encourage higher intensity land-uses and discourage lower intensity land-uses in the station areas, thereby taking advantage of the availability of transit and promoting transit ridership.

The majority of the provisions of the SAIPO will be contained in a new Section 135 of the Zoning Ordinance. Several changes have also been made to other sections of the Zoning Ordinance in connection with the new Section 135. Together, these SAIPO changes have five basic elements:

1. Establishment of a Station Area interim Protection District (SAIPD), and a Highway-Oriented Sub-Area (HOSA) along State Highway 8 within that District, in which the new SAIPO provisions will apply;
2. Provisions to allow Mixed Use Developments (residential/commercial or commercial/industrial) on individual properties in the Station Area Interim Protection District:
3. Restrictions on establishment of certain new transit non-supportive land-uses in the SAIPD and HOSA, and on expansions of existing non-transit supportive uses;
4. Provisions to allow increased density in single family residential zones, including smaller lot sizes and attached single family units;
5. Design guidelines for new non-residential development and expansion of existing non-residential development, including reduced setbacks, limitations on location and number of parking spaces. requirements for pedestrian connections to transit routes and stations. and promotion of increased intensity of use, as measured by Floor Area Ratio.

These elements are summarized below.

Station Area Interim Protection District and Highway-Orineted Sub-Area Boundaries:
Reduced scale maps showing the Station Area interim Protection District and Highway-Oriented Sub-Area boundaries are attached. These maps also show the major pedestrian routes, Light Rail station locations, and 400- and 1300- foot radii from the stations, as referenced in the SAIPO.

Hillsboro SAIPO Summary

Mixed use Developments: The Zoning Ordinance now includes a definition of this land-use as follows:

Mixed Use Developments - One or more structures, on a lot or contiguous lots, in which a combination of residential and commercial or commercial and industrial uses are permitted, but where uses not permitted in the underlying zone are limited to less than 40 percent of the overall floor area of the structure or structures.

master and/or station community plans, new zoning ordinances for each of the

---

Mixed Use Residential/Commercial Developments, on sites smaller than two acres, would be allowed as Conditional Uses in the following zones: R-7 Single Family Residential; A- 1 Duplex Residential; and A-2, A-4, and A-3 Multi-Family Residential.

Mixed Use Commercial/Residential Developments, on sites smaller than two acres, would be allowed as Conditional Uses in the following zones: C-4 Neighborhood Commercial: C-2 Central Commercial; and C- I General Commercial

Mixed Use Industrial/Commercial Developments, on sites smaller than two acres, would be allowed as Conditional Uses in the M-P industrial zone.

Mixed Use Developments larger than two acres, either Residential/Commercial or Commercia/Industrial would be allowed under the Planned Unit Development approval process.

Restrictions on Transit Non-Supportive UME The SAIPO lists 24 specific land-uses which would not be allowed as new uses in the majority of the District, and four automobile-oriented uses which would be allowed as new uses only within the HOSA. Most of these uses are land-extensive, such as golf courses or cemeteries. or low-intensity, low employment uses, such as cold storage plants or manufactured home sales. Many of the uses may not be allowed in the underlying zone itself. The uses are listed in Sections 7 and 8 of Section 135.

Increased Residential Densities: Minimum residential densities are established in the SAIPO for areas within the District. If the property is within 1300 feet of a Light Rail station, the minimum density development permitted would be 12 units per acre. Farther than 1300 feet from a Light Rail station, the minimum density would be nine units per acre. Properties may be developed in phases, but earlier phases must allow for development of the entire property at the minimum required density. Lot areas and dimensions may be reduced up to 30% to achieve the minimum density, and attached single-family and multi-family development may be allowed in single family zones.

Design Guidelines for Transit-Supportive Development: There are several sections in the new SAIPO regarding design guidelines. These are contained in Sections 12 and 13 of the new Section 135, and include the following:

Hillsboro SAIPO Summary

minimum non-residential density requirements for new development, expressed as .5 FAR (Floor Area Ratio) minimum areas for newly created lots minimum and maximum setbacks for new structures. which are in most cases less than the setbacks of the underlying zones minimum landscaping requirements provision for building entries oriented toward transit streets or major pedestrian routes

provision for pedestrian spaces (for inclusion in FAR s) guidelines for pedestrian circulation and access guidelines for location and number of parking spaces provided requirement for review by Oregon Department of Transportation on new developments on State Highways

requirements for extra-width sidewalks adjacent to the Light Rail alignment

Section 13 also includes provisions for limited exceptions to the guidelines, and establishment of Station Area Planning Agreements for the station areas.

The SAIPO is intended to discourage transit non-supportive development, and to provide guidelines for transit-supportive development, during the interim before preparation of actual site-specific Station Area Plans. The planning process for the Station Area Plans is now underway, and were expected to be completed in mid-1995. Application of the SAIPO standards will automatically expire upon adoption of a Station Area Plan for an affected property, The SAIPO also included a firm expiration date of May 5, 1996.

concerned station areas were supposed to consecutively replace the SAIPO's. Not only Hillsboro but also Washington County adopted a SAIPO. In the city of Portland itself, as well as in Beaverton, no need of such an ordinance was seen.

Station Area Master Plans (SAMP):

In recognition of the need for public-private partnerships, the city has entered into planning agreements with several private and institutional property owners, in the immediate vicinity of the 185th Avenue, 205th Avenue, and Orenco Stations. The city has coordinated planning activities, under advisement from Station Planning Advisory Teams (PAT), one of which was established for each Masterplan area. The Plans included site-specific proposals and recommendations for Comprehensive Plan changes, amendments to the Zoning Ordinance and Public Facilities Plan. As opposed to what was originally planned, these Master Plans were not adopted by the city council. Instead, zoning ordinances were directly worked out on the basis of the masterplan-concepts.

Station Community Plans:

Station Community Plans encompass a larger study area than the Station Area Master Plan areas described in Item 2 above. As such, Station Area Master Plans were part of a sub-area of the corresponding Station Community Plan. (A station community is defined as the geographic planning area which includes the LRT station site, adjacent properties, existing single family neighborhoods, apartment and townhouse communities, business centers and institutions located within the LRT station service area.) Station Community Plans were supposed to address broader issues, such as strategies for more efficient use of land within the study area, reduction in traffic congestion, and livable neighborhoods. Station Community Planning Objectives included considering the neighborhood character and respecting existing development, providing for expeditious approval of appropriate development, increasing ridership and reducing auto use, assuring a safe and pleasant bike/pedestrian environment, encouraging early development in the station areas, achieving appropriate density in station areas, being consistent with the adopted Regional Growth Concept and other subordinate plans, and being responsive to market conditions.

The plans include general policy recommendations for changes to the City's Comprehensive Plan, Zoning Ordinance amendments and proposals for a transportation network that includes bicycle and pedestrian travel facilities. The intent of long-range (year 2015) Station Community Plans was to enhance land-use and infrastructure, and incorporate transit-supportive uses and pedestrian-sensitive design into new developments located within a 10- 15 minute walk of an LRT station site.

Nine contiguous station areas in the Hillsboro LRT Corridor have been grouped into three station community planning study areas. Proposed LRT stations located within each station community planning area are noted below:

East Hillsboro Station Community Planning Area:
185th Avenue Station
205th Avenue Station

Central Hillsboro Station Community Planning Area:
Orenco Station
Hawthorn Farm Station
Fair Complex Station

Downtown Hillsboro Station Community Planning Area:
12th Street Station
Tuality Station
Central Hillsboro Station
Hillsboro Terminus Station

Project Genesis

Orenco was one of five rail based communities located in greenfields east and west of Hillsboro. Railroads have been a part of the Washington County landscape since 1840. One of the earliest lines to operate was the Oregon Electric Railroad, providing passenger service between communities for four decades.

Orenco's urban history began in 1906 with the settlement of a 1200-acre nursery, the largest one on the west coast during its time of operation and employed 150 of the towns' population of 500 inhabitants. Company officials persuaded the Oregon Electric Railroad to reroute the rail line so it would pass through the heart of Orenco town.

The City of Orenco was incorporated in 1912, grew, became the "garden spot of the Willamette Valley" and people moved to Orenco not just to work for the company but also of its beauty and convenience. The train fare from Orenco to Portland was $1.15 and took 45 minutes.

As a result of the Nursery company's bankruptcy, and the effects of the depression businesses and residents moved away during the Thirties. Train service to Orenco was discontinued in 1933, and automobiles became the primary mode of transportation for the area.

In 1938, the remaining citizens of Orenco voted to dissolve the city government. The complexion of the region evolved as nearby Portland expanded and Orenco became a bedroom community. Smaller house lots of the previous era were consolidated into larger lots, typical of suburban growth.

The closing of the Orenco Post Office in 1955, and the demolition of the Orenco school in 1961 indicated a shift toward Portland and Hillsboro to provide needed services.

Industrial sites were created to fulfill the City of Hillsboro's desire to evolve from a bedroom community and attract employment. Hawthorne Farm (west of Orenco) became Hillsboro's first planned modern industrial district, located along the rail line just west of Orenco.

Orenco and the Ronler Acres were supposed to become the second one. Therefore the city of Hillsboro had to undertake a very substantial land-use effort to purchase the Ronler Acres lots. Ronler Acres is a 350 acre piece of land that was originally subdivided into 850 single family lots in 1959, but the developer left town before building the infrastructure. As the years passed, the pressure of growth accelerated and various private attempts at assembling the land had failed, the City of Hillsboro began to study in 1988 the Ronler Acres problem. Here were 350 acres within a developable zone, surrounded by infrastructure and major investments by NEC and Fujitsu. A presentation about the city of Hillsboro puts it this way: "Ronler Acres was an island of un-developable blight that, if utilized, could significantly relieve the growth pressure on surrounding farm land, as well as contribute important strength and endurance to the City's economic base. The City solicited the opinions and advice of community groups and businesses. In addition, public meetings were held to gauge the opinion of the community and brainstorm various ways for the City to resolve the Ronler Acres gridlock. ... As a result, the City committed to forming an urban renewal agency, the Hillsboro Economic Development Council (HEDC), and the development of an Urban Renewal Plan."

The HEDC set out in 1989 to acquire 698 of the Ronler Acres lots, which were represented by 313 owners scattered all over the United States and the world, including Australia and Thailand. It was one of the largest acquisition efforts in the State of Oregon.

As the City was completing the acquisition of the land in late 1994, the Intel Corporation announced that it was looking for a research and development site. The City, in cooperation with the State of Oregon and the Portland Development Commission, proposed a number of sites, including Ronler Acres.

Intel was interested in Ronler Acres but would only locate there if it received a tax incentive from Washington County and the State of Oregon. The community turned out in force to show their support for the Intel's purchase of Ronler Acres because it had demonstrated its commitment to Hillsboro's type of smart growth goals.

The Chamber of Commerce, schools, businesses, and citizens testified about why Intel's purchase and development of Ronler Acres would benefit the community. Among these reasons were: $2.2 billion investment from Intel, 1,400 new high-wage permanent full-time jobs, 2,500 additional indirect jobs, and a $13.8 million Community Service Fee that would benefit the local community and schools, and generally lower tax rates. The Washington County Commissioners listened, agreed, and granted the tax incentive. Intel bought the Ronler Acres land in November 1994 and began their project.

Intel reimbursed the HEDC for all land costs, loaned $5.2 million to HEDC with the repayment tied to Intel construction performance, and donated $500,000 to assist in the development of a park in the area. In addition, Intel paid all regularly assessed fees and charges.

Parallel to the city, parts of this land were bought in small lots by Pacific Realty Trust (PacTrust), a commercial developer, whose usual undertakings are industrial parks and office buildings. As the southern part was never needed for the original goal, it represented a very good transit-oriented development potential while planning of the MAX Westside extension started.

PacTrust and the city of Hillsboro discussed re-zoning the area for a mix of commercial and residential uses. With PacTrust agreeing to the change of function, the city of Hillsboro sold its own Ronler acres parts to PacTrust in fall, 1996. The sales price was low, just covering all the costs of land acquisition. It reflected the “Fair Reuse Value” as opposed to the much higher “Fair Market Value” of the land gathered within the Urban Renewal District.

Illustration 7.9:Orenco Station Area under construction

Planning Process

The station was originally planned directly next to the historic neighborhood of Orenco, located on the southern side of the rail line (see Orenco station community land-use map). Despite the loss of such structures as the school, nursery packing shed and other buildings, many buildings remain intact and Orenco residents supported the establishment of a conservation district to encourage preservation and enhancement of the townsite. As the lead agency responsible for developing the Orenco Station Community Plan, the City of

Hillsboro Station Community Planning staff organized several community meetings and work sessions with neighborhood representatives during the past year, to seek public opinion during the neighborhood planning process. Alternative Neighborhood Plan Concepts noted below have been developed as a result of this effort: Concept 1: "Region 2040 Expectations", Concept 2: "Amend Existing Ordinance", Concept 3: "Orenco Townsite & Conservation District". As a result of these concepts, the station was removed westward to allow direct access to the PacTrust's developing sites north of the rail line.
This was an important condition for the Orenco Station Area Master Plan. The Plan was very accurately developed together with the city, the transit agency and the land owners. The land owners (PacTrust) contributed 50% to the planning costs. Below is the structure of the Orenco Station Area Master Plan Public-Private Partnership, which is also valid for the East Hillsboro station community

The costs of the planning procedure for these partnership stations ($870,000) were equally shared between the city of Hillsboro and the private investors.

The Work Program of November 1994 included the development of conceptual plan alternatives.

During this phase, concept plan alternatives were evaluated and a preferred concept plan alternative was selected for refinement. Design consultant services were contracted. Early on in this phase, all three consultants (market assessment, transportation and design) were brought together for an intensive work session/ "charrette" with the PAT, prior to the selection of a preferred alternative by PAT.

Two very important feasibility studies were made: the transportation study that came to the conclusion that alternatives to the extension of a regional road cutting through the PacTrust property were possible and the Economic and Market Analysis. This study was initiated through a consortium of property owners and developers in the vicinity of Orenco and Quatama / 205th Avenue station. The very critical question of this study was the land-use impacts of transit-oriented development. On the basis of a Request for Proposals issued by the Planning Advisory Team, a consultant team was selected, led by Leland Consulting Group, in association with Tashman Associates and Economic Research Associates/ ERA from San Francisco, California.

Early in the study, station community planning staff organized and facilitated a preliminary findings workshop. The consultant team to study sponsors and other stakeholders in the Light Rail corridor presented: i) market overview, ii) case studies of transit-oriented development in other suburban communities, and iii) preliminary conclusions on likely effects of Light Rail on current real estate development trends in Hillsboro.

The City of Hillsboro rendered the most important findings: "There is a strong residential market demand projected for Hillsboro with the majority of new unit demand after year 2000 by households of around two per household. - Smaller households are more likely to be a better market for multi-family and new / small lot single family housing types than has previously existed in Hillsboro. As the recipient of diversified high-tech jobs, Hillsboro can expect a rise in educational levels and this fact, coupled with the expectation of smaller household size, leads to a conclusion that many of the new smaller households will have more income per person and higher disposable income than larger households.

Table 7.1: Orenco Station Area Master Plan Public-Private Partnership

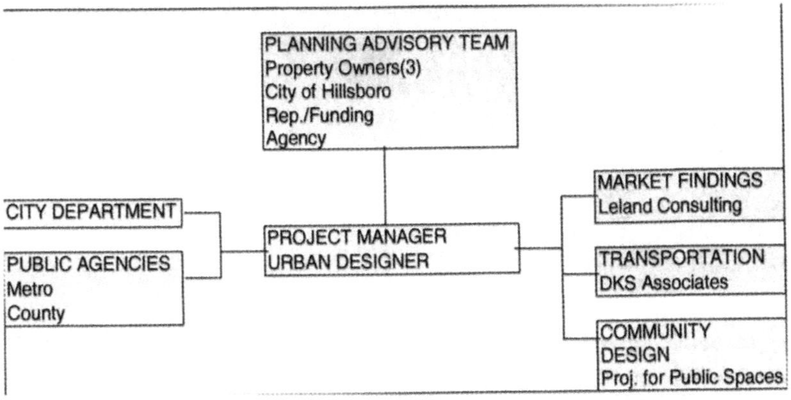

The perceived demand for residential property, coupled with the diminishing urban land supply, has caused residential land pricing to nearly double in 3 years.

Current land pricing for residential land is beginning to outstrip current multi-family feasibility given current rents and densities. - While there is a demand for industrial space, there is a significant inventory of industrial land in the Hillsboro area, which has caused a flattening of land pricing for industrial use. - Vacancy rates in existing spec industrial buildings suggest that spec industrial development is currently a high risk. - Office is beginning to pick up in the Hillsboro corridor because of land supply and tight suburban markets elsewhere. - Demand for retail space is conservatively estimated here because incomes are based on current Hillsboro trends. As Intel and associated industries phase in, however, these assumptions will have to be re-evaluated, due to the change in local per capita income produced by high wage employment

Illustration 7.10: Orenco Station Development Masterplan

The presence of rail-transit draws a higher income, more highly educated demographic group than exists in surrounding areas without transit. Significantly, the original character of the area seems not to affect this except in extreme examples.

Transit ridership issues are not necessarily the same as transit-oriented development issues, and the quality of pedestrian amenities is not causally correlated with either set of issues even though closely related. - Households near transit are smaller (around 1.6 persons) irrespective of the surrounding area household size.

Rail-transit appears to generate a seven to ten percent increase in house unit pricing near the station, with the price effect noted to around 1,800 feet from the station. In a study of BART station areas (San Francisco), office rents appear to be higher at stations and grade-down in a radius of about one and a half miles. Also at BART station areas, retail rents appear higher at transit stations, with the effect grading down in a radius of four tenths of a mile."
On the basis of this economic reassurance Masterplan and Design Guidelines were developed.

The Masterplan-phase started with a study of specific examples of how other communities have achieved, or plan to achieve densification along rail stations and transit corridors.

The study of precedents included prototypical, suburban development concepts, including Transit-oriented Developments, Neo Traditional Development, Campus Development, Urban Village, Main Street, etc., a case study of specific built projects relative to development, financing, design etc., and of development policy and standards that have been put in place, or being considered in selected communities with rail systems.

The planning results were directly translated into a description of development standards, about which the developers and the city agreed. The standards were adopted by the city council. The description contained detailed descriptions of how each of the housing complexes should look, including agreements about the façade color, the size and form of doors, windows, garages, porches, the design and plantation of front and back yards etc.

This contract and the open planning procedure, inviting not only the developers, but also the neighbors and the general public to participate, contributed to important time-savings compared to traditional planning processes. A detailed zoning plan could be skipped, and building permits could be issued almost immediately if they are based on the contract.

The total planning time needed for this process was reduced to three years instead of normally years longer. It will also avoid further slow downs for building permits, due to the normally more intense project examination.

Project design.

The entire property was divided into four different pieces, three residential and one commercial part. The centerpiece will be developed through a joint venture of PacTrust and Costa Pacific Homes, 30 acres of the northwestern residential part were sold to Fairfield Investments, 30 acres of the southwestern residential part, to Simpson Housing and the part most distant (more than 20 minutes walk) from the transit station was kept by PacTrust and is dedicated to their original purposes – a regional commercial center for a five mile area with approximately 100,000 inhabitants.
PacTrust will stay in control of the entire area even after the sale of parts of the land, reserved for residential purposes. The sales contract requires design review approvals through PacTrust. PacTrust can prevent design changes representing a risk for the integrity of the project as a whole.

The residential complex:

450 single family homes and townhouses (detached and attached) by Costa Pacific Homes and (originally) 1,400 high standard apartments by Fairfield Investments and Simpson Housing (condominium, rental), a "towncenter" with retail (small business-owned, only one exception of a chain-owned (Starbucks) facility) as well as additional 45 lofts or live/work-apartments. The different types of homes are supposed to be interspersed throughout the development.

Illustration 7.11: Costa Pacific Homes - detached home types

To determine the product and floor plan preferences for the community, builder Rudy Kadlub of Costa Pacific Homes hired Market Perspectives of Roseville, CA to conduct the market feasibility analysis, product positioning study and consumer research.

As already mentioned, Orenco Station is surrounded by five major high-tech manufacturing and research companies in what is known as the "Silicon Forest" of Washington County. A mail-return survey was developed by Market Perspectives and targeted to 1,500 employees at these companies.

With a response factor of over 30 percent, the survey determined that up to 40 percent of the likely buyers could be single-person households and a significant number of married couples, which did not have or were not planning to have children.

From this survey finding, the floor plan mix was slanted towards larger two bedroom models with several having the option of a den alcove or loft, which could be converted into an avocation space or extra bedroom.

The end result were designs for the townhomes and detached homes with richly detailed Craftsman and English cottage styles which included front porches, lots of windows, gables and garages which are tucked discreetly behind the homes along alleyways.

Consumer focus groups confirmed the market acceptability of both the exterior elevations and interior layouts for the townhomes and detached homes. The targeted buyer profiles also confirmed the standard and optional features for the homes.

Half of the entire single family complex is under construction, 166 homes have been finished, and 199 have already been sold. The buildings include town homes, cottage homes and Craftsman style homes. Sizes range from 1,200 to 2,500 square feet and prices range from $150,000 to $280,000. Seven furnished models are available for viewing. Lot-sizes have an average of 4000 square feet.

Whereas the prices per square foot are slightly higher than the regional average, the lot-sizes are not only smaller than the regional average but also far smaller than the homes in the immediate neighborhood. The fact that this is relatively new to Portland's housing market contributes to a slightly slower than expected sales speed of 8 instead of 10 units per month. Peter Bechen, PacTrust's CEO doesn't feel any serious sale problem, and is very optimistic about the remaining development activities.

The commercialization of Fairfield's and especially Simpson's apartments seems to be more problematic. The rental apartments have been changed into condominiums and the initial idea to build rental units directly at the main street between the station and the towncenter has been changed, due to the lack of rental clients in this suburban setting.

The future is not yet clear, but a change towards townhouses and condominiums seems to be realistic. It is also not clear if the originally intended southern extension of the towncenter will take place. Depending on the housing activities north and south of the station, PacTrust does though intend to realize a smaller commercial center in direct proximity to the station.

The town-center:

Essential for the development is the town-center, which gives to this neighborhood, despite its construction on a green field and its location in the region's suburban area a feeling of a real community. It consists of 56,000 square feet of retail and office space, 22 residential loft units with 20,560 square feet and 12 "live/work" units with 28,000 square feet (that will later be added through another 16 of these units with 38,000 square feet). According to Aliza Earnshaw of Portland's "Business Journal" (October 29,1999) "Main Street, U.S.A., is the model for the development's town center" The first buyers of Orenco station were drawn by the promise of walkable suburban community anchored by a Light Rail station. Now that the main street of Orenco Station is in place, the true character of the place is emerging. At last, residents of Orenco have something to walk to.

Illustration 7.12: Orenco Town Center 1999

Now a person can stroll to the Merchant of Venice, an Italian restaurant with a sophisticated menu and a fetching little bar that opens onto a quiet sidewalk and mini-plaza. Or perhaps an Indian meal would taste good tonight; Shalimar has just opened on the opposite corner, its spicy scents beckoning through an elaborately carved wooden entry, which owner Sabahat Rafiq brought from Pakistan.

There's a wine shop, Off the Vine, just up the street from Shalimar. And on the corner, facing Cornell Road, is the ultimate indicator of late 20th century American Civilization: Starbucks.

The retail businesses are moving in fast. Soon to come will be a café, a flower shop and a sporting goods store. A dentist is already doing business upstairs in an office facing Cornell, and an optician sells prescription sports goggles, along with regular glasses, a few doors from the Italian restaurant. A real estate agency and a little company are expected to move in soon".

Illustration 7.13: Towncenter Appartment Buildings

The design and the mix with the residential apartments on top of the stores were very carefully chosen: "The storefronts, and beyond them, the facing rows of mixed use residences, are wrapped in brick fasure. Beyond these lie a rectangular park, flanked by cottages painted in soft colors."

What generates such a lyrical appraisal has its price: the town center will only be profitable in its commercial part. If every office and retail space is be rented, PacTrust expects a (reasonable) return on investment rate of 11-12%. The residential components of the towncenter though will be have little or even negative return. As a consequence – despite the necessity of the center in the context of the entire development – lenders would have difficulties to finance it. PacTrust didn't rely on the $8 million that no bank would have given because it's not very profitable. It's a necessary investment

Above the shops are large windows. The ones on Cornell belong to the office spaces, the others to loft residences. "These are built and engineered to a commercial standard", said Richard Loffelmacher, PacTrust's Orenco Station project manager. "When you are going to have people living above the restaurant, you've got to make sure there won't be any noise or heat or odor coming from the restaurant below. We insulated the residences with thick concrete floors". The lofts are high-ceilinged, with generous views and substantial staircases.

Illustration 7.14: Orenco's central green area

The mixed-use housing between the main street and the cottages has a different feel. Wide steps lead from the sidewalk to handsome front doors, address numbers etched in lintel stones above, and smaller steps lead a half-flight down to a room that can be used as an office or additional bedroom.

The mix of different residence types was a deliberate decision, a departure from the more normal suburban offering of several variations on a single type of housing products coming on line – some townhouses and condominiums – available in the middle of next year". Loeffelmacher said: When you do the infrastructure right – including the town center – it lets you do a lot of different kinds and forms of housing. You can appeal to all kinds of people, and that brings a richer mix to the community.

Iverson Associates was selected to design the "for sale" product within Orenco Station. The firm studied the architecture of the traditional neighborhoods of Laurel-hurst and Ladd's Addition in Portland before designing the exterior elevations for Orenco Station.

The urban design:

In the same article Alize Earnshaw says, "Pedes-trians are the primary focus at Orenco Station". According to Bob Boileau, associate principal with Fletcher, Farr, Ayotte and project designer for the town center, this is an unusual focus for suburban development: "The pedes-trian focus is why there is so much emphasis on the straight shot from the MAX station up to Cornell Road and the town center".

Earnshaw continues: "The pedestrian experience is so important that PacTrust bore the expense of moving the Park & Ride lot that serves the station off to one side, so that disembarking passengers' first views would be of a pleasant prospect, marked by Orenco's distinctive building profile, rather than a concrete lot filled with cars."

This decision to move the parking lot is an emblem for the entire Orenco station project, where cars make way for people. There are plenty of parking spaces at the town center -- the planning team envisioned Light Rail as an amenity, not as the primary means of transport -- but cars are tucked away, behind the buildings, leaving shop doors facing the main street and open to pedestrian traffic.

"We wanted to create an outdoor living room for people to use", Boileau said. To that end, the planning team created a series of parks, ranging from tiny "pocket parks" among the houses to a 2.5 acre park east of the town center. The park give people spaces to stop and talk to one another, as do the sidewalks on the main street.

The main street itself is narrow, just wide enough for a single lane of traffic in each direction and for a row of parked cars to either side. Even the parking in the main street was added as a pedestrian amenity. "It's another layer of buffering between pedestrians and moving cars", Boileau said, "as well as an amenity for street retailers"'.

The commercial center:

The commercial center is intended to attract big box retailers in an entirely car-oriented development context. According to Peter Bechen, the commercialization of this part started well and a large grocer, a video-store, several banks, fast foods and a gas-station did already settle.

Despite this car-oriented character some important changes of the original concept have been made: The parking is less visible, due to a couple of smaller buildings that surround the north-eastern part of the site, which will directly face future residential developments. A street, also financed through PacTrust, cuts through the entire commercial development, creates a slightly more urban atmosphere and brings a bus in. As opposed to many other suburban shopping centers, this commercial center will at least be transit-accessible.

Critical elements

- The existence of the urban growth boundary, the car-access problems to downtown Portland and the relatively high parking costs in downtown Portland allow high quality alternative concepts for suburban development.

  The urban growth boundary leads to a limitation of available and developable land. One consequence is that land values increase. Portland is supposed to have relatively high land prices. Another consequence is that real estate development becomes more predictable. As every developer faces the same rules, the risk for transit-oriented developments to be competed through projects with no transit context is reduced (especially for the medium to high standard categories).

- The relatively low land price at the time of PacTrusts's land acquisition, the existence of an "Urban Renewal District" necessary for the city of Hillsboro to purchase all the land parcels of Ronler Acres and the fact that the assembled land was sold to PacTrust at the original price,

- The realization of the low revenue town center – which was possible because of PacTrust's own financing capacity,

- The possibility to avoid the original plan of the widening of Cornell Road, which took a heavy and risky effort through the PAT and many influential persons,

- The management of the public planning and zoning process through the city of Hillsboro and the involved consultants,

- The project flexibility, for example allowing the switch from rentals to condominiums at the multi-family housing units in proximity to the station,

- The readiness of the metropolitan government to accept lower housing densities than initially planned, to agree instead on a total number of housing units to be built and to accept the developers parking rations (based on a high level of mutual trust and avoiding to "create density for density's sake" (Peter Becken, PacTrust president),

- The important financial participation of PacTrust for the entire local infrastructure, including the financing of all local streets, its design, the sewer system and the costs of removing the park & ride facility at the station and the financial participation in the planning phase.

Conclusions

The New Urbanism movement achieved its first Master Planned Community of the Year honor from the National Sales and Marketing Awards at the National Association of Home Builders (NABB) convention in Dallas, in January 1999.

Orenco Station by Pacific Realty Associates (PacTrust) and Costa Pacific Homes in Hillsboro, OR was named the 1998 "best community in the nation" for its planning concept, product design and marketing excellence.

What makes Orenco Station's recognition so important is the fact the 190-acre suburban site situated on Portland's new Westside Light Rail line was created using a combined pedestrian and transit-oriented planning approach. As a consequence, it won the prestigious national award over four other master planned communities, which had more conventional sprawl-type site plans.

Orenco Station won grand prizeawards for best attached floor plan under $200,000; best detached floor plan under $200,000; best logo; best brochure; and best sales center less than 650 square feet. It was also a silver finalist for best web page and signage and, most importantly, it finally won the award as "community of the year".

Besides the rental apartments, the "for sale" residential product lines include townhomes, small lot detached cottages (average lot size of 3,750 square feet and larger detached homes on average 6,800 square foot lots. A "for sale" condominium product will soon be added to the mix.

Orenco Station has not only been an award-winning community but also a tremendous sales success. Since the opening of the models in November, 1997 and through the beginning of April 1999 until March 2000, almost 200 attached and detached homes were sold, an average of more than eight sales per month.

Illustration 7.15:
Orenco - National showcase as a "livable community"

The townhomes and small lot cottages and not the "common" suburban residential large scale lot are capturing the majority of the sales. Of the sales as of 1999, only three of the ten larger lot detached homes have sold.

Since opening, base pricing has increased an average of 15 percent and the attached and detached units within Orenco Station are priced between 15 to 20 percent higher than the direct competition even against those competitors which have larger lot sizes for their detached product.

Another interesting fact about Orenco Station is its floor plan mix for the attached and small lot detached product lines. Five of the seven floor plans being offered in both products combined have two bedroom designs - with some of the models having specialty alcove or loft spaces.

Rental apartments, now being redesigned into condominiums are apparently less requested at the moment. As a result, the market for suburban housing with higher densities still needs to be fully discovered.

The town center became the focal point of the community. This little center is one of the most important new features of the Orenco station development. It shows that mixed used development is not only socially but also economically valuable. The large big box retail complex in close proximity limits the possibilities to increase the town-center's retail diversity. The realization of 30,000 more square feet of retail space, provided by the masterplan south of Cornell road is not very likely to happen.

Orenco Station is located on the Westside Light Rail line, which connects Hillsboro with downtown Portland. The majority of the homes, apartments and town center are within a quarter to one-half mile of the station.

Precise figures about ridership development with more people moving into Orenco don't exist at the moment. As the majority of the buildings are relatively far away from the station, and many of the new Orenco inhabitants are working at Intel or other Hillsboro High Tech companies, the probability of using the Light Rail to go to work is not very high. According to other Tri-Met-sourcesm thoughm a general trend seems to exist to use the Light Rail for other than commuting purposes.

7.8 Public approval of TOD and application of TOD promoting tools as transaction cost reducing factors

The TOD approach aims at generating specific transactions to foster urban development around transit stations. The costs of these may be reduced through the way they are handled and the conditions under which they are handled.

Transit oriented development in itself leads to project-specific extra costs compared with the same amount of dwelling units, office space, retail and entertainment facilities in a greenfield development and in absence of specific design and land-use requirements.

However, the examples presented and analyzed in this chapter show that a realistic view of what both sectors - private and public - can provide, and a wide range of flexibly applicable tools have led to mutually beneficial results. If, on the other hand, the goals on either side are too ambitious or if the amount of regulation and incentives to steer and stimulate TOD is overcharged, transaction costs increase.

Independently from the above mentioned aspects, which will be summarized below, the question whether and to what extent the local public and political arena is sensitive to the problems of urban sprawl, and is therefore requesting transit oriented development, plays an important role to increase or reduce TOD-related transaction costs.

Public approval

As already mentioned at the beginning of this chapter the amount of transit-oriented development is surprising, especially because of the weak political and legal framework to support these developments on the regional level. According to many studies, transit-oriented development is a national phenomenon and not limited to the areas investigated in this report.

The comparison with the one Canadian example represented in this report and the information about other Canadian cities seems to indicate that in North America, the leading role of how to contain urban sprawl and how to promote transit friendly urban development has now switched to the United States.

These changes do not necessarily presuppose an already existing mass phenomenon. The only city that has signs of a substantial change of the urban form is Portland, OR. And yet this is only the case for the city itself and much less for its suburban area. Toronto is still North America's most transit-oriented city of the 20th century, and it has better chances of at least partly channeling suburban sprawl than most US cities.

But the difference is that at the moment, the development community and the suburban society are less ready for such alternatives than in the United States. As a consequence no current legal and financial tools to specifically promote transit-oriented developments have been forged in Canada.

It is important to mention Canada because the postwar development of Canadian cities resembles more the development of European urban areas than US cities do. Despite many successes of transit developments and transit channeled urban growth in European countries, the concept of transit-oriented development in itself has not yet been introduced. It is the concept of forging coalitions between seemingly antagonistic forces and of developing tools to promote these coalitions.

A Washington Post article cites a study about the voters' behavior on similar issues during the US elections in November 2000. The votes about specific local or state wide decisions concerning different aspects of urban and land development show that "sprawl got space on the ballots" (title of the article on February 27th, 2001). "Proposals to preserve open space and build and maintain parks were among the most popular ballot measures voters addressed in November. Voters in 38 states and hundreds of cities, towns and counties voted on 553 growth-related measures last November and passed 72 percent of them".

"What we are seeing is the beginning of a move toward broad, cross-jurisdictional coalitions," said Bruce Katz, director of the Brookings Institute's Center on Urban and Metropolitan Policy, which conducted the study. "The constituencies impacted by sprawl have not acted together in the past." Examples of the coalition approach cited by Katz included "the passage in California of a measure to extend the Bay Area Rapid Transit (BART) line to San Jose (supported by environmental groups and Silicon Valley executives), and a $400 million annual budget set aside in New Jersey to fund improvements in highways, mass transit, and pedestrian and bicycle paths".

"The report also found that while local measures to purchase open space and keep it off-limits to development passed overwhelmingly (78 percent nationwide, 98 percent in the Northeast), citizen-sponsored efforts to impose new statewide restrictions on growth fared less well".

These votes, although most of them not directly related with transit issues, indicate important changes of political priorities in a society that is more characterized by car dependence and its urban sprawl consequences than any other. The vote results also indicate that there seems to be common ground between developers and the society on which measures should be taken: they should be voluntary and not obligatory.

Yet - as mentioned earlier – the most successful example of how to actually change the pattern of urban development is Portland, OR with its growth boundary. The contradiction between the acceptance of anti-sprawl-measures and the rejection of urban growth boundaries as the most effective framework for voluntary development agreements may very well prevent substantial changes in other parts of the country. The reluctance to tax-based funding, i.e. towards allowing to build up a substantial public funding basis, increases this uncertainty.

A correlating two prong question emerges: 1) Does transit-oriented development represent a sustained change of development patterns that eventually will have a visible impact on a broader number of US cities or rather 2) Does TOD, after filling a market niche, cease to promote the further extension of transit networks throughout the country?

These questions cannot be answered in this study but they are connected with the contradiction of the voter will that has been mentioned earlier. If in this phase of building systems and creating an alternative development opportunity, the public side ceases to fund rail system extensions and if at the same time no geographical development boundaries are accepted, chances are that the current re-urbanization efforts will crumble.

Transaction cost savings through clear definition of the role of TOD

At the moment, the role of TOD is not to fill up financial gaps and thus not to directly financially contribute to system extensions. The current role of TOD for rail infrastructure extension and financing is to generate network-users, to benefit from the rail service, to request rail service and to promote a transit-oriented change of urban patterns and thus of an overall improved economic frame for rail-transit investments.

The summary of TOD case studies in Dallas and San Diego and additional locations in attachment 10.3 shows that a great variety of uses are suitable for TOD. 14 of the 29 TOD projects summarized in the case study list have substantial office portions or consist entirely of office space. 15 projects have retail portions or are pure shopping malls. In six cases, hotels were built, generally large ones. Entertainment uses including restaurants, museums, conference centers, stadiums, libraries have been explicitly mentioned as part of 7 projects. Finally, 19 projects included or consisted of different types of residential uses, most of them rental apartments, but a growing number of single family or senior housing.

The large majority of TOD projects have been developed during the nineties, though many of them are only partly completed and still in the planning phase. The project size varies very strongly. The smallest projects are usually realized by the transit agency itself or by the city government. The largest developments try to generate new urban or regional destinations and may be an important long term actor on the local and regional real estate market.

No developer appears twice, so that no company seems to dominate the market for transit-oriented development, especially not highly specialized firms like Peter Calthorpe and Associates, founders of the New Urbanism movement. Peter Calthorpe and the congress of New Urbanism have nevertheless been a great influence in defining and qualifying what a TOD is. Peter Calthorpe's projects show (for example the one in Rio Vista in San Diego), that transit-oriented development is supposed to oppose monofunctional development. As an indirect consequence, not only his own projects, but also a growing number of other transit related projects are foreseeing mixed-use developments.

The Orenco station development in Portland, OR is not an ideal type for this new mixed use concept. It is essentially a suburban residential location, but includes innovative aspects like a little town center, well-designed landscape architecture and open spaces, and some unusual aspects in the residential portion. The homes as well as all the other elements of each development phase are designed in a common architectural language and the lots are much smaller than the average suburban housing lot. The average lot size is less than 4000 square feet, and consists of a high portion of attached homes and resembles German and other European examples of space-saving housing constructions. The most interesting fact is that the smaller lots sell better than the large ones. And they sell at a substantially higher price of 15-20% more than the average detached home on a larger lot.

It is difficult to say what the most important success reasons were, whether it was the higher quality of the project itself, based on design qualities, public spaces, town center and community-facilities, the proximity of a large employer (Intel) or the rail-transit access.

The Orenco station development seems to be economically more viable that other projects with higher densities, less parking spaces, more station oriented design and other features of TOD model cases. This may serve as an indicator that transit-oriented development works best where basic market rules of real estate development, be it residential or commercial, are respected.

In most cases no precise information exists about the impact of the projects on the travel behavior and the number of passengers generated through the development. This lack of information is surprising and needs to be filled out in future studies. As no reliable passenger counts existed in most of the development sites, this deficit could not be eliminated in this report.

Transaction cost savings through the application of appropriate tools

The table "Techniques used to encourage Transit-oriented Development" shows the techniques used by the city administration or the transit agency to encourage these developments. The table includes all seven metropolitan areas (and distinguishes between New York City and New Jersey) of this report, not only those highlighted in this chapter. It is in most cases difficult to clearly separate between Transit-oriented and Transit Joint Development. For instance several of the San Diego projects presented in this chapter take place at least partly on agency property. As the city is equally interested in transit-oriented development, the built results are the same.

In almost every study city land-use regulations provide mixed use developments at transit stations. Equally unanimously city administrations are ready to grant density bonuses for transit-oriented developments. The parking requirements have not yet been ideally tailored. Some cities have strongly reduced parking requirements for the development itself, some try to reduce parking spaces in the entire area, some have maximum allowed parking spaces for the development. This last alternative doesn't seem to fit to market requirements. In case of conflict, it is therefore difficult to withhold such requirements (see above the case of the Orenco station development).

The planning and management tools to promote transit-oriented development are crucial for the success of TOD. Without adequate planning goals and promoting institutions in the transit agency itself and on the local and regional level, the chances to actually achieve transit friendly uses along urban rail lines are much lower. The most successful cities to promote transit-oriented development are Portland, OR and San Diego, CA. Both have almost entirely utilized the range of available tools to manage this process--land acquisition of the transit agency or the local community, where possible, a very focused management of transit-oriented development on the local level and within the transit agency, station area development plans through the local community, professional station development staff within the agency and, finally, additional public development agencies, whose tasks are generally not limited to transit related development but to broader tasks of the economic and urban development (e.g. La Mesa Community Redevelopment Agency in the San Diego Area or the Portland Development Corporation in Portland/OR).

The available financial tools to attract transit-oriented development are applied where the development potential is evaluated as high enough to generate substantial amounts of sales tax or property tax in a designated tax increment finance district (tif). This is particularly the case where new (Light) Rail lines through areas with high development potential are planned and realized. Public Improvement Districts or Benefit Assessment Districts are relatively rare although potentially very interesting funding tools from a European perspective. Although the possibility to set up a PID exists in Dallas, no area is situated in proximity to a Light Rail station, where this instrument has been used with the purpose to finance necessary improvements in the station area. Tax abatements due to a transit friendly location also exist as a possibility in Dallas, but no case is known where this has been used. On the other hand, as explained in chapter 4, a tool that is very often applied is a tax deductible bond for public purposes such as station financing.

Finally, several cities use instruments such as urban renewal districts to concentrate many different public tasks in station areas. San Diego and Portland have applied this instrument. These two cities also try to locate public facilities such as tourist information centers, schools, police stations, public administration headquarters and obviously conference centers and stadiums in proximity of a Light Rail line or extend rail lines into areas with public services. The localization of subsidized housing is a possibility for which relatively few experience exists. Due to generally higher real estate values in proximity of stations, this may represent a socially rather than a transit friendly instrument.

Both the application of adequate tools and a realistic view of the potential outcome of a transit oriented development are highly important to limit TOD related transaction costs. Realism on both the public and the private side may eliminate unnecessary, costly and time-consuming debates and thus contribute to the actual realization of TODs. While a wide and segmented range of infrastructure financing sources may be counterproductive for the realization and extension of urban rail systems, a wide range of TOD tools may be very productive to promote TOD.

The Toolbox has to be diversified enough to fit the requirements, which are specific to each case. But as in the case of tendering rail systems, the application of these tools requires very professional institutions and staff on the public side, i.e. a competent TOD agent. The ideal agent would be one that combines TOD and BOT competence and enthusiasm. In the scope of this study, London is the only place where the transit authority includes both competences. The regional transport executives (Verkehrsverbunde) in Germany have the potential to fulfill both roles - if they are required to do so by their principals.

Table 7.2: Techniques used to encourage Transit-oriented Development

Tools	New York City MTA	New Jersey NJ Transit	Arling-ton County WMATA	Atlanta GA MARTA	Dallas TX DART	San Diego CA MTDB	Portland OR TriMet	Toronto ON TTC
Land-use Regulations								
Mixed Use		x	x	x	x	x	x	
Density Bonus	x		x	x	x	x	x	x
Parking Regulations			x	x		x	x	x
Management Tools								
Land Acquisition			x	x		x	x	x
TOO Management			x			x	x	
Station Area Development	x	x	x	x		x	x	x
Development Agen....						x		
Financing Tools								
Tax Increment Finance (TiF)			x		x	x	x	
Improvement District					x			
Tax Abatement					x	x	x	
Coordination of Public Tasks								
Urban Renewal Districts						x	x	
Location Public facilities			x			x	x	
Subsidized Housing							x	

8. Summary and Conclusions

8.1 System extensions and dynamic ridership development

Due to the growing economic and functional problems associated with urban sprawl and car-dependency, the demand for general public transit, and, particularly, urban rail transit, is increasing in American metropolitan areas.

On the one hand, this trend is reflected through the ridership growth of the second half of the last decade. Since 1995, annual ridership has been growing by 4% every year, peaking in 1999. Between 1995 and 2000, ridership grew by more than 21%. This indicates a growth trend, beyond population, plus economic growth. It also greatly exceeds the average growth rates of car travel. Transit ridership in the US at the turn of the century was higher than in 1960, when car ownership started to increase exponentially.

On the other hand, this is reflected through a strongly increasing demand for new rail systems. More than 300 rail lines are currently being planned, expanded or newly built in metropolitan areas. The desire for modern, efficient public transit is also based on a change in the very function of inner cities; on their becoming entertainment districts, places to live for people before or after raising families, and business locations in a multi-functional setting. Moreover, the areas surrounding these cities have undergone a transformation during the past decade. According to the US Census 2000, they are now more densely populated and more urban. These trends will be reinforced by the development and expansion of rail systems, which are intended not only to contain the proliferation of automobile traffic, but also to promote denser development along rail corridors and nearby railway stations. This objective in particular still poses a formidable challenge, as residential population density in American urban areas is still very low.

The public transit infrastructure typically consists of so-called "light rail" systems, i.e. trams that serve the urban areas and city centers on their own tracks. They generally run above ground; outside the urban centers; they tend to use former or under-utilized railway lines. At high frequencies of service, they can attain passenger transport capacities approaching those of heavy rail systems (subway and metro), and considerably surpassing those of buses.

In addition to new construction and expansion of such light rail systems, which have been in use since the early 1980s, there has been a recent increase in extensions of existing heavy rail systems.

8.2 Funding possibilities, needs and forms

Public Transportation Funding possibilities and needs

Although public funds for these expansion projects increased in the Clinton era, the monies available are wholly inadequate for implementing the many projects within reasonable timeframes. While federal funding for new starts of light rail systems amount to somewhat more than 1 billion dollars (US) (out of a total budget for mass transit of 7.5 billion dollars), the projects at some stage of planning or execution that are registered for subsidies came to a total cost of 22 billion dollars in 2000. In fact, the aggregate volume of light transit projects that are in preparation in US urban areas is probably even higher.

Federal subsidies have been cut away from operation subsidies and focused on infrastructure investments. Due to increasingly complex ground transportation problems, the transportation legislation of the nineties (ISTEA and TEA 21) focused on the interconnectivity of transport systems and the support of local decision-making to develop these interconnected systems. As a consequence, funding increased for public transit investments, especially new rail systems.

The financing of new systems, new lines or system-extensions, is almost entirely based on public funding, especially federal contributions. Despite increases of the above-mentioned federal transit capital funding, the remaining federal funding possibilities are far too limited to finance all major parts of the planned new transit systems. The realization of most transit projects depends on the possibilities to leverage funding on the state and local levels.

Gas taxes are the main revenue source of these expenditures. The gas tax revenues plus additional freight transportation-related revenues are the basis of the Highway Trust Fund, which, since 1956, has provided stable funding for highway programs. In 1996, the Highway Trust Fund had total receipts of almost 26 billion dollars. About 75% of that stems from gas taxes. The federal gas tax portion was 18.4 cents per gallon in 1996, and has not changed since.

The average additional state gas tax was 19.05 cents per gallon in 1997. That leads to an average total gas-tax of 37.5 cents per gallon (about 10 cents per liter, three to ten times less than in European Countries!). Due to relatively high gas consumption per car, and relatively long average travel distances, federal and state gas taxes together generate remarkably high total surface transportation funding sources of almost 50 billion dollars(1996).

Nevertheless, the possibilities to fund public transportation with this money are limited. While it is legally possible on the federal level to use gas-tax-income for transit projects, many states (38 out of 50 US states) legally prohibit the use of car-related income for anything other than car-related purposes. Even if not prohibited, the political readiness to use portions of this money for transit, instead of highways is limited (New Jersey with a portion of 50% for transit is exceptional). As a result, the gap between public funding needs and possibilities for public transportation remains very large.

Private investors can hardly bridge this gap. It is generally very difficult to include investors in the financing of new systems or system extensions, especially if farebox-revenues are the only significant revenue-source. This is due to relatively low or uncertain ridership numbers, low fares, and high system and operation costs. Farebox-revenues never cover operation and maintenance costs. The highest recovery rate of operation and maintenance costs is 75% (Washington D.C. Metrorail, WMATA).

Barring any additional revenue source, a closer cooperation between the public and the private sector must concentrate on the following issues: to increase system efficiency, to accelerate the realization of new lines or system expansions and to contribute to lower construction and operation costs. These are issues that integrated contracting forms of designing, building, operating, maintaining and sometimes financing of rail-transit projects deal with. The number of Design-Build-Operate-Maintain (DBOM)-contracts between transit agencies and private consortia increases; however, few reliable examples exist in the transit field.

Nonetheless, the scarcity of funds permits rigorous project screening that also (and especially) helps optimize the contribution of new systems to municipal development.

For these reasons, the degree to which the average project is subsidized has diminished. From up to 90% in the 1970s, the public-grant component has fallen to an average of 50% today. This drastic decline in public funding compels municipalities to closely investigate all ways of incorporating private investment, and especially the potential impacts of proposed rail lines on real estate development.

This area appears to be particularly in need of improvement. Not only in the USA, but also in Europe, what frequently seems attainable in road construction is generally out of the question in mass transit infrastructure: Investment expenses cannot be recovered via prospective user fees. In most cases, user fees do not cover even a system's operating costs.

This gives rise to a major problem for partnerships between public and private financial backers. The private sector's financial interest in establishing the infrastructure is slight; where an interest exists, the incentive is the indirect revenue of such investment.

The interest from private investors at large focuses on the associated construction projects and vehicle orders on the one hand, and the development and marketing of properties on the other. In the reality of US mass transit systems the latter motive has been dominant. For European needs, the forms of collaboration and co-financing encountered in these arrangements offer valuable ideas for closer cooperation between public transit institutions, public sector sponsors, and property owners and developers.

Using seven metropolitan areas as examples where rail transit systems make an important contribution to transport, this report presents a systematic overview of the types and extent of planned investments: how they are to be funded, how they form partnerships with private investors. The study differentiates among three kinds of cases:

- forming new organizational and funding methods for building and operating light rail lines;
- generating partial funding by selling or leasing transit real estate (known as "transit joint development"); and

- increasing the intensity of utilization – and hence the long-term profitability – of new rail lines by means of urban development near transit stops (referred to as "transit-oriented development").

For each of these three subject areas, the study provides an overview of the legal and funding tools used, the trend in significant projects in the USA at large, as well as a closer look at a case study, and, where appropriate, a comparative discussion of analogous cases in Britain and Germany. Chapter 8.3 will summarize the financial impact of partnerships in these three fields.

Forms of private funding and private ownership in rail infrastructure development

The traditional method of incorporating private capital in infrastructure projects in the USA is to issue **municipal bonds**. "General obligation bonds" are secured by the general revenue of the municipal or state budget; "revenue bonds" are secured by the additional receipts, which the issuer expects from the project in question (revenue from government subsidies, higher property and sales tax proceeds and user fees, such as fares).

The issuance of such project-specific municipal bonds represents one of the most important instruments of municipal finance and investment policy in the USA. This is attributable mainly to the fact that bonds are usually exempt from income tax and carry correspondingly low interest rates.

The ratings of these bonds by the rating agencies (Moody's, Standard & Poor's, Fitch IBCA) represent an important assessment of risk by the capital market. Higher levels of risk are compensated by higher rates of interest. However, from the investor's point of view, these project-specific bonds are not perceived as being significantly tied to the ongoing financial success of a particular project. For borrowers, they are a source of low-interest loans, broadly comparable to the "municipal loans" common in many European countries (these are lendings by private and public sector banks to townships, municipalities or public sector institutions).

In the context of innovative tools for financing transit infrastructure, **TIFIA** has attracted the most attention. TIFIA, the Transportation Infrastructure Finance and Innovation Act of 1998, lets the Federal government guarantee or provide part of the funds to be raised in the financial markets for eligible projects. The law was passed as a component of the broader TEA-21, a general law dealing with transport finance. TIFIA's purpose is to support the funding of major transport infrastructure projects that are potentially economically viable by backing or granting loans. Projects must cost more than 100 million dollars in total to qualify.. TIFIA's loan guarantee or low-cost loan, repayable only from the fifth year after project completion, is limited to a maximum of one-third of a project's total cost.

The first five projects supported by this program (which is administered by the Federal Highway Administration) amount to a total of 6.6 billion dollars, and were selected in September 1999. Four of these are mass transit projects in the broadest sense: The relocation of Pennsylvania Station to the historic main post office in New York; the people-mover providing a link between Miami airport and regional transit; the investment program to improve the Metrorail system in Washington, D.C.; and the light rail system of San José in Puerto Rico.

For example, the capital improvement program for Washington's 103 mile-long heavy rail system involves a total cost of 2.3 billion dollars for the upgrading and replacement of rolling stock, route infrastructure and equipment by 2009. The Washington Metropolitan Area Transit Authority (WMATA) received a TIFIA credit guarantee of 600 million dollars. This backing will enable WMATA to obtain the capital market loans for the necessary construction. The loan is secured by capital contributions by the District of Columbia and the states of Maryland and Virginia.

The key benefit of the TIFIA guarantee is that it provides access to the capital market, allowing WMATA to raise funds needed for pressing projects. On the occasion of Metrorail's 25-year anniversary in March of this year, the press praised the vast success of the system, but also underscored the need for an extensive overhaul. Over the next 25 years, according to these observers, the outlay for maintenance is expected to exceed the initial cost of building the system. Failing such continued investment, the strong ridership growth, from today's 600,000 passengers a day, to 1.2 million daily in 2025, could cause the Metrorail infrastructure to deteriorate.

8.3 Financial contribution through DBOM, Transit Joint and Transit Oriented Development

The DBOM contribution to cost reduction and infrastructure financing

Significant innovation is also embodied by projects which a single private entity or group builds, operates, maintains, perhaps also finances, and, after an agreed period of operation, hands over to the public sector. In the USA, following the example of the UK, such design-build-operate-maintain (DBOM) or build-operate-transfer (BOT) agreements are increasingly being used to have public infrastructure projects – including railway lines – completed and operated on a turnkey basis by private sector consortia.

The first and most prominent US example presently is the Hudson-Bergen line, a 20.5-mile (37-km) light rail route with 33 stations in New Jersey, running parallel to Manhattan. In 1995, after 15 years of planning, the decision was made to realize the project through a private construction and operating company. For a lump-sum public subsidy, the private firm or consortium had to build and operate the line over a period of 15 years, and than transfer it to the public side, i.e. to the state-owned transit company (NJ Transit), in a "like new" technical state.

The prelude to this DBOM or BOT contract award was a two-stage process of declarations of interest, and a limited tender. The call for expressions of interest was published in June 1995. By evaluating the pre-qualifying information, the field of eligible bidders was narrowed down to five consortia. In November 1995, these five were requested to submit bids by February 1996, based on a very detailed set of specifications, a draft contract, and all relevant project information. The tender documents filled 60 binders with requirements and information concerning planning details, environmental specifications, economic conditions, ridership forecasts, a "quality service index", and other material.

Precise criteria for evaluating the expected bids were developed in advance. Technological and quality aspects were to be weighted at 40%; price – i.e. the cost to the public sector (NJ Transit) – was given a weight of 60%.

Two bids were eventually submitted. One, for 1.082 billion dollars, was a joint offer by Raytheon, a US defense and construction firm and Japanese vehicle manufacturer Itochu, which joined forces as the "Twenty-First Century Rail Corporation" consortium. The other bid, for 1.433 billion dollars, was by Siemens. The large difference in bid prices led the board of directors of NJ Transit to decide swiftly and clearly in favour of the US-Japanese consortium in August 1996.

The lump-sum contract required Twenty First Century Rail Corporation to begin revenue service on the first section of line (as defined above) by October 1999. This deadline could not be met, nor did the actual commissioning half a year later include the entire first section. These delays were not the fault of the consortium. Rather, NJ Transit was unable to make the required properties available in time, which was its responsibility under the terms of the contract. The reason lay in the long duration of the planning process for the Hudson-Bergen line. True, property owners along the waterfront were forced by zoning and building-permit regulations to keep the 30- to 50-metre-wide corridor needed for the rail route vacant free of charge (these requirements added up to about 10% of the project cost). But, the exact location of the corridor was not determined until after real estate investors had already committed themselves to many construction projects or other land-use decisions. This resulted both in pronounced jogs in the route – conceded in order to avoid having to remove buildings – and in lengthy negotiations with property owners to set the actual location of the track.

On the whole, the DBOM approach can in principle be said to have successfully expedited the project. Without the private sector being responsible for the construction, the project could have been delayed by another several years, due especially to the continual political meddling. On the other hand, the project cannot yet be considered a poster child for how to organize the delivery of public infrastructure projects by private companies. Thus, strikes against the project were: the high total cost, the lack of systematic inclusion of real estate investors, the absence of project-specific revenue risk to the operator, and the less than optimal exact siting of the track (which, however, does not result from the specifications of the operating contract).

The first 16-km section cost the taxpayers 778 million dollars. This expense includes the cost of building track and 45 rail vehicles, the purchase of properties by NJ Transit, the purchase of track, track upgrading and permits. While this amount seems to be relatively high and has not been systematically compared with the costs the public sector alone would have had, there is a strong likelihood that the financial impact of the BOT approach was positive. The amount to be paid is much lower than the payment requested from the losing bidder, no additional subsidy over the entire 15 year period will be necessary, AND, after the 15 years of operation, a perfectly functioning system will be transferred (or submitted to subsequent bids), the ridership revenue over this period will go to NJ Transit, increasing their revenue, without generating additional costs.

In order to gain a reference base by which to judge this cost and the approach to the project, other significant light rail projects in the USA and Britain were researched. These are projects where the private partner not only provides the design, construction and operation (except in the case of Portland, Oregon), but also contributes funding.

The only post-war example of privately (co)financed rail transport infrastructure in the USA was completed in Portland, Oregon. The costs of the "Airport-Max" construction, an approximately 5.5-mile (9-km) light rail link between downtown Portland and the city's airport, were about 165 million dollars (operating costs will be borne by Portland's transit corporation, Tri-Met, as operator; Tri-Met will also provide the trains). Bechtel Enterprises, a global American building group, has contributed 25 million dollars of the investment. In addition, Bechtel is providing project design and construction management at its own expense. The airport operator is supplying 32.8 million dollars of the funding, a contribution covered entirely from airport fees. The project is being financed without the usually indispensable government investment. Bechtel's interest in the project and willingness to provide capital was generated by the fact that the city of Portland gave Bechtel the development rights for, and an 85-year lease on, a large building lot of 120 acres (50 ha) near the airport. This property will be made easily accessible by the rail line now under construction. Moreover, the design and implementation by a single, private sector provider saved considerable time.

While the direct private contribution is precisely to measure ($25 million, plus engineering costs) it is difficult to evaluate the total value of the contribution. The long-term lease of the Cascade station area is in fact a substantial remuneration for this contribution. As a result, the private contribution has two effects: it accelerates the project through co-financing, engineering and construction management, and it "builds in" a very professional and powerful mechanism to develop the large airport-linked property in a transit-oriented manner.

In Europe, due to the greater importance of public transport and higher ridership figures, there is greater experience in private participation in building railways, especially in the development of attractive route corridors. As a rule, these installations involve links to airports (UK, Sweden and Norway) and new inner-city transit systems (UK). Two particularly meaningful examples are the Greater Manchester Metrolink, and the Croydon Tramlink commissioned last year in the southern London suburb.

Both systems were not directly submitted to the Private Finance Initiative (PFI), introduced by the conservative government in 1992, but followed its approach and even contributed to the elaboration and improvement of PFI. The initiative's goal is to involve responsibility for public sector investment to the private sector wherever possible and, when this role cannot be transferred completely, to conduct public investment through privately managed joint ventures. The concept calls for favoring the respective private partner that places the lowest demand on public subsidies and that provides financing, design, construction, operation and maintenance from a single source.

Greater Manchester, which has a population of 2.5 million, decided at the end of the 1980s, to build a regional light rail system (partly by rebuilding former British Rail track, partly by laying new track in the city). The executive body (GMPTE) of the Greater Manchester Public Transport Authority (GMPTA) was instructed to put out to tender an initial 31-km stretch of line for a maximum contract duration of 15 years (one-half of the 30-year period requested by the British government). The agreement gave GMPTE the right to cancel and re-tender the contract early, after three years, in the event that profit expectations were surpassed. Conversely, the bidder had the right to back out of the arrangement after three years if earnings expectations were underachieved.

The DBOM contract for the Greater Manchester Metrolink was awarded to a consortium consisting of a building company, a rail vehicle manufacturer and an operator. The contract cost was the equivalent of about 200 million dollars (USD), to be paid largely from public funds. The consortium was to contribute some 10 million dollars in the form of licence fees. No subsidies were to be paid for operating expenses. In fact, a revenue surplus was expected, of which the operator was to remit 50% to the GMPTA.

Despite high, unregulated fares, the new system, equipped with its six-minute intervals between trams, was so successful (passenger numbers more than doubled) that the GMPTE made use of the exit clause after three years. The authority re-tendered both the further operation of this first line and the construction and operation of a (largely new) 6-km extension. Four consortia, including the existing operator, were invited in 1996 to submit offers, with the contract wording similar to that of 1989. As the successful bidder was to finance about 60% of the total 250 million dollar (US) investment cost of the project – a high percentage – the DBOM contract went to a new consortium, Altram, made up of a British construction firm, an Italian tram vehicle maker, a US bank (providing venture capital), and a British operator.

This second phase was also so successful that the GMPTE again exercised its exit option. A very substantial extension project is currently being tendered. The scope of the new tender encompasses the 37-km line network created in the first two stages and 65 km of new lines, for which the legal basis had been created in the interim. The first stage of the selection process, the declaration of interest, was completed last November. The 23 prospective bidders span the full spectrum of pan-European private sector transit companies and rail vehicle manufacturers, as well as some large construction groups. The list includes: the following companies, some of which are members of consortia: Alstom Transport S.A., Stagecoach Holdings, Altram (Manchester) Ltd, Arriva Passenger Services Ltd, Ansaldo Trasporti SPA, Balfour Beatty Capital Projects Ltd, Bechtel Ltd, Connex Transport UK Ltd, Daimler Chrysler Rail Systems (UK) Ltd, Bombardier Transportation, First Group PLC RATP International Investissement, Siemens, Sir Robert McAlpine Ltd, Transdev PLC, Ernst & Young, HSBC and Via GTI.

This strong demand from potential bidders greatly strengthens the local transport authority's executive. Unlike the dramatically failed privatization of the national rail network, this privatization can be considered a sign of the self-reinforcing benefits of an adroit, competition-oriented infrastructure policy. Nevertheless, the precise financial impact compared with a purely public solution cannot be measured. The public sector comparator as an important element of PFI, has not been applied. It is evident that this unique dynamic of creating, extending and completing a large Light Rail network would not have happened without the private sector.

Similar success is evident in Croydon in the south of London, where, after eight years of preparation, a 28-km light rail network of three lines was opened for commercial traffic in May, 2000. The cost of this system, more than half of which was newly built, runs to about 320 million US dollars. Of this, 40% is financed by the successful bidder in the 1995/1996 tender process. This consortium is Tramtrack Croydon Limited (TCL), which includes the construction companies Amey and Sir Robert McAlpine, as well as Tram Operations Limited as the operator.

There are two key differences to Manchester:

1) The Croydon project was tendered out based on very detailed project information. This information was generated during the three-year preparation phase by the Tramlink Project Development Group. The Group consisted of Croydon municipal administrators, London Transport (now Transport for London, TfL), and the prospective, three-member operator consortium: Tarmac, AEG and Transdev. The preparation period also served to mobilize the requisite public funds for the project from the British government. The private collaborators were paid based on labor time.

2) The life of the concession agreement, at 99 years, is much longer. No exit clause is provided; as a result, a possible system extension – which has already been requested – can only be put out to tender subject to many restrictions.

A comparison of these projects by public funds spent per passenger per year reveals two trends:

1) Investment costs in the USA are higher than the (albeit very low) costs of British systems.

2) In both countries the economic return for the public purse tends to increase steadily with increasing experience in collaborating with private partners.

Within Britain, government funding decreased from 15.91 US dollars in 1992 for the two tender phases in Manchester to $8.80 per passenger per year in 2000 in Croydon. In the USA, a similar trend at a higher absolute level marks the progression of the three examples provided: From Westside MAX (see

Section 3 of this report), to the first segment of the Hudson-Bergen line, to the airport extension of Portland's light rail network, the cost to the public fell from $125.10 to $ 35.90 per passenger per year. However, these projects should be considered as unique cases rather than the norm, as is shown by the much lower public subsidy of 16.85 million dollars required for the first segment of the Portland light rail system opened in 1983.

Transit-oriented property development by transit companies and its contribution to financing

"Joint developments" are defined by the US policy statements for public funding as retail, residential, or manufacturing projects – or mixtures thereof – that are developed in concert with the new construction, modernization or expansion of mass transit systems. These properties may involve transit stops, stations and areas near stations. Of particular importance are areas surrounding stations.

Thanks to the success of the partnership strategy based on transit companies' own properties, the Department of Transportation in Washington made major changes to the Transit Joint Development directive introduced in 1974 (Policy on Transit Joint Development). Despite the very limited absolute level of public funds available for new starts of rail projects, this policy statement opens up opportunities to subsidize real estate purchases serving municipal development.

Unlike the earlier federal funding rules for property acquisition for mass transit projects, the profitable sale or lease of such real estate now no longer leads to the developer having to repay subsidies. This new rule applies, on one basic condition: that the sale or leasing serve the "highest and best transit use", in other words, that it serve to maximize the benefit for transit, especially as measured in passenger numbers. According to the public grant criteria, projects must be related to transit infrastructure, improve the conditions for economic development at the location in question, and enhance the efficiency of the transit system.

Three forms of real estate marketing are explicitly permitted: 1) sale, 2) temporary lease for interim uses that do not conflict with the use for transit purposes, and 3) lease in the course of "transit joint development". The third is the preferred alternative from the standpoint both of the federal funding policy statement and of the transit company, as it generates for the transit company a permanent revenue stream that serves the transit purpose.

Regardless of whether property is leased or sold, the transit system must retain effective continuing control of the project's long-term physical and functional relationship to transit.

Leasing of properties immediately adjacent to stations generally involves land that the public sector / transit system has acquired in the course of the planning/zoning process from private property owners who voluntarily sold it. As already described above, transit systems in the USA have little scope for acquiring real property through seizure by "eminent domain" for purposes that go beyond the actual, narrowly defined land use. The most important example of such a joint development policy is that of the transit operations in Washington, D.C. (Washington Metropolitan Area Transit Authority, WMATA).

As early as the 1960s, WMATA took steps to capture the expected growth in real estate value with its acquisition of properties for construction of the subway system. The total real estate holdings amount to about 2,000 hectares, one-half of which was considered capable of development. The first private development project opened in 1973, three years before the commissioning of the subway.

On WMATA-owned land the agency as a rule concludes long-term lease agreements with private developers. For strategic reasons, properties are usually not sold. The leases provide for a base lease payment rate and an income-based commission. Access agreements generally specify a monthly lease rate that increases periodically.

To date WMATA has concluded agreements for about 30 development projects. The existing contracts generate 15 million dollars of lease receipts per year. This corresponds to more than 4% of the transit authority's gross revenues. In net terms, the share is even higher.

The subsidies to be paid per annum by the WMATA member municipalities amount to 300 million dollars. The real estate income constitutes 5% of this amount. Including parking fees, it represents the largest single revenue item after fare receipts.

The revenues from public-private project partnerships will very likely recoup the entire land acquisition cost for the development of the Metrorail system, which is estimated at about 400 million dollars. Yet only 20% of this cost was funded by the states and municipalities involved. By 2003, a 200% return on investment can be expected on this local investment of 80 million dollars.

Metrorail's role as a catalyst of transit-oriented development reaches far beyond the WMATA-owned properties. The Urban Land Institute has estimated the additional regional development leveraged by the Metro system at about 15 billion dollars, or 20 billion dollars on completion of the whole 103-mile network. KPMG Peat Marwick estimates that the state of Virginia, for example, will realize a 19% annual return on investment as a result of the added development triggered by Metrorail near stations.

Such transit joint developments can be found elsewhere in the USA; although, as in Germany, the opportunity for these solutions is limited due to the dearth of real estate owned by city and regional transit authorities. Interesting approaches which cannot be examined more closely in this report are, for instance, those taken by Atlanta's regional transit authority (MARTA) and the operator of the San Diego trolley system (MTDB).

The leasing of stations and/or of space within them is rarely practised in US subways, aboveground heavy-rail and light rail stations; as most stations have only enough space to accommodate the essential transit functions. Leasing is relevant, however, with commuter rail stations, which are typically several decades old, and in many cases, are in need of renovation.

Nevertheless, the "lease and maintenance program" of the Southeastern Pennsylvania Transportation Authority (SEPTA) provides a number of instructive precedents. Fifty of the 223 stations have so far been partially or completely leased out. The tenants are retailers, offices, banks, community institutions, clubs and residential occupants. SEPTA is less interested in gaining an added source of income than in maintaining and modernizing the passenger buildings themselves, strengthening their urban function, renewing and maintaining rail platforms and keeping operating costs to a minimum. The lease contracts are very flexibly tailored to the construction and operating expenses of the particular facility. Contract durations are the longer, and lease terms are the more cost-efficient, the higher the cost of modernization and the more responsibility tenants assume for managing the transit functions.

Similar agreements are being sought in other commuter rail regions and, in some cases, are being successfully implemented in pilot projects, such as the Station Renewal Program in New Jersey.

Financial contribution through development related fees and taxes

A large number of studies have proved that, despite the automobile-oriented development environment, property values in the US have also been positively affected by proximity to rail transport. This underpins the use of financial instruments that are based on capturing this value gain.

The payment of costs by binding majority agreement of property owners in an area (based on a benefit assessment) has a longer tradition in the revitalization of inner cities in the USA. Thus, most cities have a so-called "business improvement district". Here, business owners and property owners decide by majority vote to pay a certain annual sum (whose amount differs between participants and is based on factors such as location and property size) into a local fund to cover investments required for the improvement of the area's appearance, safety etc. Such a fund is generally managed by an agency established specifically to this end.

Analogous forms of private sector participation in defraying costs also exist for other purposes, such as the co-financing of transport investment or of investment to improve urban areas near rail transit stations. Those property owners that stand to benefit from a proposed infrastructure investment pay a percentage of the value gain expected to be created by the public investment. The private shares in the cost differ with the amount of benefit likely to accrue to the party in question. For instance, they are higher in the immediate vicinity of stations than at the edge of the business improvement district.

The establishment of such a district requires a certain foundation in property law that exists in very few US states. The areas may be known by names such as Special Improvement District (such as in New York), Transit Improvement District or Benefit Assessment District (e.g. in California), Local Improvement District (e.g. Oregon) or Public Improvement District (in Texas, where city councils too have authority to institute such districts). On the whole, the tool is seldom used, owing to the requirement of majority approval and the administrative effort involved in establishing such an area.

Still, some of the projects that do exist have raised funds effectively. In the financing of the first 4.4-mile Metrorail section in the Southern California Rapid Transit District in Los Angeles, the benefit levy yielded receipts totalling 130 million dollars, or 10% of the funding required for the project. However, a California Supreme Court decision at the beginning of the 1990s prohibited the continued use of this system. A corresponding change in legislation now expressly exempts owners of residential properties from benefit assessments. As it is commonplace for US projects to be scuttled by the courts in this manner, there has been no empirical study of long-term application of this tool.

Notwithstanding this legal uncertainty, such forms of private sector participation have borne fruit elsewhere. In Portland, Oregon, for example, the main mall areas along the light rail tracks downtown were built with the help of private funds. Unlike the example just given of Los Angeles, admittedly the private contributions were only in the seven-figure range, but these were multiplied by obtaining government grants.

According to the literature and to conversations with staff of the US Department of Transportation, above all bus systems were funded by this method. In the shopping districts of cities as Minneapolis, Seattle and Denver people are comfortably moved by buses. In Dallas, a separate bus lane on the main shopping street was paid for, and is now being maintained, with contributions from the adjacent property owners. The amount paid varies according to distance from the bus route.

The transit impact fee is a one-time contribution to a revolving fund for the financing of new mass transit infrastructure and services that developers are required to pay in certain areas. Based on the literature and interviews, however, such a fee has so far been charged only in San Francisco. There it contributed substantially to funding the community share of costs for the downtown BART stations.

A funding tool that is much more frequently employed is tax increment financing (TIF). The amount of property tax or sales tax remitted from a certain area (defined by the community) around the future stations is frozen at the pre-project level (tax rates would otherwise rise as a result of the area's development). All property tax revenue exceeding this base level is used to fund local infrastructure. How the funds are allocated is at the discretion of the community; proceeds generally not only used to pay for rail transport infrastructure. Still, some of the TIF districts established by many communities have played a very important role in funding new rail transit systems or new or upgraded stations (see below). Frequently, proceeds from sales tax instead of from property tax are frozen; all additional sales tax revenue is then used to fund the rail infrastructure or other community projects.

The TIF district is also often declared to fund urban investment in transit stops or to secure municipal bonds based on the associated tax revenue growth. The case of Portland, Oregon is an outstanding example. For instance, the funding of the entire community share of the planned northern section of the light rail system (Interstate MAX) is covered by the prospective added-tax proceeds.

Financial contribution through increased ridership

The projected benefits of access and development influenced by light rail lines also underlie a number of planning tools that are all designed to increase urban density around transit stops. Among these techniques are both regional planning tools used by the Metropolitan Planning Organizations (MPOs), and municipal laws on the planning building projects.

These, and an array of other instruments, are employed where transit-oriented projects are to be promoted or funded. Transit-oriented developments are continually growing in number and have become one of the foremost approaches of urban and regional development policy in the United States.

A stellar example is San Diego. At 14 stations, development projects were implemented on properties of the transit authority, the city or private owners that brought more than an additional 60,000 passengers per day into the rail system.

In Portland, the first, 15-mile Banfield line east of downtown, which started service in 1986, generated considerable momentum for the redevelopment of the multifunctional city center, but had little effect on the development of the suburban area through which that it passes. This is attributed primarily to the fact that the area in question was already largely built up and held little scope for new development.

The extension of this section of track was designed to prevent this problem from recurring. The 18-mile Westside MAX, opened in 1998, runs through a mostly undeveloped corridor with substantial development reserves of more than 1,000 hectares that belonged to a handful of large companies; chief among them Nike, Intel and large developers. Each of the 20 stations of the Westside line offers more development area than all stations on the Banfield line combined.

At an earlier stage of planning, master plans, investment blueprints and implementation strategies were developed for all stations of the Westside line. The plans for the principal development areas were prepared jointly with the property owners and developers. The resulting agreed plans were protected by conservation orders.

This planning has special significance against the backdrop of the "Urban Growth Boundaries (UGB)" in Oregon. The UGB defines clear geographic limits for construction development of urban regions, including that of Portland as the state's largest conurbation. In order to define and monitor this boundary and implement the planning for it, Portland's Metropolitan Planning Organization was vested with sweeping authority that far exceeds the regional planning authority wielded by counterparts in other US states. The regional planning authority, known as Metro, is controlled by elected officials from the communities of metropolitan Portland and has at its disposal a highly diversified tool kit for supporting development along the transit corridors inside the urban growth boundary.

In its "Metro 2040" plan, the Authority spells out its intention to locate one-third of all new residential areas and two-thirds of all office locations near stops on the regional rail network. All municipalities of the metropolitan area are required to formulate their land use plans in such a way as to achieve these objectives, and must align their detailed planning and the issuing of building permits with these goals. In 1991, the Authority produced a transport planning directive, by means of which the average per-capita vehicle miles travelled were to be reduced by 20% over the subsequent 30 years, by co-ordinating construction use planning and transit development. Analysis of national statistics reveals that in the past decade, unlike most US urban areas, average trip length in the Portland area already stabilized.

In close consultation with the regional transit company, Tri-Met (Tri-County Metropolitan Transportation District), Metro commissioned an experienced planning consultancy to advise the municipalities along the corridor of the Westside-MAX, and hired an experienced developer to coordinate all means of obtaining public funding.

In the development of the Orenco Station project as well, the planning consultants figured prominently. On about 80 ha of land, Orenco Station represents a model version of a suburban residential community, centered on the light rail station functionally and in design terms, and given life by a mixed-use town center.

The owner is a development company, Pacific Trust (or PacTrust), which actually bought the area in the early 1990s for commercial development for a relatively low price. This land, adjacent to an important location of chipmaker Intel, was re-zoned in connection with the planning for the light rail line. The developer's management has since been deeply involved in executing a pilot project that has acquired national significance.

2,000 housing units, most of them single-family homes, as well as retail space, a town center, green areas and other features are to be developed on this area. The total investment comes to about 500 million dollars. One quarter each was sold to smaller residential developers, subject to strict specifications; the lion's share of the project remains with PacTrust, which sold 200 houses in several construction phases between November, 1997 and March, 2000.

Some remarkable trends emerged at Orenco Station. The sale price of the PacTrust units, located about 50 minutes by light rail from downtown Portland, rose more strongly than elsewhere. Unusually, most of the units sold were townhouses; their average property size of about 350 square metres is extremely small by the standards of US middle-class suburbs. Another striking fact is that all buildings follow a unified style of urban architecture and, combined with the similarly novel, park-like open spaces, create an impression of a town with a strong community orientation.

Another important aspect was the creation of a town center with a (limited but sufficient) range of stores as well as with restaurants, smaller live-in offices, and a number of urbanesque apartments that each occupies the whole of one storey. Viewed in isolation, this town center amounts to a property development that will at best be profitable in the long run, which is why banks have been unwilling to finance many projects with a similar focus, including in Greater Portland. At Orenco Station, the town center was self-financed, a fact that contributes to the very long-term expectation of a positive return.

In many ways, the Orenco Station project constitutes a partnership between private developer and public institutions (municipality of Hillsboro, Tri-Met, Metro). This collaboration has several facets:

- The financial side: Even at the early, master-planning stage, PacTrust shouldered 50% of the cost. The developer is also handling all development work.

- The organizational side: From the onset of planning of the light rail line, the company and public agencies have worked on the new development together.

- Collaboration in transport matters, as a concrete contribution was made towards accomplishing the (already described) shift in the modal split in favour of public transit. For PacTrust, its involvement in the project-to-date has paid for itself, making the precedent transferable in principle to many other proposed developments.

8.4 Comparative institutional analysis - the regulatory framework

In order to draw conclusions for the applicability of the study findings in Germany, it is necessary to distinguish between the regulatory framework of Transit PPPs, the solution of property rights problems, the transaction cost gains, and the relationship between principal and agent under the PPP regulatory system.

The study's focus was the question as to how far the public sector may benefit from a closer cooperation with the private sector. The following analysis serves a pubic sector view.

With reference to the classification of public tasks that PICOT and WOLFF (1994) have established (see chapter 1), public rail transit can be classified as "a specific task with (relatively) low strategic relevance" – more complex, but basically comparable with the task of building a road network. Based on the research presented by Picot and Wolff, it can be said that the statement quoted on page 12 "once an agreement on the classification of tasks is obtained, there is hardly any need for discussion of the appropriate form of procurement" appears as very simplified and neither takes into account the highly political meaning of the precise form of the procurement method nor the very specific demands of each single case.

The impact of specific financial, land-use, planning, transport and PPP-related legislation and policies)

Generally (if not exclusively) the key public partner initiated the PPPs, due partly to the fact that the public sector occupies a central position in transit and urban development. Thus, public bodies wishing to attract developer interest to sites close to rail transit, should have clear development and transport policies, and in turn identify certain sites as favorable for certain types of development, while excluding other sites away from transit.

The following overview of the different public policies and strategies will determine the regulatory frame under which transit PPPs take place. This framework is partly set by the local authorities and public transport companies, and in part by superordinate public institutions.

The following three tables (Table 1.3-1.5) will list such financial, land-use and PPP-related policies respectively and indicate their effect on the projects studied (for easier reference, they will be numbered consecutively throughout the tables). Please note that these policies are evaluated only in so far as they have a direct influence on PPPs or with regard to TOD and TJD, since a favorable environment for such projects can be helpful in attracting developers.

The overview shows that there are comparatively few policies, which have actively favored the inception of the PPP examples studied. Most of the legislation, policies and strategies which have influenced the case study processes related to TJD or TOD activities have necessarily achieved the combined effect of fostering PPP-based TOD or TJD activities.

They have simultaneously increased transit ridership and positively served the public. However, the study has identified a variety of hard (legislative and financing) and soft (strategic and policy-related) tools, which could be considered for adoption by national, local, or transport providers' decision-making levels where they do not already exist. Such activities should not be seen as an end in themselves or a panacea for problems associated with public spending powers and/or sinking rail transit ridership (HÖRHAGER, 1998); each individual situation requires meticulous planning and only if all or most of the requirements can be met and if the public bodies can rely on the continued provision of benefits to the general public throughout the duration of the project, should public administrations consider entering into a PPP. If the requirements can be met, PPPs can provide a very helpful tool for creating synergies, which the public sector alone cannot achieve.

Table 8.1: Financing acts and policies

Country and administrative level	*Policy/* Strategy	Content & *Effect on PPP(s) studied*
Germany – federal	Municipal Transport Financing Act, 1988 (Gemeindeverkehrs-finanzierungsgesetz)	Provides up to 90% of capital investment cost for e.g. construction or extension of urban rail services if these "serve to improve the transport conditions in the community" if they are in agreement with local land-use plans; *very little direct effect on TOD or TJD activities as benefits necessary for funding are very loosely defined and land-use plans need not necessarily favor such projects; some services along, which TOD or TJD have been constructed would not have been built without the federal financial support, though*
Great Britain – national	Section 56 of Transport Act, 1968	Enables Secretary of State for Transport to give capital grants to large new public transport infrastructure projects where there are considered to be exceptional reasons for spreading the cost beyond users and local taxpayers; *no direct effects of TJD/TOD activities but helped to finance some new urban light rail systems*
USA - federal	Transportation Infrastructure Finance and Innovation Act, 1998 (TIFIA – see chapter 1)	Considered a useful tool for leveraging funding (but not necessarily as part of PPP) for major projects; *no direct effect on U.S. case studies as all projects were conceived before passing of Act*
USA - federal	FTA Policy on Transit Joint Development, 1997 (see Chapter 1)	Provides financial support for clearly defined TJD or TOD projects; *no direct effect on U.S. case studies as all projects were conceived before passing of policy*

Source: GAFRON et al. 2002 based on the authors' research

Table 8.2: Land-use, planning, and transport policies and strategies

Country/ administrative level	*Policy/* Strategy	*Content & Effect on PPP(s) studied*
Germany – federal	§ 34 BauGB (building and development law)	Gives planning authorities flexibility to speed up planning procedures under certain conditions; shorter time spans attractive for privately financed developments; *positive effect on TOD and TJD*
Great Britain - national	Section 6, Town and Country Planning Act 1990	Allows local authorities to designate certain areas under their control as enterprise zones, where relaxed planning procedures are supposed to attract developers; *positive effect on TOD activities as both in Docklands and Salford these areas were provided with rail transit – this is not a requirement, though*
Great Britain - national	Planning Policy Guidance 13 Transport, 2001	Recommends maximum (rather than minimum) parking requirements for new developments; *no effect on TODs investigated as these were either conceived earlier or the recommendation was not followed*
USA – Ballston (county)	Rosslyn-Ballston Corridor Alternative Land Use Patterns, 1972	Proposed to concentrate future development around 5 metrorail stations in that corridor, partly to protect existing neighborhoods from commercial intrusion; *positive effect on TOD projects*
USA – Ballston (county)	Ballston Sector Plan, 1980	Designated Ballston as a new mixed use center with high density residential and commercial use within 400 m radius from metrorail station; subsequent zoning provided major density incentives for half commercial/half residential projects; street level retail facilities were required in all buildings; *positive effect on TOD projects*
USA – Friendship Heights (county)	Special Zoning District, 1970's	Allowed an optional doubling of density under special hearing and design review procedures; was supported by Planning Board; *attracted developer for TOD project*
USA – Orenco Station (metropolitan authority)	Urban Growth Boundary	Lead to a limitation of available and developable land, land values increased but also real estate development became more predictable; reduced risk of non-transit linked competition to TOD developments; *positive effect on TOD activities*
USA – Orenco Station (public transport provider)	Strategic Plan 1993-1998	Recommended land-use intensification along bus and light-rail corridors to increase ridership and accessibility; also recommended that 85% of new developments should occur within urban growth boundary and within 5 min. walk from transit stops; *positive effect on TOD activities*

Country/ administrative level	*Policy/* Strategy	*Content & Effect on PPP(s) studied*
USA – Orenco Station (state)	Oregon Transportation Rules, 1994	Require that vehicle miles traveled are reduced by increasing development densities and improving pedestrian access to transit and facilities; *positive effect on TOD activities*
USA – various regional transit agencies	transit joint development policies	Aim to attract TJD or TOD to real estate owned by the transit agency (often in the form of very extensive park & ride facilities) to increase transit ridership and bring financial gains for the agency; *positive effect on TJD/ TODs activities though mostly adopted after inception of case studies*
USA – various regional transit agencies	1-for-1 parking replacement policies	Require any parking spaces lost to TOD or TJD to be replaced by the developer; this generally needs very expensive under or above ground multi-story constructions; *negative effect on TOD activities as many developers cannot afford the cost*

Source: GAFRON et al. 2002 based on the authors' research

Table 8.3: PPP-related policies and strategies

Country and administrative level	*Policy/* Strategy	Content & *Effect on PPP(s) studied*
17. Great Britain – national	Private Finance Initiative, 1992 (see Chapter 5)	Aims to deliver higher quality and more cost-effective public services by encouraging partnerships and involving the private sector more directly in asset provision and operation; national government provides help with financing if a financial benefit to the public sector can be expected; *positive effect on PPP activities; however, assessment criteria have been criticized and several PFI projects are estimated to be significantly more expensive for the public sector in the long term than full public financing would have been*
18. USA - national	Transit Joint Development Guidelines (see Chapter 6 and Attachment 10.2)	Aims to initiate public land acquisition for transit- oriented development. *Rarely used, but potentially attractive for those communities that start new systems or that want to develop specific station areas.*

Source: GAFRON et al. 2002 based on the authors' research

The impact of different financing models

Depending on its set-up and the contributions of the partners involved, the PPP approach constitutes a specific approach to financing transit services and urban development projects. However, one of the aims of this project was to determine whether there were any innovative approaches to financing PPPs that were different in the way private or public funds were normally raised. Only one public financing mechanism related specifically to PPPs has been identified – the Private Finance Initiative in Great Britain (see Table1.5); all other approaches were not specific to PPP projects. As far as information was made available, private sector capital was also generally raised through the conventional route of bank loans based on risk assessment, which considered the real estate market and/or the forecasts for the development of transit ridership. As the example of Bernau-Friedenstal (and general experience) showed, such forecasts are not always sufficiently accurate to guarantee the financial success of a project nor the continued existence of the investors.

The public sector was generally more interested in obtaining the facilities (rail transit services or elements of urban development) achieved through the PPPs as well as perhaps the associated revenue streams, fare box earnings, and increases in local taxes associated with the projects (depending on the conditions of the PPP agreement). It was interesting to find, however, that the overall assessment of the impact of the projects, particularly on transit ridership and modal shift, was often sketchy at best (see also chapters 5, 6, and 7).

In general, the public side provided capital for the majority of transit-related investments and none for the private development projects. This is slightly different for the BOT projects. While in the U.S., the largest BOT-project (Hudson-Bergen) was entirely publicly financed, and another project was to a large extent (AirportMAX) publicly financed, the British projects called for a substantial amount of private capital. In the beginning of the project a relatively small portion of the total financing of the initial phase of the Manchester Metrolink was allotted, and was strongly increased to finance the Metrolink extension through Salford Quays and the Tramlink in London-Croydon. Public capital was used as part of the PPP agreements for the respective projects.

As far as station development projects are concerned, the most important contributions of the public sector were not financial ones, but rather those which the private sector could simply not provide. These would include certain areas of land (particularly near existing rail infrastructure) or favorable policies, regulation, and planning conditions. Similarly, the public sector is generally responsible for ensuring the provision of rail transit facilities (if not necessarily for actually providing it). It is thus up to public bodies to give out concessions for such services, and as the examples in this study have shown, private companies generally make a profit out of such projects (e.g., Manchester Metrolink; Croydon Tramlink; Hudson-Bergen-line).

The most structured approach to provide financing for PPPs is the PFI procedure, adopted by the national government in the United Kingdom. Under these agreements, the national government pays a local authority participating in a PFI an up-front sum, which the authority then has to use to cover the cost of the unitary charge paid to the private partner for the duration of the contract (usually between 20 and 30 years, in the case of the Croydon Tramlink this amounted to 99 years). In the case of the Docklands Light Rail (DLR), which was begun before the PFI concept, this charge was agreed to in the form of a daily fee that first the Development Corporation and then the DLR company paid to the operators of the service.

In order to secure public interests, payments are generally performance-related, and private partners should be certain that they will be able to meet their targets. In the case of actual public transport services, the case studies showed that it pays to use technology which is tried and tested and with which at least one of the partners already has gained some experience.

If innovative (and thus unfamiliar) solutions are called for, both the public and the private partners should allow sufficient time to test new systems and to deal with operational problems, as unforeseen delays reduce the level of service to the public – and the amount of money paid to the private side.

A more indirect way of supporting the financing of a project is the provision of tax incentives for private companies. This can stimulate up-front investment, which is of greater benefit to the public than the tax revenue, as the latter can be lost as a result. Taxpayers (both businesses and residents) that would otherwise have located elsewhere could actually be attracted to a transit friendly area.

The impact of planning conditions

Planning authorities, which are interested in securing development in a certain location with quick completion, are sometimes prepared to relax planning conditions or to prioritize certain processes if a greater public benefit can be expected. This was the case in most of the U.S. examples; in almost every

U.S. case, transit-oriented development was further encouraged by granting permissions for higher buildings than originally intended so as to increase floor space and revenue income.

The role of property rights, transaction costs and the principal agent relationship

On the basis of the neo-institutional analytical methods, which are described theoretically in chapter 1, the following three subchapters summarize the most important findings about the impact of specific institutional settings or changes of these settings.

8.5 The transfer of property rights

The transit-supportive completion and the transfer of property rights was an essential element in achieving partnerships. This applies to the supply of developable land, the provision of necessary land use rights, and the private management skills in maximizing the (transit) developmental impact of the land.

The availability of land, needless to say, is a major issue for TJD and TOD projects. Table 1.8 therefore shows who originally owned the land on which the PPP projects were built, who purchased the land and how it was incorporated into the PPP agreement. The table shows that in most cases the land was at least partially owned by the local authority (or a public development corporation) to begin with and in almost every case the public transport organization was the original owner. Only in 2 cases was the land originally completely in private ownership and in another 3 it was partly owned privately. There is not one example where a local authority and/or public transport organization was involved in the land transfers. Thus it seems as though public bodies play a very important part in securing land for PPPs. This fact is noteworthy since theoretically the public partners could play other roles as well, such as offering financial assistance, favorable planning conditions, or making other contributions. The prominent role regarding land matters should not lead to the conclusion that PPP developments necessarily remain in (partial) public ownership, since in 7 cases the land actually was privately owned completely.

The existing results indicate that it is very important for public bodies (local authorities as well as public transport operators) to ensure that land parcels, which are in locations that are expected to be of importance for future urban redevelopment (such as the Orenco station site), are not split up or given over to development, which is not well integrated with existing or future rail transit facilities. It depends partly on the interests of the landowners (if not a public agency), but it can also be steered through land use zoning and planning regulations. The advantage of a PPP might be that the local authority can offer an existing land owner – or potential buyer - favorable conditions for development (such as accepting higher density or different uses or increasing the land's value through tax incentives connected to certain types of development) and, in exchange, obtain a development which furthers goals of integration between land use and rail transit and creates synergistic effects in favor of the general public.

It may, on the other hand, be worthwhile for the local administration to actively pursue the purchasing of existing land parcels that can be used for future PPPs. If such purchases are planned once the decision for future development has already been taken, the owners are likely to sell at the expected value of the development rather than at the value determined by current use. Such increased prices can even be expected for land parcels that never will be built on, but instead will be reserved, for example, as compensation areas, a legal requirement in some countries (such as Germany) when greenfield land is developed.

If the public administration is the landowner, the situation is a slightly different one. It can use the property as leverage for attracting the type of development and developer that would be integrated best within the existing or planned rail transit facilities. By entering into a PPP rather than simply selling off the land, the public body could possibly be able to retain more influence regarding the nature of the development and its future use.

All the above applies to both a public administration and a public transport operator. There was less evidence in the UK and Germany of public transport operators actually using their land to initiate rail-oriented PPPs – even though they were often involved in the transfers. In particular, it was found that operators of rail-based public transport in Europe had no explicit policies to do so, while the WMATA in Washington D.C., for example, not only owns large tracts of land adjacent to its metrorail station, but also has developed its own

Joint Development Policy and *Guidelines* (WMATA, 2002) that deal with issues such as *"determining the relative marketability of various joint development sites and improving prospects for development of less viable sites" (ibid,* p.1).

The absence of such integrative policies on a national level in Europe can partly be attributed to the restructuring of particularly the national rail operators in Europe in the wake of legislative changes on the German national or on the European level. In Germany and Great Britain, this left the organizational units responsible for real estate management, apart from those, which were providing the actual transit services. As a result of this division and the operation of the newly formed companies on a market basis, there is considerably less incentive today for cooperation between the parties, since they each are individually responsible for their own profit and loss calculations, which do not necessarily register synergies created through strategic cooperation.

In eight cases, the land was originally entirely publicly owned; and in only two cases was it originally entirely privately owned. In five cases, public bodies owned at least part of the land before the beginning of the project. In those two cases where the land had originally been completely in private hands, it was the public bodies that purchased the individual parcels in order to secure the continuation of the project.

There were different models for making this land available once it had been assembled:

- sold to developer (either at cost price or with a profit)
- lease given to developer for duration of PPP/PFI agreement
- land use rights transferred to developer for duration of PPP/PFI agreement free of charge
- combining public and private land parcels into a public/private development company

Table 8.4: Land owner, Land buyer

COUNTRY	PROJECT	ORIGINAL OWNER OF LAND / BUYER OF LAND FOR PPP
Germany	Bernau-Friedenstal, nr. Berlin	*original owner*: national rail company (DB AG), local authority *buyer*: private developer
	Hennigsdorf, nr. Berlin	*original owner*: national rail company; very small part owned by local authority *buyer (of local authority portion)*: rail company, all leased to private developer
Great Britain	Croydon, Greater London	*original owner*: national rail company, private owners *buyer*: private consortium (cost-free transfer from rail company, purchase from private owners)
	Salford Quays, Manchester	*original owner*: local authority, private developers *buyer*: land was included in PPP agreements free of charge
USA	Ballston, Washington D.C.	*original owner*: public transport operator, private land owner *buyer*: private developer
	Bethesda, Washington D.C.	*original owner*: public transport operator, local authority *buyer*: private developer
	Friendship Heights, Washington D.C.	*original owner*: public transport operator *buyer*: private developer
	Orenco, Portland OR	*original owner*: many private land owners *buyer*: local authority assembled land parcels, sold on at cost price to private developer

Source: GAFRON et al. 2002 based on the authors' research

Sales usually resulted if the land was to be used for transit-oriented development, as such developments were generally either sold or rented to other users once completed. A lease was given for some transit-joint development, because at least parts of such developments (station buildings, access, etc.) had to be secured for public use in the long term. Similarly, land was included in PPP agreements for the duration of the contract (e.g., the concession to operate a public transport service) if it was to be used for the rail transit infrastructure.

The benefits to the private sector are obvious; companies can avoid the potentially lengthy processes of securing land parcels from a variety of different owners and also public bodies, in some cases, can forcibly buy small but important tracts of land if a greater common good can be identified (e.g., through compulsory purchase order in Great Britain). Where land was given free of charge, it usually was real estate to private developers would not normally have access, because it was zoned for transit purposes.

Leases or sales were made below the free market value of the land, since the public bodies were interested in securing developments that would fulfill some of their own urban and transport planning goals, thereby placing certain restrictions on the use of the land. Also, if land was purchased or leased as part of a PPP agreement, the developer could be certain of the intended use of the area and also of the overall support in favor of the particular use from the public side. This contrasts with a free market situation, where land is bought on a speculative basis and plans for future development depend on the granting of planning permission or on other future developments, which are not assured.

8.6 Transaction cost analysis

The study thoroughly examines how transaction costs can be reduced through PPP under certain conditions.

As already mentioned, the evaluation of advantages and disadvantages of the PPPs studied is largely based on the information derived from the stakeholder interviews combined with the results of other peoples' research on these projects, if available.

The interviewees commented on the process of getting the partnership together and implementing the project because they had had first-hand experience of such a process.

Studies conducted by other researchers provided some insight into the broader impact of such projects – in respect to passenger numbers and economic development, for example.

As can be expected, the benefits and dis-benefits discussed are often quite specific to the context and set-up of the case studies; these specific aspects are presented and analyzed in chapters 5, 6, and 7.

Getting partners together

There was a general agreement among the interviewees that it was important to *get all the partners involved* together as early as possible. For the public bodies (as well as for the private partners) this meant that they knew from the beginning whom they would be working with and what the interests of the different stakeholders were.

It also helped the public bodies secure influential allies (such as the national government, a specific ministry, the regional planning authority, or an important investor) right from the start. Having support of such partners strengthened the public bargaining position, as it demonstrated a wider interest in the aims of the project.

The importance of having *clear goals and mutual development aims* between the different parties right from the start was emphasized more than once. In some cases, where this had not been the case, the people involved stated very clearly that in retrospect they would have preferred greater clarification of many issues from the beginning.

In the case of the Manchester Metrolink (Salford Quays extension), for example, it became apparent that the design specifications for the hard and soft elements (platforms, plantings, etc.) had not been clear enough, leading to lengthy discussions with the contractors. Had the local authority and the public transport provider agreed on these elements from the beginning, high-quality results, which would satisfy the requirements for such a high-profile project, could easily have been ensured.

Further, it was considered very important to not forget to *involve transport and civil engineers* as early as possible, since it was both very useful to harness the respective expertise of drawing up plans, as well as making communication later on much easier, when those directly responsible during the construction phase were aware of the development aims from the start.

Finally, the actors in the Washington D.C. projects found that the clear TJD-friendly policies of their regional planning authority had *created a good sense of awareness in the private sector* for the potential benefits of such projects, creating the desire to become more involved.

Working with partners and the contract (communication, conflict and problem solving)

The proceedings for the case studies in Germany (Bernau-Friedenstal and Hennigsdorf) were initiated during a time when the respective national rail companies were undergoing restructuring to become a private (but publicly owned) enterprise. In both cases there were initial difficulties on the side of the local authority to identify the people responsible for different aspects of the project within the newly formed operators of trains and stations as well as the infrastructure companies, as responsibilities were shifting. It is important to identify all stakeholders as early as possible (both the partner organizations as well as all colleagues involved), to prevent processes from having to be repeated if the *person "really" responsible* had not been *consult*ed, for example.

According to the interviewees it was also considered very important that any *contract between partners* was *as specific as possible* and, if feasible, should be based on a very detailed brief for the purposes that the development should fulfill and the expected design details. Examples where lack of initial clarity led to unnecessary expenses and delays included: specifications for the services a private station operator had to provide – such as "working toilets" – but uncertainty regarding the definition of when the service was working satisfactorily and when it was not; design specifications for the materials to be used on an on-street light rail platform and subsequent disagreement on whether access ramps were part of the platform and should be built to the same specifications.

Ideally, such details as mentioned above should be incorporated in the brief at the tender stage even before concessionaires or contractors are determined, since they still could be included in the contract.

The interviewees also said that a *willingness to be flexible* was important in creating an overall vision without getting too tied down by discussions about details. It is much easier to agree on compromises from a common basis (such as a detailed brief), should any problems be encountered rather than when different ideas about certain issues arise at the beginning of the discussion.

Many of the interviewees *found that "chemistry" between the people* representing the different partners and their readiness to communicate on a common level was important during the process. To consciously create such conditions is not necessarily possible, but it would be valuable to select people who not only understand the concerns and working mechanisms of their own organization but who also have, if not develop, a feeling for the often very different operating structures of the partner organizations.

On the evidence obtained, it was found that openness toward constructive communication could be more helpful than the single-minded determination to push one's own goals without compromise. In addition, communication in regular intervals between different groups working on the same project (e.g., financial and creative sections) is necessary. In projects which extended over several phases (as with most Light Rail lines) it was found that overlap between contracts left some of the interface responsibilities unresolved, leading to disputes between contractors regarding the allocation of responsibilities for either non-performance or under-performance.

Several of the case studies involved more than one contract; there may have been an urban planning contract between a local authority and a developer but at the same time other valid *contracts between developers and operators* (of stations or services, for example), possibly resulting from a maintenance contract between the operators and another firm. It is very important to ensure from the beginning that these different documents are well *coordinated in terms of their requirements and obligations* placed on the contractual partners. The timing of different activities (operation, maintenance, and repair, for example) needs to be planned carefully if a smooth operation of facilities and services is to be guaranteed.

The contributions of the partners

The *additional investment capacity of the private sector to urban development and transport projects* is considered a major advantage from a public point of view. The second major advantage cited is the fact that the private sector is expected to provide greater efficiencies in terms of project management and delivery, since it is geared toward using the twin resources of time and money to its own greatest possible benefit (which is generally financial).

In the case of Bernau-Friedenstal for example, STRATHMANN (1999) concluded that it was the initiative of the private investor, interested in using the light rail stop as a marketing tool for the new housing development, which made the timely completion of the stop or at least the entrance building) possible. This initiative not only provided funding, but also included a very active involvement in the planning process as well as frequent communication with the various parties in the public sector. Similar evaluations were obtained in the Croydon Tramlink Project.

There is also evidence, however, suggesting that going into partnership with a private company not always is completely wholly beneficial for public bodies. Especially with regard to the PFI process in the UK the formalities of the PFI agreements dictated by the national government were said to have resulted in exceedingly higher than necessary public sector expenses

It was further found that the desire of the private sector to create profits was sometimes in conflict with the desire of the public sector to achieve certain aims, like attracting a particular type of business into a new location by offering financial incentives or by offering cheap public transport services[21]. Such conflicts were generally resolved through compromises, but in some cases remained unsolved. It is advisable for the public sector to be clear about its goals from the beginning and also to be aware of the financial implications these might have for private partners.

It can neither be expected that the private sector will agree to participate on a minimum profit basis nor that it will accept all the financial risks involved. On the other hand the examples examined have shown that the public sector should be able to get more out of a PPP than merely the construction of a new facility. In cases like Hennigsdorf or Orenco Station there was some up-front public investment[22] which facilitated the contributions by the private sector (or was the condition for such contributions) and resulted in an overall development benefit that is generally agreed to have far exceeded the initial public financial input. Thus, in Hennigsdorf, an already completed high-quality urban space served as an attractor to the private investor, whose project then provided the fourth frontage for the upgraded square as well as for an improved pedestrian and cyclists' connection underneath the rail tracks. And in Oregon the complicated process of land assembly for the Orenco Station Development through the public administration ensured that the resulting package was large enough for the private investors to provide the public spaces (streets, parks, etc.) in the new development while still making a profit.

Potential bankruptcy on part of the private developer is another important factor to consider. Ideally, this should not ever happen; yet, there is no way of guaranteeing that it will not. The case of the commuter rail stop in Bernau-Friedenstal is one example. Here, the private developer of the associated

[21] which might operate in direct or at least indirect competition with those run by a private company
[22] for the pedestrian passage across the station and the squares at either end; for the square in front of the station building and for the purchase of land from over 600 individual owners respectively

residential quarter went into receivership before the station or the development had been fully completed. Fortunately, the main elements of the station had already been built, and it was operational as a stop to be used by those who had already moved into the completed units – only the entrance building and associated small shops were still missing. Particularly in the case of transit services and associated facilities, bankruptcy of the private developer or operator can cause the public sector having to carry the full risk to ensure the continuation of a service it legally is obliged to provide. If proper securities are not in place, such an eventuality could burden the public bodies with very considerable financial and organizational responsibilities that they are unprepared for. But even without a severe failure such as bankruptcy it should be borne in mind that "private enterprises recognize very well how they can lure the state [...] and where it will not leave them hanging [...], even if their housekeeping is at fault" (JUNGCLAUSEN, 2002). This may seem like a negative assessment; such a strong feeling indeed was not expressed in any of the case studies. However, it was made clear that as little room as possible should be left for the post-contractual interpretation of the specific obligations of different partners.

Project process and form

The issues discussed concerning the project process and its overall character are assigned to the following broad categories:

- land use mix
- timing
- technical aspects
- design
- overall functionality.

The evaluation of the above categories differed somewhat within the case studies. While in Friendship Heights, for example, the provision of a varied land use mixture was seen to have provided great benefits to the users (which might also be able to absorb "less valuable" uses such as an existing lorry filling station), it was also acknowledged that elements such as an extension of existing retail facilities and office spaces was a necessary addition in order to support the public transport elements of the project within a PPP, which were continuously considered a top priority by the local authority and the public transport provider.

Timing was mentioned as an important factor in several of the case studies. Due to negative experience with the Dockland light rail system, which at the time was the first computer-operated driverless light rail, the Tramtrack Croydon consortium wanted to avoid technical novelties as much as possible. They had decided to buy a vehicle, which was already operating well in another city (Cologne, Germany) and only needed minor modifications, rather than testing and adapting a completely new design. Yet they had decided not to doubletrack parts of the network to avoid some of the associated difficulties of moving existing structures. Due to the high demand and increasing service frequencies this doubletracking of parts might now have to be done during operation of the service, a much more costly and time-consuming process. Although under the contract any problems related to the vehicles and upgrading of the line will be the responsibility of the private consortium, the public sector should bear these points in mind, as any disruption or delay to the service poses a disadvantage to the users.

The timing of different elements of a PPP is particularly crucial, since the private and the public sector normally operate on very different time scales. If the public sector provides a firm deadline for the completion of its own parts of the project (such as the provision of a new rail service), it can possibly expedite the execution of other parts of the project as well. If the provision of certain facilities is conditional to the completion of other elements of the project, it is also more likely that those deadlines will actually be met. This mechanism, though, can pull both ways. Delays are always possible (whether or not the development project is a PPP), and private developers should not expect public bodies to provide additional funding to bridge delayed revenue income, for example. For this reason, securities for at least a year's delay should always be included in the budget.

Aesthetic and design aspects were also mentioned by several interviewees. It was recommended to ensure high-quality design even if costs would be slightly higher, because the aesthetic aspects of a new facility played an important role in its reception by the public and thus its enrichment of the urban landscape. In some cases it was found that clever design could even reduce costs, for example by combining the electricity poles and street lighting poles along the route of Metrolink in Manchester.

Functionality is important in any urban development, possibly requiring even more attention with PPPs, as many different elements have to be incorporated into a functioning unit. In Hennigsdorf, functionality - to some degree - had to make room for the interests of the developer, as the new building did not offer many passenger-oriented facilities (such as waiting rooms, luggage lockers, or toilets) apart from a small ticket office. The transfer between trains and buses is not very direct, as the marketability of floor space in the new building took precedence over considerations in favor of passenger convenience.

In two U.S. examples it was also found that pedestrian links to the stations remained unsatisfactory (Ballston, Friendship Heights), while the Orenco Station development received major awards for planned communities, with the pedestrian-friendliness of its central area playing an important part. It is important to think and act beyond the new development as much as possible. A pedestrian-friendly facility that is not well integrated within its surroundings is not likely to be very successful.

Changing plans in the face of developing realities is a normal process in the context of urban development. The question is to what extent and on which basis such changes should be allowed at all.

Take-up of new facilities by users of urban development projects and/or passengers of rail services is vital in measuring the impact and potential success of the case studies. From the point of view of the public partners, the public facilities should be well received (such as rail transit service and associated infrastructure), since local tax revenue is also an important motivating factor for fostering new developments, it is also beneficial for the authority involved if residents and businesses rent new floor space as quickly as possible.

8.7 Principal-agent relationship

One of the vital prerequisites for a successful PPP is initiative and willingness – even enthusiasm – on the part of the relevant public administration, and in some cases, on the part of the public transport operator. This often jibes with a perception on the part of the administration that there is a need for a certain project from an urban development point of view, either because of existing economic and/or population growth or because of a desire to improve the own area as a residential and/or business location. From the developer's point of view, who is interested in benefiting from the synergies of a PPP, it is important not only to locate land parcels with interesting development potential, but also to be aware of the readiness of the public agencies to make active contributions in exchange for a development which fulfills explicit policy goals of integrating land use and rail transit.

The stronger the belief that the activity of a public agent or his private counterpart can "make a change", the easier it will be to actually achieve a stated goal. This trivial statement does certainly not only apply to transit PPPs, but to administrative and economic activities in general. The cultural background of focusing and achieving goals presumably is better in an entrepreneurial country like the USA than in a country with a strong dominance of the public sector such as Germany[23]. It is not up to transit policy, though, to increase the enthusiasm of public and private partners to work together; moreover, the overall reform of the public sector, the public debate about sustainability, and the dynamics of the economy have to be considered in a wider sense.

Specific contributions to the evaluation of the PPP-relevance of public agents' activities and their ability to add value stems from the observation of BOT-projects.

The findings of the U.S. and UK cases of this study are supported by the existing research results. In order to improve the value of public money, the agent has to become more competent to be able to adequately specify the desired output of a potential PPP, and to develop contracts on that basis.

The public agent is both agent and principal in one. In the case of public urban transport, the principal is generally the local community represented by the municipal, regional, or state council/parliament and its respective administration. In the context of this study, the problem of hidden information and hidden action of the agent, as very systematically described by STROHBACH (2001, pp. 253-275), has no relevance. The interest in achieving best values for money is unanimous. The problem of agency costs is greater; yet the study delivers no relevant findings. The agent is actually principal in relation to the (private) contract partner; an equal and an adverse

[23] This assumption is substantiated by quantitative differences: the share of public economic activities being at 35 % of the total GDP in the USA compared with approximately 48 % for Europe as a whole (EU-Ecofin 2002) and in Germany a total of 6.7 million public employees (in 1991) out of 80 million inhabitants (Picot/Wolff 1994, p.223) with very little incentives to improve output quality.

interest characterizes this, consisting of making a deal with the private partner (equal) and obtaining the service for a minimum amount of public money (adverse). In order to produce optimal results, a contract is concluded between both partners. This contract is based on a tender that very precisely describes the requested service, so that the assumption of hidden information or hidden action has to be assessed very thoroughly in a competitive process. Tendering, competition, and complex contracts reduce the interest and possibility of the private contract partner (here: agent) to hide information. The competence of the public agent to formulate adequate procurement procedures and to conclude contracts is thus vital.

The results of an Arthur Andersen and Enterprise LSE report about the impact of PFI in the UK (ANDERSEN 2000) confirm this. The report is based on reports of the National Audit Office (NAO) about 11 specific PFI-projects and on a review of public sector project managers' opinions about the success of "full-business-case" PFI-contracts, i.e., PFI-projects after completion of development and construction work, and after the beginning of service delivery and the payment commencement of unitary charges.
The report quotes industry (i.e., private PFI-partners) comments regarding the *over-reliance of public agents on advisors*, although the report also states that the industry generally concedes that the public side has improved its ability to work with PFI and the private PFI partners.

The *procurement process* is seen by the NAO as a "key element in delivering value for money in PFI projects" (ibid, p.16); the procurement is based on tendering and competition, and requiring competitive tension. The costs for the private bidders to participate at tenders are so high that it may discourage them from participating. In order to maintain the competitive tension, the NAO recommends considering "refunding the unsuccessful bidder's costs" in specific cases.

The public sector managers, when asked to rank the PFI aspects according to their contribution to increase value for money, attributed primary importance to the following aspects: the *risk transfer* towards the private sector, the *output-based performance specification*, the *long-term nature of contracts*, the *performance incentives* and the possibility of measuring them, *competition* and the skills of private sector managers. *Secondary importance* was attributed to aspects such the quality of advice to the public sector and the bidders, the transparency of the process, and, surprisingly, to the *cost of capital* and the *release of hidden values* (such as realizing the value of surplus under-utilized land – as in the case of transit-joint and transit-oriented development). They even evaluated their own management skills as being less important, an evaluation with which the study's authors disagreed: "Our experience, however, of working with bidders is that the quality of the public sector project development team and its advisors is considered a key factor in deciding whether to bid and also in the eventual successful award of the contract in a timely manner" (ibid, p. 37).

The study concludes that "in the early days of the PFI it was a familiar part of the rhetoric that the private sector management skills would deliver efficiency improvements, which would more than compensate for the perceived additional cost of private sector finance. There is now greater emphasis on *recognizing and exploiting the respective skills of the public and private sectors* and combining the two in effective partnership" (ibid, p. 32)

The PPP transit study included four cases of private management of the construction and/or the operation of new light rail lines. The impact of the relation between the public agent and the private sector, and especially of the behavior and the efficiency of the public agent on the project result, can be defined quite clearly in each of these projects (see chapter 5).

8.8 Transferability of institutional patterns and financial achievements

Building partnerships the USA

If the experience in dealing with problems of urban sprawl and implementing new rail systems can be generalized: building partnerships between the public and the private sector in the USA, appears to be easier than in most European countries, where the cooperation between both sides has no long history. While in many cases, the separation between the public and the private side seems to be even deeper than in Germany and other European countries (example New York City area); in others, where they occur, partnerships are less ideologically charged. They are a sign of a strong capability to react flexibly and pragmatically to problems when they occur.

In many areas where transportation problems are particularly strong, astounding partnerships have emerged to resolve these problems. They include partners as diverse as leading economic firms and organizations, public administrations and non-governmental interest groups. A tremendous effort has been undertaken to start new rail systems in cities and metropolitan areas where none has ever existed, as well as in cities where earlier streetcar networks were shut down many decades ago.

Especially in "younger" urban areas of the South and the West, such partnerships may very well be initiated through private investors and institutions of the private sector.

Relevant traditional financial tools and new financing initiatives

The most important traditional financial tool for public investments is a project-related **municipal bond**, as described in chapter 3. The study did not focus on this instrument, because the connection between private investor and public project/ public investment is indirect, and in many cases the project for which the bond is issued is not essential for the bond-buyer. Nevertheless, this tool has some instructive aspects for future local public lending in Germany and other European countries. One is the project-related character of the bond. To a certain extent, the profitability of the bond for the bond-buyer depends on the economical viability of the project. The second instructive aspect is the fact that the specific bond undergoes a rating procedure, which gives relatively clear hints of the project-inherent financial risks. The third aspect is the fact that the degree of tax-deductibility of bond-related income depends on the geographical proximity of the investor to the project. Bonds bought by inhabitants of the issuing municipality are generally tax-exempt; they are tax-reduced for inhabitants of the same state, etc.

The right to issue bonds represents a possibility for local municipalities to obtain relatively cheap money from the financial market. But bonds increase local debts, which may in many cases accumulate to an unhealthy degree. Therefore, independent from the legal difficulties in the German framework of municipal finance, an implementation of this tool may not generally be recommended. But the feasibility of project-related municipal bonds may be examined. This instrument may contribute to a greater variety of public lending and, in adequate cases, implement a market rating for public investment projects. It may also create a relationship of the bond-buyer with the specific project that may generate an investor-like behavior.

The problem of higher land costs in proximity of urban rail transit stations, especially in suburban areas, is one of the key obstacles for transit-oriented residential developments and transit-oriented single-family housing. While this problem can be resolved in specific property constellations (see below transit joint and transit-oriented development), it may in many others be reduced through adequate lending conditions. Living near transit will reduce transportation costs and increase the possibility for homebuyers to afford a higher monthly mortgage rate.

The calculation of transportation cost savings is the basis of the "**Location Efficient Mortgage**" (LEM). According to this method (based on available statistical information about land use, population density, public transit stops, car ownership and driving levels), a lender can predict how much a household in a particular location will spend on transportation. The difference in transportation cost between an urban, transit-friendly located household and the suburban counterpart can be added onto buyer's qualifying income.

After only one year of practical experience with the LEM in four US metropolitan regions (LEM-mortgage-provision of approx. 1 billion US dollars), Fannie Mae, the national home-financing service, has agreed to apply the method nationwide. The success of this tool is reason enough to consider an implementation in Germany. The role of Fannie Mae in the US to secure the specific bank loans, could be played by state-owned home financing services. The potential impact of the LEM in the German context has to be investigated before defining pilot-cases for its implementation. On the basis of these recommendations, research on this issue is now being conducted[24]

The **Transportation Infrastructure Finance and Innovation Act** (TIFIA) of 1998 will accelerate new business opportunities for public-private partnerships, as well as investment opportunities for bond investors in transportation projects. The federal government estimates that TIFIA could provide up to $10.6 billion in leveraged credit assistance for new transportation projects over the next five years, from a total budget authority of $ 530 million.

While the TIFIA assistance is small in comparison to the national gap between funds needed and funds available for transportation projects, it represents an innovative approach to transportation financing, a significant increase in

[24] At the European Center of Transportation and Logistics, Technische Universität Hamburg-Harburg, in 2002 a dissertation under the auspices of Dr. Carsten Gertz has been started.

available funding for this purpose, and a potentially wide range of new debt transactions.

As in the case of privately pre-financed public projects, the TIFIA credit assistance can accelerate the realization of privately managed public projects. But, as opposed to actual pre-financing, TIFIA-assisted loans have only exceptionally, in case of project failure, been publicly, i.e. federally, re-financed. Due to careful project-rating procedures, these cases are likely to happen only rarely.

As no project has been defined by the time of the PPP-study start, TIFIA could not be investigated in the context of this study. But after two years of implementation experience, and on the basis of initial experience with 10 selected projects, TIFIA may provide a useful expertise for the application of loan guarantees as an instrument of promoting privately managed surface transportation projects in Germany. It should therefore be carefully studied and its transferability should be evaluated.

Relevant DBOM experience

Only very few DBOM projects have been started in the public transportation field in the USA. This may, at least partly, be related to the fact that public transportation companies in the USA are still being seen as a branch of the transportation economy that is reserved for pure public management. This is comparable to the current situation in Germany, where publicly owned companies monopolize the market of their "home"-area.

However - two new lines represent a nationally closely surveyed new approach of sharing the task with the private sector: the Hudson-Bergen Light Rail line, and the Light Rail extension to the airport in Portland, OR (AirportMAX). They will soon be followed by other examples, including the very well known "Tren Urbano" project in San Juan, Puerto Rico. Each of these projects are major investments, and rank among the most important surface transportation projects nationwide. The US has relevant turnkey projects and initial experience with this new type of cooperation. Their sheer existence is relevant from a German perspective and has already generated increasing interest in the turnkey approach. One of the reasons is the already mentioned similarity of the institutional and "mental" framework of public transport and public investments in general between the US and Germany.

The two investigated US projects have very different issues and approaches:

1) The **AirportMAX**, an extension of an existing, publicly operated system, is comparable to current extension projects for Light Rail systems in Germany. The contract with the construction firm Bechtel to design and build the extension has financial and organizational advantages, which might be applicable in the German context. Construction costs are clearly defined; the private side has to carry the risk of cost excess and the period between the project decision and the project realization can be minimized. The additional element of realizing a public real estate asset through a long-term lease to the construction firm is very instructive. It is on the one hand, a specific and focused form of commercialization of a public asset, and, on the other hand, an intelligent and potentially transferable transit-land-use-connection. The fact that the AirportMAX contract has not been tendered, but negotiated with only one firm, is, under the EU-regulatory framework, not directly transferable though. It would be possible to tender both the construction of the line and the transit oriented maximization of the real estate value. But it will be extremely difficult to link both goals in one tender. Tendering procedures for public tasks and investments have to be in accordance with the German law "against obstacles of free competition", (Gesetz gegen Wettbewerbsbeschränkungen) that requires a very detailed description of the project. In the German context it would make sense to separate both issues and tender them consecutively.

2) The **Hudson-Bergen Light Rail** system has not only been built and equipped through a private consortium, but is also operated by this consortium. This is a completely new approach to the US transportation sector. No comparable project exists so far in Germany. Through a costly and time-consuming procedure, the tendering has been extremely carefully prepared. Due to an extensive planning period before the turnkey decision (more than a decade), political influence led to an alignment with so many obstacles that a technically smooth result would not be achievable. The tender preparation costs were so high and the financial result, measured in public investment per rider, is so unattractive, that neither the procedure nor the result look very tempting from a German perspective. And yet it may represent a procedure that is directly applicable under the German regulatory framework, unlike the British PFI-procedure.

The lessons to be drawn from this experience are similar in the USA and Germany: If the turnkey contract for this line will not remain a single or rare event in America's transportation field, future tendering procedures will increase the number of bidders (only two in the case of the Hudson-Bergen-line) and contribute to substantial financial gains for the public sector. A comparison of the American projects with British cases makes clear how important the experience in dealing with the private sector is.

The preparation, implementation and improvement of the "**Private Finance Initiative (PFI)**" of the British government led to a series of projects in which the risk-reward ratio between the public and the private side was gradually improved. In many cases, it has achieved a level that is hardly to improve for the public side. These benefits have been achieved on the basis of long-term contracts. Each of these contracts are still in their early phases so no definite conclusions can be drawn over the life of the contract. But as has been described in chapter 5, initial experience is so encouraging that the introduction of a similar strategy would be highly recommendable. In fact, the treasury departments of several German state governments have started such initiatives. Their major interest results from the possibility to substantially increase the public investment-capacity with private money.
The **Manchester Metrolink** had been started before the introduction of PFI in 1992. It has inspired PFI and yet it has specific characteristics that distinguish it from the broad PFI-mode and from the **Croydon Tramlink** in particular. The most important difference is the much shorter contract period, allowing for a more flexible regime.

One of the major differences from the American projects is the transfer of the ridership-risk to the private side in Manchester and London-Croydon.

The second major difference is the fact that due to the accumulated experience on the public and the private side, the number of bidders gradually increased. In the most current case of the substantial system extension in Manchester, almost the entire "who's who" in transportation, construction and consulting expressed interest to participate in the tendering procedure. This maximization of potential bidders could be achieved despite the sharp financial, technical and security requirements of the Greater Manchester Public Transport Executive, one of Europe's most experienced Public Transport Authorities.

The third difference is the fact that on the basis of the public acquisition of Rights of Ways, the bidder has the chance to influence every aspect of the project, from the early design phase on. This is reflected in the concession agreement. One example, the concession agreement of the first extension of the Manchester Metrolink, is therefore attached to this study (see 10.1).

The fourth difference is related to the urban structure of the Manchester and Croydon area. The cities themselves but also their suburban areas are much more densely urbanized than typical metropolitan areas in the USA. As a consequence, the number of transit riders per Kilometer/Mile is substantially higher than in the US.

The result of these differences from the first turnkey experiences in the USA, contributes to a much lower public investment rate per passenger. As shown in chapter 5, the investment per yearly rider is at least four times lower in the UK projects. This, and the entire background of the decade-long experience with PFI, are the reasons why the UK-experience appears more relevant for future improvements of German urban rail systems than the US experience. The US, on the other hand, is an example of how to start the turnkey approach, despite important technical and political obstacles.
German public transport as well as road-building sectors can strongly learn from the British BOT-experience.

The use of transit property for transit purposes

As described in chapter 6, there are inspiring types of transit property related development partnerships in Germany. However, those projects are elaborated randomly and without clear goals from the property owner side.

Despite all of the differences with German transport and urban development structures, the US experiences reported are highly important to develop a closer connection between the traffic purpose of German rail transit companies, and the commercialization of their respective properties.
The following practices, derived from the experience in the case studies, mainly in Washington D.C., an Diego, Portland, OR, Southeast Pennsylvania and New Jersey, appear to be particularly relevant:

- Publications of lists of available real estate properties adjacent to stations and requests for development proposals (see as a significant example the WMATA transit joint development guidelines in attachment 10.2). Transit Agency's (or other public body's) support of selected developers to obtain the necessary local zoning rights, in order to accelerate the issuing of building permits and to encourage improvements of the management and the appearance of the urban context of the proposed development.

- Priority for lease-contracts, but openness to all other forms of contracts with private developers or private real estate users. Flexibility in defining which part of the real estate property is subject to a contract with a private side.
- Possibility to use federal transit funds to acquire real estate, necessary to spur urban development in proximity of transit stations.

As opposed to the complex legal, organizational and cultural obstacles to BOT-projects and PFI in particular, Transit Joint Development would be directly applicable in Germany. Is has not been applied because regional and municipal transit agencies don't own property that could be used for Joint Development purposes.

The Deutsche Bahn AG is the only public transport agency with substantial real estate property. The most important reasons why this property has (mostly) not been used for Joint Development are

- the role of this property to generate income for the National government to cover the costs of the Deutsche Bahn transformation into a "private" company and
- the distance from regional and local development concerns.

In order to actually apply the joint development experience of the US in Germany, it would thus be necessary to transfer the property of Deutsche Bahn real estate to local communities and state governments. This is subject to ongoing research[25] and political debate. It is already happening in several places due to the creation of "real estate pools" around rail stations.

The use of transit for development purposes

In most cases, in the US as well as in Germany, transit agencies don't dispose of real estate property other than the property directly related to the transit infrastructure. In these cases, it is necessary to encourage transit-oriented development of private or other public land property adjacent to stations. Transit-oriented development can increase urban density and diversity at transit stations and may thus contribute to increasing transit-ridership and increasing fare-box revenues. In some regions, development patterns focused on transit corridors contribute to a long term reshaping of metropolitan areas.

---

[25] see for example the dissertation currently undertaken by Gerhard Wulfhorst, Rheinisch-Westfälische Technische Hochschule in Aachen

Of the seven regions studied, those with the most transit-focused development in the postwar years are Toronto, Portland Washington, DC and, more recently, San Diego. All of these regions have attracted considerable development in the downtown areas served by new transit systems, as well as certain city and suburban nodes of commerce and business. Important development at inner city and suburban stations occurred also in St. Louis, Atlanta and Vancouver.

Development in station areas has either been driven by market forces that value the particular locational attributes of public transit or spurred by specific public policies, programs, and regulatory settings and/or by transit-agency actions (e.g. joint development). In the past, real estate cycles almost always interrupted the development process.

The following problems, successes and tools of transit-oriented development are pertinent to the German perspective:

- Driving forces to promote transit-oriented development differ strongly. Associations, developers, private landowners, politicians, the transit agency or strongly devoted individual administrative staff members may be pushing new development patterns. But they will all be unsuccessful without the understanding or support of the local community. Local governments play a fundamental role in promoting transit-focused development. As the guardians of land-use regulation, local governments can encourage transit-focused development. They can elaborate comprehensive planning policies and zoning provisions that encourage a transit-supportive development-pattern. These planning and regulatory actions, which sometimes must override neighborhood opposition, are an absolute necessity to attract private investment in station areas. Taking more initiative, local governments can work with transit agencies to undertake redevelopment activities, infrastructure improvements, and joint development projects. Public development corporations, created to manage and promote station-oriented development, have proven to be effective in various cities, including the Portland and the Washington D.C. area.

- The stronger the regional support for transit-oriented policy, the better the transit effects and the urban and regional reshaping possibilities. The lack of binding regional plans and the institutional and geographical fragmentation of American metropolitan areas are the main reasons why the strong economic and political impulse for transit doesn't translate into an increase of the share of public transportation, and a sustained transit-oriented urban development. Even on the state level, the political support and funding coordination for transit-oriented development is very often insufficient. Also – the weaker the regional coherence, the weaker the cooperation of private real estate owners and developers with transit agencies is. The weaker the regional agreement about the transit orientation, the weaker also the acceptance of value-capturing measures to achieve private contribution to the financing of transit-improvements or new transit lines. Many of these weaknesses may be mitigated once reliable public support for transit-focused development will be built up. Some encouraging signs for growing public support and its development consequences are visible. The best example is Portland. Despite the fact that any form of government influence limiting the use of private property is politically very risky, the support of Oregon's Urban Growth Boundary seems to grow, not only as a result of several public referendums on this issue, but also as a result of a mind-building process within the development-community itself. The reason is that once land acquisitions and marketing strategies correspond to the given framework, the urban growth boundary prevents incalculable competition. In addition other examples are highly inspiring from a German perspective, such as Atlanta, GA. The development-community itself, in conjunction with the state Governor, claims the necessity of a more transit-oriented regional development. The existing level of traffic congestion and the dependence of the most important (federally funded) development projects on agreements with the US Environmental Protection Agency seem to be the most important factors that led to this new mind-set.

- If accompanied by an adequate and aggressive TOD-policy, today's Light Rail systems may have a similar development impact as the Heavy Rail systems, especially in suburban areas.

- Transit-oriented development requires adequate methods of risk-analysis through the financing sector. One specific aspect is related to the fact that transit-oriented development projects tend to cover a greater diversity of uses. The interdependency of these development-elements needs to be evaluated. Uses cannot be regarded and estimated separately. It may thus make sense to take a greater than usual development risk in one sector in order to attract demand for other development-elements. The other aspect is related to the evaluation of the transit service as a development-promoter. For both aspects, evaluation methods need to be developed that permit a quantitative estimation of specific TOD risks and opportunities. Due to different development frameworks in the US, Germany and other European countries, the method or the specifically relevant factors may differ greatly.

Learning from US experience with transit joint and transit oriented development, and exchanging experiences in this area between European and American responsible parties, appears to be one of the most fruitful contributions to the promotion of public private partnerships in the field of urban rail transit on both sides of the Atlantic.

8.9 Final remarks

The financial potential for PPP in Germany in the field of public transport (and in many other public sectors) is enormous! Due to the country's size, it's economic importance, and the amount of public money involved, the absolute potential in Germany is much higher than that in Great Britain. In absolute terms, it is comparable to the US potential, because the size of its public transport markets is equal. As opposed to the UK, where public-private cooperation is already substantial, the potential for PPP in both Germany and the US is very far from being achieved. These remarks focus on the financially most important type of partnerships for the construction and management of new rail lines. Compared with that, the financial importance of transit-oriented partnerships, that focus on the utilization of those infrastructures, has a long-term character. As has been shown it is their political impact in terms of shaping transit friendly urban structures that makes these partnerships so interesting, less their potential to deflate public budgets.

Generally, the financing of public transport in Germany is so strongly segmented that it can be characterized as *the* socio-administrative counter-example of British pragmatism.

It is divided by law into a wide range of specific funding purposes, including capital investment, transport service, individual price reductions, other social issues, and, last but not least, the diverse funding purposes of urban development and economic development.

A detailed investigation of public transport related funding flows in the state of Brandenburg (HICKMANN/BERSCHIN 2002) quantifies the inefficiency of this costly system. It underlines the findings of other studies (e.g. DEUTSCHE BANK RESEARCH 2001) that significant funding portions are not aiming at improving the public transport system, but rather at maintaining a monopolistic market of local transport companies, each entitled to direct company-related public payments. The suggested solution to this is to combine funding sources, and to pay lump sums to the local authorities, so as to tender public transport services on the European market. This can be approached within the existing legal framework, but completed only after overhauling the legal system on the national level.

The payment of public funding out of a single source, and the "all- inclusive" character of this funding, with no additional operational subsidies over a number of years, is the basic financial pillar of PPP's for public transport investments in the UK, and for the most current light rail projects in the US. The analysis of the US and British cases underlines the strong financial advantage of such a solution. The British cases show that it may be possible to build a whole new system, and to subsidize its construction and service over at least 15 years (up to 99 years), with the monetary equivalent of an annual triennial subsidy for regional rail transport in Germany that covers only operational and infrastructure maintenance expenses, but no infrastructure renewal or extension.

This study is being conducted at a time of fundamental change in the management and financing of public transport in Germany and all over Europe. The first step in Germany was the railway reform of 1994, described in chapter 7. One of its main characteristics was the so- called "regionalization", through which the responsibility for procurement and financing of regional railway service was delegated to the regional level (a step that needs to be followed by the ownership and financial responsibility for the regional railway network). A similar process will follow for Bus and Light Rail transport.

The identity of political and financial responsibility for regional rail transport has already led to a strong increase of the efficiency of the public monies involved. However – the identity of political and financial responsibility is only a necessary, and not a sufficient condition for the maximization of the value for public monies. This is also valid for the US, where regional rail transport and public mass transport, in general, were under state responsibility (and ownership) for a longtime. The additional necessary condition is competition among different transport providers. This presupposes the clear separation between the public transport authority and the ownership of public transport companies.

The changes initiated so far will in the future be clearly directed through two processes: increasing budgetary deficits and the competition-oriented legal framework on the EU-level.

As a consequence, a new share of roles between the public and the private sector will be implemented. Due to deep rooted German (and other country's) traditions of Social Welfare/Protection, the market conditions for the private sector will be characterized by more strongly regulated public requirements (e.g. fixed PT tariffs) than in Great Britain outside London. Social Welfare/Protection will secure a structurally higher public financial contribution than in the US and Great Britain.

As the second British case (London-Croydon) and the US cases show, these preconditions will not hinder or diminish a radical redefinition of the roles of each sector. In order to prepare for this change, the study delivers a systematic overview of cooperation possibilities between both the public and private sectors, and evaluates their financial and political impact.

The questions and solution-models of this study are characterized by the technical and economic specificities of Public Transport. However, several core results are transferable to other fields of public tasks, including other modes of transport (e.g. turnkey-projects for toll roads) and urban and regional (economic) development.

If the institutional conditions for the realization of those (and potentially more) public tasks fit to this new share of roles, the quality of public services can be maintained or improved even if public budgets continue to be reduced. Necessary basic changes of public institutional structures include:

a) an increase in professional competence for tendering public tasks,

b) an adequate legal and organizational framework for PPP oriented public procurement and public-private informal cooperation (see also SCHUPPERT 2001),

c) a repeal of segregated and segmented public funding in favor of holistic funding approaches aiming at securing the profitability of public projects, and, last but not least,

d) an implementation of a culture of cooperation on the basis of increasing and continuing PPP-experience.

This study has presented and analyzed a wide range of possibilities to achieve or approach these goals. A detailed analysis of the transferability of specific tools and methods is necessary. This will be the task of further research projects, of which two have already been initiated through this study (EU-study of transit oriented development – PPP Transit – and a dissertation about location efficient mortgages).

9. Sources

9.1 List of Interviews

- G.B. Arrington, Jr., Tri-Met, Director of Strategic and Long Range Planning, Portland/Oregon
- Jean Banker, Metropolitan Transportation Authority, Capital Program Funding, Assistant Director
- John Barden, Parsons Brinckerhoff Denver, Director of Visualization
- Peter J. Basso, DOT, Assistant Secretary for Budget and Programs and Chief Financial Officer
- Rajiv Batra, Urban Design Collaborative, Portland/OR, Principal
- Peter Becken, PacTrust, Pacific Realty Associates, Portland/Oregon, President and Chief Executive Officer
- Chris Bertram, Subcommittee on Ground Transportation, Senior Professional Staff
- William S. Beetle, State of New Jersey, Trenton/NJ, Department of Transportation, Division of Transportation Systems Planning, Director
- Brenda Myers Boehlke, Parsons Brinckerhoff Herndon/VA, Principal Professional Associate and Vice President
- Gerry Bogacz, New York Metropolitan Transportation Council, Assistant Director
- Theodore von Briesen, Parsons Brinckerhoff Milwaukee, Assistant Vice President
- Ann Catlin, DOT, Federal Transit Administration, Real Estate Specialist
- Donald H. Camph, Aldaron Inc., Public Policy Advisors to Industry and Government, President
- Peter C. Cap, P.E., Parsons Brinckerhoff Newark, Vice President
- Yuval Cohen, Parsons Brinckerhoff New York, Chief Economist, Vice President
- Daniel Corbett, United States Senate Committee on Environment and Public Works, Professional Staff Member
- James Croy, Georgia Regional Transportation Authority, Director of Transportation

- Rita Daguillard, DOT, Federal Transit Administration, International Program Manager
- Thomas G. Dallessio, State of New Jersey, Office of the Governor, Policy Advisor
- Steve Davies, Project for Public Spaces, New York, Vice President
- Walter Deriso, Synovus, Vice Chairman, also: Chairman of the Georgia Rail Passenger Authority
- Robert Dorey, chairman of Tramtrack Croydon Limited, London-Croydon
- John Diebold, The John Diebold Institute for Public Policy Research, New York
- John Driscoll, Harvard University, Cambridge/MA, Graduate School of Design, Unit for Housing and Urbanization, Assistant Director
- Robert Dunphy, Urban Land Institute, Washington D.C., Senior Resident Fellow, Transportation
- Mark Evans, Siemens Transportation Partnership Puerto Rico, S.E., Director, Project Administration
- John Fawkner, Transport for London, Head of Department International Relations
- Nuria Fernandez, DOT, Federal Transit Administration, Acting Administrator
- Daniel V. Flanagan Jr., Transrapid International-USA, Washington D.C., Managing Director: National Center for Innovations in Public Finance at the University of Southern California
- Martin Garrett, Altram, Managing Director, Manchester/UK
- Sten Gdowski, Parsons Brinckerhoff Newark, Senior Supervising Architect
- Mike Georgiou, Serco Metrolink, Managing Director, Manchester/UK
- Robert C. Gilbert, BellSouth, Director Atlanta Metro Plan
- Mark W. Gordon, NJ Transit, Newark/NJ, Senior Director Real Estate
- Marianne Ginsburg, German Marshall Fund, Washington D.C., Senior Manager
- Sigurd Grava, Parsons Brinckerhoff New York, Technical Director of Planning, Principal Professional Associate, Vice President. Columbia University, New York City, Professor at the School of Architecture and Planning

- Jacquelyne D. Grimshaw, Center for Neighborhood technology, Transportation & Air Quality, Coordinator
- Marc Guichard, Metro Regional Government, Portland/OR, Transportation Department, Associate Regional Planner
- Jane Hayse, Atlanta Regional Commission, Director of the Department of Transportation
- David Heymsfeld, US House of Representatives, Washington D.C., Committee on Transportation and Infrastructure, Democratic Staff Director
- Dilawez Hoda, Monroe Center LLC, Hoboken/NJ, Managing Member
- Julie H. Hoover, Parsons Brinckerhoff New York, Professional Associate, Senior Vice President
- Geoff Inskip, Greater Manchester Passenger Transport Executive, Director of Finance, Manchester/UK
- Suzan Kedron-Lyn, Jenkens & Gilchrist, Attorney
- Fred Kent, Project for Public Spaces, New York, President
- Roy Kienitz, Surface Transportation Policy Project, Washington D.C.
- Allan Kiepper, Parsons Brinckerhoff, Senior Vice President, New York/NY
- William M. King, Metropolitan Transportation Authority (MTA), Office of Construction Oversight, Deputy Director
- Gary D. Kuykendall, Virginia Department of Rail and Public Transportation, Richmond/VA, Transportation Engineering Program Supervisor
- Pierre Laconte, Union Internatonale des Transports Publics (UITP), Brussels, Belgium, External Affairs Advisor to the President, Honorary Secretary General
- Jack Limber, Metropolitan Transit Development Board (MTDB), San Diego/CA, Deputy General Manager
- Richard D. Loffelmacher, PacTrust, Pacific Realty Associates, Portland/Oregon
- Rick Mariani, NJ Transit, Newark/NJ, Models Stations Program, Director
- Paul Marx, DOT, Federal Transit Administration, Office of Policy Development, Financial Analyst
- Scott McIntosh, Transport for London, TfL representative for the Croydon Tramlink project, London/UK
- Bud Melton, Bowman-Melton Associates, bicycle and pedestrian planners, trail consultant, Dallas/TX

- Henry L. Michel, Parsons Brinckerhoff New York, Chairman Emeritus
- William W. Millar, American Public Transit Association (APTA), President
- Neil D. Muller, Muller, Bohlin & Associates, Highland Park/NJ
- Chris Mulligan, Greater Manchester Passenger Transport Executive, Chairman, Manchester/UK
- Alvin Mc Neal, Washington Metropolitan Area Transit Authority (WMATA), Washington D.C., Property Planning and Development, Manager
- James L. Oberstar, Member of Congress, Committee on Transportation and Infrastructure, Ranking Democrat
- Cynthia Nikitin, Project for Public Spaces, New York, Project Manager
- Jeffrey P. Ordway, Bay Area Rapid Transit District, Oakland/CA, Real Estate Service, Manager of Property Development
- Anna Pace, Urban Planning & Development Services, Toronto/Ontario, Canada, Program Coordinator, Transportation Planning
- Robert M. Paley, Metropolitan Transportation Authority (MTA), New York, Real Estate Department, Director
- John Pucher, Rutgers University, New Brunswick/NJ, Bloustein School of Planning and Public Policy, Professor for Transportation Planning
- Sharon Pugh, DOT, Federal Transit Administration, Office of Planning Innovation and Analysis, Transportation Planner
- Jeff Rader, Georgia Regional Transportation Authority
- Prof. Tony Ridley, Imperial College, London/UK
- Martin E. Robins, Rutgers University, New Brunswick/NJ, Center of Transportation Policy, Director
- Peter M. Rogoff, United States Senate, Committee on Appropriations, Subcommittee on Transportation and Related Agencies, Staff Director – Minority
- Marcel Rommerts, European Commission, Brussels, Belgium, Directorate Generale VII – Transport
- Janette Sadik-Khan, Parsons Brinckerhoff New York, Senior Vice President
- Sarah J. Siwek, Sarah J. Siwek & Associates, Transportation & Environmental Consulting, President
- James B. Snyder, Arlington County/VA, Department of Community Planning, Housing and Development, Planning Division, Current and Comprehensive Planning Supervisor

- Effie Stallsmith, DOT, Federal Transit Administration, Office of Planning, Special Assistant
- Ralph L. Stanley, Bechtel Enterprises Portland/OR, Vice President
- Jennifer Tabakin, Metropolitan Transportation Authority (MTA), Office of Construction Oversight
- Helen Tapp, Regional Business Coalition, Atlanta/GA, Executive Director
- Karen Trapenberg Frick, Metropolitan Transportation Commission, Oakland/CA, Transportation Planner
- Jean-Arnold Vinois, European Commission, Brussels, Belgium, Directorate General VII – Transport, Transport R&D Intermodal and Strategic Aspects – COST, Head of Unit
- Jean Vivier, Union Internationale des Transports Publics (UITP), Brussels, Belgium, Programs and Studies Department, Head of Department
- Edward Verde, Focus Realty Advisors, Dallas/TX
- Paul Vespermann, MARTA, Director of Real Estate
- Alexandros E. Washburn, Pennsylvania Station Redevelopment Corporation, New York, President
- Richard A. Weaver, American Public Transit Association (APTA), Washington D.C., Manager Planning and Programs
- Bernard L. Weinstein, University of North Texas, Center for Economic Development and Research, Director
- John Williams, Post Properties, Chairman and Chief Executive Officer
- Nigel H.M. Wilson, Massachusetts Institute of Technology (MIT), Center for Transportation Studies, Professor of Civil and Environmental Engineering
- Mariia Zimmermann, DOT, Federal Transit Administration, Office of Policy Development, Policy Analyst
- Jeff Zupan, Regional Plan Association, Senior Transportation Planner

9.2 List of Literature

- 1000 Friends of Oregon: The LUTRAQ Analysis of Alternatives, Portland/OR 1992
- Agenda 1998: Clinton-Gore Livability Agenda: Building Livable Communities for the 21st Century, Washington, September 1998
- American Public Transit Association (APTA): Building better communities – coordinating land-use and transit planning, Washington 1989
- American Public Transit Association (APTA): Transit Fact Book 1999, Washington 1999
- Anas, Alex; Armstrong, Regina: Land values and transit access: modeling the relationship in the New York Metropolitan Area, an implementation handbook, Urban Mass Transit Transportation Program, Washington D.C. September 1993
- Aoki, Masahiko: Toward a comparative institutional analysis, Cambridge 2001
- Arthur Anderson, Enterprise LSE: Value for Money Drivers in the Private Finance Initiative, report commissioned by The Treasury Taskforce, London 2000
- Audirac, Ivonne; Thompson, Gregory: A Literature Review of TOD - Transit-oriented Development: Challenges and Opportunities for Reshaping Urban Development Patterns, Florida DOT, Department of Urban and Regional Planning, Florida State University, November 1988
- Barzel, Allan: Economic Analysis of Property Rights, 1989
- Basso, Peter "Jack": speech at the 1999 ARBTA conference – Innovative Financing, Washington D.C., Nov.2nd 1999
- Bates report 1997: PFI to be re-invigorated, London 1997
- Beckmann, Klaus; Perian, Thomas; Wulfhorst, Gebhard: Staedtebauliche Chancen und Risiken bei der Entwicklung von Bahnflaechen – Handlungserfordernisse des Bundes, Berichte Stadt Region Land des Instituts für Stadtbauwesen, RWTH Aachen, Aachen, Oktober 1999
- Bernick, Michael; Cervero, Robert: Transit-Based Development in the United States: A Review of Recent Experiences, UC Berkeley, IURD, working paper 611, Berkeley 1995
- Bookout, Lloyd W.: Neotraditional town planning – cars, pedestrians and transit, in: Urban Land, February 1992

- Bragado, Nancy S., Transit Joint Development in San Diego: Policies and Practices, March 1999, forthcoming in the Transportation Research Record.
- Bundy, Emory: Remarks for a conference on: Sprawl and Congestion – is Light Rail and Transit-Oriented Development the Answer? Center for the New West, Colorado Springs, June 17, 1999
- Calthorpe Associates et al.: Design for efficient suburban activity centers, phase I Report, FHWA, Washington D.C. March 1997
- Cervero, Robert: The Transit Metropolis, A global inquiry, Washington D.C. 1998
- Cervero, Robert; Hall, Peter; Landis, John: Transit Joint Development, Institute of Urban and Regional Development (IURD) at Berkeley-University, monograph 42, 1992;
- Coase, Ronald H.: The Nature of the firm, Economica 4, 1937, 1-44
- Colliers International, San Diego County Market Profile, in: ULI Urban Land Institute, Market Profiles 1999 North-America, Washington D.C., 1999
- Collins, Mary A.; McDaniel, James B.: Report on Innovative Financing Techniques for Transit Agencies, Transit Cooperative Research Program, Legal Research Digest, August 1999, number 13
- Deakin, Elizabeth et al.: Real Estate Trends and Transit-oriented Development, Institute of Urban and Regional Development at Berkeley University, IURD working paper 688, 1997,
- Deeming, Eryn: Growing with Transit: Creating Transit Supportive Development in an Automobile-Focused World, Master-thesis MIT, Cambridge/MA 1999
- Deutsches Seminar fuer Staedtebau und Wirtschaft (DSSW): conference about "operating and financing of regional train stations" in Potsdam 1998, DSSW-Schriften 29, Bonn/Berlin 1998
- Deutsche Bank Research, Sonderbericht: Öffentlicher Personennahverkehr auf dem Weg in den Wettbewerb, Frankfurt/M 5.1.2001
- Dorey, Robert: Croydon Tramlink, 28 km system aims to improve quality of life for residents, from: UK Transport Projects, London 1998
- Dorey, Robert: The Croydon Tramlink Concession, presentation at the conference Light Rail 99
- Dueker, Kenneth J.; Bianco, Martha J.: Light Rail-transit Impacts in Portland: he first ten years, Transportation Research

- Dunphy, Robert: Transportation and Growth: Myth and Fact, Urban Land Institute, Washington, DC, 1996
- Dunphy, Robert: Moving beyond gridlock, Urban Land Institute, Washington, DC, 1998
- Ehrenhalt, Allan: New Recruits in the war on Sprawl, in: New York Times, April 13th, 1999
- Eggertsson, T.: Economic behavior and institutions, Cambridge 1990
- Erlei, Matthias et al.: Neue Institutionenoekonomik, Stuttgart 1999
- EU Select Committee Final Report on the Financing Options for the Trans European Networks, 1997
- Faber, O.: Metrolink Monitoring Study – Volume Two: Demand Modelling, Pre and Post Implementation The Department of Transport and GMPTE, Manchester, 1996
- FANNIE MAE, James W. Rouse Forum on the American City, Rouse Forum Survey: A rise in Downtown Living, Washington D.C., January 1999
- Federal Highway Administration (FHWA): Our Nation's Highways – selected facts and figures, Washington D.C. 1998
- Federal Highway Administration: Metropolitan America in Transition: Implications for Land-use and Transportation Planning, Searching for Solutions, A Policy Discussion Series, Number 10, Washington 1994
- Federal Register, DOT, FTA, Section 5309, Notice: FTA New Starts Criteria, Washington D.C. December 1996
- Federal Register, Part V, Department of Transportation, Federal Transit Administration: Job Access and Reverse Commute Competitive Grants: Notice, Washington D.C., November 6, 1998
- Federal Register, Public Law 91-646, with 1987 Amendments, including changes through 6/1/1993, part 24: Uniform relocation assistance and real property acquisition for federal and federally assisted programs, Washington D.C. 1993
- Federal Register, Public Law 91-646: Uniform Relocation Act, Federal Highway Administration, Office of the Right-of-way, Washington D.C. January 1971
- Federal Transit Administration, Livable Communities Initiative: Planning, Developing, and Implementing, Washington D.C. October 1997
- Federal Transit Administration, Office of Planning, TPL-22: Overview of the revised Section 5309 New Starts Criteria, Washington D.C., September 1997

- Federal Transit Administration: Planning for Transit-Friendly Land-use, A Handbook for New Jersey Communities, Washington D.C., 1994
- Federal Transit Administration: Transit-Supportive Development in the United States: Experiences and Projects, Washington D.C., 1993
- Fejarang, Robert A. "Impact on Property Values: A Study of the Los Angeles Metro Rail," Transportation Research Board, Washington, DC, 1994
- FHWA-Statistics: State Motor-Fuel Tax Rates, 1983-97
- FTA-report: "Innovative Financing" 1998
- Furubotn, E. Pejovich: Property Rights and Economic Theory: A survey of recent literature, in: Journal of Economic Literature, 1972, pp. 1137-1162.
- Furubotn, Eirik; Richter, Rudolf: The New Institutional Economics: An Assessment, in: Furubotn, Eirik; Richter, Rudolf (editors): The New Institutional Economics, a collection of articles from the Journal of Institutional and Theoretical Economics, Texas 1991
- Gafron, Philine et al.: Public Private Partnerships around Urban Rail Transit – lessons from case studies in Europe and North America, final draft of a study for the EU-Commission, DG TREN, fifth research framework, Hamburg 2002
- GMPTA/E (Greater Manchester Passenger Transport Authority & Executive): Metrolink 2000, information: Metrolink – unprecedented success, Manchester/UK 2000
- Goldberg, V.: Regulation and Administered Contracts, Bell Journal of Economics, 94, 1976, pp.691-719
- Gomez-Ibanez; Meyer, John: Going Private, the international experience with transport
- Grava, Sigurd: Mobility demands of the Urban Field, in: transportation quarterly, 2/1999privatization, Brookings Institution, Washington, D.C. 1993
- Guichard, Marc: Transit-Oriented Development Implementation Program, Metro Regional Government, Portland/OR, January 1998
- Guiliano, Genevieve: The weakening Transportation-Land-use Connection, Access, number 6, 1995
- Hayek, F.A: Law, Legislation and Liberty, Vol.1, London 1973
- Heinz, Werner (Hrsg.): Public Private Partnership – ein neuer Weg zur Stadtentwicklung?, Berlin 1993
- Hickmann, Gerd; Berschin, Felix: Vorschläge zur Neuordnung der ÖPNV-Finanzierung: Leitbilder für eine Fortentwicklung der ÖPNV-Finanzierung in

Deutschland und Reformvorschläge für die Bundesländer Brandenburg und Sachsen-Anhalt, Schlussbericht (unveröffentlicht), November 2001

- Hickling Lewis Brod, Inc. (HLB): Transit's Value in Neighborhoods: Working Paper 1, April 8, Federal Transit Administration, Washington, D.C. 1996
- HM Treasury (Her Majesty's Treasury): Private Opportunity, Public Benefit, Progressing the Private Finance Initiative, London/UK 1995
- HM Treasury (Her Majesty's Treasury): Public Private Partnerships, The government's approach, London/UK 2000
- Hoeveler, James K.: Accessibility vs. Mobility: The Location Efficient Mortgage, URL-document, www.cnt.org
- Hörhager, A.: Förderung europäischer Verkehrsprojekte am Beispiel der Europäischen Investitionsbank Volume B218 Proceedings of Seminar X/98, Public Private Partnership im Verkehr – eine Alternative für Auftraggeber, Auftragnehmer und Nutzer', Deutsche Verkehrswissenschaftliche Gesellschaft, Essen,1998
- Inskip, Geoff: Metrolink – on the move, in: PFI Journal, Volume 4, issue unknown, 1999
- Inskip, Geoff: Metrolink – on track for expansion, in: PFI Journal, Volume 1, issue 4, 1996
- Institut d'Amenagement et d"Urbanisme de la Region Ile de France (IAURIF): Four world –cities transportation study, French version, Paris 1998
- International Council for Local Environmental Initiatives (ICLEI): Local Government Implementation of Climate Protection, Nagoya 1997
- Irish Business and Employers Confederation First Report on Public Private Partnerships IBEC, Dublin, 1998; available from http://www.ibec.ie
- Jennings, John, "Major Transit Initiatives for Centers," APA New Jersey Planners' Journal, Fall, 1997
- Jungclausen, J.F.: Kunden hinter Gittern Die Zeit, 6.6.2002, p.27
- KPMG Peat Marwick: Fiscal Impact of Metrorail on the Commonwealth of Virginia, Executive Summary and Final Technical Report, Arlington, VA 1994
- Kumkar, Lars: Wettbewerbsorientierte Reformen der Stromwirtschaft, Tübingen 2000
- Kyrein, R.: Schaffung und Mobilisierung kostengünstigen Baulandes in Public Private Partnership Proceedings of SLR Jahrestagung/BDLA

Bundeskongreß 1998, Vereinigung für Stadt-, Regional- und Landesplanung e.V., Berlin, 1998

- Landis, John, Subhrajit Guhathakurta, William Huang, and Ming Zhang (LANDIS et al.): Rail-transit Investments, Real Estate Values, and Land-use Change: A Comparative Analysis of Five California Rail-transit Systems, UC Berkeley, Institute of Urban and Regional Development, Berkeley, July 1995
- Leland Consulting Group (et al.): Market Findings, Hillsboro LRT station area development, executive summary, Hillsboro 27 June 1995
- Lerner-Lam, Eva: "Hardwiring Coordination in Transportation and Land-use Decision Making: Making it work in San Diego, California", in ITE 1989 Compendium of Technical Papers (Washington, D.C.: Institute of Transportation Engineers, 1989)
- Levy, Brian; Spiller, Pablo T. A framework for resolving the regulatory problem, in: Regulations, institutions, and commitment: comparative studies of telecommunications, Cambridge (USA), 1996
- Levy, S.M.: Build, Operate, Transfer. Paving the Way for Tomorrow's Infrastructure, New York 1996
- Luczak, Marybeth: New Jersey Transit maps a still bigger role for rail, in: Railway Age, October 1999
- Manvel, Evan: Beyond Highways-Only, The Earmarking of State Motor Fuel Taxes for Highways and Recommendations for a Progressive Response, Surface Transportation Project, April 1998
- Marks, Stephen D.: Case Study of the Hudson Bergen Light Rail Transit (LRT) Project, Rutgers University, Newark, NJ 1999
- McNeal, Alvin R. and DOGGETT Rosalyn P.: Using Real Estate Assets to Help Finance Transportation: The Washington Metropolitan Area Transit Authority's Public/Private Land Development Program, Transportation Research Board, Washington D.C., January 1999
- Mead, Susan: Smart growth – public-private partnerships – transit villages, Jenkens & Gilchrist, P.C., Land-use practice group, Dallas/TX 1999)
- Metrolink: Greater Manchester Metrolink Extensions Strategy; Manchester, UK, 2000
- Metropolitan Toronto: The Transit/Development Connection, Toronto 1987
- MOBILITY 2020, The Metropolitan Transportation Plan Executive Summary, North Texas Council of Governments, Arlington TX, 1996

- Monsees, Jan/ Schneewolf, Dr.Rainer, Bedarfsanalyse für die Einrichtung eines S-Bahnhaltepunktes in Bernau-Friedenstal, in: Verkehr und Technik 1998, Nr.4, 145-153
- Moore, Terry; Thornes: The Transportation/Land-use Connection. American Planning Association, Chicago 1994
- MSWV aktuell 3/2000: Beiträge zu Hennigsdorf und Fürstenwalde, Potsdam 2000
- MTDB, Designing for Transit, San Diego 1993
- MTDB, Policies and Procedures No. 19: Joint Use and Development of Property, San Diego 1984
- MTDB-Brochure: Joint Development Major Project, Summary, San Diego 1998
- NAO (National Audit Office: Examining the value for money of deals under the Private Finance Initiative, London/UK, 1999
- National Census, Estimates of the Population of Metropolitan Areas, December 1997
- Nelson, Dick; Niles, John: Market Dynamics and Nonwork Travel Patterns: Obstacles for Transit-Oriented Development? Annual conference of the Transportation Research Board, Washington D.C., 1999
- Nelson, Dick; Niles, John: Measuring the Success of Transit-Oriented Development, National Planning Conference of the American Planning Association, Seattle, WA, April 1999
- NJ Transit, "Hudson River Waterfront Study: Draft Transportation Plan Technical Report," April 1986
- North, Douglas C.: Institutional Change and Economic History, Journal of Institutional History, 145,1989, pp. 238-245
- North, Douglas C.: Theorie des institutionellen Wandels. Eine neue Sicht der Wirtschaftsgeschichte, Tübingen, 1981
- North, Douglas C.: Institutions, Journal of Economic Perspectives, 1991, pp. 97-112
- Northstar Corridor, Environmental Impact Statement Project Scoping, July 1999
- Northstar Corridor, Federal Funding Request for Fiscal Year 2000, Minneapolis 1999
- NY Times, December 29th, 1999: New Jersey weighs tax rise on gasoline despite big surplus

- NY Times, October 12, 1999, B1: Hudson towns wary of railroad's reach
- NY Times, October 12, 1999: Information Superhighway Is Just Outside the Beltway
- NY Times, March 5, 2000: Saying Goodbye to the 'Burbs': A Developer Heads Downtown
- New York Times, May 1st, 2000: Approval Expected for Transit Spending Plan
- New York Times, May 4th, 2000: Ambitious Plans for Transit
- O'Toole, Randall: The Vanishing Automobile, Thoreau Institute, Portland 1999
- Park, Munsun: The Role of Transit Agency in Station Area Development: A case study of Tren Urbano, Puerto Rico, Master-Thesis at MIT, Cambridge 1999
- Parsons Brinckerhoff Inc., Notes February 1999, Doing Portland Proud
- Parsons Brinckerhoff Inc.: Transit and Urban Form, Volume 1 and 2, Transit Cooperative Research Program, Report 16, Washington D.C. 1996
- Parsons Brinckerhoff Portland/OR: Land-use Impacts of Transportation: A Guidebook, Transportation Research Board, National Cooperative Highway Research Program (NCHRP), Report 423A, Washington D.C. 1999
- PB Farradyne: Major Investment Study I-66, summary, Rockland, MD, 2000
- Peirce, Neal R.; Guskind, Robert: Breakthroughs – re-creating the American city, New Brunswick 1993
- Picot, Arnold; Wolff, Birgitta: Institutional Economics of Public Firms and Administrations, Journal of Institutional and Theoretical Economics, 150/1, 1994, pp.211-232
- Porter, Douglas R.: Transit-Focused Development, TCRP Synthesis #20, Washington D.C.1997
- Porter, Douglas: web-page about transit-oriented development in North America, URL www.peak.org, 1999
- Price Waterhouse Coopers: Market Profile New York City, in: ULI, Urban Land Institute: Market Profiles 1999 North-America, Washington D.C. 1999
- Project for Public Spaces (PPS), The Role of Transit in Creating Livable Metropolitan Communities, TCRP-Report 22, Washington D.C., 1997
- Public Securities Association (PSA): Fundamentals of Municipal Bonds, New York 1982

- Public Works Financing, December 1997, Volume 113: Portland Light Rail Partnership
- Pushkarev, Boris; Zupan, Jeffrey: Public Transportation & Land-use Policy, New York 1977
- Pushkarev, Boris; Zupan, Jeffrey; Cumella, Robert: Urban Rail in America – An exploration of criteria for fixed-guideway transit, New York, NY 1982
- Real Estate Research Corporation: Market Profile 1999 Washington D.C., Metropolitan Area, in: ULI Urban Land Institute: Market Profiles North America 1999, Washington D.C. 1999
- Regional Plan Association (RPA): A region at risk – summary of the third regional plan for the New York - New Jersey – Connecticut Metropolitan Area, New York 1996, p. 11
- Regional Plan Association (RPA): RX – Regional Express Rail, New York October 1996
- Regional Plan Association: The Renaissance of Rail-transit in America, New York, NY 1991
- Regulatory incentives, in: Regulations, institutions, and commitment: comparative studies of telecommunications, Cambridge (USA), 1996
- Ridley, Tony; Fawkner, John: Benefit sharing: the funding of urban transport through contributions from external beneficiaries, 47th International Congress of the International Metropolitan Railways Committee, Lausanne 1987
- Royal Lepage Professional Services, inc.: Real Estate Market Report 1999 of the Toronto Metropolitan Area, in: ULI Urban Land Institute: Market Profiles North America 1999, Washington D.C., 1999
- Schelte, J.: Beiträge zur Raumordnung Nr. 97 - Räumlich-struktureller Wandel in Innenstädten Dortmunder Institut für Raumplanung, Fakultät für Raumplanung, Universität Dortmund; Dortmund, 1999
- Schuppert, Gunnar Folke: Grundzüge eines zu entwickelnden Verwaltungskooperationsrechts, Regelungsbedarf und Rechtsrahmen für Public Private Partnership, Gutachten im Auftrag des Bundesministeriums des Inneren, Berlin Juni 2001
- Securities Training Corporation: Municipal Bonds, New York 1998
- Sedway Kotin Mouchly Group (SKMG): Joint development entrepreneurial study for the Bay Area Rapid Transit, San Francisco, CA, May 1996
- Skidmore, Owings & Merrill et al.: Planning for transit-friendly land-use - a handbook for New Jersey communities, Federal Transit Administration, Washington D.C. 1994

- Soberman, Richard, Understanding GO Transit: Transition to the Greater Toronto Services Board, Toronto 1998
- Soberman, Richard: The Track Ahead, Organization of the TTC under the new amalgamated City of Toronto, Toronto 1997
- Solari, Stefano: Economic order, institutions and the state: the many approaches to comparative institutional analysis, 2000
- Spiller, Pablo T.; Vogelsang, Ingo: The institutional foundations of regulatory commitment in the UK: The case of telecommunications, Journal of Institutional and Theoretical Economics, Volume 153, 1997, pp. 607-629
- Sriver, Jeffrey: Factors influencing land development around rail-transit stations, Master Thesis at the Department of Civil and Environmental Engineering at MIT, Cambridge 1993
- State of New Jersey, Department of Community Affairs: Smart Growth Planning Grants, URL www.state.nj.us/osp/
- Strathmann, Ludger: Der Beitrag privater Investitionen zur Entwicklung und Nutzung von Schienenverkehrshaltepunkten im Einzugsbereich von Ballungsräume im deutsch-französischen Vergleich, Diplomarbeit, TU Berlin, Dezember 1999
- Strohbach, Hannes: Build-Operate-Transfer-Modelle zur Finanzierung von Infrastrukturinvestitionen, Frankfurt a.M. 1999
- The Diebold Institute for Public Policy Studies, Inc.: Infrastructures for the 21st century – a progress report on the information-based infrastructure project, New York 1992
- The Oregonian, July 8, 1998: Harvard study gives black mark to Light Rail
- Thompson, Gregory L. and Ivonne Audirac, TODs Importance to Transit: Transit's Importance to TODS: Planning Scenarios for Sacramento, paper presented at the Transportation Research Board meetings, January, 1999.
- Transportation Research Board, Record No. 1466 (Planning and Administration): Issues in Land-use and Transportation Planning, Models, and Applications, Washington D.C. 1994
- Tri-Met, Facts about Tri-Met, Portland September 1999
- Tri-Met: At work in the field of dreams, Light Rail and smart growth in Portland, Portland 1998
- TTC, Service Planning: Encouraging Increased Transit Use – Density of development and rapid transit access issues, Toronto 1999
- University of Toronto, Joint Program in Transportation, Data Management Group, The Transportation Tomorrow Survey, Toronto, 1998

- US DOT FHWA, highway statistics: State motor-fuel tax rates, 1983-97
- US DOT, FHWA 1998: Our Nation's Highways, selected facts and figures, Washington D.C. 1998, p. 37)
- US DOT: ISTEA, TEA 21 & USDOT's Strategic Plan: A continuous and connected vision, URL-document, www.fta.dot.gov, Washington, D.C. 1999/1
- Vaccari, Michael A.: Overview of Innovative Financing: Highway and Transit, in: Transportation Research Board, Record No. 1527 (Transportation Law): Transportation Law Issues 1996, Washington D.C. 1996
- von Spee, Monika, Finanzierung und Trägerschaftskonzepte für Regionalbahnhöfe unter Einbeziehung privater und kommunaler Partner, in: Trägerschaft und Finanzierung von Regionalbahnhöfen, Hrsg.: Deutsches Seminar für Städtebau und Wirtschaft, Bonn 1998, 29-30.
- Vuchic, Vukan R.: Achieving intermodal balance for efficiency and livability of cities, presentation at the UITP/APTA/CUTA-conference in Toronto, May 1999
- Weinstein, Bernard; Clower, Terry et al.: The Initial Impacts of the Dart LRT System, University of North Texas, Center for Economic Development and Research, July 1999
- Welsh Chester Galiney Matone Inc. and Sitar Company, ONCOR International: Market Profile Northern New Jersey, in: ULI, Urban Land Institute: Market Profiles 1999 North-America, Washington D.C. 1999
- Williamson, Oliver E.: Corporate Finance and Corporate Governance, The Journal of Finance, 1988, pp.567-591
- Williamson, Oliver E.: The Economic Institutions of Capitalism, New York 1985
- Williamson, Oliver E.: Transaktionskostenökonomik, Hamburg, 1996
- Winston, Clifford; Shirley, Chad: Alternative route: toward efficient urban transportation, The Brookings Institution, Washington D.C. 1998
- WMATA, Joint Development Guidelines, Washington D.C., Nov. 1995
- WMATA, Joint Development Solicitations, issued March 22, 1996, February 11, 1999, July 29, 1999
- WMATA; New York Avenue Metro Rail Station, Environmental Assessment & Section 4(f), April 2000, Progress Draft
- Wulkan, Alan; Snyder, Gregg: The role of land regulations in successful transit investments: case studies of success, Parsons Brinckerhoff, 1997

9.3 Sources of Illustrations

Title page	New Light Rail Station in Dallas/TX, DART, InMotion, DART-Journal Autumn 1999
Illustration 2.1	Geographical Overview about study areas in the USA, Kümmerly+Frey, Rand McNally, Westermann, Internationaler Atlas 1990
Illustration 2.2	Geographical Overview about study areas in Europe, Kümmerly+Frey, Rand McNally, Westermann, Internationaler Atlas 1990
Illustration 3.1	LEM zones Chicago, URL: www.cnt.org
Illustration 3.2	Illustration 3.2 relationships between transit oriented development, transit joint development and livable communities
Illustration 4.1	Commuter Rail System of the Tri State Area New York – New Jersey – Connecticut, Institut d'Amenagement et d'Urbanisme de la Region Ile de France (IAURIF) 1998
Illustration 4.2	New York Express Rail System – RPA concept, Regional Plan Association 1996
Illustration 4.3	Major NJ Transit Investment Projects, NJ Transit
Illustration 4.4	Metrorail system map, WMATA 2000
Illustration 4.5	Technology Centers in the Washington, D.C. Area, New York Times, 12.10.1999
Illustration 4.6	Dulles corridor Bus Rapid Transit, URL: www.vdot.state.va.us
Illustration 4.7	MARTA Metrorail system, MARTA 1999
Illustration 4.8:	Infrared aerial photo of Fulton, DeKalb, Cobb and Gwinnet County Regional Business Coalition, Atlanta/GA 1999
Illustration 4.9:	same area, 21 years later, Regional Business Coalition, Atlanta/GA 1999
Illustration 4.10	Atlanta postcard, Atlanta/GA 2000
Illustration 4.11	Atlanta Highway Interchange (Morland), Atlanta Regional Commission, Regional Transportation Plan, Draft, Atlanta/GA 1999

Illustration 4.12	MARTA skyway, PowerPoint-presentation of Paul Vespermann, MARTA, Director of Real Estate, Atlanta/GA 2000
Illustration 4.13	Real Estate Developer John Williams, President of the Atlanta Chamber of Industry and Commerce, New York Times, March 5th 2000
Illustration 4.14	Williams' (PostProperties) early and recent development locations, New York Times, March 5th, 2000
Illustration 4.15	DART journal, InMotion, Spring 2000
Illustration 4.16	DART rail system map, URL: www.dart.org, 18.11.2002
Illustration 4.17	San Diego trolley, MTDB-brochure, 1999
Illustration 4.18	San Diego trolley 2, MTDB-brochure, 1999
Illustration 4.19	San Diego Skyline, URL:www.sandiego.com
Illustration 4.20	MTDB transit corridor plan, Bragado 1999
Illustration 4.21	Tri-Met system (present and future), URL: www.trimet.org
Illustration 4.22	Interstate MAX alignment, URL: www.trimet.org
Illustration 4.23	Willamette River Road before ..., photo-archive, Metro-government
Illustration 4.24	...and after removal, photo-archive, Metro-government
Illustration 4.25	Portland City Center, view of Mount Hood, photo-archive, Metro-government
Illustration 4.26	Toronto Commuter Rail Network, URL: www.toronto.com
Illustration 5.1	Prospectus picture of the MGM Grand Bally's Monorail extension, presentation brochure of MGM Grand Bally, Las Vegas/NV, 2000
Illustration 5.2	Alignment of the Vegas Monorail, presentation brochure of MGM Grand Bally, Las Vegas/NV, 2000
Illustration 5.3	Alignment of the AirportMAX, Information brochure of Bechtel, Portland/OR 1999

Illustration 5.4	Cascade Station Masterplan, Information brochure of Bechtel, Portland/OR 1999
Illustration 5.5	Weehawken Terminal, beginning of the 20th century, photo-archive, Parsons Brinckerhoff Inc., Newark/ NJ 2000
Illustration 5.6	End of the 20th century: View from the HBLRT to the World Trade Center on the other side of the Hudson, photo-archive, Parsons Brinckerhoff Inc., Newark/ NJ 2000
Illustration 5.7	HBLRT Final Alignment and construction segments, NJ Transit Annual Report 1999
Illustration 5.8	LRT alignment through historic neighborhoods in Jersey City, Duffy 1998
Illustration 5.9	HBLRT in service, May 2000, 21st Century Rail Corporation, photo archive
Illustration 5.10	HBLRT, Initial Operating Segment, 21st Century Rail Corporation, NJ Transit: Hudson-Bergen Light Rail System Map, Newark 1999
Illustration 5.11	HBLRT final alignment of the initial segment as a result of influences and compromises, NJ Transit, information brochure, Hudson-Bergen LIGHT RAIL, Volume 1, No. 2, January 2000
Illustration 5.12	PFI fields 1992-1998, Jacob/Kochendörfer 2000, 35
Illustration 5.13	Greater Manchester Metropolitan Area, Greater Manchester Local Transport Plan (GMLTP) 1999
Illustration 5.14	Manchester Metrolink, phase 1, stations and Inner-City Map, URL: www.gmpte.gov.uk
Illustration 5.15	Manchester Metrolink, phase 2, Salford Quays extension, Gaffron et al. 2002, Appendix D
Illustration 5.16	Metrolink system extensions, URL: www.gmpte.gov.uk
Illustration 5.17	Croydon – a City inside of Greater London, Westermann, Rand McNally World Atlas 1990
Illustration 5.18	Croydon Tramlink network as of May 2000, URL: www.tfl.gov.uk
Illustration 6.1	Cover of the Joint Development Solicitation 7-2000, URL: www.wmata.org
Illustration 6.2	Example of the 7-2000 solicitation – Brookland, CUA URL: www.wmata.org

Illustration 6.3	Joint Development Project at Friendship Heights Metrorail Station, Parsons Brinckerhoff, Inc, 1996
Illustration 6.4	Metro Center Project at Bethesda, Parsons Brinckerhoff, Inc, 1996
Illustration 6.5	Arlington County Metro Corridors, PowerPoint presentation of Chris Zimmermann, Arlington County Board Member, 2001
Illustration 6.6	Ballston (Parkington) in the 1960s, PowerPoint presentation of Chris Zimmermann, Arlington County Board Member, 2001
Illustration 6.7	Ballston (Parkington) in 2000, PowerPoint presentation of Chris Zimmermann, Arlington County Board Member, 2001
Illustration 6.8	Joint Development at Ballston Metrorail Station, PowerPoint presentation of Chris Zimmermann, Arlington County Board Member, 2001
Illustration 6.9	Arlington County at the end of 1960s, before Metrorail, PowerPoint presentation of Chris Zimmermann, Arlington County Board Member, 2001
Illustration 6.10	Ballston-Rosslyn corridor in 2000, PowerPoint presentation of Chris Zimmermann, Arlington County Board Member, 2001
Illustration 6.11	Development Projects in the Area North of Massachusetts Avenue, WMATA 2000
Illustration 6.12	Future central BellSouth locations, the author, on the basis of a Metrorail system map of 2000
Illustration 6.13	Construction works at Sandy Springs, PowerPoint presentation of Paul Vespermann, January 2000
Illustration 6.14	Lindbergh station development plan, PowerPoint presentation of Paul Vespermann, January 2000
Illustration 6.15	The station as the urban center, PowerPoint presentation of Paul Vespermann, January 2000
Illustration 6.16	S-Bahn-Station Bernau-Friedensthal, Strathmann, December 1999
Illustration 6.17	Hennigsdorf: S-Bahn and Commuter Rail Station, Strathmann, December 1999
Illustration 7.1	Cover of a DART magazine, InMotion, DART-Journal Summer 2000 issue

Illustration 7.2	Transit accessible area at Cedars Station, DART information about the Cedars station, Dallas/TX 2000
Illustration 7.3	Old Sears Warehouse at Cedars Station, DART information about the Cedars station, Dallas/TX 2000
Illustration 7.4	DART system extension, North Central Corridor, DART information about the North Central Corridor, Dallas/TX 2000
Illustration 7.5	Development at Mockingbird Station – rehabilitation and new buildings DART information about the Mockingbird station, Dallas/TX 2000
Illustration 7.6	Amicus Partners at Plano's future development site, DART photo archive
Illustration 7.7:	Development potential at West MAX station areas, URL: www.trimet.org
Illustration 7.8	Plans for Beaverton Round, Metro, Transit-Oriented Development Implementation Program, Program Summary, Portland/OR 1999
Illustration 7.9	Orenco Station Area under construction, slide-presentation of Richard D. Loffelmacher, PacTrust, Pacific Realty Associates, Portland/OR 2000
Illustration 7.10	Orenco Station Development Masterplan, Information brochure of the City of Hillsboro, autumn 1999
Illustration 7.11	Costa Pacific Homes - detached home types, information brochure of Costa Pacific, autumn 1999
Illustration 7.12	Orenco Town Center 1999, slide-presentation of Richard D. Loffelmacher, PacTrust, Pacific Realty Associates, Portland/OR 2000
Illustration 7.13	Towncenter Apartment Buildings, slide-presentation of Richard D. Loffelmacher, PacTrust, Pacific Realty Associates, Portland/OR 2000
Illustration 7.14	Orenco's central green area, slide-presentation of Richard D. Loffelmacher, PacTrust, Pacific Realty Associates, Portland/OR 2000
Illustration 7.15	Orenco - National showcase as a "livable community", slide-presentation of Richard D. Loffelmacher, PacTrust, Pacific Realty Associates, Portland/OR 2000

10. Attachments

10.1 Excerpts of the Manchester Metrolink Concession Agreement

3.1 The provisions of the Concession Agreement are outlined below

Part 1 - General

3.2 This part grants to the Concessionaire the right to operate and the obligation to maintain Phase 1 and Phase 2 during the Concession Period, which will run for 17 years and 3 months. The Concessionaire will begin operations on Phase 1 on the 27th April 1997 after the Award of Contract to enable a smooth transition of operations from the existing operator and to enable the Concessionaire to obtain acceptance of its safety case. The Concessionaire will begin operations on Phase 2 once construction work has been completed, and provision is made for sectional completion and commencement of operations.

	Altrincham - Central Area	Bury - Central Area	Eccles - Central Area
Mondays to Thursdays 6.00 a.m. - 7.15 a.m. and 6.30 p.m. - 11.30 p.m.	12 minute intervals	12 minute intervals	12 minute intervals
Fridays 6.00 a.m. - 7.15 a.m. and 6.30 p.m. - 12.30 a.m.	12 minute intervals	12 minute intervals	12 minute intervals
Mondays to Fridays 7.15 a.m. - 6.30 p.m.	6 minute intervals	6 minute intervals	12 minute intervals
Saturdays 6.00 a.m. - 9.30 a.m. and 5.30 p.m. 12.30 a.m.	12 minute intervals	12 minute intervals	12 minute intervals
Saturdays 9.30 a.m. - 5.30 p.m.	6 minute intervals	6 minute intervals	12 minute intervals
Sundays and Bank Holidays 8.00 a.m. - 10.00 a.m. and 5.00 p.m. - 10.30 p.m.	15 minute intervals	15 minute intervals	15 minute intervals
Sundays and Bank Holidays 10.00 a.m. to 5.00 p.m.	12 minute intervals	12 minute intervals	12 minute intervals

Part 2 - Operation of Metrolink Services

3.3 Clause 4 specifies the minimum services to be operated by the Concessionaire unless otherwise agreed by the Executive. The minimum service intervals on Phase 1 are based on the existing timetable, except that a slightly increased frequency is required on Sundays and Bank Holidays during normal shopping hours and later services are required on Friday and Saturday nights. These minimum service intervals are as follows:

3.4 The earliest and last services are also specified. The existing service pattern on Phase 1 has been retained (involving alternate through journeys between Altrincham and Bury during peak hours), while all services on Phase 2 will depart from or terminate at Piccadilly. The Concessionaire has to use reasonable endeavors to ensure adequate connections at Piccadilly Gardens and Cornbrook. In order to meet expected demand without overcrowding, certain minimum flows of light rail vehicles are required during peak times Mondays to Fridays, by operating higher frequencies.

These requirements are as follows:-

8.00 a.m. - 9.00 a.m.
12 Light Rail Vehicles from Altrincham to the Central Area
11 Light Rail Vehicles from Bury to die Central Area
8.00 a.m. - 9.00 a.m.
7 Light Rail Vehicles from Piccadilly to Waterside
5.00 p.m. - 6.00 p.m.
12 Light Rail Vehicles from die Central Area to Altrincham
11 Light Rail Vehicles from die Central Area to Bury
7 Light Rail Vehicles from Waterside to die Central Area

3.5 An incentive regime is imposed under Clause 6 to incentivise the Concessionaire to operate the timetabled services. This involves die potential payment of an incentive fee to the Executive in respect of each 28 day period unless at least 98% of the timetabled mileage is operated during that period. The incentive fee payable increases gradually up to a maximum of £ 80,000 (index linked) if in any 28 day period less than 75% of the timetabled mileage is operated. For the purposes of calculating the incentive fee, services that are more than 12 minutes late at their destination (or 6 minutes late in the case of peak services), services that do not run their entire course or do not stop at all scheduled stops and services that do not consist of a double unit where a double unit is scheduled, all count as cancelled services. However, failure to provide services arising from matters beyond the reasonable control of the Concessionaire will not result in any incentive fee being payable.

3.6 The Concessionaire is free to determine the level of fares and range of tickets on Phase 1 and Phase 2, provided that the Concessionaire will be required to continue participating in the existing concessionary fare scheme applying to the Metrolink system on the terms set out in Schedule 1 of the

Concession Agreement. In. addition, the Concessionaire is under an obligation to negotiate arrangements with the operators of local passenger railway services and where possible with bus operators, to participate in through ticketing and multi modal travel arrangements respectively. If necessary, the Executive can require the Concessionaire to enter into such arrangements on terms that will involve no net financial loss to the Concessionaire, which in the event of dispute is to be determined by an independent expert. Similarly, the existing arrangement enabling holders of rail tickets from railway stations within Greater Manchester to Manchester City Centre to travel free of charge on Metrolink services within the Central Area will be continued if required by the Executive, on payment of quarterly payments that result in no net financial loss to the Concessionaire.

3.7 The Concessionaire is required to make effective use of the passenger information system at Metrolink stops, which in the case of Phase 1, is being upgraded.

3.8 The existing and any new proposed Metrolink car parks may only be used for car parking free to Metrolink passengers and the Concessionaire will be expected to discourage parking by others.

3.9 The Concessionaire is required to comply with all health and safety legislation and to take all reasonably practicable measures to ensure the safety and security of passengers, including by the use of a CCTV system at all Metrolink stops.

3.10 The Concessionaire is required to draw up detailed operating manuals, which will be identical to or be based upon die existing operating manuals, and will supply copies of these and of any updates to the Executive.

3.11 The Concessionaire is required to obtain all necessary licenses and approvals, including from HM Railway Inspectorate, and to comply with all applicable legislation, including in particular die Acts and Orders specifically relating to Metrolink. The Executive has made by-laws relating to Phase 1 and it is anticipated that these will also cover Phase 2.

Part 3 - Maintenance of Metrolink System

The Concessionaire is required to maintain, renew and repair die Metrolink System as necessary throughout die Concession Period so that there is no impairment or loss of function, no undue wear and no reduction in safety. Detailed maintenance manuals for Phase 1 have been agreed and will need to be provided for Phase 2. Copies of them and of any updates will be provided to the Executive. The Concession Agreement also requires the

Concessionaire to comply with certain specified maintenance and cleaning obligations, including routine daily cleaning of Light Rail Vehicles and more thorough cleaning on a monthly basis, as well as periodic repainting of painted surfaces.

The concessionaire must aim to minimize disruption caused by maintenance work and to inform passengers and the Executive of any anticipated disruption to services. The Executive has a right to inspect the Metrolink System to ensure that the Concessionaire is complying with its maintenance obligations and in the event of default can carry out necessary remedial work at the Concessionaire's cost.

Part 4 - Financial

3.14 The Concessionaire will retain all fare and advertising revenue. The location of advertising is subject to the Executive's approval. The Concessionaire's advertising rights are limited to advertising at Metrolink stops and on Light Rail Vehicles. The contract with J.C. Decaux U.K. Limited places limitations on the Concessionaire in relation to advertising at Metrolink stops on Phase 1.

3.15 The Concessionaire will be responsible for all costs and outgoings in connection with the operation and maintenance of the Metrolink System and will be required to indemnify the Executive against any claims and liabilities, which arise as a result of the Concessionaire' s operation and maintenance of the Metrolink System.

3.16 The Concessionaire is required to take out insurance, in the joint names of the Executive and the Concessionaire covering third party legal liability, property damage and 24 months loss of income on the part of the Concessionaire. Levels of cover may be reviewed and adjusted from time to time taking account of Inflation and other relevant factors.

3.17 The Concessionaire will be responsible for the payment of all insurance premiums and will be required to take out its own Employer's Liability Insurance and any other necessary insurances. In respect of the joint names insurance, the Concessionaire may choose the levels of excesses/deductibles up to agreed limits of £30,000 per claim and £300,000 per annum in aggregate.

Part 5 - Use of Assets

3.18 The Concession Agreement provides for separate property licenses to be granted by die Executive to the Concessionaire in respect of Phase 1 and, when completed, Phase 2. In respect of Phase 2 the license is presently incapable of being completed pending completion of the acquisition of all necessary property rights by the Executive. However, the principle on which the licenses will be based is that the Concessionaire must comply with all of die Executive's obligations to third parties and be subject to all applicable restrictions that arise from the terms upon which die Executive has itself acquired the property rights to enable the construction and Operation of Metrolink. Such obligations are contained in die Metrolink Acts, the agreements between the Executive and British Rail in respect of Phase 1 contained in Volume 7, Parliamentary Undertakings and agreements with property owners. The licensees will grant to the Concessionaire only those rights that are necessary to enable it to operate and maintain the Metrolink system and no more, all other rights being reserved by the Executive, subject to these not interfering with the operation and maintenance of the Metrolink system. For example, the Executive has reserved the right to use spare capacity in all relevant cable ducts, development rights and lineside advertising rights. If the concession is terminated then the Phase 1 property license and the Phase 2 property license will (for tax reasons) transfer to a new Concessionaire or a subsidiary of the PTE rather than simply expire.

3. 19 The Executive has granted to the Concessionaire a separate license permitting the Concessionaire (and Serco as operator) to use the Metrolink trademarks, which are registered in the name of the Executive. The license reserves to the Executive all rights appropriate to the Executive's status as registered holder of the trademarks. Unless agreed by the Executive, the Concessionaire cannot use any other marks in connection with the operation of the Metrolink system.

3.20 The Concessionaire is restricted from making any additions, alterations, amendments or other modifications to the Metrolink System without the consent of the Executive. Any such modification will belong to the Executive unless otherwise agreed.

3.21 As well as approving the size and location of advertising space at Metrolink stops and on Light Rail Vehicles, the Executive will be entitled to use up to 5% of the advertising space available at Metrolink stops and inside Light Rail Vehicles for the display of information notices.

Part 6 - Records, reporting and audit

3.22 The Concessionaire will maintain proper financial, operating and maintenance records, including records of Metrolink services that have not run in accordance with the timetable.

3.23 The Concessionaire will be subject to various reporting obligations, including immediate reporting of serious accidents and of significant faults of the system. Information concerning ticket sales and service defaults relevant to calculating any incentive fees payable are to be reported on a 28 day cycle. Accounting Information is to be reported quarterly and reports covering Information such as the number of incidents involving personal injury or damage to the Metrolink System and estimates of patronage will be required. The Executive will be able to require the provision of general information relating to the operation of Metrolink and the carrying out of the Concessionaire' s obligations wider the Concession Agreement. The Executive will also have a general right of access to the Metrolink System in order to carry out passenger surveys and other research, with which the Concessionaire will be expected to co-operate where necessary

Part 7 - Termination And Its Consequences

3.24 The Concession Agreement will be terminable without compensation in the event of certain specified breaches by the Concessionaire and in the event of the Concessionaire's insolvency. In addition, and in order to enable the future expansion of the Metrolink System, the Executive has the right to terminate the concession on not less than three months notice and on payment of compensation to the Concessionaire, where it has awarded a contract for the construction of any extension. In respect of the operation of any extension, the Executive will first seek agreement with the Concessionaire as to the terms on which the Concessionaire would agree to operate the extended system. Only in the event of a failure of negotiations with the Concessionaire held over a minimum of three months will the Executive seek competing tenders. The proposed compensation formula in the case of network expansion is based on the Concessionaire's anticipated loss of profits for the remainder of the Concession period based on profits immediately prior to termination discounted to the date of termination but subject to a minimum payment to ensure the Concessionaire can repay all of its borrowing in relation to the project. Any disputes about compensation will be determined by an independent firm of accountants.

3.25 Termination of the concession in the event of network expansion will however not be possible before four and a half years following the Phase 1 operating date, in order to give the Concessionaire a minimum period to operate Phase 1 and a "settling in" phase on Phase 2. If any future extension is constructed and capable of operation within this minimum period then the Executive may require die Concessionaire to operate and maintain the extension on terms specified by it. If the extension is loss making, the Executive will compensate die Concessionaire for its net costs and pay a "management fee" of 100,000 per annum. If the extension is profitable, the

management fee will be 20% of the profits subject to a £ 100,000 per annum minimum fee, with the Concessionaire paying die remaining profits to the Executive. Either party may terminate any such interim arrangement after the aforesaid four and a half years, subject to the payment of compensation.
3.26 As a protection for the Concessionaire, if it incurs unexpected net losses in excess of £5 00,000 (index linked) in any year as a result of any new and onerous legislation relating to die Operation or maintenance of the Metrolink System, the Executive will either reimburse losses in excess of that sum or, at its option, terminate the Concession Agreement on no less than 2 months notice and on payment of compensation to the Concessionaire.

3.27 Whether the concession terminates by expiry or by earlier termination, the Concessionaire is obliged, following termination, to pay the Index linked sum of £5 00,000 to fund a technical assessment of the state and condition of die Metrolink System and any remedial works that may be required. If this involves expenditure in excess of that sum, and this is due to the default of the Concessionaire, then the Concessionaire will in addition pay that excess. If the contrary applies, a refund will be made.

3.28 Subject to the comments above about the Phase 1 and Phase 2 licensees the entire Metrolink System will revert to the Executive on the expiry or early termination of the Concession Agreement. In respect of assets not comprised in the Metrolink system and acquired by the Concessionaire and contracts in connection with the operation of the Metrolink System, the Executive will have the Option to acquire these from the Concessionaire at a value to be calculated on a specified basis and subject to determination by an independent expert in the case of any dispute.

Where the Concessionaire wishes to ensure that the Executive will be under an obligation to acquire any particular asset that it wishes to purchase, provision is made for this to be agreed with the Executive and where appropriate a specific valuation of that asset can also be agreed.

3.29 As well as transferring all relevant assets on termination, the Concessionaire will be expected to transfer all records and documents and to ensure that the Executive or any successor operator has a license to use all copyrights and other intellectual property used by the Concessionaire in connection with the operation or maintenance of the Metrolink System.

Employees will transfer to the Executive or the successor operator under the Transfer of Undertakings (Protection of Employment) Regulations 1981 and the Concessionaire will be required to give appropriate indemnities in respect of outstanding claims. However, the Concessionaire may be required to procure that employees who are also directors of the Concessionaire do not transfer and will be expected to pay all costs associated with the termination of the employment of such persons if required to do so.

Part 8 - Obligations Associated with Network Expansion and Change of Operator

3.30 The Concessionaire will be expected to co-operate with the Executive and provide all necessary information in connection with future Metrolink extensions and to co-operate with contractors engaged in the construction of extensions so as to minimize disruption and facilitate die efficient construction of the extensions.

Metrolink will be permitted to prospective tenderers for future extensions and the Concessionaire will be expected to co-operate in the smooth transfer of operations to any successor and not to take actions designed to prejudice that transfer.

3.31 In respect of the operation of future extensions, the Executive recognizes the desirability of continuity of operations by one operator. As noted above, it would therefore anticipate, subject to statutory constraints and the requirements of the Department of Transport, seeking to agree a mutually acceptable basis upon which the Concessionaire would take on the operation of any future extension without this element going out to competitive tender. However, if no mutually acceptable basis can be agreed but the Executive does not wish to terminate the Concession Agreement, it will have the option to introduce a second operator on any future extension. In those circumstances, die Concessionaire will be obliged to permit the second operator to operate in die Central Area and use any necessary Metrolink assets subject to die operator compensating die Concessionaire for any resultant increase in its net costs resulting from that use.

3.32 The termination provisions in relation to the Concession Agreement are complex and are summarized in the report.

Part 9 - Schedules of the Concession Agreement

3.33 There are 8 Schedules to the Concession Agreement dealing with the following matters:-

- Schedule 1 –

Concessionary Fares Scheme - this requires the participation of Altram in the Concessionary Fares Scheme with reimbursement from the PTE so that the operator suffers no financial loss. The PTA/E are free to amend the Scheme as they see fit.

The concessions are:-

Children - half fare all day
Elderly - half fare to 9.30, 9.30 onwards - 35p
Free Passes - Blind, Mentally Handicapped etc (no difference between bus and rail)

- Schedule 2 –

Phase 1 License, which gives the operator the right to use all Phase 1 assets

- Schedule 3 –

Phase 2 License, which gives the operator the right to use all Phase 2 assets

- Schedule 4 –

License for Metrolink Marks, which gives the operator the right to use the name Metrolink

- Schedule 5-

This sets out the calculation of compensation where termination of the concession occurs

- Schedules 6 and 7-

These give the PTE a legal charge over die Metrolink system to prevent Altram disposing of any of the Metrolink Assets

- Schedule 8 –

This gives the PTE a right to super profits where the returns to Altram exceed certain limits.

10.2 WMATA Joint Development Policies and Guidelines (Excerpts)

as of November 16, 1995, revised on June 17, 1996,

1.0 Introduction

Joint development is a means of securing transit compatible public and private development at, and adjacent to, Metrorail stations to enhance ridership and revenue of the Washington Metropolitan Area Transit Authority (WMATA) and Legal Jurisdictions. WMATA has been involved in joint development agreements for projects at the following Metrorail Stations: Rosslyn, Farragut North, Van Ness-UDC, McPherson, Bethesda, Friendship Heights, Metro Center, Dupont Circle and Ballston.

Joint development at WMATA means the development by lease of land and related interests in real property owned or controlled by WMATA at or near Metrorail stations. Due to its physical or functional relationship to the Metrorail station, the property has significant potential for commercial, residential development, alone or in combination with adjoining real property to further WMATA's development-related goals.

The goals of WMATA's joint development program are:

* Attract new riders to the transit system by fostering commercial and residential development projects on WMATA owned or controlled land and on private properties adjacent to Metro stations;

* Create sources of revenue for the Authority to operate and maintain the transit system by expediently negotiating joint development agreements between WMATA and public or private development entities; and

* Assist the WMATA local jurisdictions to recapture a portion of their past financial contributions and to continue making subsidy payments by expanding the local property tax base and adding value to available local revenue

2.0 Purpose

The purpose of these policies and guidelines is:

* To provide a process to disseminate information about WMATA's Joint Development program to the development community and the general public;

* To identify the roles and responsibilities of the WMATA Board of Directors, the General Manager, Local Jurisdictions and developers in the joint development process; and

* To define the six step joint development process and procedures.

3.0 Scope of Policies and Guidelines

These policies and guidelines apply to joint development projects to which WMATA is a party. They do not apply to:

* "System interface" projects: Projects which have direct connections between WMATA's facilities and adjacent development owned by others. These projects are managed by WMATA's Department of Design and Construction (DECO), Office of Real Estate (REAL).

* "Adjacent construction" projects: Projects which are administered by DECO's Office of Engineering and Architecture (ENGA).

* "Interim leasing" of WMATA-owned land. These leases are managed by DECO's Office of Real Estate.

* "Sale of excess property." This program is administered by DECO's Office of Real Estate.

4.0 Policies of Local Jurisdictions Affecting Joint Development

WMATA coordinates closely with local jurisdictions to protect its property interests and to implement its joint development program. Many of the policies which influence joint development activity in local jurisdictions are generally contained in various planning, land use and related documents, such as comprehensive plans, sector or station area plans, zoning ordinances and maps, adequate public facilities ordinances and capital improvement programs. Interested parties may obtain these documents and plans by contacting the jurisdiction involved.

5.0 Major Roles and Responsibilities in the Joint Development Program

The WMATA joint development program is implemented by the combined efforts of the Board, the General Manager and WMATA staff, Local Jurisdictions and Developers. Their major responsibilities are outlined below:

5.1 The WMATA Board of Directors

The WMATA Board of Directors establishes policies on behalf of WMATA for joint development, exercises specific approvals within the joint development process, and maintains oversight of the joint development program. The Board has specific responsibilities to approve the Joint Development Work Program and the joint development agreement.

5.2 General Manager

Jurisdictions in the WMATA Transit District include: the District of Columbia, Arlington, Fairfax, Montgomery and Prince George's Counties, and the Cities of Alexandria, Falls Church, Fairfax and Rockville. Each contributes to the planning and implementation of joint development projects.

* Copies of the draft Joint Development Work Program are sent to the jurisdiction's Chief Executive and relevant Board member for jurisdictional review and comments.

* Jurisdictions participate with WMATA and consultants in conducting joint development studies.

* WMATA coordinates with jurisdictions in the preparation of the Disposition and Joint Development Plans and in the preparation and issuance of Offering Documents.

* After approval of the Joint Development Agreement by the WMATA Board, jurisdictions review and approve (or disapprove) the developers' site and project plans through local policies, land use plans, zoning, and development-related capital improvements.

5.4 Developers

Public and private development entities, landowners or their agents may participate in early planning as well as in implementation phases of joint development projects.

* Developers may propose the introduction of a station or site into the draft Joint Development Work Program through coordination with local jurisdictions and WMATA.

* Developers may participate or otherwise cooperate in station area planning conducted by local jurisdictions and WMATA.

* Developers may propose mutually beneficial solutions to local jurisdictions and WMATA regarding station area development issues such as improved access to Metro, programming of capital improvements, phasing and land assembly.

* Developers may respond to joint development offerings in the form of proposals to WMATA.

* Developers or other interested parties may initiate unsolicited proposals for a WMATA property at any time.

* A developer selected to build a joint development project will negotiate agreements with WMATA based on the Offering Document and the accepted developer's proposal.

* A selected developer will plan, construct and operate a joint development project in accordance with pertinent joint development agreements and jurisdictional laws and regulations.

* A selected developer will, with WMATA's assistance, obtain all necessary zoning and plan approvals from the local jurisdiction.

6.0 Joint Development Process and Procedures

This section describes the "normal" process and procedures followed for joint development. The six stages are illustrative; they are not mandatory; and may not be necessary for each joint development project.

6.1 Preparation of the Joint Development Work Program

The Joint Development Work Program is prepared on an annual basis in coordination with jurisdictions. The Work Program includes a list of all joint development sites by jurisdiction, site descriptions and current joint development status. The draft Joint Development Work Program is prepared by the General Manager and approved by the WMATA Board of Directors by June 30 of each fiscal year.

Procedurally, a given year's work program evolves as follows:

* REAL issues a draft Joint Development Work Program to each jurisdiction by March 31, of each year.

* Jurisdictions review the draft work program and transmit to REAL their comments by April 15 of each year.

* Real discusses the submitted comments with the jurisdiction, if required, to resolve any issues which may exist. All discussions will be concluded by May 15 of each year.

* During each fiscal year, REAL submits a draft work program, comprised of each jurisdictional element, to the General Manager for approval by June 1.

In preparing the annual draft Joint Development Work Program, REAL will normally perform physical inspections, evaluations and internal screening of each potential joint development site.

6.2 Board Approval of Joint Development Work Program and Authorization of the General Manager to Initiate a Joint Development Site Marketing and Procurement Process.

By June 30 of each fiscal year, the General Manager submits to the Board, WMATA's recommended Joint Development Work Program and all jurisdictional comments. The General Manager recommends fiscal year funding authority to the Board for the inclusion of joint development activities.

A request for authorization to initiate a joint development procurement process is normally included in the work program package to the Board.

6.3 Preparation and Issuance of Offering Document

The Offering Document is intended to solicit joint development proposals from developers on a competitive basis.

Drafting of the Offering Document is initiated by REAL. Concurrently, WMATA Offices and the affected jurisdictions are consulted for comments. The local jurisdiction advises WMATA as to planning, urban design and other guidelines which will apply to the proposed development site.

The Offering Document is transmitted to the General Manager for approval. If approved, the Offering Document is then issued by WMATA.

Issuance of the Offering follows WMATA's established joint development procurement procedures. Normally, these procedures include:

* Advertisement of the offering in local and national newspapers for two weeks;
* A pre-proposal conference, if needed, to respond to questions from prospective respondents;

* A proposal due date, generally 30 to 90 days from the date of issuance of the Offering Document;
* Proposal review and evaluation by a Contracting Officer appointed panel, and
* Recommendations from the panel to the Contracting Officer.

6.4 Evaluation and Selection of Proposals

The Contracting Officer appoints a panel to evaluate submitted proposals in order to determine if they are in accordance with the Authority's established procurement procedures, to determine the capability of the development entity and the feasibility of the proposal based on the criteria in the Offering Document. Project evaluation criteria for projects will emphasize the Board's stated goals for Joint Development.

6.5 Negotiations and Execution

Negotiations shall be conducted with the selected developer or developers by the Contracting Officer and/or hi/her representatives. Competitive negotiations will be used in all cases where WMATA receives more than one acceptable proposal or more that one that can be made acceptable. Other WMATA offices will be consulted as required. The WMATA Board members from the affected jurisdiction shall be advised of the status of the negotiations as required.

6.6. Board Approval of Selected Development Proposal

The General Manager will recommend selection of the development proposal and approval of the agreement to the WMATA Board of Directors. Upon ratification and authorization by the Board of Directors, the Contracting Officer shall execute the joint development agreement, as negotiated.

After execution of the joint development agreement, the development entity is required to submit the proposed joint development project site plan for review and approval by DECO and the Department of Operations, prior to submission to the local jurisdiction, to ensure compatibility with Authority facilities and operations. All site plans and required subdivision actions will be subject to approvals by the local jurisdiction in accordance with local ordinances and regulations.

DECO will develop and administer a program of inspection in accordance with the terms of the executed agreement. To the maximum extent possible, all inspection and enforcement activity will be coordinated with local jurisdiction inspections on those private improvements which may incorporate WMATA facilities.

10.3 Summary of TOD case studies in New Jersey, Dallas, San Diego, and Toronto

Station	Developer	Completion	Uses	Project Size	Invest-ment Size	Transit Impact
New Jersey						
Secaucus Transfer	Allied Junction Corporation	2000 - 2015	Office/Retail	5 mio sq ft	$ 450 Mio.	12,000 - 16,000 rail passengers expected
Dallas/TX						
West End, Akard, Pearl	HBE Corporation others	1996 - 1998	Entertain-ment, Restaurants, Retail, Hotels, Office	Office: > 500,000 sq ft Hotels: > 2000 rooms	> $ 250 Mio.	
Kiest	Affordable Housing corporation others	after 2000	Retail, Housing (Senior and Single family)	160 acres		
Mockingbird	UC URBAN Phoenix Property	2000 - 2002	Hotel, Office, Retail Housing	10 acres > 600 apartments		
Cityplace	Cityplan company		Hotel, Office Housing	230 apartments 300 room hotel 43 story office tower		
Illinois	DART	1996 - 2000	Retail, Museum	30,000 sq ft	$ 26 Mio.	
Cedars Station	Matthews Southwest	1998 - 2000	Housing, Retail, Entertainment	30 acres 450 left apartments	> $ 100 Mio.	
Galatyn Park	Hunt Petroleum Nortel Networks	2002	Office, Housing, Retail, Hotel, public Institutions	500 acres, Urban Center: 25 acres		expected job growth: 50.000 employees are potential DART-riders
Plano´s 15th Street Station	Amicus Partner	2003	Housing, Conference Center, Retail	3,5 acres 250 apartments	$ 16 Mio.	

San Diego/CA[26]						
Imperial Station	MTS/James R. Mills Building	1989	Office	2,7 acres 180,000 sq ft	$ 35 Mio.	[1)] 1995, more than 17.000 daily ons/offs [2)] Yearly lease revenues [3)] savings in construction and financing costs for the station
America Plaza		1991	Office	3 acres 34 stories approx. 600,000 sq ft		[1)] 1995: more than 7.500 daily ons/offs [2)] 80 % of the $ 5.2 Mio.capital costs of the station was financed by the project developer
Convention Center	Unified Port District of San Diego	1989 (phase I) 2001 (phase II)	Convention Center	phase I: 760,000 sq ft assembly facility phase II: 940,000 sq ft assembly facility	phase I: $ 160 Mio. phase II: $ 216 Mio.	according to the conventions and special events hold
Santa Fe Depot	Catellus Corporation	2000 - 2008	Office, Hotel, Residential		$ 815 Mio.	1995: more than 7,000 daily ons/offs including Amtrak, Coaster Commuter Rail, Trolley Blue Line
Fashion Valley	Fashion Valley shopping Center/ERE Yarmouth	1997	Retail		$ 116 Mio.	1995: more than 8,500 daily ons/offs

[26] based on information of a folder: MTDB Joint Development Major Project Summary, San Diego 1999

Rio Vista	Cal Mat Properties (Peter Calthorpe)	phase I/II: 1995 phase III: 2000	Retail/Residential	phase I: 250,000 sq ft retail phase II: 464 apartments phase III: 1,754 apartments, 30,000 sq ft office, 325,000 sq ft retail		1995: 530 daily ons/offs Developer dedicated the right-of-way for the LRT alignment and the station
Qualcomm Stadium	City of San Diego	1998	Stadium	Stadium size: 73,000 visits parking capacity: 19,000		the Trolley serving 10 % - 20 % of a capacity crowd deporting the stadium within 1/2 hour
47th Street	WKB General Partnership	1989	Residential/Day Care	144 apartments 3,000 sq ft day care center		1995: more than 1,225 daily ons/offs
Lemon Grove Depot	City of lemon Grove	1986	Trolley Depot Chamber of Commerce Visitor Information Center		$ 291,547	1995: more than 4,400 daily ons/offs
La Mesa	La Mesa Village Plaza Associates others	1991 - 1992	Office, Retail, Residential	244,000 sq ft		1995: over 1,800 daily ons/offs
Amaya	ITEC Properties assistance from : la Mesa Community Redevelopment Agency	1987	Residential	384 apartments		1995: more than 667 daily ons/offs
Grossmont Center	CCRT Properties assistance from: La Mesa Community Redevelopment Agency	1991	Retail/Entertainment	15,3 acres regional shopping male		1995: more than 3,300 daily ons/offs

24th Street	Sweetwater Union High School District	1997	Adult School Residential Retail	24,000 sq ft school building to serve 3,000 students a day, 40 apartments , 6,000 sq ft retail	$ 3,2 Mio.	1995: more than 6,500 daily ons/offs
Bayfront/E Street	City of Chula Vista	1986	Transit Center with Visitor Information Center	1,600 sq. ft. Information Center 255 Park & Ride Spaces	$ 6,5 Mio.	1995: more than 4,400 daily ons/offs
Gresham	Gresham Central Apartments	1998	Residential	2.5 acres 30 apartments		
Beaverton Central		not finished	Office, Retail, Residential	100,000 sq ft office 59,000 sq ft retail 53 townhomes 54 apartments 200 seat-theatre		
Beaverton Creek		1997	Residential	840 townhouses and apartments additional 112 acres of vacant land		
162nd Street			Residential	42 apartments 1.7 acres		
Orenco Station	Pac Trust others	1998 - 2005	Residential, Mixed Use Town Center, Retail	190 acres, including shopping center, 2000 single family houses, apartments towncenter 100,000 sq ft officel	$ 500 Mio.	

Toronto/ON						
High Park		1975	Residential	533 Apartments		
North York Centre		late 1970´s	Hotel, Office, Retail Library	Office towers, 250 Hotel rooms, Shopping Galleria	$ 250 Mio.	
Scarborough Centre		1990 - 2000	Office- and High-Rise-Apartment-Towers, Retail			

GPSR Compliance

The European Union's (EU) General Product Safety Regulation (GPSR) is a set of rules that requires consumer products to be safe and our obligations to ensure this.

If you have any concerns about our products, you can contact us on ProductSafety@springernature.com

In case Publisher is established outside the EU, the EU authorized representative is:

Springer Nature Customer Service Center GmbH
Europaplatz 3
69115 Heidelberg, Germany

Batch number: 10725993

Printed by Printforce, the Netherlands